The Journey of a Warrior: General Alfred M. Gray

Second Edition

29th Commandant U.S. Marine Corps (1987-1991)

Colonel Gerald H. Turley, USMCR (Retired)

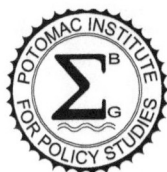

POTOMAC INSTITUTE PRESS

The Journey of a Warrior: General Alfred M. Gray, Second Edition
29th Commandant U.S. Marine Corps (1987-1991)

Potomac Institute for Policy Studies
901 N. Stuart St, Suite 1200
Arlington, VA 22203
www.potomacinstitute.org
Telephone: 703.525.0770; Fax: 703.525.0299
Email: webmaster@potomacinstitute.org

Second Edition
ISBN: 978-0-9852483-8-3 cloth; 978-0-9963960-5-9 pb; 978-0-9963960-9-7 Kindle

First Edition
ISBN: 978-1-4697-6132-9 (sc)
ISBN: 978-1-4697-6132-3 (hc)
ISBN: 978-1-4697-6132-6 (sc)

Dedication

To my dear wife, Bunny Turley,
who was there from the beginning,
who patiently listened, smiled, and cheerfully encouraged
me all along the way for more than 67 wonderful years.
A truly special lady, she is the wind beneath my wings.

The Author

TABLE OF CONTENTS

PREFACE

General Alfred Mason Gray Jr. is beyond a doubt the most unforgettable man I have ever known. I have had the unique opportunity to have served under him, been responsible for implementing a couple of his visionary ideas, been his confidant, sometimes his "Napoleon's Corporal" and, at times, his personal critic, a friend in time of need, and always an admirer of his vision, drive, and selfless devotion to his Corps of Marines.

This book brings to the fore the journey of a most unusual individual: a warrior, a leader, a thinker, and a patriot. It is not written as a biography but rather as retrospective of a unique Marine whose impact on his institution was both nontraditional and perhaps underappreciated. The U.S. Marine Corps is better for his unselfish and dedicated journey to faithfully serve this great republic of the United States of America.

Again, this is not a biography. Rather, it is an effort to capture the picture "before the colors fade," based on my personal observations and those who were close to Gray during the later stages of his career as he made what I believe were some lasting changes to the Marine Corps. Long-term effects and interpretations of trends will require the perspective of distance. It will be the charter of later historians to record and provide testimony to how successful one man's vision and capacity to lead fundamentally changed the Marine Corps in preparation for the 21st century.

His ultimate task was that of changing the underlying relationship of each Marine in the Corps. His call was for every Marine to elevate the position of the Corps in that historic relationship and to accept a more subordinate individual role to that of the institution. These were strange and potentially disquieting concepts for those careerists who were secure in a peacetime environment and complacent posture. Gray's initial changes generated a strong positive reaction among many Marines, and confusion, discord, and discontent among others.

Initially unappreciated by many because he was "rocking the boat," his fundamental belief was that change was vital to the survival and future viability of this more than 200-year-old institution. His efforts were intended to enhance and refocus the institutional strengths of the Marine Corps, to engender Marines to look inward at their profession for a deeper and better understanding of the essence of their covenant with their Corps. The focus of this book is the Marine Corps, its activities, and the events Gray encountered during four decades of military service.

As the 29th Marine Corps Commandant, Gray's stewardship coincided with a series of the most dynamic changes in world order since World War II, to include specifically the end of the Cold War. In the forefront of world events was the breakup of the Soviet monolith, the dismantling of the Berlin Wall, and the unification of East and West Germany.

As fate would have it, the nation went to war in the Persian Gulf only months before Gray's tenure as the 29th Commandant ended. The Iraqi invasion of Kuwait resulted in the United States entering into an international coalition force of more than 600,000 in the Middle East to first contain and then drive out the Iraqis, and finally reestablish Kuwaiti national sovereignty. The United States ultimately deployed 540,000 men and women to southwest Asia to support this international force. The Marine Corps deployed an excess of 85 percent of its air, ground, and logistics forces to the Central Command's theater. By February 1991, more than 96,000 Marines were positioned on land and in amphibious task forces steaming in the Persian Gulf and the Mediterranean Sea, ready to strike the Iraqi forces. Gray, sometimes working openly but often behind the scenes with his in-country force commanders, was involved in every aspect of his Marines' special needs and contingency war plans. It was a truly historic battlefield for Marine forces that, for the first time ever, were fighting and executing maneuver warfare against a massive, armor-equipped force. History was being made by a new breed of Marines.

The Persian Gulf War was, in reality, the "test" of Gray's ideas and visions, his decade of procurement efforts and upgraded training programs. Throughout the deployment and force buildup phases, he involved himself beyond his strict mandate as a Service Chief. Gray had extraordinary knowledge of joint-, combined-, and coalition-type operations at all levels and was always willing to share his thoughts where appropriate. He was acutely aware of his responsibilities to President George H.W. Bush and to the nation as a member of the Joint Chiefs of Staff, and he quietly provided his advice throughout the period. It was no surprise to those who knew him to see Al Gray assume a take-charge attitude and respond to this newly arising crisis. He had always been operationally oriented, often finding himself in the middle of conflicts and crises. In this situation, he continued to operate in the same manner: making decisions and influencing actions across the broad spectrum of the Marine Corps' involvement in pre-paring for combat against the Iraqi forces.

I retired from the Marine Corps in 1981. The Corps had been great to me and my family. I had advanced to the rank of Colonel and recognized that that would be the limit of my advancements. After completing 32 years, it was time to step aside and let younger officers step forward. My personal situation since the mid-1980s had taken a strange twist in my post-military career planning. A completely unex-pected series of events would rekindle my friendship with then-Major General Gray. In 1984, I received a presidential appointment from President Ronald Reagan to serve as a Deputy Assistant Secretary of Defense. This unexpected and sudden appointment originated with James Webb Jr., who had just recently been confirmed as the Assistant Secretary of Defense (Reserve Affairs). Jim Webb had asked me to serve on his staff. These two men, Webb and Gray, both battle-scarred warriors and decorated heroes, would become the principal figures in my professional life in the subsequent ten years.

After resigning from the Department of Defense in mid-1987, I was approached by Gray to serve as a special consultant to his office.

I accepted his gracious offer. Throughout the next four years, I was privileged, and many times honored, when he allowed me to share in his vision, discuss his plans, attend his conferences, and observe his leadership challenges as he served as the 29th Commandant of the Marine Corps. He would go on to become one of the most effective Commandants of the Marine Corps; the most influential in the last 50 years. This is his story, his journey as a warrior, and my reflections as I saw it from a special vantage point and from three decades of reflections.

Before the colors fade any further, and hopefully, before the precious Lord extends his hand at the river's edge, I have long felt compelled to record and share this extraordinary experience. It has not been purely a labor of love but a deep respect for a man who made historic differences in a military service, and the nation is better for it. During the past 25 years, I have devoted hundreds of hours researching and writing this manuscript. Only during the last five to six years have I periodically shared my writing with him. His immediate demand was to ensure factual accuracy when presenting historical matters and events. His near-photographic recall drove me back to a number of primary source documents where, indeed, I had cited flawed sources. On several occasions, he did not agree with all of the personal *reflections* I had written, but he never asked or implied I should change any personal observations. As when I served with him, when we quietly disagreed, we expressed our opinions, accepted our difference in views, and moved on. I never forgot that he was the one charged with awesome responsibilities, and I was but a contributor to his tasks.

General Alfred M. Gray was the right man for the right time, as the Marine Corps transitioned into the 21st century. Since his retirement from the Marine Corps, the intensity of his activities has not diminished. He serves as Chairman of the Injured Marine Semper Fi Fund, which provides comprehensive assistance to wounded servicemen and servicewomen and their families throughout their long periods of recovery. He remains a steady visitor to the hospitals and bases where many recovering warriors convalesce. In his continuing commitment to education and his firm belief that all members of the armed forces must pursue a "lifetime of learning," Gray has served on numerous college boards of trustees and is Chairman Emeritus of online American Military University. He also serves as Chairman of the Marine Corps League's Youth Fitness Foundation, Chancellor of the Marine Military Academy, and Director of the Marine Corps-Law Enforcement Scholarship Foundation. In many ways, Gray's stature has increased as he progressively has become a national asset and has repeatedly been called upon by leaders of industry and the highest levels of our government agencies.

ACKNOWLEDGMENTS

Special acknowledgment must go to two talented individuals, Jean B. Reynolds and Jeffrey J. Seeley, who devoted hundreds of hours to update, and immensely improve the clarity, accuracy, and quality of the second edition of this fascinating Marine warrior narrative.

This book would not have been completed without so many people who freely gave their most precious commodity—their personal time and intellect. The process of researching and conducting many interviews spanned nearly two decades. I remain forever grateful for their patience and tireless assistance, especially James A. Lasswell, who led the team devoting hundreds of hours to polish my drafts. Lieutenant General George Flynn, Major General Michael M. Myatt, Brigadier General James R. Joy, and Colonels Nicholas Reynolds, William Wischmeyer, William Bond, and James McGee all helped raise the quality and depth of details to bring forth these *reflections* on one of the most interesting individuals I have ever had the privilege to meet and serve with.

General Alfred Mason Gray approved and provided open and complete access to his personal papers, which are located in the General Alfred M. Gray Research Center at Quantico, Virginia. More than 250 cartons stuffed with valuable documents were screened. However, this robust nest of trivia and priceless correspondence was only the tip of the iceberg in researching materials, as nearly 100 individuals eagerly brought forth personal papers and shared vignettes of encounters with Gray.

The Research Centers' Chief Archivist, J. Michael Miller, and his staff were repeatedly sought out to "find" those one-of-a-kind "must have" documents. Equally supportive was the Director, Charles P. Neimeyer, PhD, and Robert V. Aquilina from History Division, Marine Corps University, who responded freely to my many requests for assistance from both staffs. They never faltered, never failed to come through with professional assistance.

Major Edward F. Wells, a polished Marine Corps historian, provided multiple articles and writings on former Marine Corps Commandants, giving new insight into their historic tenures.

Edited by Jean B. Reynolds and Jeffrey J. Seeley.

CHAPTER 1
The Test

"This shall not stand."

George H.W. Bush
President of the United States
August 5, 1990

This was a time like no other in the 200-plus years of Marine Corps history. It was a time when combat-ready Marines were leaning forward in their battle positions. They were preparing, not for an amphibious assault across some enemy-held beach, but to conduct a massive, two-division mechanized attack. Their staging positions were miles from any ocean waters. It was a moment in time when the 29th Commandant of the U.S. Marine Corps was visiting his nearly 90,000 Marines and Sailors in their forward positions just days before the 1991 war against the Iraqi tyrant, Saddam Hussein.

Marine Commandant General Alfred Mason Gray Jr., a warrior and world traveler, was visiting his Marines and Sailors who were assembling for war on the cold winter and windy desert sands of Saudi Arabia. His two divisions, strengthened by the equivalent of two aviation wings, along with a large logistical support team, had been equipped and trained to exploit the latest technological advancements against an army equipped with aged Soviet-made tanks and artillery. In addition, the force was prepared for the possible Iraqi employment of biological and chemical weapons of mass destruction (WMDs). Munitions had been distributed to the leading elements of the assault battalions. Radios had been synchronized. The field medical hospitals were preparing for the inevitable flow of wounded. All were in position and prepared for the auspicious test ahead.

The Christmas holidays were tense, but not in a wholly unpleasant way. Something close to war fever gripped the country, and that hadn't been seen for generations. The Fox News affiliate in New York City seldom referred to Saddam Hussein by name anymore; he was usually "the Butcher of Baghdad." Kiosks in shopping malls sold T-shirts with smart-ass, dimwitted legends like "I'd fly 5,000 miles to smoke a camel" under a cartoon of an F-15 leaving a smoking hole (pieces of camel visible) in its wake. Lee Greenwood's song "I'm Proud to be an American" got a lot of airplay, and a new version included voiceovers from family members saying the names of the units their loved ones served in, such as "USS *Saipan*, 24th Infantry Division," and so on. All were pronounced in the various flat, serious, hinterland accents of the people who volunteer for America's wars. People were apprehensive, but they were proud of their military, too, and confident in them.

United States President George H.W. Bush had given the Iraqis a deadline. They were to leave Kuwait by January 15, 1991, or they would be expelled. An American-led coalition was preparing to make good the ultimatum, and they were clearly almost ready to do so. The danger that Iraqi troops might overrun Saudi Arabia and the minor Persian Gulf states had receded. That danger had seemed very real back in August, when Bush had drawn his line in the sand with the bayonet of an 82nd Airborne trooper. The 82nd's great military advantage was its deployability, but against a determined attack by heavy mechanized forces, it was a plate-glass window: valuable, easily shattered by a hard blow but, if shattered, a guarantee that some vandal would pay.

There is another interesting factor in the overall combat posture of the earliest units into Saudi Arabia. The U.S. Army's phased buildup in the Middle East resulted in an initial lack of major armored assets in Saudi Arabia. Once their heavy tank and mechanized divisions were alerted, it took time to embark their equipment. Then, when fully loaded, the ships had to transit from Texas ports to Saudi Arabia. In some cases, their arrival times were 30 to 45 days later. It was during this initial buildup phase that the Marine Corps had the only American armored units in the Persian Gulf, aboard maritime prepositioning ships and the amphibious ships offshore. These few armored assets had to be considered as General Norman Schwarzkopf's regional strategic reserve. Fortunately, Saddam Hussein held back in attacking the growing U.S. forces. Significantly, the Army accelerated the buildup of their own prepositioning afloat capability after what was to become known as the "First Gulf War."

But eventually, heavy numbers of Army forces arrived in strength, the U.S. Air Force moved tactical fighter wings into airfields in the Saudi Arabian Desert, and the Navy's air armada arrived aboard carriers. Along with the carriers came a vast naval surface fleet equipped with the untested cruise missile shooters—and, grandest of all—the USS *Missouri* and the USS *Wisconsin*, the world's last two battleships.

With the American forces were troops from a surprisingly disparate set of allies referred to as "coalition troops." Some were old allies such as the British and French, but they also included Arab troops, Italian fighter squadrons, and, harbingers of what President Bush unfortunately would call "the New World Order," welcomed oddities such as Polish naval units and a Czech chemical decontamination regiment.

And, of course, the U.S. Marines were there on the ground opposite Kuwait City, as well as afloat in the Persian Gulf, menacing the Iraqi seaward flank. They were part of more than half a million U.S. personnel in Saudi Arabia, nearly ready to eject Saddam Hussein from oil-rich Kuwait.

It had begun on August 2, 1990, when Iraqis, emboldened by misreading an American ambassador's remarks on inter-Arab disputes, overran and annexed Kuwait. Kuwait was now Iraq's "19th province," something the Iraqi press led its citizens to believe Kuwait had always been. The war was not aggression; it was a rectification. The Kuwaiti army was relatively small and unprepared. As the Emir, Sheik Jaber al-Ahmed al-Sabah, his family, and his ministers fled, and many civilians became refugees, Iraqi forces sustained the momentum of their attack until they reached the Persian Gulf and the ill-defined Saudi border. There they stopped and consolidated. It was unclear whether this was, in fact, a final objective, or whether it was nothing more than an operational pause.

Kuwait's rich oil fields were under the complete control of the Iraqi Army and the fields immediately to the south in Saudi Arabia and the other Gulf states were under its guns. Saddam Hussein now controlled, either directly or indirectly, much of the oil reserves upon which the developed world depended. President Bush declared the Iraqi attack "aggression" and said that it would not stand. There had been initial skepticism over whether he would find support for his resolve in the United Nations and among the world's seven major economic powers (let alone Congress), but President Bush made good. Working through the United Nations, Western nations, and some Arab countries, he assembled a coalition of forces in Saudi Arabia and afloat in the Persian Gulf. As these ground and air forces arrived in Saudi Arabia and moved into desert assembly areas, they joined in a series of training exercises in preparation to recapture Kuwait and expel the Iraqi forces.

Gray's vision of how the Marine Corps had prepared itself to fight on battlefields during the last decade of the 20th century was to be demonstrated by the Marine Corps' performance during DESERT STORM. All military forces change over time in order to remain a viable instrument of their nation's national security strategy, and so it was with the Marine Corps, which had undergone any number of changes in its 200-plus years of service to the nation.

Many Marine Corps senior leaders skillfully contributed to this restructure and expansion of Marine Corps operations forces global capabilities. But when closely studied, one individual's vision and boundless energy was singularly responsible for the Marine Corps' transformation from a conventional warfare mindset to one focused on the emerging threats that demanded expeditionary forces capable of operating in the Information Age. Gray was that man.

During the entire decade of the 1980s, Gray had been the leading advocate for this change within the Marine Corps and was often both the architect and its overseer. Every component of the historical air-ground logistics team had, in one way or another, been significantly impacted by his efforts. During the 1980s, when either a new concept or doctrine was proposed or tested, he was there. When decisions had to be made about new equipment, such as the M1A tank, and the Light Armored Vehicle (LAV), he was there driving the development and testing the High Mobility Multipurpose Wheeled Vehicle (HMMWV or Humvee). For example, he was active in the procurement and mounting of a 25mm turret gun on the LAV. Additionally, he was the most vocal advocate in the procurement of new engineer barrier breaching technology. When Headquarters Marine Corps (HQMC), under Commandants Robert Barrow and Paul X. Kelley, were aggressively pursuing procurement of the revolutionary V-22 Osprey helicopter and the Navy's development of the LCAC (landing craft air cushion), Gray was there helping, working with Congress and various agencies to get vital long-term funding. For more than a decade, Gray assisted, cajoled—perhaps even schemed a little—to mold and equip a different Marine Corps to enter the 21st century.

For example, the Marine Corps initially elected to wait until the first major modifications to the M1 tank turned it into what was designated as the M1A2. Later, for Marine Corps budgetary reasons, there had to be a further delay in programming for their allowed numbers. When the 1990 Persian Gulf crisis arose, Gray requested the Army provide an accelerated delivery of a tank battalion's worth of M1A2s. There was a compelling reason for this request, as the Army's Reserve units were not scheduled to receive the M1A2 until long after the Marines were positioned against the immediate Iraqi threats. Gray was aware of the increased lethality and survivability of the M1A2. He wanted the best armor capability for his Marine units to meet and destroy Iraq's

Sixth Armored Division.[1] It would have been unconscionable not to seek and equip his Marine tank battalions with anything less than the most advanced capabilities. His request was quickly approved. This changed the Army's initial modernization plans. However, at the procurement and operational decisionmaking levels, Gray's request was a rational and timely request. With the procurement of the M1A2, there was also an immediate need generated for specialized crew and gunnery training.[2] Headquarters Marine Corps designated the 4th Tank Battalion—a reserve battalion—to receive the necessary crew training. Later, during the ground war, this particular unit scored hundreds of tank "kills."

As the nation began positioning its forces in the Gulf, there would be many Admirals and Generals entering the forthcoming battle space. But Al Gray would have a unique position among them, as they had only recently been assigned to their commands. All were exceptionally capable, but each had had no time to make major adjustment to their forces. They had to fight with the forces provided. In essence, these component commanders had their horses harnessed, their stirrups set and ready for their leader to ride. U.S. Army General Norman Schwarzkopf, the overall senior American commander, had but to get into the saddle, raise his warrior's sword, so to speak, and unleash the unprecedented might of his forces to move forward from their lines of departure. He and the commanders from the U.S. Air Force, Navy, and Army would fulfill their responsibilities in a superb manner.

To continue with the metaphor, Gray's uniqueness was that he had "birthed the Marine Corps horse." In doing so, he had trained it to function in a maneuver warfare mode that he had defined in his seminal doctrinal document, *"Warfighting."* He was the untiring advocate for a new Marine Corps armed, trained, and equipped to operate on an asymmetric battlefield with initiative and audacity. Lastly, he was instrumental in upgrading all tactical command and control systems to operate over vast distances to include near real-time position reporting from all maneuver units. It was a totally new Marine Corps for the 1990s. As the leading advocate for change, he was undaunted by seemingly overwhelming issues where a lesser determined person would have tired of fighting the perpetual scarcity of fiscal funding, an immovable bureaucratic maze, and accepted less than his visionary convictions mandated. All who encountered Gray during this trying decade learned to never underestimate his vision and dogged determination. He had truly affected the quality and power of a new *expeditionary force* that was about to unleash this reinvigorated air-ground logistics team just hours away.

Gray's initiatives must be seen in the context of overall changes in the Department of Defense during the same period. In 1986, Congress passed the Goldwater-Nichols Act which dramatically changed the way the four Service Chiefs interacted with the Chairman, Joint Chiefs of Staff (CJCS), and the geographical Combatant Commanders. While the Joint Chiefs of Staff (JCS) still have major roles to develop and enforce their respective service policies, plans, and projections, their primary role as a Joint Chief would be to present their best advice and thoughts on all military matters to the Secretary of Defense and the President. Combatant Commanders would report directly to the Secretary of Defense through the Chairman of the Joint Chiefs of Staff.

General Al Gray was completing the fourth and last year of his tenure as the Commandant of the Marine Corps. Now, as had happened often during his four decades of service, Marines were preparing for war. As Commandant, Gray was not to be in the operational chain of command. However, because of his executive responsibilities, he remained responsible for logistical planning and remained in charge of the Marine Corps Reserve forces. The senior Marine on the ground was Lieutenant General Walter E. Boomer, and that placed Gray in a coaching role. This time he wasn't giving them orders, except indirectly, insofar as his position on the Joint Chiefs involved him in the war. The Marine Corps' battle orders now came directly from the Commander-in-Chief, Central Command, General Norman Schwarzkopf, and down his functional chain of command to his Joint,

Land, Air, and Maritime component commanders. Fortunately, there was open and mutual respect between Schwarzkopf and Gray. On several previous occasions, Gray had openly supported Schwarzkopf at the Secretary of Defense/Joint Chiefs level on various strategic matters. Furthermore, Gray was adamant that the Marine Corps would meet all of General Schwarzkopf's requests for forces in a timely manner.[3]

The Commandant of the Marine Corps recruits, trains, equips, and organizes the Marine Corps. He is responsible for their readiness, their doctrine, and their esprit de corps. In reflection, Gray was probably more innovative than most of his predecessors. On his watch, the Corps had undergone some fairly far-reaching changes; he had not been merely a caretaker Commandant. Certainly he was not the only individual, but he was the principal driving force. The new Corps he had helped birth, train, and equip was now about to be tested, and Gray was certainly quietly overseeing the final preparations.

Now in Saudi Arabia and in the Persian Gulf region, he was visiting as many of his 96,000-plus Marines and Navy personnel as he could reach in the forward areas of deployment. Everywhere he went, he was received with spontaneous cheers and the open admiration of the young Marines. Having himself served in the ranks, he was admired as "our General." He was their friend and exemplar, and they, as among troops everywhere, each seemed to have an "Al Gray" story. When he moved to a unit, Gray would climb up onto a tracked vehicle or a truck and, from his field-expedient rostrum, tell the troops how proud he was of them. Their preparations had been tireless, and the weather was almost as extreme as they had endured at Twentynine Palms, California, during earlier desert training exercises.

Once, when he finished speaking, a young Marine yelled out from the crowd, "General Gray, sir, would you reenlist me?" The troops fell silent, waiting for his response. Their General or not, no young Marine lightly intruded into any General's schedule. And reenlisting is a serious thing. They all knew that the act of reenlisting was an important ceremony of mutual commitment between the Corps and the young enlisted Marine who was taking the first step toward "making it a career." A reenlistment was usually administered by their immediate unit commanders.

Gray was up to the moment. "Sure!" he yelled back. "Come up here." The others cheered and then roared. As the Marine pushed his way through the crowd, other Marines shouted, "How about me, General?" Before Gray moved on to the next unit, at least ten Marines had taken their reenlistment oaths. Gray had experienced this type of request before, and working with the Sergeant Major of the Marine Corps, Dave Summers, they had developed a simple signaling code that confirmed their unit commanders agreed with the troopers' requests for reenlistment. Gray left this unit, as he did most, with the charge to all to "take care of your buddies and take care of yourselves." It came from the heart, and his Marines knew it. Warriors tend to be emotional.

The battles that would begin in a few days would be fought by the "warriors" Gray had trained (and often reenlisted). Gray had started calling them "warriors" many years prior to his tenure as Commandant, extending to the Corps as a whole a name he had begun to apply to the Marines under his command when he was still a junior Colonel, in order to emphasize to Marines and others what the Corps was fundamentally about.

This was an "All-Volunteer Force," no novelty for the Marine Corps, to be sure, which had rarely in its history taken conscripts, and Gray wanted no one to mistake joining the Marine Corps as a casual undertaking but as a deep commitment to serve one's country. So they had been recruited, to be sure, for their unprecedented level of education, test scores, and lack of police involvement, but present in most was a burning desire to be called "Marine."

They were equipped with new generations of weapons and equipment that had replaced most of the seemingly eternal standbys from

Vietnam, Korea, and World War II, from the Jeep to the M1911 .45-caliber pistol. Their weapons now included the spooky, powerful M1A2 main battle tank, the nimble troop-carrying Light Armored Vehicle (LAV-25), a long-ranged brute of a gun-howitzer in the M198, an aviator's mud fighter in the AV-8B Harrier ground attack aircraft, and their accompanying suite of precision-guided bombs and anti-tank missiles. New also were laser rangefinders, Global Positioning System (GPS), satellite communications, unmanned aircraft with video cameras, and night-vision systems for infantry units, all integrated into what arguably the best-trained Marine air-ground team ever assembled. Much of this hardware had been conceived, developed, purchased, and fielded through the personal involvement of this intense and frequently controversial man. Gray had also seen to it that Marines had thought through just how they were to use their equipment. Three new doctrinal publications, *Warfighting, Campaigning,* and *Tactics,* had short introductions from the Commandant himself. Gray played a significant and active role in drafting these publications. Later he often referred to the books as "my" conception of how Marines would fight. There was little chance of ducking responsibility for that doctrine no matter how carefully it had been staffed.

Now, after five months of intense training and logistics preparation, the 1st and 2nd Marine Divisions, reinforced, were leaning forward in their assault positions. Offshore in amphibious shipping were the 4th and 5th Marine Brigades, 16,000 strong and ready to come from the sea. This naval force, afloat on 36 amphibious ships was actually serving as the strategic reserve for the growing coalition forces and was under the leadership of Major General Harry Jenkins and Brigadier General Pete Rose. This combined arms force was led by Marines who had "grown up" together in the Corps and had served together in Vietnam as company and battalion commanders. Likewise, they had served together in the smaller wars, interventions, and operations since Vietnam: Grenada, Lebanon, and Panama. But this test was different. This was going to be a test of Gray's warfighting philosophy and all that he had done to shape the Marine Corps. If he hadn't done it well, no 11th-hour patching would make it hold up.

Years before Gray became the Commandant, he had already embedded, where he could, prescient changes in Marine Corps force structure, doctrine, and operational capabilities. As a relatively junior General officer, he had exerted a surprising influence on the Corps as a whole and, of course, as Commandant, he had fundamentally changed its culture. The time passed quickly. In 1975, the year Saigon fell, a newly-promoted Brigadier General Gray was assigned to command the 4th Marine Amphibious Brigade in Norfolk. New Brigadier Generals wished for such a challenging assignment. The 4th Brigade had forces afloat in the Atlantic, and it habitually trained for North Atlantic Treaty Organization (NATO) missions, in particular, the reinforcement of Norway in the event of a Soviet attack on the West. The 4th MAB (Marine Amphibious Brigade) offered a good fulcrum for someone interested in moving the Marine Corps in certain directions.

During the three years he commanded the 4th Brigade, Gray planned and executed 18 major amphibious exercises on the Northern European littoral, in the Mediterranean, and in the Caribbean. The United States had turned away from its engagement in Southeast Asia—the first military defeat in its history—to devote what limited attention and energy it had to NATO. The nation had long held a NATO-first policy (directly formed from the Europe-first strategy of the Second World War) and a strategy to match it. The operational doctrine designed for NATO's central front had proven ill-suited to Vietnam, and it was an uneasy beginning of a long period of change that would begin with a doctrine called "active defense." During the Cold War, NATO forces, in which American divisions figured prominently, faced a massive Soviet armored threat, one that could move with unprecedented speed and violence, and, as they had shown in Czechoslovakia in 1968, they were capable of strategic surprise. It was assumed the Soviets could crash through the three great approaches—the North German Plain, the Fulda Gap, and the Hof Corridor. NATO would contain the penetration and then go over to a counteroffensive that would restore the sovereignty and territorial integrity of its members. Most people who thought about it believed that NATO would be forced to employ tactical nuclear weapons early in such a war. The Europeans, especially, believed it and looked upon the American troops in Germany (a sorry lot, in the early days of the volunteer Army) not so much as an effective warfighting force, but as a guarantee that the American strategic deterrent would continue to be extended to them.

The first Marine Amphibious Unit (MAU) to participate in any NATO exercise did so in 1975, shortly before Brigadier General Gray assumed command of the 4th Marine Amphibious Brigade. The initial MAU deployment was a reinforced infantry battalion supported by a battery of 105mm field artillery and a tank platoon of five M-60 tanks. In previous exercises, the Marine ground combat elements had consisted of reinforced dismounted infantry battalions and were assigned only minor roles because they lacked both the mobility and firepower to move quickly and engage the enemy forces. The MAU units were often bypassed by the fast-maneuvering opposing forces, or simply isolated. They ultimately contributed little to the NATO exercises beyond their physical presence in a spuriously "joint" combined arms environment.

This lack of understanding of amphibious forces' strategic capabilities grated on senior Marines for a lot of reasons. The NATO arena was the big game; the Soviet Union was the big opponent. If the Marine Corps couldn't make a useful contribution to NATO, it was unclear why we should bother having a Marine Corps at all. Marine Corps senior leadership felt a critical need to demonstrate to the European Theater Commanders that the Marine Corps could update its task organization and play a viable role on the strategic flanks of Europe. It could do this only if it undertook to remake itself, just as it had remade itself into an amphibious force between the world wars.

Gray's position in the 4th MAB gave him an opportunity to think about how this might be done. A prolific reader and a student of what was beginning to be called "maneuver warfare," now Gray began to systematically change the structure of his MAB units. He increased the mobility of his ground units with additional trucks, amphibious assault vehicles, and tanks. He tinkered with new task organizations, developing a new emphasis on "maneuver warfare" training programs, and he executed a series of NATO exercises on both the northern and southern flanks.

For exercises in Denmark and Germany, the 4th MAB's Marine Air-Ground Task Force (MAGTF) had been revised. The traditional structure of the Air Combat Element had been augmented by increasing the numbers and types of fixed- and rotary-winged aircraft providing close air support. He particularly emphasized the role of anti-armor helicopters. With a more robust anti-armor and close air support capability, the MAB's command element and air-control units formed a NATO-specific, effective air element totaling more than 45 fixed-wing aircraft and 28 helicopters. The ground combat element was also progressively strengthened, building up to a reinforced infantry regiment, supported by one battalion of field artillery, a tank battalion of 58 M-60 tanks, and 80 amphibious assault vehicles, plus highly mobile reconnaissance units designed for deep penetrations.

Gray also looked at how the other NATO players were equipped. He was particularly attracted to West Germany's military family of wheeled light armored reconnaissance vehicles, capable of speeds of 70 miles per hour on roads. He had acquired three years' experience in contesting the speed and maneuverability of several NATO nations' reconnaissance vehicles. He realized that the Marine Corps needed a vehicle with similar capabilities and he was determined to find it, and quickly.

Based upon these European maneuvers, he began conducting some rudimentary mechanized operations at Camp Lejeune, North Carolina, and at Fort Pickett, Virginia. These increasingly represented departures from the Marine Corps' historical tradition of enclave, linear warfare, in the direction of "maneuver warfare." He recognized that to effectively operate on a maneuver warfare battlefield, broad mission-type orders at all levels would become necessary. This perception was a major change from the Marine Corps' traditional conventional warfare doctrine. Senior commanders' intent would now have to be understood by leaders at every level. This realization caused him to make drastic changes in his MAB's training. His concept of maneuvering on the battlefield downplayed the traditional Marine Corps doctrine of a fixed battle line of interlocking battalions, reinforced in depth by reserve forces and artillery units. In contrast, maneuver warfare necessitated highly mobile forces, structured to exploit an evolving battlefield. This generates increased reconnaissance dependence above the battlefield via helicopters. For the ground forces, especially on the flanks, he used the aged amphibious P-7 assault vehicles as armored vehicles, with them playing a "poor man's cavalry" role to fix the enemies in position for the main force to execute a narrow line of advance to attack.

The adoption of maneuver warfare as a warfighting doctrine was greeted by Gray's seniors within the Marine Corps with skepticism and great concern. Yet his 4th MAB's operational performances were repeatedly applauded by European allies and the Supreme Allied Commander Europe for their ingenuity and increased combat capability within the NATO theater. By 1977 and through 1978 his 4th MAB was playing a principal role in NORTHERN WEDDING/BOLD GUARD, a major NATO exercise. The culminating exercise event was the 4th MAB's successful counterattack through an opposing force of more than 250 tanks and mechanized vehicles.

It was to be Gray's last opportunity to demonstrate with the 4th MAB that Marine Corps units could adapt to maneuver warfare. Under his strong leadership and broad mission planning concept, Regimental Landing Team-2 (RLT-2) executed a counterattack that penetrated the enemy's lines before dawn, on a narrow front, rolling up much larger armored forces and then exploiting the enemy's battlefield disarray by advancing some 26 miles in four hours. No other Marine Corps Brigade had ever successfully accomplished such a mission.

A voracious reader of history, Gray had begun his early discussions at the philosophical and doctrinal level. He sought to create an intellectual dialogue among Marine officers who could transform the Corps from a force suited principally for enclave warfare into one capable of defeating an enemy across the spectrum of conflict. Gray's innovation was formed by his love and knowledge of history. It represented the best of the Marine Corps tradition. It was in the context of a broad debate about the future role of the Marine Corps that Gray deployed and led his brigade under a transformed conception of conventional warfare. There were many new lessons learned during his extended command of the 4th MAB. Gray was not a forgetful man, and would store these experiences away to recall later and use the knowledge gained as new situations arose.

Upon his selection for promotion to Major General and subsequent reassignment to the Marine Corps Development Center at Quantico, Gray was able to reflect on the experiences of his MAB command and consider how to equip and train the Fleet Marine Forces (FMFs) better for maneuver warfare. He had full responsibility for research and development funding, a special team of program managers, and the resources and developmental mission to make his impact on preparing the Fleet Marine Forces for modern war.

One of his first actions was to find a suitable Light Armored Vehicle (LAV). He did this, in June 1980, by acquiring six Swiss-built LAVs. Both six- and eight-wheeled versions were shipped to the Marine Corps Ground Combat Center at Twentynine Palms, California. After a short but intense field test, the eight-wheeled model was accepted by the Marine Corps, and small unit level training began. In doing so, the Marine Corps began to develop a maneuver warfare doctrine which ultimately led to significant organizational changes in infantry, reconnaissance, artillery, tanks, and Amphibious Assault Vehicle

(AAV) units. The current conventional warfare doctrine was based on confronting an enemy where traditional linear defense was based on fixed lines, the depth of the battlefield, and superior firepower. This concept would be extended into a fourth dimension—time—for the essence of maneuver warfare is the ability to decide and act faster than your enemy can respond.

Gray recognized that, in changing established Marine Corps doctrine, the organizational structure of the Marine divisional units would also change in terms of size, equipment, and training requirements. He also set his eyes on the Marine Corps' training and education programs. He had gained enough professional recognition in the 4th MAB that military people were willing to listen to—if not necessarily approve of—his ideas, and his recognized leadership and operational experience let him begin an intensive dialogue through the Marine Corps schools at Quantico on how the Corps might change to better serve the nation through the 1990s and beyond. Gray was never reticent about this. He vociferously expounded on the need for change, and he relished his opportunities to address officers at these schools. Little did he realize then, as the Commanding General, 2nd Marine Division, that before he completed his last assignment (as the 29th Commandant), the very concepts of maneuver warfare and upgraded training programs he was stressing would be tested in the 1991 Gulf War.

Circumstances in the Gulf had brought together, in the form of DESERT SHIELD and later DESERT STORM, the largest concentrations of U.S. Marine Corps forces since the peak of the Vietnam War. But in the 20 years subsequent to that conflict, the Marine Corps had grown more in Gray's short era than during any similar period in Marine Corps history. The Corps had become a modern fighting force that had survived a period of self-examination and implemented a fresh commitment to what Gray preferred to call "the warrior ethos."

As Gray moved from his ground combat units to the amphibious ships offshore to the aviation squadrons and to the logisticians supporting every one, he had opportunity to reflect on his work for more than a decade when he undertook to prepare the Marine Corps to fight on any battlefield through the year 2000. As the primary architect who had years earlier laid out the training of the 1st Marine Expeditionary Force's air, ground, and logistics teams, he was about to see the proof of his vision of a modern Marine Corps prepared to fight as a high-tech force. He felt confident.

Time was short. It was obvious to everyone, and particularly to Gray, that soon his Marines would be ordered forward to breach the Iraqi obstacles. Like any reflective officer before battle, he ran through the things he could still do to prepare his Marines for battle. However, his authority and period of responsibility was essentially over. The combat test of his vision was at hand. It weighed heavily on him, because Marines would live or die according to how carefully he had trained and equipped them. Now time and events would determine how well he had fulfilled his charge.

Gray had earlier made a study of mine-clearing and obstacle-breaching equipment and had become convinced that several Israeli systems were far superior to the standard American products. Characteristically indifferent to the inevitable criticism the decision would incite, he directed the emergency procurement of specially designed bulldozers to perform the critical initial breaching quickly for his 1st and 2nd Marine Divisions. His personal and aggressive involvement in this procurement issue would be instrumental, no doubt, in saving the lives of Marines and Army Soldiers who led the assault through the Iraqi minefields.

The complexity, depth, and massive expanse of the barrier deeply concerned him. It was positional warfare of a kind Marine forces hadn't seen since their modern emergence on the Western Front in 1918. The Iraqi obstacle system was ominous and appeared as a broad field in disarray via a carefully structured barrier defense. Even from a distance he could see hundreds of exposed anti-tank and anti-personnel mines. Many could be assumed—with the force of knowledge—to be booby-trapped as well, all to make any breaching force pay for its advance with time and blood. Each mine represented a potential casualty. Lethal, dumb, and with the deadly vigilance of all simple machines, they looked to Gray like silent sentries warning that intruders would be killed or maimed in the most casual, impersonal way imaginable. He wondered how many more were just below the blowing sands. Gray was no stranger to minefields. During the Vietnam War, he had, on two different occasions, crawled and probed his way through an anti-personnel minefield, at night, under heavy artillery and mortar fire, to rescue injured Marines.

Minefields and other types of barrier systems are normally covered by enemy fire. They need to be breached as close to "in-stride" as possible, because the barrier systems are designed to restrict all movement so the enemy can fix your positions with deadly artillery. In contrast, the attacker wants speed and mobility, because battles are won by "executing," as officers say in the coach-speak popular among them, faster and more violently than the enemy. Accordingly, the American forces needed to breach quickly in order to exploit the superior speed of their maneuver forces, and to avoid being caught stationary before an obstacle by Iraqi long-range artillery. The ultimate outcome of the pending war could well be decided in the first hours of battle.

Gray was completely confident the Marine forces would break through the barriers, but at what cost to his Marines and Sailors? Mines were of special interest to him. He understood their potential and their threat. In this he was not alone. Mines were not novelties to Marines, and their comrades in the Army considered support of mobility, including specifically and prominently breaching mined obstacles, the first mission of their combat engineers—but countermine warfare tended to lack a strong constituency within the services.

He was always interested in learning from the best in the business. Gray stood out, however, in his willingness to maneuver around the laborious and glacially slow defense acquisition system to get Marines the equipment they needed to breach minefields effectively. The acquisition system is typically American in its legalistic fondness for due process, fair business practices, and meticulous accounting, and it is victim to the lowest bidder's shortcomings. This time-consuming approach to procurement is the evolutionary product of innumerable negotiations and compromises among alert, stubborn, and legally well-advised players in Congress, industry, and the executive branch. It serves many excellent purposes, but absent a national emergency on the scale of a world war, the system is not usually a supple instrument for quickly fielding the smaller and more easily overlooked critically needed tools of the military. The Marines had to close with the enemy rapidly to fix their forces in place, while the Army's troops on the western flank enveloped the Iraqi armor. Gray would do everything legal, or almost legal, to support his warriors.

Gray's daily routine, no matter where he was, was to separate himself from the business of the day with an evening walk. Dipping tobacco or snuff was effete and cigarette smoking wasn't for Gray. Neither were part of his ritual but chewing tobacco was. Gray used his "off" time to think and reflect as he walked several hundred yards away from the last group of Marines he was visiting, and he stood looking north across the desert dunes toward Kuwait and Iraq. Just a short distance away was the forward edge of the barbed wire fence the Marines had put in place to prevent anyone from prematurely entering the enemy's minefields. The hastily placed red signs were hung from the top strands of barbed wire and were swinging with the light, hot breeze to mark the ominous minefields. From the numerous briefings Gray had received about the Iraqi minefields, he could visualize that just over the berm lay the series of mine barriers the leading Marine elements would have to breach to place their "cleared" lane boundary markers.

As the sun was setting on the final evening before Gray was to return to the United States, he again separated himself from the other officers and enlisted men and went for one more walk. The troops and others were quick to notice this solitary routine. They watched him, but carefully so as not to disturb or distract him. He walked close to the barrier of wire and tank barrier ditches, looking over the windswept berms. He could visualize the neglected and now poorly hidden and half-exposed landmines that marked the Kuwaiti border.

A soft breeze was blowing the desert sand around his field boots. It was the type of fine-grained sand, almost rouge-like, that had blown across the Middle East deserts for thousands of years. His thoughts also caused him to reflect on the seemingly endless wars that had crossed the surrounding deserts. He valued the military commander's need to "know his enemy" to better understand how best to fight and win on any battlefield. As he strolled along, he searched his mind for any new thoughts about the waiting enemy.

Gray, being a quasi-history student, was aware that the nondescript desert he was now walking across had long been the violent scene of innumerable long-forgotten battles. As a tireless reader, he was rekindling his knowledge on the long and ancient history of the whole region. Since the earliest of recorded history, the Kuwaiti and Iraqi deserts had served in a strategic position at the crossroads of three continents: Europe, Asia, and Africa, and the particular geographical features had played an overwhelming role in its history. From ancient Mesopotamia came the greatest advances in mankind's evolution.[3] Here had lived the first people to practice agriculture and the domestication of animals more than 6,000 years ago. Its strategic position placed it on the ancient but busy Silk Road to China and on the camel caravan routes to India.[4] It was the pivotal crossroads for both commerce and unwanted wars. It was a land passageway ideal for invading armies to move through. The Arab world is the junction between Africa and Asia and Europe.[5] From ancient invaders such as Genghis Khan to Alexander the Great, and the more recent armies of World War I and

World War II, Europe had moved through Kuwait and Iraq to hold and/or occupy, the Crescent Valleys.[6]

Gray knew that both Iraq and Kuwait had been subjected to near-continuous invasions. Iraq's lands were the largest of the Fertile Crescent countries rimming the northern edge of the Arabian Peninsula. The region lay between the plateau of north Arabia and southwestern Iran and Turkey, forming a lowland connection between East and West. Its broad, fertile valley had been a Mecca for the earliest civilizations, with nomadic tribes settling between the two major tributaries: the Tigris and Euphrates Rivers. Many contributions to civilization were made by Iraqis, such as the development of writing—based originally on pictographs.[7] Through their observations of celestial bodies, they created the first accurate calendars based on the 12-month lunar year and the cycle of 60 minutes and 12 hours that we still use to tell time. These advances also made the region the target of uncountable invaders. From Roman Legions to Alexander the Great and many other armies, including British forces during the 18th century, all contrived to fight across the desert sand Al Gray was now looking over.

Gray's lonely walk over the undulating terrain brought him upon a small sand dune. He climbed and looked again at the vast minefield. He spat tobacco across the wire and moved on. The heavy feeling of a forthcoming war was in the air. But this was to be a war like no other. This time, there would be no camel caravans or slow-moving hordes of dusty Arabs invading another Arab nation. Instead, it was to be a campaign known for advanced technologies like jet aircraft sweeping across the skies, day or night, at speeds greater than 500 miles per hour and armed with precision-guided bombs to strike key bridges and high-value targets, or large Iraqi communications centers. Far at sea, U.S. naval gunfire and electronically guided Harpoon missiles were set to strike hundreds of inland targets. On the ground, the most sophisticated M1A2 Abrams tanks were to break through the minefields and lead multiple armored attacks across Kuwait and on into Iraq. Infantrymen were equipped with precision-guided anti-tank missiles. Night-vision devices had been placed in the hands of the assaulting formations to ensure around-the-clock combat operations. It was to be a different war like no other that had ever occurred before. The Information Age had arrived.

Most Marines had long held Saddam Hussein partly responsible for some of the terrorist actions in Lebanon (terror that Gray had anticipated years earlier), and Marines are always mindful of their comrades, their history, and their heritage. It was time for his "soldiers of the sea" to "Suck it up and go!" A few hours later, as his plane rolled down the runway and lifted off toward Washington, it must have felt like the loneliest moment of his life. He prayed for his Marines and Sailors.

I, Colonel Gerry Turley (USMCR, Retired), was originally scheduled to accompany Gray on this trip to the Middle East. In serving as a special consultant to his office, I had often traveled with him across the States and overseas. However, on this trip, there was limited seating on the government aircraft, and he felt that it was more important that his two Fleet Marine Force Commanders, Lieutenant Generals Carl Mundy and Robert Milligan, should join him on the trip. He was right asking me to remain stateside. Gray recognized the value of having his Commander, Marine Forces Atlantic in lieu of simply taking me, a retired Marine Corps Colonel. This would be his third trip to meet with his Marines and Sailors before they jumped off in the attack to recapture Kuwait. I wanted to go, to see, listen, and learn, but he needed others far more important, and I fully understood his decision to not take me along and hoped I did not show my personal disappointment. Though the General and I had become quite close over the previous three and half years of his command, he never wavered from always seeking "what is best" for his Marine Corps. The Corps was always first consideration, true friends and professionals understood this trait.

After Gray's return, he shared some of his observations. I later spoke with several Marines who had moved with him and had listened to his informal talks with different units. They observed how he usually climbed up on a tank or truck so he could see all those gathered around. They related how he was always up for every troop encounter and noted his tendency to routinely separate himself, seemingly to ponder his thoughts. Being a complex man of many personality traits, including tenacious determination, there would be much to see and observe during the next four years.

CHAPTER 2
The Character of the
29th Commandant

*"If Marines don't have a lifelong idea of learning, then
they will not rise to the top of their profession; nor
will they maintain the ... professional confidence that
[they] ... need; that then is needed for tomorrow."*

> General Alfred M. Gray
> 29th Commandant, U.S. Marine Corps
> November 17, 1989

He is not a tall man, but broad and stocky, with the powerful upper body and swaggering gait of an athlete, holding his frame erect to the limit of his five feet, eight inches. Today, 29 years after Al Gray became Commandant, he seems younger than most who have spent nearly 41 years in uniform, his thinning white hair cropped clean on the sides, short on top, capping a broad smooth face. His light complexion, coupled with his reckless and penetrating blue eyes are immediately noticed by even the most casual observer.

But what distinguishes Gray from his peers—even at a first meeting—are several distinct character traits that have strong roots in his life experiences. Foremost is his direct, plainspoken approach that is more typical of what one would associate with a "working man" than that of a former Service Chief and member of the Joint Chiefs of Staff. Typically, Gray would reflect about "what ordinary folks are thinking" and about how what was being discussed "down at the 7-Eleven" were metaphors for common knowledge and concerns.

Perhaps this grounding in everyday people is the result of Gray's early life. Alfred Mason Gray was born on June 22, 1928, in Rahway, New Jersey.

During World War I, his father, Al Sr., had joined the Navy as a seaman and served aboard troop ship USS *Edgar F. Luckenbach*, which made eight trips to France. Two of his father's brothers also served in the Navy aboard minesweepers during the war period. Al was proud of his father's military service.

When the 1918 Armistice was signed, Al Sr. was honorably discharged and returned home to Staten Island, New York, where he resumed his job as a brakeman and later conductor with the Pennsylvania Railroad.[1] Al senior would eventually serve the railroad more than 44 years, the last 25 years making the New York City to Washington, DC run on what was then known as the Congressional Limited. When the Stock Market crashed in 1929, hundreds of thousands of people were suddenly without jobs, and few had future aspects for employment. Fortunately, his father was able to keep his railroad positions all through the Depression. But for the greater Gray family, it was a time of some despair. In the best Scotch-Irish family tradition, when Al senior's wife's two brothers lost their jobs and their families became financially destitute, they were invited to live in the already-crowded Gray home. Throughout the long years of the Depression, Al senior repeatedly and graciously opened his home to his wife's brothers and their families, as well as his wife's parents. More than that, he often took the few extra dollars he had put aside and used them to assist others through their even more difficult Depression-related circumstances.

There was one "interesting" trait that his father exhibited at the end of every railroad run between cities. He would go through the train's compartments and gather up the day's newspapers, magazines, and perhaps an occasional book that passengers had left behind. He brought these materials home for others to read. The Gray home, in an era of few personal pleasures, became a mini news center, where the reading of local and worldly news events became the highlight of many evenings. At this time, young Al was between four and ten years old and was obviously in the center of these nightly reading and discussion activities. Perhaps it was this occurrence that kindled the spark that began his lifetime habit of reading and learning about worldly affairs.

Early on, I had the opportunity to pass a copy of my draft manuscript to Gray. He called me and suggested we meet to discuss my writing, as he felt there were some inaccuracies in regard to his family history. This was to be his and my first-ever detailed discussion about the book. His focus was on ensuring the accuracy of the manuscript. I gladly agreed to this. I requested permission to bring along two other veteran Marines who have assisted me over the years. He agreed to this and even allowed us to bring our small tape recorders.

As Gray shared this very personal moment from his early life with us, he reached across his desk and picked up a large family album. It was a pictographic history of his forefathers that had probably been published in the 1930s. He pointed out the pictures of his father and all of his uncles. It was a rare moment when Al Gray ever spoke to anyone about his family. It briefly opened a window on his early life. I had known him for more than 30 years, and this was the most open discussion we ever had on his family and early life. I was highly honored. When he spoke of his father, he fondly recalled him as a "hardworking person with the finest of work ethics. He was a caring person, and always observant of opportunities where he could perhaps help others."[2]

Another key figure in Gray's life was his mother, Emily. His exceptionally close relationship with her was to last throughout her life. Her impact on his life was profound. Her examples of kindness to others strongly influenced his manner and character. Before he was born, the Gray family had experienced grief as their first child was stillborn, and a second daughter, Lurene, died of pneumonia at age one.

When his father died in 1968 while Al was serving in Vietnam, he came home to make arrangements for the funeral, settle family affairs, and make arrangements to take care of his mother. Years earlier, Al had assured his father that should anything happen to him, he would make caring for his mother his most important priority. The importance Al placed on his family and his relationship with his mother is reflected in the fact that she came to live with him while he was on active duty whenever he was stationed in the States. They became an inseparable pair and were highly visible at each of his duty stations, characterized by evening walks together—always accompanied by the ever-present black Labrador, a breed for which he retained a love throughout his life. Even after he was married in 1980, his mother continued to live with him and his wife, Jan, until Emily's death in 1988.

Gray always had a respect and a thirst for knowledge and education that was to set him apart from his contemporaries throughout his career. He read voraciously and, even more importantly, he felt it was essential that every Marine think and exploit life experiences in the conduct of their duties. He became an avid reader of military matters. The *Marine Corps Gazette* was always close at hand and was a source of provocative articles. He recognized and appreciated that it attracted many well-known authors about military affairs, people such as B.H. Liddell Hart, J.F.C. Fuller, S.L.A. Marshall, Reginald Hargreaves, Samuel B. Griffiths, Lynn Montrose and Robert D. Heinl, as well as hundreds of serving or retired Marines who, like Gray, were committed to enhancing the Corps' capabilities and studying the history of warfighting. From these extensive readings, and from his experiences commanding the 1st Battalion, 2nd Marines, and later the 2nd and 4th Marine Regiments, he molded his warrior philosophy.

Probably one of the most important articles that covered the first 20 years of Gray's career was Brigadier General F. Paul Henderson's *THE FMF: An Alternative Future and How to Get There*. The article looked ahead one to 15 years to what Marine Corps warfighting capabilities could be if it chose to focus on what today would be called "transformation." It went a long way toward integrating the diverse "truths" that Gray had been gleaning from his reading and practical experiences into a unified style of warfare. He thought at length about what was needed to fulfill the charter of the U.S.

Marine Corps to win battles across the spectrum of conflict. Ideas about warfighting, such as those below, became fixed in his mind and affected his crucial considerations.

- Act boldly and decisively.
- Act more quickly than the enemy can react.
- Support maneuver by fire.
- Avoid enemy strength; exploit enemy weakness.
- Avoid patterns and obvious actions.

Gray became convinced that new emerging threats and advanced technologies were rapidly changing the world as we knew it. He became a visionary and disciple for change in the way Marine forces trained and operated. The changes he advocated and the compelling rationale he presented began to cause other, more senior, leaders to rethink traditional amphibious and expeditionary doctrines of the Marine Corps. He became a catalyst for change focused on increasing the operational capabilities of deploying forces. It was a hard message for many traditionalists to accept and, as a result, he was often looked upon as a bit of a rebel. However, few had the courage to directly challenge his views of the future requirements for a 21st century Marine Corps.

Throughout his career, Gray never seemed to miss an opportunity to stress education. As a regimental commander on Okinawa in the mid-1970s, he designed training schedules for his battalions so that he could maximize the opportunities for his non-high school-graduate Marines to attend off-duty courses and complete their high school education. As Commandant, he would initiate a "Commandant's reading list" and encouraged Marines of all ranks—including his Generals—to prepare themselves intellectually for their responsibilities. He had the foresight to establish the Marine Corps University around a world-class research center that bears his name: the Alfred M. Gray Marine Corps Research Center in Marine Corps Base Quantico, Virginia.

Gray became a master at giving broad mission-type orders. He did it deliberately because he wanted his juniors to think. Seldom did a professional military education class or a planning session go by without him stressing that "everyone should think and be aware of your commander's intent at least two command levels above your own position. You've got to fight smart," Gray would often say to his audiences, shaking his fist while focusing his intense gaze on his listeners.

His family and early experiences influenced him in other ways as well. While his father was making his daily run to the nation's capital, young Gray was heavily influenced by his grandfather, John Zust, who was born and raised in Switzerland and traveled to Latin America as a young man. Fluent in many languages, he provided Al Jr. with a hardworking role model who began each day long before dawn. He had lived in the Amazon jungle, had visited Cuba, and spent hours relating his many worldly travel experiences to his grandson, which almost certainly evoked a lifelong interest in the world at large for Al. In 1946, when he entered Lafayette College, young Al Gray found that most of his classmates were older combat veterans of World War II. He gravitated to these returned warriors, finding he was comfortable in their acceptance, fascinated by their "war stories," and intrigued by their depictions of unique experiences in far-off lands.

Al Gray enlisted in the Marine Corps shortly after the outbreak of the Korean War. On a day late in October 1950, young Al Gray stepped boldly down from a crowded bus parked in front of the Marine recruit receiving barracks in Parris Island, South Carolina. He and the other new recruits were greeted by shrill, barked commands from an assembled gauntlet of drill instructors demanding all the best in speed that the young men possessed. Thus began for Al a lifelong adventure and a love affair with the tough and unrelenting world of the professional Marine Corps.

Little did he realize, at the time he joined the Marine Corps, that it had just overcome a fight on the home front for its very survival. As Al Gray and his fellow platoon recruits rushed to the faded yellow footprints on the asphalt drill field, they were oblivious to the haunting and arising events that would ultimately affect their lives in future years. Much to the surprise of the recruits, the broad spectrum of military indoctrination into the Marine Corps was heavily embellished with the long history of the Corps. Once instructed on the Uniform Code of Military Justice, the next subject was the history of the Marine Corps, its ethos, legendary warriors, and the meaning and privilege it is to wear the eagle, globe, and anchor emblem on their uniform collars. They were repeatedly reminded that the emblem must be earned and never given. It was not until they completed basic training, on graduation day that they were even called "Marine" for the first time or permitted to wear their first set of Marine Corps emblems. Regardless of their ultimate length of honorable service, they were taught that the title "Marine" would remain with them always.

There was even more of an awakening as each recruit met and learned to work with each other. They learned that "no man is an island"—one does not walk alone. Although each person travels a personal journey in life, he does so by walking, learning, and working with others. Most of life's encounters are short-lived while others last a lifetime due to work, personal responsibilities, or location. Through this life-cycle process, some become leaders while others are content to follow. Most will not journey far from their home regions; a few—very few—become world travelers intimately aware of the world's happenings around them.

Even before boot camp, Gray had a good knowledge of history. He had grown up during the first half of the 20th century, where the newspapers had been filled with depictions of war. Hundreds of millions of people had been killed, maimed, or displaced across Europe as the result of two world wars.

With the unconditional surrender of Germany and Japan, the United States began a massive demobilization of its military forces. Defense budgets were drastically reduced as the U.S. Army's residual forces that were spread across Europe shifted from combat to performing occupation duties in a more casual, peacetime training environment. When Japan surrendered, U.S. Army and Marine forces were the first foreign troops to enter and assume military control over a bewildered population still endemically shocked from the atomic bombs that had vaporized two major cities. History shows that the Marines and Soldiers who entered Japan were unopposed, as promised by the emperor, and the rebuilding of a new, democratic Japanese government began.

The successful launching of a peacetime posture over both former belligerent nations only caused Congress to further reduce the military. For the Marine Corps, their portion of this reduction was the most severe, as the Army, a newly established Air Force, and the Navy were collectively defending their roles, missions, and dwindling resources, leaving the Marine Corps to go it alone. The mighty battles across the Pacific Ocean were forgotten. By the end of World War II, the Marine Corps' strength had expanded to nearly 600,000 with six divisions and supporting air wings and logistics organizations. By 1949, the Corps' strength was less than 80,000 and headed for even more reductions. Survival of the U.S. Marine Corps as a major military force was in doubt.

However, because the Soviet Union was aggressively attempting to expand their Communistic philosophy around the world, the concept of peace was becoming a fading dream. More significantly, both the Soviet Union and Communist China had followed the United States into the Atomic Age and began developing an arsenal of atomic weapons, fully capable of destroying America's major metropolitan areas. Lest there be any mistake about the concept of peace, on June 27, 1950, North Korean forces crossed the 38th parallel and invaded South Korea. President Harry S. Truman led the United Nations in opposing this unprovoked aggression. He authorized the mobilization of the Marine Corps and the Army National Guard. Within days, Army units, then serving in occupied Japan, began to arrive and moved to South Korea's defense. A new war, supported and supplied by international

Communism, led North Koreans to launch a series of ground attacks that quickly overran most of South Korea. The United Nations, defying the Soviets' opposition, committed units to rescue a collapsing army. The aging British Prime Minister, Winston Churchill, warned the world that the conflict "runs the risk of turning into a full-fledged Third World War." Nearly halfway around the world, these forces and conditions would ultimately confront U.S. military forces.

It was ironic that President Truman's mobilization of U.S. forces in response to the Korean situation ultimately saved the Marine Corps. The U.S. Army's operating forces were employed in occupational duties across Europe and Japan and were not immediately ready to deploy. The Marine Corps leadership, recognizing the situation, quietly proposed organization of a "brigade of Marines" to be immediately sent to reinforce the collapsing South Korean army. Time was critical. The proposal to send Marines to Korea was approved, and within weeks, a brigade of Marines was assembled on the West Coast, boarded waiting transports, and headed to stabilize the Pusan perimeter in another Asian war.

On September 15, 1951, the United States swung to the offensive in support of their Republic of Korea allies with a daring amphibious landing at Inchon, Seoul's port city. It reversed the Communist momentum, as the naval assault far behind their lines caused the North Koreans to abandon their advance and retrograde back to their home territory. With this repositioning of forces, the war entered a stalemate, a war of attrition.

These world events had a profound impact on the initial years of Private First Class Al Gray's Marine Corps life, though it would be more than two years before then-Lieutenant Gray would deploy to Korea. Completing boot camp, Private Gray was assigned to the Marine Corps Communications School at San Diego. Upon completing the radio operators' course, he sought out and was accepted into the newly activated Amphibious Reconnaissance Platoon at Camp

Pendleton, California, one of the Marine Corps' most elite units. Its mission was to conduct both reconnaissance and combat missions.

The unit's primary mode of entry was at night from a submarine. Each entry required extensive physical training and attention to the smallest detail in all training evolutions. It was rare for any unit to have an enlisted Marine like Gray, with three years of college, in their ranks. After only a short period in the company, Gray was recognized as a "comer" and quickly advanced in grade.[3] Staff Sergeant (later Sergeant Major) Neal King served as Gray's platoon sergeant. He recalled, "Corporal Gray was the senior communications man and, in essence, became the platoon's communications sergeant. It didn't take him long to make sergeant, because he got involved in everything the unit did."[4]

Gray's leadership ability was not solely the product of his Marine Corps experience. While in high school in Point Pleasant Beach, New Jersey, he had exhibited early signs of natural leadership abilities exemplified by his selection as captain of his school's football, basketball, and baseball teams. Many years later, Charles Bertolatus, a veteran Marine and one of Gray's oldest and lifelong close friends recalled, "We were probably the smallest public high school in the state to field athletic teams, and 'Peanuts' was a natural leader even then. He made us excel."[5]

In the Marine Corps, his trademark leadership style emerged while at Camp Pendleton. On one occasion, he was marching two columns of Marines along Basilone Road when a truckload of loudly jeering prisoners passed through his column of men. Gray stopped the truck and ordered the prisoners out. He saw that the truck had a number of power lawnmowers. Gray ordered them started and then ordered the prisoners to mow the hillside. His own Marines sat and watched the event, smiling. When the hillside was completely mowed, he allowed the driver to take the prisoners to their previously assigned work area.

Without Gray's knowledge, the incident was reported up the chain of command and finally reached the desk of Major General Graves

B. Erskine, a strict disciplinarian and seasoned veteran of World War II. Distant staff officers were upset by Gray's "irresponsible" actions and were out to see that some severe action be taken against him. The incident wouldn't come to rest until Gray was called to appear before General Erskine. At a rigid position of attention, Gray explained his rationale for his actions. He told of the jeering prisoners who were mocking his "good" Marines, and it was more than he could accept. Gray closed off his comments with something like, "General, I believe you would have taken the same or even more drastic action had that happened to you." It was said that General Erskine didn't smile very often, but, as the story goes, this time he did. He told Gray that he agreed with the appropriateness of his actions and proceeded to excuse him to return to his duties. The word quickly got around the base brig, and no other jeering-prisoner comments incidents occurred.

Within 20 months Gray had advanced to the rank of sergeant, a rapid promotion cycle even in wartime. Recognized as a superior non-commissioned officer (NCO), he was recommended for the meritorious NCO commissioning program. The officers and NCOs that young Gray followed were the men who put a lifelong stamp on this fledgling leader. Beginning with the recruiting officer who swore him in, Medal of Honor recipient Major Louis Wilson, who would subsequently rise to become the 26th Commandant of the Marine Corps, they included great Marines such as Kenny Houghton and Mike Ryan—who both later became Major Generals—and the colorful Gunnery Sergeant Ernie De Fazio, (later Lieutenant Colonel) who was a real pioneer in the amphibious reconnaissance field. These Marines and others like them set high standards before him and insisted he fully measure up. They were mentors and leaders. They showed him how important it was to pay close attention to their Marines, to genuinely care for them and their welfare. These left two indelible marks: high standards and a focus on troop welfare that would become his lifelong trademarks.

They also established a model for mentorship. Gray's approach became that of a teacher or coach; a persuader rather than a distant parade-ground commander. There was casualness in his manner, and his confident delivery and animated expressions seemed to create a wave of energy about him. Perhaps because of his enlisted history, he was able to relate on a personal level with enlisted Marines. His charismatic nature, athletic agility, and casualness were disarming. He would be humorous and casual and then become solemn as the individual came to attention, prepared to recite the Oath of Allegiance. For those advancing in rank, he would remind them of the importance of their new responsibilities and admonish them to "take care of your men." As a former sergeant, he was aware of the tradition of "pinning on the stripes," so each individual promoted would then receive a light punch on the upper arm to make sure that the new chevrons were firmly emplaced. It was another way of bonding with his Marines, as all would declare they were personally promoted by Gray. He had a gift for making important events for his Marines fun and memorable. Recognized early by his senior staff of noncommissioned officers and his reconnaissance unit commander Captain Francis "Buff" Kranze, he was directed to attend the Officers Candidate Screening Course in Quantico.

Gray became a master at sizing men up and then challenging them to excel—if he saw a need. He thrived on giving broad, mission-type orders and then carefully observing how different individuals responded to his guidance. Gray was unpredictable and often showed up at the most unexpected places at the least expected times. His energy levels remained exceptionally high. Seldom did he need more than three to four hours' sleep at night.

His entrances were low key, often through a side or back door, but his mere presence caused him to be noticed. Heads turned. There was something about him that attracted crowds. He disliked the attention and artfully tried to downplay it. When he spoke, it was most often of themes not often addressed by others, like, "What is best for the United States?" or "How can we do this thing?" or "How can the

Corps better serve this great nation?" Inquisitive by nature, he was always searching for new ideas, new thoughts.

Gray was not reluctant to talk about the big and serious issues or admonish leaders at all levels to "take care of yourself and your men." He remained uncompromising in his belief that each Marine must subordinate himself to his Corps. Careerism in any form remained unethical to him. He reminded everyone, "All the Corps promised you were challenges and recurring duty in the Fleet Marine Forces—not an easy life with tours in Paris or Hawaii." He meant it.

This uncompromising focus on the profession is also likely a product of his life experiences. Gray did not marry until he was 52 years old and already a Major General. There was no competition for his time or his intellectual efforts. Instead, he was solely focused on preparing for his profession. In addition, in part because he was a bachelor, he was available for an unusual range of assignments throughout his career that would give him an extraordinary background by the time he was a General officer.

Having completed the Marine Corps Officer Basic School in Quantico, in 1952, he attended the U.S. Army Field Artillery Officer Basic Course at Ft. Sill, Oklahoma. He had requested infantry duty but had been turned down because the Marine Corps needed Forward Observe artillery officers. Moving to his first leadership assignment, Lieutenant Gray went to Korea in early 1953 and was assigned to a firing battery in the 2nd Battalion, 11th Marines, 1st Marine Division. Later, he served as an artillery forward observer in direct support of the infantry companies in the 1st Battalion, 7th Marine Regiment. In October 1953, he was promoted to First Lieutenant. It was in Korea where he learned to work with other units, striving to quickly fit in with the team to achieve the maximum benefit from the effects of combined arms. He volunteered for a second tour and stayed in Korea as an infantry officer. Gray then joined A Company, 1st Battalion, 7th Marines, serving first as a platoon leader, and then company executive officer, and later as a company commander.[6]

In Gray's subsequent journey of service to Corps and country, his character was to be molded by the diversity of command assignments and combat actions culminating with three Purple Hearts and other events that spanned the spectrum of military activities, including a series of operational crises, peacekeeping missions, and humanitarian actions. The image is of an individual who possesses the drive and persistence that ultimately will cause major changes within a 200-year-old institution that prides itself on tradition. One is reminded that character is, in essence, a life-building experience that reaffirms that each individual is really a "product in development." So it was with Al Gray, because, as he encountered new situations, he grew in stature, knowledge, maturity, and with professional wisdom. The first aspect is to appreciate his ability to grasp the importance of electronic information-gathering, and his use of sensitive command and control systems. Time and time again his ability to influence actions came because he had intimate knowledge of how to exploit various communications modes to achieve success. He quickly realized the value and power of real-time information in any decisionmaking process.

Over the years, Gray witnessed repeated examples where unit commanders neglected their communications planning and security measures. From the beginning, he had an appreciation for the importance of firepower, communications, infantry tactics, and intelligence that enabled him to begin building a personal philosophy about the Corps and warfighting. He saw that the Corps was a force-in-readiness, organized as a balanced combined arms team, designed specifically for forcible entry from the sea but able to task organize as necessary to be useful across the full spectrum of conflict. Gray accepted this charter as a fundamental definition of his new profession. He realized that, in the broadest sense, his job could be thought of as doing whatever he could do to ensure these capabilities were realities, adjusting and refining them as necessary to meet changing threats and technologies.

Perhaps the most significant of the character traits Gray exhibited was "courage." The word suggests firmness of resolve, identity, and commitment in the face of opposition that can require both physical and moral courage. Courage has long been listed as one of the four classic virtues, along with prudence, justice, and temperance. His personality and commitment to excellence made him stand apart from others. President John F. Kennedy's *Profiles in Courage* declared courage to be the "most admirable of human values." And Ernest Hemingway, in a treasured phrase, called it "grace under pressure." There would come a hundred or more times when Al Gray could have backed down or remained silent and accepted the status quo, but his vision for change and his steadfast determination to better prepare the Marine Corps for the 21st century never faltered. Gray could be stubborn and demanding when he felt he was right. He was a crusader who was true to his beliefs. As a General of Marines, he was well known throughout the Corps, yet his personal life stayed private. Intimate friends were few. He remained a loner in a world of busy men. As history has recorded, wherever he went, "things happened."

When professional challenges arose, he seemed to become electrified. When faced with unexpected challenges or unpredicted situations, he seemed to have prepared himself for just such an occasion years earlier. In each situation, Gray seemed to comprehend the total situation, arrive at a pivotal moment, and quickly gravitate to a primary leadership role. He would begin making assessments and quickly proceed to stabilize the situation. He led in the style of a teacher or a coach rather than taking the I'm-the-senior-guy-here, so-I'm-in-charge approach. He was adept at building teams.

Gray's energies and vision of what needed to be done to prepare the Marine Corps for the future never faltered. The Corps is better for his dedicated efforts. But one of the greatest challenges he faced was not on the battlefield but on the home front. The Persian Gulf War of 1991 was, in reality, the "test" of all the ideas, vision, and programs he had fostered over the previous three decades.

Throughout all deployments of Marine Corps units into Saudi Arabia and the Gulf region, he involved himself extensively in the detailed planning for which Marine Corps forces would be used. Quietly and behind the scenes, he was involved in determining when and how his forces should arrive in the crisis area. He had always taken great care in monitoring the readiness of all deploying forces before sending them off to a regional commander. But now, as the Commandant, he knew his role must become that of a "distant coach," for once his Marine forces deployed, they would be placed under a regional commander's operational control. This was a sensitive situation for him personally, as he wanted to ensure that the capabilities of the Marines onboard the amphibious task force and Marine land-based forces were fully exploited by the joint service commander. There was also tension in the Joint Chiefs of Staff arena because Gray's extensive expeditionary and operational experiences gave him broader insights into how to more effectively achieve theater-level objectives. He was not shy about speaking out about the potential problems the vast array of all the American and coalition forces would be facing in the deserts of Saudi Arabia and Kuwait.

Although there have been numerous attempts by his admirers and critics to describe Al Gray, one description in particular stands out. Brigadier General Edwin H. Simmons, USMC Retired, Marine Corps Historian Emeritus, appears to have best captured his character when he wrote, "General Al Gray is imaginative, iconoclastic, articulate, charismatic, and is compassionate. His Marines love him."[7]

CHAPTER 3
The Early Years of Marine Corps Service

"Good ideas are not adopted automatically. They must be driven into practice with courageous impatience."

Admiral Hyman Rickover
U.S. Navy

The character of the Cold War had a profound impact on newly commissioned Second Lieutenant Gray's early career. When he became president in January 1953, Dwight D. Eisenhower traveled to South Korea in a new attempt to end the war. He was not successful. Although an agreement was finally reached to halt the combat actions, a peace treaty was never signed by the North Korean leaders. The long, bitterly contested war may have quickly faded from public view, but "America's forgotten war" was only the first stage of the Cold War that would dominate U.S. strategy for the subsequent 35 years.

Nuclear stalemate made conflict through surrogates or "wars of liberation" the Soviet's preferred methods for disrupting vulnerable countries. The early signs of war were appearing specifically in Southeast Asia, and French colonial rule over the Vietnamese, Laotian, and Thailand regions was under challenge. Communist-inspired insurgent leaders were seeking aggressively to eliminate all foreign forces. By May 1954, French troops lost a key battle in the brutal 55-day siege of Dien Bien Phu and surrendered to the Soviet-supported Viet Minh.

The French signed an agreement that divided Vietnam in half along the 17th Parallel. No one doubted the Viet Minh and sympatric southern Viet Cong forces intended to unite all Vietnam under a Communist regime. As the remnants of the beleaguered French departed in 1961, newly elected U.S. President John F. Kennedy made a first commitment of 16,000 U.S. military troops to South Vietnam's defense. This would be the beginning of a commitment that would send 1.5 million Americans to South Vietnam in a distant Asian war that would last six years and eventually cost more than 54,000 American lives.

The impact on Gray was immediate. Rather than a normal assignment with the operating forces, his background as a commander with communications knowledge made him a prime candidate for assignment to a number of special intelligence-collection billets that were far out of the mainstream for the typical ground officer. There is an old Marine adage that says, "Bloom wherever planted." Al Gray personified this creed better than any other Marine officer of the times. His career was replete with nontraditional assignments that many would have thought were "non-career-enhancing."

Many years before Gray enlisted in the Marine Corps the Navy launched its own radio surveillance and intercept program. From 1928-1941, a total of 176 (150 Navy and 26 Marines) enlisted radio operators were specifically trained at a unique school located on the roof of the old Navy Department building in Washington. Known as the "Top of the Roof Gang," they were trained to intercept and analyze foreign radio communications. This group of dedicated skilled operators formed the vanguard of the naval cryptology. Though many Marines have served in this special unit over decades of service to the nation, they still often refer to themselves as the "Top of the Roof Gang."[1]

Then-First Lieutenant Gray's firm grounding in the communications field as an enlisted Marine, and as an artillery officer, plus his natural affinity for the exploding technical field of special communications, security, and radio surveillance made him an ideal candidate for special assignments. He volunteered to join a new and challenging endeavor. After graduation from Communications Officers School, he became a student at the Naval Security Group (NSG) Training Center in California, where 120 Marines were undergoing Morse Code intercept training. Selected but not yet promoted to Captain, he was tasked with forming two units. These two units would become the nucleus of what is known today as the Marine Cryptologic Support Battalion.

From 1956 until 1961, Captain Gray served overseas in highly specialized classified assignments. He became proficient in several Asian languages and was deeply sensitive to both the verbal and written communications that link the nations of the world together. He also gathered a rare insight into the multifaceted world of signal intelligence, counter-electronic methods and technologies, and the critical need for operational security. Equally significant was his appreciation for all aspects of communications that enable a commander to first control and then maneuver his forces. These were to be the first cryptologic units since World War II, and field operations began in May 1956.[2] Gray began to learn as much as he could about the complex operations in northern Japan and similar facilities in the Pacific area. His command conducted sensitive operations in the Yellow Sea, just off the 38th parallel of the Korean Demilitarized Zone. He served in various supporting assignments such as special project officer for the construction of the U.S. Electronic Intelligence Activity in northern Japan. He conducted and supervised other special operations and organized a Navy emergency ground defense force of more than 200 Sailors.

Upon completing his tour in the Far East, he was assigned to Hawaii to activate the First Composite Radio Company, where he would serve from September 1958 until May 1961. Gray was later recognized for his:

> Effectiveness and contributions of tactical SIGINT [Signals Intelligence] by commanding Radio Company detachments, support eight Marine Amphibious Brigades and three Marine Amphibious Force exercises, [and] providing all-source information to commanders and their staffs and instruction [sic] them on the use and potential of special intelligence.[3]

These were the early efforts at what would become the central theme of Marine Corps cryptologic operations, providing support to the warfighter. In May 1961 he was assigned as the officer-in-charge of the Naval Security Group (NSG) Detachment, in support of Headquarters Marine Corps. One of his priorities was to place particular emphasis on improving Marine Corps cryptologic linguistic capabilities. These early efforts were validated in future years as Marines returning from duties with NSG commands brought back invaluable linguistic and cryptologic skills to be applied to tactical operations. His purpose in emphasizing dissemination of the latest sensitive information down to the most forward-deployed units was to ensure tactical employment by the warfighters. This and other projects became Al Gray's legacy to the Marine Corps cryptologic program. At the same time, his interest in the tactical employment of intercepts continued at every level of his future many commands. In spring 1964, Major Gray would command the first Marine Corps ground unit to deploy to South Vietnam. It was a unit which was specifically organized and tasked to conduct a sensitive mission of high value to the National Security Agency (NSA) and the entire Intelligence community. Known as Marine Advisory Group One, the unit conducted overall counterinsurgency training and operations for the South Vietnamese Irregular Force from a base in Northern I Corps, located in Quang Tri Province, South Vietnam, on the Demilitarized Zone (DMZ) border.

Equally significant was his appreciation for all aspects of communications that enable a commander to control and maneuver his forces. Over the years, Gray witnessed repeated examples where unit commanders neglected their communications planning and security measures. He had learned firsthand that, to be a viable commander, one must be able to communicate in the most secret mode, otherwise unit commanders were relegated to being just another officer in field exercises, or in combat. The three Cs (command, control, and communications) and interrelated intelligence matters were later to become the principal areas of attention for Gray in the diverse staff assignments or command positions he was to hold as a Marine.

The 1960s were to be a dynamic change for the nation's youth. Long hair, mod dress, drugs, sexual freedom, and anti-establishment ideas exploded everywhere, as affluent kids embraced a counterculture fueled by rock music and sincere yearning for brotherhood and peace. It was an unforgettable era.

Another characteristic of the period was racial unrest, beginning with "black sit-ins" in Greensboro, North Carolina, just as John F. Kennedy was sworn in as president. When President Kennedy opened the 1960s with a challenge to Americans to commit them to public service and seek new frontiers, he and his beautiful wife made it seem like a return to the mystical time of Camelot. Neither he nor the nation foresaw how the decade would be turned upside down as civil and antiwar movements drew millions of people into the streets when public protest raged. Bloody riots erupted, and the national colors were repeatedly burned in protest.

The Soviet Union shot down a U.S. U-2 spy plane as it crossed over their airspace. The pilot, Gary Powers, was captured, and the Soviets announced to the world that they had physical proof of America's spying missions. Nearly simultaneously, they placed a man in space, exulting their own technological advancements which rivaled those of the United States.

In late 1962, President Kennedy was confronted with the Soviet Union's attempt to place missiles in Cuba. It resulted in a standoff between two nuclear powers that could have erupted into WW III. The Cold War was getting hotter.

Marine Colonel John Glenn Jr. was blasted into space to orbit Earth three times before returning. And, in August 1962, the Reverend Martin Luther King gave his now famous "I Have a Dream" speech on Washington's National Mall attended by more than 250,000 people. The country was in a restless mood, and dramatic changes were taking place.

In Selma, Alabama, more than 700 people were arrested for protesting against their restrictive voting rights. In Watts, California, five days of deadly fires burned down hundreds of businesses and private homes. Literally miles of urban developments were leveled, and military units were deployed to halt the destruction and rioting. President Kennedy authorized sending 16,000 U.S. troops to serve as advisors to the Communist-threatened South Vietnamese forces.

Al Gray's journey was certainly affected by the social and strategic changes taking place around him, though his assignments continued to be focused on the emerging field signals collection and emergence of the Radio Battalion as a key Marine Corps national asset. Then-Captain Gray was assigned to support Headquarters Marine Corps (HQMC) in Washington. He was assigned as the special operations and plans officer, in the G-2 (Intelligence) division. As such, one of his tasks was to carry the "Red Book," which contained the most sensitive intelligence (SIGINT) material, to selected officers for their daily update on world affairs. This assignment placed him in almost-daily contact with the Commandant of the Marine Corps and his most senior Generals.

Never content with fragmented incidents and data, Gray routinely spent many extra hours studying and collaborating events to present the most accurate assessment. He became so knowledgeable and sensitive to a turbulent world's secretive events that his personal insights were often sought by his seniors. This close interaction with the most senior General officers in the Marine Corps broadened his knowledge as to the executive management level thought process as to how major decisions were approached and ultimately resolved. This close personal interaction was a rare opportunity of seasoning for a young officer, and it would be of immeasurable value to him in later years. Gray was promoted to Major in February 1963.

During this period at HQMC, there had been one unpleasant staffing situation that deeply affected Gray for a long time. Apparently, during one of Gray's daily special intelligence briefing sessions with General Wallace A. Greene and the Commandant, there was a discussion on the potential value of activating a Marine Support Battalion (MSB), which would be similar to the Navy's Naval Security Groups. Greene, who had a long career in the intelligence field, had informally tasked Major Gray to personally study the issue of developing battalion-sized special intelligence capabilities. Greene believed such a unit could better serve his Marine commanders and their operating forces. Because of the sensitivity of the issue, very few were aware of the Commandant's tasking. Later, when Gray was ready to brief the Commandant, Lieutenant General Leonard F. Chapman, the Chief of Staff, HQMC, became aware of the issue and opposed the development of a Marine Support Battalion. His concern was that the activation of units requiring nearly a thousand men would ultimately erode the shrinking pool of combat-arms personnel. A planning session was scheduled. Later, when called upon, Gray presented his proposal recommending the activation of a Marine Support Battalion, known today as the Marine Cryptologic Support Battalion. It was a long session, with deep deliberations on the potential risks, challenges, and benefits to be achieved. After all the issues were discussed, the Commandant looked over and said to Gray, "Make it happen." Chapman, always the professional gentleman, quietly accepted his Commandant's decision. It would be years later before he and Gray would ever again speak about the MSB decision.

While serving at Headquarters Marine Corps and on other sensitive assignments, Gray traveled extensively. These trips took him to Guantanamo Bay in Cuba, as well as to the Republic of South Vietnam. It was during this period that he began to work closely with Major Paul X. Kelley, who was assigned to the reconnaissance branch of the Development Center. Unknowingly, two future Commandants of the Marine Corps were building a close relationship that would carry them through their long careers as Marine officers. Historical records show that Gray was one of the first Marine Corps officers to enter the Southeast Asian theater prior to America's major military buildup for the Vietnam War. On November 6, 1964, then-Major Gray was awarded his first Bronze Star Medal, with Combat V. His citation simply read:

> For meritorious achievement as the commanding officer of a specially organized survey unit. Much can be read into this award. However, because of the sensitivity of the mission; the what, where, and why that made his contribution noteworthy remain to be told.[4]

During the latter half of the 1960s, the war in South Vietnam would eventually cause President Kennedy and later, President Lyndon B. Johnson, to commit more than 525,000 men to a distant war that would be the subject of anti-Vietnam War protests across the nation. Al Gray's earlier experiences in South Vietnam and the strong acquaintances he made with the South Vietnamese military officers would repeatedly serve him well in his later combat tours. Years later, as fate would have it, a then-Colonel Gray would be one of the key on-the-scene decisionmakers during South Vietnam's 1975 evacuation crisis. History also records that Gray was the last American to leave South Vietnam, by helicopter, from the Defense Attaché Office (DAO) when that country was taken over by the North Vietnamese.

To further exacerbate the national unrest sweeping the land, on November 22, 1963, President Kennedy was assassinated in Dallas, Texas. The nation was emotionally shocked with disbelief and grief. But even greater violence erupted as Martin Luther King Jr. was killed by a sniper's bullet in Memphis, Tennessee, in April 1968, only to be followed by the June 1968 killing of President John Kennedy's younger brother, Robert F. Kennedy, who was a U.S. Senator from New York. The impact of the raging violence and killing of these renowned leaders engulfed every community. Each tragic event only led to more rioting and protest of the Vietnam War. So severe was the prevailing violence that President Johnson decided not to run for reelection. Richard M. Nixon was elected president in November and took office in January 1969. He won the election on his promise to bring our military home from the Vietnam War "with honor."

In September 1965, Major Gray joined the 12th Marine Artillery Regiment, 3rd Marine Division in South Vietnam. Initially, he served as the regiment's communications officer. Shortly thereafter, he was reassigned as the regiment's S-3 (Operations and Training) officer, normally a senior Lieutenant Colonel's billet, and remained filling the Communications billet for several months. Always seeking the greatest challenges, and taking advantage of Army aircraft assigned to the 12th Marines, Gray also concurrently served as an aerial observer, rendering direct fire support to the I Corps Tactical Zones maneuver units while flying in observation aircraft. He was seemingly ubiquitous in supporting the division's active deployments and combat operations against the Viet Cong and North Vietnamese Army (NVA) forces.

During these assignments, now-Lieutenant Colonel Gray (promoted in October 1967) and his close friend, Major Alex Lee, a distinguished infantry and reconnaissance Marine, took the lead in developing concepts and doctrine for the employment of sensor technology within the Marine Corps. These sensors and related activities were employed throughout Southeast Asia to stem the infiltration and enemy use of the Ho Chi Minh Road/Trail network in Laos and the Demilitarized Zone (DMZ) area. He returned to South Vietnam again for six months in 1969 in conjunction with surveillance and reconnaissance matters.

The expanding Vietnam War captured Gray's imagination and energies. As a bachelor, he elected to remain in the combat zone until four tours were completed. Without fanfare and relatively unnoticed, he remained in South Vietnam for more than three continuous years, while his peers normally served one or two separate one-year tours. Serving as the Commander, Composite Artillery Battalion over U.S. and Free World Forces in Northern I Corps, his multinational battalion was of mixed artillery pieces, collectively positioned just south of the boundary dividing the two Vietnams, the DMZ. On May 14, 1967, his fire support base came under heavy incoming artillery and rocket fire from North Vietnamese artillery and their supporting infantry forces.

During his unit's reaction to the barrage, a three-man listening post patrol became disoriented and inadvertently entered a minefield. One Marine was killed when he detonated a mine, and a comrade was seriously wounded. The third Marine was too terrified to move, afraid of tripping any of the anti-personnel mines that were hidden in the rice paddies. When Gray was informed of his Marines' situation, he immediately entered the minefield, exposing himself to enemy artillery fire and the well-concealed, randomly placed booby-traps and anti-personnel mines in order to rescue the two Marines. It took many hours for Gray to carefully pick his way in and then carry the wounded Marine to safety. He instructed the traumatized second trapped Marine to "follow in my footsteps." For his heroic actions under enemy fire, and for the saving of two Marines, he was awarded the Silver Star Medal.[5] Portions of the citation read as follows:

> For conspicuous gallantry and intrepidity in action ... During the night of 14 May 1967, three Marines were en route to their assigned night listening posts. One of the Marines inadvertently detonated a mine which killed him and seriously wounded the other comrades. ... Upon learning of the accident Major Gray immediately proceeded to the area and unhesitatingly entered the mined areas to assist them. Disregarding his own safety, Major Gray calmly and skillfully probed a cleared path forty meters through the unmarked minefield to the side of the wounded men and administered first aid to the injured Marines. ... When stretcher bearers arrived, he directed the safe evacuation of the casualties from the minefield. ... His timely and heroic action ... in the face of great personal danger ... was instrumental in saving the lives of two Marines.

But that wasn't the end of his minefield experiences. On the night of June 27, 1967, three Marines on their way to a listening post of the Composite Artillery Battalion's perimeter inadvertently entered a South Vietnamese emplaced and unmarked defensive minefield. After penetrating some distance into the minefield, one of the Marines detonated an anti-personnel mine, seriously injuring two Marines. Upon learning of the incident, Gray immediately proceeded to the scene. Cutting through the wire, Gray entered the minefield with complete disregard for his own life and proceeded to probe a small safe lane to the wounded Marines. Only after the safe lane was clearly marked did he allow members of the rescue party into the minefield. His citation for a Bronze Star read:

> His prompt action unquestionably saved the life of one of the two men who had lost considerable blood. … The example set by Gray that night was in keeping with the highest traditions of the Corps and exemplified the highest standards of courage and leadership.[6]

In July 1967, Gray was transferred from the 3rd Marine Division after 22 months with the 12th Marines. He had just extended his tour and was in line to command an infantry battalion. Instead, he was ordered to Da Nang by Lieutenant General Robert Cushman, the Commanding General of the 3rd Marine Amphibious Force, to take command of all 1st Radio Battalion elements in Vietnam. Cushman wanted to improve overall intelligence operations throughout the five northern provinces of South Vietnam and he was well aware of Gray's experience. He had served as Gray's boss when he was dual-hatted as both the G-2 and the G-3 of Headquarters, U.S. Marine Corps in the 1963-64 timeframe. Then-Lieutenant Colonel Gray had just extended his tour again when his father died in January 1968, and he returned home on emergency leave. After taking care of matters at home, he was denied the opportunity to return to Vietnam and was assigned to a highly classified billet with the Defense Communication Planning

Group (later the Defense Special Planning Group) in Washington. At the end of October 1968, Gray reported to the Marine Corps schools at Quantico where he was assigned to the Development Center as the Combat Surveillance Officer and later as Head, Intelligence, Surveillance, and Reconnaissance Branch.

The 1970s would take Al Gray through a broad spectrum of assignments. First, he was a student at the Marine Corps Command and Staff College, Quantico, from August 1970 to June 1971. As the senior Marine, Gray was designated class president of the 1970 command and staff course at Quantico. Shortly before graduation, the class had a formal mess night, and Gray was seated at the head table, between the commanding general of the college, Colonel Samuel Jaskilka, and General Leonard Chapman, who was then the 24th Commandant of the Marine Corps. Throughout the evening there was banter among the senior officers, with Gray often the topic of discussion. At one point, General Chapman turned to the other Generals, saying, "Gentlemen, there is nothing you need to tell me about the character of Lieutenant Colonel Gray. I know him well." Scott Laidig, a longtime personal friend, recalled Gray later telling the story of this encounter. He remembered Gray saying he was uncertain about what Chapman might be thinking and could only hope for the best. Then the Commandant turned back to Gray and said, "You know, Lieutenant Colonel Gray, there is something I need to say to you. When you were briefing General Greene on the Radio Battalion proposal, and I was opposing you on that issue, you were right and I was wrong." This caught Gray completely off guard but emotionally relieved his feelings from a long-ago but not forgotten difference of opinion between two professionals. It is interesting to note that in future encounters, whenever Chapman's support was either needed or desired, he could be counted on to provide Al Gray with unwavering, unconditional assistance.

From the Command and Staff College, Gray was assigned to the 2nd Marine Division, where he assumed command of the 1st Battalion,

2nd Marines in June 1971. There were many unforeseen leadership challenges in which Gray was to demonstrate his extraordinary talent and ability to command. It was an explosive time when few "careerist" officers were seeking infantry command assignments. The late 1960s and early '70s were times of endemic racial discontent throughout the nation, as well as in all military services. High rates of unauthorized absences and drug-related incidents were common statistics within every organized unit. Approximately 1,000 Marines were illegally absent on any given day from the 2nd Marine Division. Racial tension was high in the Corps, and it was just as stressful throughout local communities. At night, in the troop areas, even in certain barracks, it was not prudent for duty watch-standers to enter a darkened squad bay alone. Many incorrigibles became even more violent after being awarded unfavorable discharges. While waiting for their discharge documents, they often initiated even more serious offenses. Military discipline and traditional values were replaced by near anarchy. Unit training programs existed only on paper.

This snapshot view of military disarray was not confined to the 2nd Marine Division; it was evident throughout the Marine Corps and other services. It was influenced by the anti-Vietnam War movements, in addition to the racial unrest and general misconduct so prevalent in the entire American civilian society. In the years to come, this particular era would become recognized as one of the darkest and most disruptive periods in America's military and civilian history.

In spite of these endemic unrest conditions, Gray sought a command, fully realizing that he had a difficult task ahead in preparing an infantry battalion that was then scheduled to deploy to the Mediterranean in only three months. Gray discovered that several of his rifle companies had recently returned from the Washington area, where they had been deployed for OPERATION GARDEN PLOT and assigned to the unpleasant mission of military forces staged to counter civil unrest. The companies had been positioned near the nation's capital and prepared for riot-control purposes, attending to major anti-Vietnam War protests, and the subsequent Dr. Martin Luther King rally.

Gray's four infantry companies were all commanded by Captains. Commanding Bravo Company 1st Battalion, 2nd Marines (more commonly identified as B1/2) was Captain James G. Magee. He, too, had only recently joined the battalion. Jim was quick to discover, with great dismay, that Company B, 1st Battalion had previously been designated as the Second Regiment's "casualty and discharge company" and was populated with the worst-of-the-worst of the regiment's hardcore malcontents and individuals who were awaiting discharge. Almost all of his non-rated Marines had at one time or other been noncommissioned officers (NCOs) but had been court-martialed for serious offenses after reporting to the 2nd Division. Most were combat veterans from Vietnam.

Magee's earlier arrival into the 1st Battalion proved beneficial to Lieutenant Colonel Gray, as he had already begun the long process of bringing structure and discipline to the small group of good Marines in the company. Magee was also taking disciplinary actions against the many wayward discontents. In taking command, Magee assembled his company and informed them that their unmilitary appearance and conduct were not acceptable to him or to the U.S. Marine Corps. He told them, "We are no longer a discharge pool; we are now really Bravo 1-2, and we are scheduled to deploy to the Mediterranean in September. Anyone without an expiration of enlistment before March 1972 is going to deploy." Magee later recalled, "This bit of news caused 30 Marines to go into unauthorized leave status by the following morning."[7]

The word on the Bravo Company's future deployment and resulting sudden surge in unauthorized absences of enlisted Marines spread like wildfire throughout the rest of the battalion with the same alarming results. All the ills of the Vietnam War had infested stateside military organizations. Besides the disciplinary problems, the 2nd Marine Division was critically short of reliable junior noncommissioned officers, staff NCOs, and junior-grade officers. Equally significant was the lack of funds to maintain a high state of readiness in combat-essential equipment. There were no maintenance funds to repair rifles, machine guns, or other weapons systems. Nor were there resources to buy the most basic troop care necessities like toilet paper. The few concerned officers and NCOs were so embarrassed they would spend their personal money to bring in rolls of toilet paper and place them in the troops' heads. There seemed to be no end or appropriate solution to the lack of suitable troop conditions at Camp Lejeune.

Under such emotional and stressful conditions leadership was virtually nonexistent, as there was open disrespect for routine military leadership. Racial polarity, open drug use, and crime were the order of the day, both on and off duty. Unauthorized absences ran to more than a hundred in each of the division's nine infantry battalions at Camp Lejeune on any Monday morning, as the troops challenged each other, playing guns in the woods, shouting, "Bang, bang." They were without training ammunition, or for that matter, without apparent purpose. "We've been to 'Nam! What's the purpose of all this field training?" became a common outcry.[8]

It was during Bravo Company's deployment to Panama for "jungle reconnaissance training" that Gray took command of the battalion. By the time Magee's company completed the Panama deployment, he felt the company had responded well to training. His young NCOs and officers had begun to exert their fledgling leadership. The company was taking form and as their unit commander, Gray was also motivated by the positive changes. Magee was having his first morning formation after returning to Camp Lejeune when Gray unexpectedly appeared in front of the company. It was a mild shock to everyone, as battalion commanders just didn't show up at dawn formations. Gray welcomed them home and confirmed that "we" are deploying to the Mediterranean in mid-September, and they would hear more about how "we" were going to prepare for this adventure in the next few days and weeks.

Later that morning, Gray gathered the five company commanders together with the battalion staff for his first commander's conference to lay out his objectives. He tasked these officers to collectively come up with a plan to meet his objective of "doing everything passably, but some things very good." Gray then met separately with his company commanders in the battalion executive officer's office. Magee remembers the look of surprise on Gray's face when he asked them collectively, "Are you ready to deploy?" and two of his company commanders said they'd been in the battalion for two years and were just worn out. They hoped to get out of the battalion prior to the Mediterranean deployment. Gray was explosive, vividly shocked. He responded with something like, "You don't want to command Marines? Then you damn well won't! I only want players on the team who want to be here!" At Gray's behest, both were moved out of the battalion by the weekend. Gray received a new senior Captain, John J. (Jack) Sheehan, who took over A Company.[9]

By the end of the week, the staff and company commanders had put together a rudimentary plan to meet Colonel Gray's objectives and after a few modifications it was approved. This was the beginning of changing a docile, ineffective battalion into a fully capable battalion landing team (BLT) with all the reinforcing elements necessary to go aboard ships and deploy to the Mediterranean.

Next, BLT 1/2 began training for several Tactical Evaluation Tests, which were only 60 days away. The nearly impossible task of bringing the battalion up to full strength and locating sufficient serviceable rifles, machine guns, and mortars was a tedious daily, often hourly, logistical management task. With some marginally serviceable crew-served weapons, the battalion trained hard and did well enough to barely pass the field evaluations, known as the TACTEST. Just before deployment, they received an 11th-hour surge of new privates and private first class recruits directly from the infantry training regiment.

Gray attacked this festering unit morale problem as if executing a frontal attack. He went where his junior officers hesitated to go—the barrack squad bays—even with escorts. Gray often walked alone, entering barracks at any time of the day or night, and he would often directly confront the recalcitrants who positioned themselves to prevent anyone of authority from entering any troop billeting spaces. In September, his battalion was reinforced with artillery, tank, reconnaissance, and logistics units in preparation for deployment to the Mediterranean. Organized as a battalion landing team of more than 2,000 Marines and Sailors, his combat-ready force served as the ground combat element of the 24th Marine Amphibious Unit (MAU). It was Gray's first venture and exposure to Europe and the Middle East.

In the final days before embarkation, the battalion's officers and staff NCOs searched the Operational Readiness Afloat support facility for its available "spares" to bring the battalion's equipment inventories up to the minimum levels authorized for units to deploy. This was one of the first signs that Gray's challenges to get ready for an important deployment were having some effect on his junior leaders.

Through all these pre-deployment efforts, morale remained low as the battalion moved to Morehead City, North Carolina, to embark on amphibious shipping. Several of the rifle companies brought their disciplinary malcontents and marginal Marines aboard because it was mandatory that they have a minimum number of Marines in each unit to claim a C-2 rating in personnel and operational readiness. However, before they had barely lost sight of the U.S. coastline, Gray called his company commanders to his stateroom. He told them he would have a C-130 aircraft in Rota, Spain, to take back the worst 68 Marines they were forced to deploy with and that he wanted each of his companies to work with the battalion adjutant during the crossing to complete the discharge packages on the "chosen 68."[10]

As Gray had promised, when the battalion landing team got to Rota, the battalion's worst 68 troublemakers were flown back to Camp Lejeune for discharge. Then Gray talked to the assembled BLT on the dock and was frank and challenging. "We just sent home the bums who didn't want to be Marines—who have been dragging this BLT down and holding us back. We're where Marines should be: at sea, at the point of the spear, where the action will happen. If there is trouble over here, we have to be ready. We are going to train hard, take care of each other, learn our business, get some good liberty, and act like Marines. You either shape up and keep up, or this will be the last time you'll go ashore during this cruise." From that time on, BLT 1/2 transitioned into a tough, disciplined, and spirited unit.[11]

During the deployment, Gray went from ship to ship to see "his Marines," appearing in troop compartments or down in the holds late at night, helping serve chow on the mess decks, always punching troops on the shoulder and telling them. "If you have a problem, come see me." This was a personal mannerism he would perform throughout the remaining years of his active service. It was his charismatic way of leading men and showing them he cared about each of them. The troops seemed to light up around him, no matter how hard he pushed them. They knew, and saw, that even though Gray had a soft heart for the enlisted Marines, the word was out. "If you screw up, you'll never see land 'til we get back to America." He didn't make a show of being "the man," but he was, indeed.

"The deployment was the best of nine Mediterranean deployments I made during my career," said Captain Magee.[12] The battalion went everywhere, had an amphibious landing every three weeks or so, and trained with the French Foreign Legion in Corsica for three cold, snowy weeks in December. They joined in with the Turkish naval infantry and with the United Kingdom Marines for a landing exercise in Turkey, and with the San Marco Tactical Group (Italian Marines) in Sardinia. In Crete with the Greek Raider Forces, they trained in their own amphibious skills, both day and night, in Sardinia and in Spain.

With all the landing activities, there was an occasional mishap. The most interesting event occurred when the BLT staff mistakenly bivouacked one of the companies in the wrong location on the Island of Corsica. When the farmer who owned the land discovered a thousand-plus Marines had destroyed his crops, he threatened to blow it into an international incident. It cost the BLT every gallon of gasoline and oil container they had, and two companies abreast tilling the soil with their expeditionary entrenching shovels and several Amphibious Assault Vehicles (AAVs), trying to till the farmer's land that they had nearly stripped of vegetation and cork bark during the three weeks ashore. A very collegial, humorous Gray soothed the anger of the farmer, pouring his coffee and offering him cigarettes and C-rations while periodically talking on the radio to the companies working the fields. At one point, Gray urged a company commander to "have the men till the ground like hell, so we can get out of here before this guy demands a Jeep!" It was a zestful comment, but the troops loved it.

CHAPTER 4
The Final Collapse of South Vietnam

"Leave no Marine behind."

U.S. Marine Corps Ethos

Professionally, Gray was in a league by himself. In February 1972, 20 years before it became fashionable, the 24th Marine Amphibious Unit and BLT 1/2 conducted a night-coordinated, over-the-horizon surface and air assault amphibious landing in Carboneras, Spain. The Amphibious Assault Vehicles (AAVs) were in the water for almost two hours after they splashed out of the flooded well deck of the amphibious ship, and before the helicopters were launched for deep raids and troop unit insertions. These deep helicopter assaults inland were designed by Gray to plan and execute special mission-type operations.

This was the beginning of special operations-type maneuvers in all of Gray's later deployments. With these special operations, Gray was moving his Marines into new crisis-response capabilities years before it was officially approved by Headquarters Marine Corps.

BLT 1/2 landing teams were taking peacetime training to the limit, and the exercises came off without a hitch. Gray would later say, "This was our graduation exercise. We should have been able to do this before we deployed."[1] This was the beginning of what was to become the Marine Amphibious Units' Special Operations Capable (SOC) program. As Rear Admiral George Milligan, the flotilla commander, said later that after the Mogadishu raid to rescue the entrapped U.S. Embassy and other mission personnel during the 1991 Gulf War, "It seems as if Al Gray saw such a future special training capability back as early as 1972." Gray's vision and determination to expand the Marine Corps mission capabilities have been validated many times over the past two decades. There were to be even more benefits from special operations capable forces in other regions of the world in the years ahead.

Always a dedicated reader, Gray still managed to crowd in his own specialized research on the littoral nations and their military forces. As the most forward-deployed amphibious force, the 24th Marine Amphibious Unit (MAU) participated in amphibious landings and field exercises in both the eastern and western Mediterranean.

It was an exciting and challenging time for Gray as he honed his leadership style and his BLT's readiness with seemingly endless training evolutions. While on this deployment, Gray was selected for Colonel. His assignment to an infantry battalion, and later to command of the 2nd Marine Regiment marked a major change in Gray's assignment pattern. Since the day of his commissioning as a Second Lieutenant, he had aspired to become an infantry battalion commander. His career until this time had been one of the most diversified among his peers. Yet he was relentless in following the activities of the Marine Corps operating forces that were spread around the world and standing in harm's way. His unique planning actions and aggressive leadership, both as battalion and regimental commander, were the culmination of his military experience in a lifetime of study and his wide variety of assignments.

The opportunity to command one of the Corps' nine infantry regiments, and then to do so successfully, placed Lieutenant Colonel Gray back into the mainstream of the Fleet Marine Forces. Traditionally a much sought-after command assignment, this meant he was to assume one of the most-desired assignments of any of the Corps' 540 Colonels. After years of professional service in the more technical fields, Gray was to discover that it was in the combat commander's role where he found his true fit in the Marine Corps. His appointment, while still only a "selected" Colonel, clearly demonstrated Gray's professional credibility, creative energies, and field leadership. It led to his recognition as an exceptional field officer by the higher levels of the U.S. Marine Corps.

Recognizing the astute intellectual and professional skills of then-Major Jack Sheehan, Captain James Magee, and others, Gray transferred several of these officers from the 1st Battalion to his regimental staff. Comfortable with these officers' styles and proven ability to plan and execute complex operations on short notice, he quickly injected an accelerated training pace throughout the regiment.

Gray led the regiment through a series of major exercises, including the cold-weather exercise ALPINE WARRIOR at Camp Drum, New York. Later elements of the regiment deployed to Twentynine Palms, California, to participate in ALKALI CANYON, a major combined arms, live fire exercise. Gray's energy levels never faltered as he seemed to plan and design more and more field training exercises. There were also numerous Gray-initiated regimental field exercises in the North Carolina region. Gray's focus was always on warfighting, as well as being prepared to conduct other unexpected fast-response missions. All these training evolutions were executed in addition to providing other BLT-sized deployments for a number of contingency requirements in the Mediterranean and Caribbean regions.

Typically, Gray developed close professional and personal ties with such gifted young officers as Major Ernie Cook, M. "Doc" Smith, and Jack Sheehan, plus Captains James Magee, Tony Zinni, and legions of others. These trusted relationships would be maintained for years and through a number of job assignments. This, too, was characteristic of his leadership style. He always remembered the "best and brightest" leaders, and once found, tended to find them again and again as his own assignments evolved.

Hundreds of Marines, in enlisted and officer ranks, individually bonded with Gray. They were especially proud to have served with him and didn't hesitate to tag themselves as "Gray guys." He fostered loyalty from his key subordinates and exhibited his own loyalty to them thereafter.

Several important events will demonstrate how this special bond of loyalty would be fostered in all his future assignments. Although it was unspoken, this bond of loyalty would pay off for Gray many times and in many ways during the remaining years of his Marine Corps career.

From August 1973 until June 1974, Colonel Gray attended the Army War College at Carlisle Barracks, Pennsylvania. This concentrated, top level school for the Army's most qualified Colonel and prospective General officers introduced him to the specifics of operational level planning in the European theater, the problems within the North Atlantic Treaty Organization (NATO), and the intellectual perspectives of his Army peers. History-astute Gray was aware that, years earlier, Major General John Lejeune, who became the 13th Commandant of the Marine Corps, had paved the way for Lejeune's command of an Army division in World War I by his attendance at the Army's War College. While at that college, Gray showed a strong interest in the Army's armored and mechanized doctrine and field operations. Again, he confirmed his belief that, no matter what type of operation was to be conducted, in order to be an effective commander one must have reliable and operational secure communications.

Shortly after graduating from the Army War College, Gray received command of a second infantry regiment—a rare opportunity for any Colonel of Marines. He focused all training evolutions at the regimental level. The 4th Marine Regiment, 3rd Marine Division was based on the island of Okinawa, 500 miles south of mainland Japan. Regimental commanders were often dual-hatted with the responsibility as camp commanders. In Gray's case, he was charged with the responsibility for the effective operation and security of Camp Hanson, located on Okinawa, Japan. The camp, with 8,500 personnel, was the largest of the Okinawa camps and included eight separate battalions in addition to the 4th Marine Regiment. The top priority assigned personally by Fleet Marine Force Pacific Commander, Lieutenant General Louis Wilson, was to take control of the many disciplinary and racial problems that had plagued Okinawa for years and restore order. In an unprecedented step, Major General Houghton, the Commanding

General of the 3rd Marine Division, assigned operational control of all the Hansen units to Gray. Additionally, Major General H.A. Hatch, who commanded all Marine Bases on Okinawa, gave Gray wide latitude in dealing with the Japanese government and civilian personnel. This mission was completed to everyone's satisfaction in four months.

The U.S. forces had been withdrawn from South Vietnam since 1973 under President Nixon's Vietnamization program. The Vietnam conflict had ended in an impasse for the Free World forces, who had served and fought there for six years. But the internal strife between the North and South Vietnamese had continued. All the while, the United States observed the growing threat from the North Vietnamese against the demoralized South Vietnam.

There were ominous signs the North Vietnamese Army was gathering its forces in potential attack positions. Gray's established modus operandi was to scrutinize every piece of the intelligence communities' classified message traffic. It was just his way to know, better than anyone else, what was going on. This extra pursuit of information enabled him to assess the credibility of the emerging threat and the potentially worst situation. Were there any options, should a crisis occur? Again, fate seemed to place Al Gray in a command position at a time and place where a crisis would soon erupt.

Within a few months, Gray would further expand his command responsibilities to also become the Commanding Officer, 33rd Marine Amphibious Unit (MAU). In the late fall of 1974, Al Gray was designated as the Primary Ground Security Force Commander for any South Vietnam helicopter evacuation requirements.

During early March 1975, U.S. diplomatic intelligence agencies and military forces in the western Pacific monitored the deteriorating military situation. The South Vietnamese government and its military forces failed to respond to requests for the latest military situation on the advancing North Vietnamese armies.

In January 1975, the situation in Cambodia continued to deteriorate, and U.S. contingency plans were reviewed. At the request of Air Force Lieutenant General John J. Burns, the commander of U.S. Forces Support Activities Group and the 7th Air Force located in Thailand, Al Gray flew there for discussions and then into Phnom Penh, Cambodia, to speak with Ambassador John Guenther Dean and review their plans. Gray thought the plans were much too complex and that they should be simplified. With the Ambassador's concurrence, Gray returned to Thailand and briefed General Burns, who also agreed with Gray's assessment. Gray then drew up a simple plan utilizing two soccer fields as the primary and secondary landing zones for helicopters. This plan was ultimately executed to perfection by the 31st MAU as OPERATION EAGLE PULL on April 11, 1975, with the evacuation of 296 Americans from Cambodia.[2]

On March 26 Major General Carl W. Hoffman, Commanding General of the III Marine Amphibious Force on Okinawa, activated the Headquarters, 9th Marine Amphibious Brigade under Brigadier General Richard E. Carey, a seasoned Marine aviator who had also served as an infantry officer in Korea. Headquarters was activated for planning contingency operations and had forces assigned for that purpose. These included battalions from the 4th and 9th Regiments as well as Marine Air Group (MAG) 39 and Logistics Support Units. If, and when required, the ground combat command elements would be commanded by Gray and his staff assembled on Okinawa. As Regimental Team 4, it had assigned four infantry battalion landing teams—1st and 2nd Battalions, 4th Marines, and the 1st and 3rd Battalions, 9th Marines. Brigadier General Carey and his staff were briefed on the overall deteriorating situation in South Vietnam, and all commenced planning.

On March 27, General Hoffman activated the 33rd Marine Amphibious Unit (MAU) for operations and deployment with Amphibious Group Bravo to the South China Sea off the South Vietnamese coast. The 33rd MAU was initially comprised of BLT 1/9, Logistics Support Units 1/9, and two helicopter squadrons, HMM-165 and HMM-463, and they embarked on amphibious shipping during the period March 27-30 en route to the operating area. This dual designation of the Commanding Officer (CO) of Regimental Landing Team-4 (RLT-4) for planning and the CO 33rd MAU for operations with its nearly unprecedented responsibilities was to keep Gray extraordinarily busy for the next several weeks.

Meanwhile, battlefront conditions continued to deteriorate in South Vietnam. It was becoming apparent that South Vietnam's government and military were in danger of a total collapse. General Hoffman, back at III Marine Amphibious Force (MAF) Headquarters, had prepared for the worst and dispatched additional units to assist in the possible rescue of South Vietnamese leaders who had been supportive of American forces while they were in Vietnam. These American Navy and Marine forces were not only committed to an uncertain future but one of historic proportions.[3] In days, it was to become one of the most extensive humanitarian evacuations in history. Throughout this period, Marine helicopter squadrons from other Marine Force Pacific assets were assembling and moving toward South Vietnam by air and sea. Additionally, Air Force helicopters had been embarked on the carrier USS *Midway*. It was a time of confusion. The normal rumor-mill stories were rife with possible operational commitments. The absence of any U.S. forces in South Vietnam further exacerbated the information flow and complicated the emerging crisis situation.

On April 4th, General Carey, the Commander of the 9th Marine Amphibious Brigade (MAB), accompanied by Gray, flew to Subic Bay in the Philippine Islands to continue planning and join up with the assembling naval forces under the 7th Fleet. Carey joined his naval counterpart, Rear Admiral Don Whitmire, aboard the Amphibious Task Force Commander's flagship USS *Blue Ridge* on April 10th. Meanwhile, Gray, after completing actions required to convert the aircraft carrier USS *Hancock* for helicopter operations and embarking BLT 3/9 aboard, sailed on the *Hancock* to the operating area. After cross-decking from the *Hancock,* he joined his 33rd MAU command and his naval counterpart aboard the USS *Dubuque* in the South

China Sea and proceeded to station off Vung Tau, South Vietnam. On April 9th, six additional squadrons were placed under his operational control. On April 13, the 33rd Marine Amphibious Unit (MAU) reported to his 9th MAB for planning. However, Gray still had full responsibility for the impending helicopter operations until April 18, when the 33rd MAU was deactivated and the forces placed under the operational control of the 9th Marine Amphibious Brigade. At the time, Regimental Landing Team 4 (RLT-4) was formed with Gray designated as Commanding Officer.

By April 19, a restructured and powerful MAB had been formed at sea under General Carey in a highly complex orchestration of ships, helicopters, combat equipment, supplies, and personnel within the 7th Fleet. On April 20, General Carey, as Commanding General 9th MAB and as Commander, Landing Force, reported to Commander, Amphibious Task Force 76 for operations on station off the coast of Vung Tau. Both the 9th MAB and RLT-4 issued their operations plans. Concurrent and parallel planning had continued at a rapid pace for weeks. The next ten days were to be even more hectic as the North Vietnamese and Viet Cong forces tightened their noose on Saigon.

By April 28, a U.S. naval task force of 18 ships was positioned off the southern coast, a short helicopter distance from Saigon. The 9th MAB had the strength of more than 6,000 Marines, including Navy corpsmen and a fleet of 80 helicopters. Gray's three reinforced infantry battalions, which had deployed as separate Marine Amphibious Units, had all been deactivated and reconstituted as the 4th Regiment. This gave Gray immediate control over all Marine ground forces. Additionally, a unique organization was hastily developed. The Amphibious Evacuation Security Force was organized to provide security aboard the Navy and Military Sealift Command (MSC) ships awaiting the potential South Vietnamese refugees. Gray recognized that the Saigon situation demanded some special operational capabilities, and his force began to train for uncommon missions.[4] Despite the obvious complexity and uncertainty of the fluid situation, the transition went very smoothly. From the very beginning, Gray, in concert with General Carey, his commanders, and their superb staffs had worked diligently to prepare for a worst-case scenario. Additionally, he had operated with many of them before and they shared mutual confidence in each other. Gray also had great rapport with many of the naval officers within the naval task force for they had served together as well. Furthermore, his exceptional knowledge of both naval and air operations, as well as his previous experience with Air Force operational capabilities, strengthened the entire planning process. Prior to joining the 9th MAB, Gray had been making daily reconnaissance trips into Saigon and the surrounding region including the Vung Tau peninsula. Returning each night to the *Blue Ridge,* Gray briefed Admiral Whitmire, the Amphibious Task Force Commander, General Carey, and their staffs on the situation and various challenges that would confront the mission.

A major requirement for the 9th MAB was to form a properly structured brigade from the somewhat disparate units that were embarked aboard the amphibious shipping while at sea. This had never been done before and required detailed planning by all concerned. Gray took the lead here and after several days of cross-decking equipment and personnel by helicopter, and great work by the Navy personnel aboard the ships, a doctrinally sound Marine Amphibious Brigade (MAB) was ready for any contingency that might come their way. The MAB could also count on overwhelming air support available from the U.S. Seventh Fleet and the U.S. Seventh Air Force operating out of Thailand.

Initial requirements for evacuation covered the entire spectrum from being prepared to lift out a small number of "stay behind" people engaged in conducting or supporting special activities all the way to evacuating a million and a half people. Over time, as the Air Force-managed airlift from *Tan Son Nhut Air Base* continued to fly thousands of people out of the Saigon area, and as the situation became somewhat clearer, the numbers were adjusted downward.

Potential evacuation sites initially included the Defense Attaché's Office (DAO) Air America complexes at *Tan Son Nhut*, the Newport Pier, and the Can Tho Region along the Bassac River on the South China Sea. This latter turned out to be the largest site where hundreds of thousands of refugees as well as remnants of the Army of the Republic of Vietnam (ARVN) units had fled. It was also home for the Vietnamese marines and posed the most difficult evacuation challenge in terms of size and complexity. To make matters even more challenging, the U.S. Embassy was never considered a primary evacuation site for the Ambassador or any of his advisors. It had only a rooftop landing site, which was restricted to no larger than a CH-46 troop helicopter capable of carrying only 18 passengers. All Embassy and security personnel were supposed to be moved to the DAO Complex by vehicle or Air America helicopters prior to evacuation.

Based upon Gray's earlier extensive reconnaissance of the entire region, including numerous visits to key personnel, his overall concept of operations as it evolved from a MAU to Brigade conducting joint operations was for RLT-4 to reinforce and secure the Defense Attaché Office compound, the Air America complex, and the adjacent *Tan Son Nhut Air Base*. The plan included provisions for emergency evacuation of up to 100 personnel from the Embassy in case all of their people had to be moved to the DAO complex. Additionally, the Ground Security Force elements as well as ship security units were to be dispatched to the Newport Pier facilities if required. Likewise, if Can Tho was utilized, Ground Security Forces elements could be introduced by waterborne units and helicopters.

Depending on the situation in the Vung Tau peninsula area, this could require up to a brigade-sized landing over the beaches with a combination surface and helicopter evacuation. From the operational and tactical standpoint, the MAB had overwhelming air support from the 7th Fleet and 7th Air Force assets. Additionally, naval gunfire support was available and they could control the prerequisite air space. In addition to his three reinforced infantry battalions, Gray also had his 1st Battalion, 4th Marines at Subic Bay building a refugee camp as a reserve and two additional battalions on "Air Alert" on Okinawa, should General Carey deem them necessary. Gray gave full credit to the superbly detailed planning by the combined 33rd MAU and 9th Marines planning staffs and their Regimental Landing Team 4 (RLT-4), 3rd Marine Aircraft Group (MAG-39) and Brigade Logistics Support Group counterparts, under General Carey, for finalizing the operation plans. Both 9th MAB and RLT-4 Operation Plans, including the RLT-4/MAG-39 complex Helicopter Assault Tables and related scheduling activities, were promulgated on April 20 and were continually refined consistent with the dynamic situation ashore.

Gray knew command arrangements always tended to be complicated and often unresponsive to critical time-sensitive demands as forces came together in a crisis. He was determined to keep the plans simple for execution. OPERATION FREQUENT WIND was unique in its complexities, in part because the Ambassador was attempting to maintain a routine of "business as usual" and deny that any threat existed. The Ambassador felt it was important to demonstrate that the American presence would remain and not be seen as preparing to evacuate. This hampered final preparations and was of considerable concern to General Carey and Gray.

Gray firmly believed, then and now, that the order to evacuate by helicopter was finally issued at 1000 hours on April 29th and was well more than a day later than it should have been. Furthermore, it was flawed in that it expected an L-Hour (landing hour) of 1100, allowing only one hour for proper loading and launching of the Ground Security Force and the long trip, which approximated 55 to 75 miles from the ships to the South Vietnamese coastline. In a hasty conference with Admiral Whitmore and General Carey, Gray estimated a possible L-Hour of 1400 hours, and the critical decision was made to go with it. Everyone had been put on alert at first light and plans were executed quickly and smoothly. General Carey and Gray landed in their command and control helicopters at the primary DAO Complex evacuation site at 1330 hours and observed enemy artillery and rocket fire striking the air base as they landed. They quickly established an austere forward command post and made preparations for the arrival of the large CH-53 helicopters and the Ground Security Force.

The first wave landed at 1402 hours and within 30 minutes Lieutenant Colonel George Slade's 2nd Battalion, 4th Marines had secured the DAO/Air America Complex plus the adjacent *Tan Son Nhut* area critical for protection. Now more than a thousand people were on their way to safety. After inserting Ground Security Forces, flight plans called for a simple "daisy chain" flow of Marine and Air Force helicopters throughout the day and night until the evacuation was completed. As operations progressed smoothly at the DAO Complex, South Vietnam Army units including the military police were performing in a superb fashion. Based upon this situation, the decision was made to use the remaining two battalions of the Ground Security Force Battalion, 1/9, commanded by Lieutenant Colonel R.I. Bond, and Battalion 3/9, commanded by Lieutenant Colonel R.W. Loehe. Two other Marine officers who would play vital supporting roles through the evacuation were Lieutenant Colonel Bob White and Major R.K. Young, both from the 9th Marine Amphibious Brigade's (MAB) S-3 Operations Section.

General Carey and Gray became concerned about the situation at the American Embassy. The DAO Compound command center had been neglected and did not have communications with the Embassy. Additionally, the Airborne Command and Control Communications Center under the control of Brigadier General Earl J. Archer, USAF, did not seem to have a firm understanding of the Embassy situation either. A few weeks before, Major Keane, the senior officer from the Marine Security Guard, with his headquarters in Hong Kong, had deployed to the American Embassy in Saigon to oversee their Marine Security Guard operations. At 1600 hours on April 29th, Major Keane called Gray on one of his tactical nets and asked for a reinforced platoon to come to the Embassy and assist with security and crowd control. Gray immediately dispatched the highly skilled reconnaissance platoon to provide assistance.

It must be noted here that both General Carey and Gray had received repeated assurances from Ambassador Martin that he would not require them to evacuate people from the Embassy but would remove all his people to the DAO Compound via Air American helicopters. Gray and Carey continued to worry about the overall situation as they could obtain only fragments of information. At about 2100 hours, Gray asked General Carey to return to the USS *Blue Ridge*, and in concert with Admiral Steele, Commander Seventh Fleet, get the Embassy closed down. General Carey agreed and departed the DAO Complex, leaving Gray in charge.

The overall operation continued to go smoothly at the DAO Complex throughout the late evening hours. Gray attributed this to superb professional efforts by the aforementioned DAO and Army and Marine planners. After carefully briefing and screening all evacuees, placing them on appropriate helo lift schedules, and tending to their personal needs, all personnel remained calm throughout the ordeal. There were some unusual and isolated incidents, but they were to be expected and were promptly handled by the Ground Security Force and South Vietnamese army soldiers that were operating outside the DAO perimeter.

Although steps had been taken to clear the Embassy and terminate operations there, time was now becoming most critical as the North Vietnamese Army (NVA) was now employing American-made antiaircraft weapons against the evacuation helicopters. These weapons had been turned over to the South Vietnamese at the *Tan Son Nhut Air Base*. The weather was also turning bad and could possibly hinder final operations. Gray thought this was good, as they could operate in marginal weather and it would certainly hamper enemy marksmanship.

Gray decided to go to the Embassy himself to check on the situation. However, when he attempted to use his command and control helicopter, he discovered that someone had ordered it to return to the ship as it was thought it would not be needed. Gray was furious, since only the large CH-53 helicopters were coming into the DAO Compound, and they were too big to operate on the Embassy roof. In the years ahead, Gray would never forget the unintended consequences of tactical decisions being made by someone at a distant headquarters without coordinating with the senior commander on the ground.

Suddenly an order came down directing the helicopter evacuations to cease all flight operations because the pilots had passed their maximum number of safe flight hours. This further angered Carey and Gray as it jeopardized the mission and safety of all concerned. In Hawaii, thousands of miles away, Lieutenant General Louis Wilson, who commanded all Marine forces in the Pacific, quickly informed his forces that no Marine helicopters would stop until all the Marines were brought out. With this decision Marine CH-53s quickly resumed flying to continue operations at the DAO Complex so that the disruption was minimal. The order was also rescinded for the Air Force helicopters.[5]

By now, Gray believed that the Embassy had been shut down, and he was ready to execute the final steps of the plan to complete the evacuation of Saigon. Gray and his combat engineer demolition team began the systematic destruction of the large DAO Headquarters, additional vital areas, sensitive communications satellite terminals, a radar system, and other specialized equipment. As the last Ground Security Force Marines embarked aboard the helicopters, Gray and his team burned $8,000,000 in U.S. currency that had been stored in 55-gallon drums. Then they torched the entire complex.

Frank Snepp, in his book *Decent Interval: An Insider's Account of Saigon's Indecent End* captures the hectic final moments of Colonel Gray's actions in the DAO:

> At approximately 11:30 p.m. Colonel Gray and a handful of Marines still at the DAO began the final, systematic destruction of the headquarters building and its vitals. ... Several

minutes later Colonel Gray and his men triggered delay-action thermite bombs scattered around the bottom floor of the head-quarters building. ... Then they dashed out to the helo-pad, climbed aboard, and were lifted off. Later, the heat was so intensive that the roof of the fabled bastion of American power in Vietnam crumbled and collapsed like a ribbon of cheap tin.

After ascertaining that all his Marines were aboard the waiting helicopters, Gray climbed into the last helicopter at about 0230 hours thinking that the mission was finally complete. As he stood in the rear of the CH-53 for the long ride back to the ship he watched the huge fires they had started. He reflected on what had transpired with mixed emotions. On one hand, they had successfully carried out the largest helicopter evacuation in history, yet he had great empathy for his for-mer allies and the South Vietnamese people they were leaving behind.

After about 90 minutes, Gray landed on the USS *Blue Ridge* and was moving from the landing spot to the command center. He noticed Lieutenant Colonel George Slade embarking on a CH-46 helicopter. Gray was stunned to find not all Marines were out of the Embassy yet and that George was going back to help. Gray told him to move over, and they both began the long flight back to Saigon.

En route, Slade brought Gray up to speed on what was going on and they discussed the actions to be taken. Apparently Ambassador Martin had departed the Embassy at 0458 hours aboard a CH-46 and was aboard ship. As Lieutenant Colonel Slade and Gray approached the final leg of the flight into the American Embassy, the word was passed that everyone had gotten out. At around 0750 hours, the last 11 Marines had lifted off the Embassy roof and were en route to one of the ships. Gray and Slade gave each other a "thumbs up" smile and returned to the flagship. OPERATION FREQUENT WIND was complete and had accomplished its purpose: 978 Americans, 1,120 third party nationals, and several thousand South Vietnamese civilians were lifted to freedom and flown to ships offshore. The exhausted

Marines had successfully flown 680 sorties before returning to the U.S. armada.

Upon returning to his stateroom office on the *Blue Ridge*, Gray was shocked when Major Keane informed him that the bodies of Corporal Charles McMahon and Lance Corporal Darwin Judge had not been brought out of Saigon after they were killed in action. These two Marines had been assigned to the DAO Complex to provide additional security prior to the evacuation. Neither the 9th MAB Advance Party in charge of the DAO Complex at the time nor the Navy/Marine staffs aboard the *Blue Ridge* had informed Gray of any casualties. Stressed and exhausted, Gray could not hold back his temper. He was furious at this turn of events because Marines never leave their fallen comrades behind. To have not been informed was one thing but to not bring these fallen Marines out was inexcusable.

Gray quickly ascertained that both bodies had been evacuated from the DAO Complex on April 29th by a civilian/military team via ambulance to the Saigon Adventist Hospital in accordance with State Department policy and Embassy procedures. The hospital facility also functioned as a morgue and prepared the bodies for air transport back to the United States. Rumors that these Marines had been transported to the carrier USS *Midway* were proven false, and, of course, all flights from the *Tan Son Nhut Air Base* had been terminated. At this point, Gray turned his efforts to bringing the fallen Marines home. It was another of many tragic lessons learned, and it reinforced his position over the years that there is a point in all such operations when everything must be turned over to the military for evacuation.

Another thorny issue that was to consume much of Gray's thinking and actions was the problem with L-Hour and the perceived delay in starting helicopter evacuation operations. Higher command echelons apparently could not answer questions satisfactorily and word was received that a team from the Joint Chiefs of Staff (JCS) was meeting the amphibious task force upon its arrival at U.S. Naval Base Subic

Bay, Philippines. The stated purpose was a "Lessons Learned" session which is a polite Pentagon term for an investigation. Since Gray had been the driving force behind the overall concept from the beginning, he developed and gave the briefing and answered all the key questions put forth by the JCS team. Apparently the group from Washington was satisfied, and nothing more was required.

Finally freed up, Gray again focused his efforts on trying to bring Corporal McMahan and Lance Corporal Judge home. He had previously spoken at great length with Ambassador Martin about the situation and gathered his thoughts on the dead Marine issue. Gray then quietly "disappeared" for a few days to think through the challenge. It is known that he traveled to Manila to speak with Wolfgang Lehman who had been the Deputy Chief of Mission in Saigon. Gray also traveled as required to other locations to seek assistance from the international community and had several discussions with his former friends in the intelligence community. Closure to this tragedy came eleven months later after long and tedious negotiations led by the late Senator Edward Kennedy resulted in the release of their remains and the long flight home for burial.[6]

Marine Corps Historical Publications later recorded that Gray's recommendation to establish their own separate control system "proved to be invaluable."[7] It is interesting to note here that, in later commands, Gray's first operational priority was to demand that his subordinate commanders concentrate on establishing secure and effective communications networks. To violate this mandate was cause for immediate and strongly worded chastisement.

With the 4th Marine Amphibious Brigade's mission complete, the armada of ships turned toward the Philippine Islands and Okinawa. It had been a whirlwind of tragic events but ultimately thousands of South Vietnamese were rescued. Many eventually migrated to the United States. However, for the 4th Marine Regiment, it signaled a return to normalcy and unit training for future operations.

Gray's role in rescuing American citizens from the Saigon area, as well as his untiring and caring assistance to Vietnamese citizens may never be fully documented. However, he was the dominant decisionmaker and most aggressive U.S. military officer to be directly involved in the chaotic atmosphere and the highly emotional evacuation from a dying nation. For his heroic achievement in connection with OPERATION FREQUENT WIND, the evacuation of Saigon during the period of April 11 to May 2, 1975, while serving as the Commanding Officer, 4th Marine Regiment, he was awarded his 4th Bronze Star Medal. The citation reads, in part:

> Under constant threat of small-arms fire and enemy artillery and rocket fire impacting nearby, he directed the destruction of all vital communications equipment and facilities in the defense attaché's office compound, ensuring that no operations equipment remained for use by the enemy.[8]

Upon Gray's return to Subic Bay, Lieutenant Colonel Chuck Hester, who commanded Gray's 1st Battalion, 4th Marines, called on him for an update. The reception and processing of refugees was going smoothly. However, Hester had received a strange request from the Naval Command Post. Hester was told to have two platoons prepared to go aboard ship and be prepared to board a merchant ship that had been seized. Gray and Hester went immediately to the Naval Command Bunker to find out what was going on. En route, Gray ran into Admiral Mickey Weisner, Commander of the Pacific Fleet, with whom Gray had worked on earlier assignments. Weisner requested Gray and Hester join him for a briefing on a crisis that had arisen. The American merchant ship SS *Mayaguez* had been seized in the Gulf of Thailand near Cambodia, and American forces were being dispatched to save the crew and recover the ship.

Hester and Gray then discussed the situation with Captain Walt Wood, who commanded D Company, 1st Battalion, and would provide two platoons and lead the unit. Walt Wood was an experienced commander with a distinguished record in Vietnam, where he was awarded the Navy Cross. Gray assigned Major Robert Porter, from his 4th Marines staff, to be the overall Officer-in-Charge. Porter also had extensive experience in both infantry and intelligence matters. Furthermore, as Gray's Intelligence Officer, he had the requisite clearance and access to special intelligence data, should that be necessary.

Gray then returned to brief Admiral Whitmire and General Carey on what had transpired. On May 13th, Gray and his 9th MAB (Marine Amphibious Brigade) were again activated for contingency planning. An austere staff embarked aboard the USS *Hancock*, and assigned forces included 2nd Battalion, 4th Marines (BLT 2/4), Heavy Helicopter Squadron 462 (HMM-462) and Logistics Support Unit 3rd Battalion, 9th Marines (LSU 3/9). At General Carey's request, Gray was additionally assigned as Chief of Staff, and preparations began for contingency operations in the Gulf of Thailand. The 9th MAB headquarters, along with BLT 2/4, reinforced by Company K from the 9th Marines and HMM-462, embarked on USS *Hancock* and LSU 3/9 embarked on the USS *Mobile*.

The force sailed toward the operating area. Rapid concurrent and parallel planning by the Navy/Marine team was continuous en route. Initially, assigned missions were to seize the Poulo Wai Islands and occupy the port of Kampong Som, seize Koh Tang, and recover the SS *Mayaguez*. Later when the situation changed and other plans of action were required, the decision was made to insert BLT 2/9 Marines with Air Force heavy-lift helicopters from U-Tapao in Thailand to Koh Tang, a distance of 190 nautical miles. Monitoring events over the Airborne Battlefield Command and Control Center command network, flexible plans were developed to extract forces from Koh Tang Island by helicopter and/or landing craft from selected beaches and landing sites.

Meanwhile, confirmation was received on May 15th that the recovery of the SS *Mayaguez* had been successfully carried out by Major

Porter and Captain Woods's Marines plus the superb efforts of both the USS *Holt* and the USS *Wilson*. With the operations complete, 9th MAB returned to Subic Bay and was deactivated on May 22, 1975.

CHAPTER 5
The Carolina MAGTF

*"The key to understanding the MAGTF is recognizing
that Marines are inherently Naval Forces and come
from the sea. Together with the Navy, they comprise
the Naval Services of the United States."*

Colonel Gerald H. Turley
USMCR (Retired)
Author, *The Journey of a Warrior:
General Alfred M. Gray*

Gray always strove to develop both military and educational programs. He saw the need and authorized individual Marines to continue
their education rather than participating in unit training. On Okinawa,
he, along with several other commanders, established policies for any
Marine or Sailor to attend high school and college classes when the
33rd Marine Amphibious Unit (MAU) and his 4th Regiment redeployed to Okinawa. This enabled him to place his young Marines back
into their educational programs. There were a few leaders who resented
his elevation of formal education opportunities to the regiment's highest priorities, but no one openly challenged his decision. Many other
commanders could have instituted the same type of service but didn't.

In sharp contrast, Gray revealed another side of his personality. As
a Marine he was universally acknowledged to be a proven warrior,
but as a man he was equally recognized as a person interested in all
aspects of his men and their betterment. Several years after Gray left
the 4th Regiment, his special education program remained in effect.
Enlisted Marines and Sailors were able to continue their education
while still preparing for deployment into harm's way.

In August 1975, Colonel Gray returned to the United States and was
assigned to Headquarters (HQMC) U.S. Marine Corps Staff as Deputy
Director, Training and Education Division. Following three command

billets and top level school, it was another "fast-track" assignment, leading to his selection for Brigadier General in November 1975.

"You know who the last Lieutenant Colonel was to command this regiment, don't you?" were the first words then-Brigadier General Al Gray ever said to me. It was to be our first eyeball-to-eyeball meeting and the beginning of many more close encounters. I looked up from my desk in my office as the Commanding Officer, 2nd Marine Regiment and saw General Gray leaning against the doorjamb wearing his field equipment, his goggles resting on his helmet. I came to my feet and assured him that I was indeed familiar with the fact that he had done so before moving out to take over the 4th Marine Regiment in Okinawa.

We chatted for a few minutes, mostly about the regiment, and Gray took his leave. It was not lost on me, even at the time, that Gray was clearly there to size me up, and the fact that he came to me straight from the field rather than summoning me to his office, as most Generals might have done, was another indication of his approach to leadership.

At this point in 1977, Gray had been in the dual command billets of Landing Force Training Command, and 4th Marine Amphibious Brigade (MAB). Both of these commands were located in Norfolk, Virginia, but Gray was often away from his office supervising the combined arms training of elements of his command.

This dual assignment was the perfect assignment for Gray to broaden his exploration of warfighting beyond battalions and regiments and into landing forces and Marine Air-Ground Task Forces (MAGTFs) as part of combined and joint forces. Not only did he have the formal school facilities at his disposal, he had the operational command that was most involved in high-level joint exercises in support of the growing U.S. interests in sea-based maneuver warfare against the Soviet threat. The last U.S. forces had been withdrawn from Southeast Asia. American policymakers were refocused on the European theater and the expanding Soviet threat. As fate would have it, Gray would be thrust into the European arena of military operations at the very time a dynamic shift in U.S. national security policy was being implemented. It would be into this emerging arena of European joint operations for the U.S. Marine Corps that Gray would be asked to train and deploy Fleet Marine Forces (FMF) and validate the importance of the Navy's unappreciated maritime strategy along the northern and southern flanks of the European continent.

This was to be a pivotal field assignment, not only because of the emergence of the Navy and Marine Corps team as a contributor to the North Atlantic Treaty Organization (NATO) theater with larger sized forces, but also because it put Gray at the leading edge of amphibious combat development. Historically, Marines had never played a significant role in NATO exercises. Gray was to find that there was a series of annual NATO exercises where he would deploy battalions and up to brigade-sized forces, formed from East Coast units of the 2nd Marine Division, 2nd Marine Aircraft Wing (MAW), and 2nd Logistical Support Group. Later, as opportunities arose, he added reserve units from the 4th Marine Division and 4th Marine Aircraft Wing to these NATO exercises.

Even as I, Colonel Gerry Turley, assumed my command of the 2nd Marines, I was well aware that chances were good that I would be reporting to this young, innovative Brigadier General who was so fascinated with warfighting and maneuver warfare. The stories about his relentless focus on warfighting and amphibious warfare were often discussed among my peers. Typical of his interest in all things that might relate to his capabilities were his battles with the Navy over command and control.

The 4th Brigade Headquarters was located on the USS *Mount Whitney*, designed and built as a one-of-a-kind command ship for control of amphibious operations, with supposedly sufficient communications systems to support both the landing force and the amphibious task force communications requirements during an amphibious operation. However, several factors made the ship's communications systems totally inadequate for support of Marine Air-Ground Task Force (MAGTF) operational communications.

First, the ship's shared radio frequency power system provided marginal service for any terminal that was not supported by a highly technical control facility. Such a facility was impossible to field in that environment with the mobile crews operating the newly established satellite terminals. Thus, the 4th Marine Amphibious Brigade (MAB) initial command and control effort was only marginally successful.[1]

Gray recognized that the main issue appeared to be more basic operator skill training to include informing the men on the general scheme of maneuver, and then explaining how the overall system worked. Undaunted, he knew that with additional experience for the young Marines operating the equipment, immeasurable value would come to the brigade in later exercises. This personal assessment was to prove true the following year when the 4th MAB participated in the North Atlantic Treaty Organization exercise DISPLAY DETERMINATION-77 in Saros Bay, Turkey.

Gray envisioned a completely operable communications capability for every deploying MAGTF. These capabilities would result in a force that, while remaining the world's best in amphibious warfare, would also become adept in extended operations ashore. This deployment concept presented a whole new thought process for his Marines and meant that his forces, projected from the sea, would also be equipped and trained as a highly proficient mechanized force, ready for continued maneuver warfare ashore. This would require the utmost performance from the aging air and ground command, control, communications, and intelligence (C3I) systems supporting his 4th Marine Amphibious Brigade—just the kind of challenge that excited Gray. He also knew that to be an effective commander he must have a reliable communications system, and he was going to perfect it in spite of the age of the system.

He and his staff identified two major areas of concern. First, the Navy relied heavily on "high frequency" or HF radio communications and emphasized HF systems in all ship construction. This Navy fabrication policy was also included in the construction of the command and control ship USS *Mount Whitney*. In sharp contrast, the backbone of the Marine Corps' tactical communications was the "very high frequency," or VHF, radios. Gray knew that VHF radios were reliable with little extra operator intervention beyond turning them on and setting the correct frequency. Additionally, he was aware the Navy's longer-range high frequency operated in the frequency band that required strict attention to antenna and frequency management, something mobile Marines couldn't afford to constantly attend to. During Gray's endless visits to the ship's controlled spaces, he discovered that there were very few VHF radios installed on the USS *Mount Whitney* to support landing force operations.[2]

The second unexpected discovery was that the Commander, 2nd Fleet, who was also double-assigned as the Commander, Striking Force Atlantic, had moved his headquarters aboard the USS *Mount Whitney* at roughly the same time Gray took command of the 4th Brigade. The relocation of the Navy staff had absorbed significant communication resources previously available to the landing force and the amphibious task force commanders. The net result was a significant shortage of shipboard radios to support any type of large-scale amphibious operation. Gray's long and varied experience in tactical and highly classified communications systems enabled him to reassess the ship's communications deficiencies and equipment shortfalls. He quickly gained the necessary understanding of the problem and used his ever-compelling command influence to establish a standard procedure for installation of tactical radios aboard ships in support of the landing force. These adjustments resulted in major improvements in communications during the many amphibious landings he would later plan and conduct during his command of the 4th MAB.[3]

In spite of his best efforts, it rapidly became clear that, even with functioning tactical radios installed aboard ships, the distances between ships and intervening terrain when his Marines were both moving ashore and on to inland objectives often precluded reliable communications at critical times. To overcome the continuing communications problems, Gray routinely took to the air in his small Huey helicopter to regain communications through the improved line of sight that altitude gave him, as well as achieving actual visibility of the operations area. He soon developed a pattern of spending significant time in the air where he could gain better situational awareness and monitor firsthand his forces' tactical dispositions. Always an upfront leader, he sought the opportunity to share the operational experiences of his Marines and Sailors.

Although the Marine pilots were amiable to Gray's concept of an airborne command and control platform by allowing him to use their aircrafts' radios to contact ground forces on ground frequencies, it soon became clear that he needed a 24-hour platform capability in the air to monitor and talk on several frequencies without interfering with the helicopter pilot's own communications system. To adequately command and control his maneuvering air and ground forces, he identified separate frequencies to receive intelligence, control forces, and monitor the use of supporting arms. The magnitude and complexity of resolving the inability to have the real-time situation of his forces would have caused many a professional communications officer to just accept the problem as being unsolvable. Gray knew better.

He advanced a concept for the development and employment of an airborne command-and-control system with multiple integrated radios that would meet the needs of the MAB commander without interfering with the pilots' radio use. Initially, he had his communications personnel simply strap two tactical radios together for him to carry aboard the helicopter, providing him with two or more channels of voice communication. This led to a later design that upgraded archaic Airborne C4I (command, control, communications, "computer" and intelligence) systems to support commanders in airborne command and control in extended operations ashore. He never stopped experimenting until he achieved solid communications with his ground forces.

It is important to understand that, at that time (1976-78), there were no automated command and control (C2) systems available to project control of ground forces when Gray took command of the 4th MAB. Ground force situation awareness was maintained on paper maps hung on a tent wall, using acetate overlays updated with grease pencil annotations showing force locations and various tactical situations. This paper map process was a holdover relic from command posts of World War II and Korea. It was an archaic manpower-intensive monitoring process that would not be able to accurately portray the near real-time location of mobile, fast-maneuvering ground forces. He knew that accurate and timely situational information was dependent on reliable communications, which were extremely difficult to maintain continuously in ship-to-shore and follow-on operations ashore. Furthermore, because of the extended ranges to his forces and intervening terrain, Gray's headquarters lost communication.

There had to be a more reliable communications system for the brigade to operate effectively. The aging VHF radio systems, which had served Marines so well in Vietnam, had an inherent capability to retransmit signals from another radio, thus allowing for extended ranges. But this condition also required an inordinate number of radios to set up a relay system. It was an outdated command and control system and a patchwork system at best.

Over time, Gray's airborne makeshift vehicular mobile radio and radio relay systems finally achieved the ability to effectively monitor and control his mechanized fast-moving maneuver forces. His airborne retransmission systems were early forerunners of the retransmission systems to be used by forces in the 21st century to track unit locations and progress when satellite communications are not available.

With an eye to the future, Gray convinced the Marine Corps Development Center (MCDC) at Quantico to provide two field satellite communications terminals for use during the 4th MAB NATO exercises in 1978. These were to be used with the gap filler satellites during the 4th MAB's deployment while conducting three separate and distinct operations in three different countries.

It was not entirely a surprise to me when, in early 1978, the Fourth MAB published the activation order for NATO exercise NORTHERN WEDDING/BOLD GUARD to be held during September and October on the northern flank of Europe and named my regiment as the nucleus for Regimental Landing Team (RLT-2). My regiment was joined by Marine Aviation Group-15 (MAG-15) and a large logistics support element.

Shortly thereafter, Gray assembled the MAGTF's senior officers and many enlisted Marines and Sailors at the amphitheater directly behind the 2nd Marine Division Headquarters. Dressed in his camouflaged utilities, he presented the image of the very experienced field commander that he was and set himself apart from the normal persona of his contemporary Generals. As he casually walked to the small podium, he made little of his entrance, asking all to move in close around him and sit on the grass. Nearly 1,500 individuals moved en masse as he took the microphone and made a few humorous comments. As he relaxed them, he let them know who he was, advised them that he was in command, and told them that there was much to be done before their deployment to the NATO arena. He proudly welcomed them to membership in "The Carolina MAGTF."

The purpose of his meeting was twofold: first, to lay out an ambitious training schedule, and second—unknown to all those present— he had made this same appeal to every other 4th MAB deploying force as his method of motivating them for the challenges about to occur. Always speaking as a teacher/coach, he sought to stimulate their performance by welcoming them to "The Carolina MAGTF." Actually, there was no such formal organization, but he used it to create bonds with units and with his 4th MAB staff. He was quietly ignoring the most senior officers and staff noncommissioned officers and spoke directly to the junior Marines and Sailors surrounding him. They were the ones who would later be executing his various amphibious and mechanized maneuvers once ashore. The hundreds of Marines sitting casually on the grass were caught up in his enthusiastic and challenging speech. They liked what they heard, and it was obvious they liked this new Brigadier General. He made them feel that membership in "The Carolina MAGTF" was something special. In their minds, this was not going to be just another shipboard deployment. We all had been alerted beforehand that Gray would be a demanding taskmaster.

In addition to laying out a very intense and challenging operating tempo, Gray advocated the need for the Marine Corps to modify its traditional conventional doctrine and begin training in mechanized operations. Accelerating the traditional slow speed of the ground forces maneuvering elements would also have great impact on the aviation and logistics elements in how they would support MAGTF operations ashore. He challenged all present—looking specifically at me as his ground combat element commander—to recognize how the world threats were changing and insisted that, to best meet the emerging unrest, it was time to expand the Corps' operational capabilities to include maneuver warfare. These were indeed strange words for tradition-bound Marine officers, especially coming from a Marine Corps General officer, but incredibly exciting. Gray made it clear that he was not focused on readiness indicators like the percentage of Marines that had fired on the rifle range or equipment readiness figures; instead, he was focusing on warfighting and succeeding at the operational level of war. It was a heady discussion for us all.

For the ground elements, there was an awesome challenge to prepare for the NATO deployment. Gray's command guidance to the Regimental Landing Team was to organize and begin to build an armor-mechanized training capability that didn't exist in the Marine Corps at that time. He wanted a two-battalion-level mounted assault force capable of fast-moving maneuver operations. His innovative concept was to utilize large numbers of the amphibious assault vehicles (AAVs), commonly called AMTRACs, as armored personnel carriers. The AMTRACs were specifically designed for the transfer of men and equipment from the ship to the beach. Once on the beach, the AMTRACs were often used to move men and supplies forward. The Amphibious Tractor Battalion guarded the movement of any tractors away from the immediate beach areas and resisted all attempts to utilize their AAVs in any type of offensive operations. Their stated concern was for troop safety when riding over rolling terrain.

To overcome the battalion's restrictive policy, it was necessary to appeal to the Division for allowing a policy change. At my request, the Commanding General, 2nd Division had the operational command of the AAV passed to my 2nd Regiment, with full authority for developing new operational maneuvers. With additional planning guidance from Gray, we were able to begin developing our concept of mechanized operations. We quickly discovered that there were no training manuals, established standard operating procedures, or common hand-and-arm signals for maneuvering between tank and AAV units.

Fortunately, one company commander had just completed the Army's Career Course at Fort Benning, Georgia. Captain Sam Brinkley's rifle company was selected to develop basic tank-AAV coordination and mechanized operations. He did a superb job training all of us. The biggest challenge was to transition the vehicle into a more combat operating platform. There was a single machine gun position on the right forward corner, but more firepower was needed. To accomplish this, the troop space hatches were tied open, so that each corner of the troop area was designated as a fighting position. The troops' rucksacks and other equipment laid inside the troop compartment seriously restricted their movement. To overcome this, my decision was to hang all but their essential fighting equipment on the outside of the AMTRAC. Gray approved this conceptual use of the AAV (Figure 1) as a maneuvering and fighting vehicle.

90

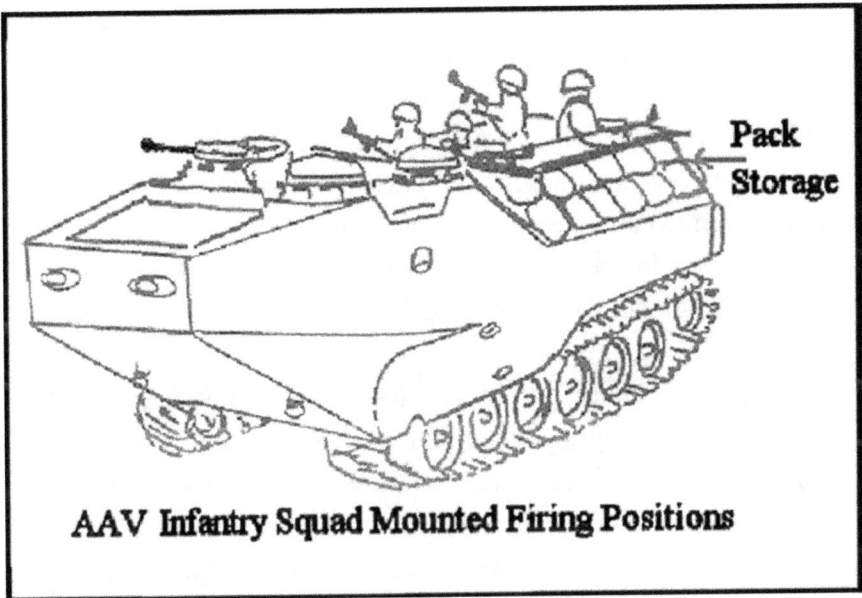

Pack Storage

AAV Infantry Squad Mounted Firing Positions

Figure 1
Support for RLT-2 maneuver warfare operations for
NORTHERN WEDDING/BOLD GUARD (1978).

With these field-type adaptations to the amphibious tractor, we could become mobilized. It was the first step in developing our new maneuver capabilities. Next, we began with both crew and infantry unit personnel training to the basic maneuver and combat techniques and mechanized operational training began for the regiment. There were many miscues. Our time and space for planning fires accelerated the need for a more rapid response from our combined arms team. But repeated training scenarios began to prove fruitful. As with any new training program, changes were in the works, being thought of, or being tested. Each rifle company spent a week learning the basics of maneuvering and mounted infantry tactics.

During these early months of testing and evaluating our maneuver training, one member of Gray's MAB staff was often with us. Major Mike Myatt was the Brigade's Assistant Operations Officer (G-3Alpha). He offered timely suggestions and was able to keep Gray fully informed on our progress and unexpected problems. Unknown at that time, and years later, as a Major General Commanding the 1st Marine Division in the 1991 Iraqi War, this mechanized maneuver knowledge Myatt gained while in the 4th MAB would play a vital role in his maneuver warfare battle plans.

Through every major training evolution Gray was there, mostly making silent observations, but never so distant as not to notice the improving mechanized techniques and how we could make it better or execute tanks and AMTRAC maneuvers faster. He became our primary instructor, our teacher. Like me, he sometimes became frustrated because there were no satisfactory Marine Corps publications available to help standardize our training. We rediscovered that operational changes do not come easy. Any new officer personnel changes on the battalion or regimental staff routinely set us back to the most basic steps. We needed to get common information to all unit leaders, down to the squad level. Once this was recognized, a small operational handbook was provided to every platoon and all squad leaders.

The regiment had been assigned one Marine Corps Reserve Infantry battalion as the second progressively larger exercises were conducted, all exploiting the newly created mechanized capabilities of mechanized maneuver force. To train the 3rd Battalion, 24th Marines, located in the Chicago area, it was necessary to fly each infantry company to Camp Lejeune for three days of basic mechanized training. On their return to their home stations, each unit continued mechanized training under their Battalion Commander, Lieutenant Colonel Mitchell Waters' supervision. Through his professional leadership, with units in different cities, and his untiring professional efforts, his battalion later performed on a par with the regiment's own 2nd Battalion. Mitch Waters proved to be an exceptional leader and went on to become a Major General and the acknowledged leader of the Marine Corps Reserve forces. He saw to it that the active and reserve General officers were one in their thoughts, priorities, and actions.

To test the Regimental Landing Team readiness, Gray held one final field exercise, where free maneuvering and rapid response planning (RRP) performed to his expectations. We were absolutely exhausted, but all were especially proud when Gray said, "I think you're ready." But ever Gray, he also challenged us to "tighten it up a bit." His quest for excellence enabled him to recognize from our state of training that we were capable of becoming even more proficient. He was raising the bar again. It was typical Gray.

After eight months of continuous training in mechanized operations that were modeled specifically after the European areas they would be operating in, Gray used all elements of the MAGTF and expressed his appreciation for everyone's extra effort. They were proud to hear his encouraging words. His forces were ready and it was time to deploy. In a highly choreographed motor march, the 4th MAB's men, vehicles, and equipment descended on Morehead City, North Carolina, to embark. The flotilla included various amphibious-type ships loaded with troop-carrying helicopters, tanks, and amphibious assault vehicles, and more than 16,000 Marines and Sailors. Gray embarked his supporting staff on the USS *Mount Whitney*. Once all personnel were accounted for, the amphibious ships joined with the Navy's surface warfare ships and set a course for the North Sea, where they would join with other NATO Naval and Royal Marine Commando units. Three distinct and separate exercises were to be conducted during a very short period of time.

Gray's 4th MAB units were scheduled to conduct an initial amphibious landing on the Shetland Islands in the United Kingdom and make another amphibious assault across the beaches in Denmark, followed by a fast redeployment into Northern Germany for the final and major NATO exercise event. The successful execution of these three important exercises would serve to confirm that a U.S. Marine

Corps MAB-sized force along with the Navy's combat-ready ships would be a formidable fighting element in the NATO theater.

The first event was an amphibious landing on the Shetland Islands. At first light on September 8, 1978, two battalions of the 2nd Regiment simultaneously executed a helicopter assault into the northern section of the main island, as the 3rd Battalion made an amphibious landing along the southern end of the island. High sea states and extremely wet and windy weather conditions made the planned assault in the Shetland Islands questionable to just before H-Hour. Gray reviewed the weather forecast and sea states and directed that the RLT-2 launch as scheduled. The assault vehicles and helicopters, battered by strong winds, executed a near-flawless ship-to-shore movement. Gray was everywhere aboard the amphibious command and control ship, USS *Mount Whitney*, carefully monitoring every existing activity via the multitude of communications channels and radio/radar systems in order to detect the slightest indication of his assault units encountering any serious difficulties. It was a situation that demanded a commander to be intimately involved in every phase of the operation. He was not wanting.

The weather was overcast, around 40 degrees, with rough seas. Both rehearsal day and D-Day operations were hindered by a steady freezing drizzle. Wet, cold but determined, the Marines moved to seize their various objectives. Throughout the maneuvers ashore, Gray was frequently overhead in his helicopter observing the infantry battalions, and later, seemingly everywhere, on the beach monitoring the backloading process. After 48 hours, his units and a British commando unit seized their final objectives and returned to their ships offshore.

With the last helicopter aboard and battened down, the naval task force proceeded through the choppy North Sea for another amphibious landing, on Denmark's southern coast. An initial course of east/northeast was set, which would allow the ships to move toward the Danish Coast by passing close to Ireland and then Scotland. The weather remained cloudy and cold, with a rolling North Sea making the trip uneasy on still-wet and tired Marines. The second phase of the 4th MAB operations was to be a helicopter and amphibious assault on Denmark's southwestern shore, a 36-hour operation in conjunction with Danish Homeland Defense Forces. Upon concluding this exercise, 4th MAB forces would then move more than 100 miles by aircraft, ships, and European trains deep into Western Germany to a new tactical position close to the Iron Curtain separating East and West Germany. Once there, the Regimental Landing Team-2 would stage their forces for the NATO NORTHERN WEDDING/BOLD GUARD-78 exercise.

On the second morning of the transit from the Shetland Islands, there was an exceptionally unusual event. The U.S. Navy's ships were steaming east/northeast at about 15 knots, and holding a straight course. Several alerts passed over the ships' intercom systems to the more senior Navy and Marine officers that there had been sightings of Russian warships operating in the local area. Most of the Americans thought nothing of it at the time it was announced. At about 1100 that morning, it was announced over the U.S. amphibious task force ship intercoms that a large Russian flotilla of warships had been identified some 20 miles ahead, and they were steaming directly toward the American ships.

Out of curiosity, I, along with other off-duty Marines and Sailors went topside to stand along the ship's rails and watch. Few, at that time, imagined the two fleets would see much of anything. They were wrong. As the two fleets closed, the Russian ships were slicing through the greenish rolling ocean at about 25 knots toward the U.S. ships, which were proceeding at 15 knots. They closed on each other very fast and were on a direct approach toward each other. It was surreal. It seemed like an I-dare-you game. It soon became apparent that the ships were going to pass at very close range.

The U.S. ships held their course, as did the Russian ships. The 4th MAB's Marines and Sailors, standing along the now-crowded railings of the different ships, looked on in astonishment as the lighter gray-painted Russian ships held their course and swept straight through the U.S. fleet. Ships were passing a mere thousand meters apart. There was no communication between the American and Russian ships. The Russian ships were all buttoned up tight, as if preparing for actual combat operations. No Russian naval personnel could be seen. The strange affair was all over within a few moments, and the flotillas steamed their separate and opposite ways.

The power of the Soviet fleet was readily apparent. Sleek, fast-moving heavy cruisers and smaller ships displayed their naval guns and guided missile systems. It was an iconic moment that reminded both navies that the Cold War remained ever so present. For the hundreds of Marines and Sailors observing the ships' passing, it proved the importance of their year of hard training, should any conflict ever break out between these two mighty naval task forces.

But the 4th MAB's encounter with the Russians was not over. Colonel Dwayne Gardner, the MAB's communications officer recalled that nearly four weeks later, after the NORTHERN WEDDING/BOLD GUARD exercise, the flagship USS *Mount Whitney* spent four days in Hamburg. Gray was away. While he was gone, the fleet commander invited the Russian attaché to come aboard the USS *Mount Whitney*. The attaché brought a Major General and a Colonel from the Russian army. These two officers were given a tour of the MAB staff's Landing Force Operations Center, the Supporting Arms Coordination Center, and the ship's Combat Operations Center (COC). Colonel Dwayne Gardner recalled, "When Gray came back aboard and was told of the Russian's visit, he told the staff that the Russians were the enemy and they had no business in these sensitive spaces, and that we should have kept them out. There was no doubt in Gray's mind that the Russians were the enemy."[4]

Gray had honed his air-ground team with months of virtually continuous training to peak the 4th MAB's operational capabilities. Their first operation had met Gray's expectations. Now approaching the Danish Coast, high sea states in the English Channel were still threatening to halt the amphibious landing. A 24-hour delay might be necessary. It had to be a commander's call. Not taking the importance of his decision lightly, Gray spoke on the radio to me as his RLT-2 commander, and to his aviation commander, Colonel Jake Moore. Moore reported that the helicopters could operate off the rolling decks and were prepared to go as planned. Time was pressing for a decision. Would it be "Go!" or "No go!" for the amphibious tractors to leave the ship's well decks?

The sea state was close to the maximum safe operating level for the Amphibious Assault Vehicles (AAVs). It was a tense period of analyzing all the possibilities and the potentially hazardous conditions to which the troops would be exposed. The landing ship docks' well decks were flooded and the troops were already embarked in their AAVs. All waited for the final signal to splash the tractors.

It would be the ultimate test of peacetime training conditions, demanding the best from the amphibious vehicles and the highly trained and keyed-up Marines. With helicopters already circling overhead watching for the assault vehicles to splash, the total force on board the battleship gray vessels waited for the emergence of AAVs to signal the landing is a "Go." It rested with me as RLT-2 commander to decide whether to launch the assault waves. Gray waited for my decision.

I deeply felt the responsibility for this decision in such marginal sea conditions, but confidently shouted "Go!" The AAVs entered the stormy English Channel and turned toward the Danish Coast. The surging seas prevented the AAV crews from seeing the beach-line, so Cobra helicopter gunships flew directional pattern directly over the churning assault vehicles, guiding them to their assigned beach two miles away. The AAV drivers had only a limited view of the beach of only a few seconds while cresting from one wave to the next. It was a difficult ship-to-shore movement. The landing of the 2nd Battalion, 2nd Marines, under the Command of Lieutenant Colonel Michael Sheridan, was accomplished within a minute of its schedule and almost dead center on Green Beach. And it didn't take long for some seasick Marines and Navy corpsmen to storm out of the AAVs. The traditional roar of assaulting Marines crossing a beach was perhaps just a little louder than usual as they released their pent-up emotions after the bobbing ride they had just experienced. Once ashore, the Marines joined with the Danish forces. Within hours, all objectives were seized. The exercise was declared over, and a success.

The 4th MAB's Marines immediately began preparing for the final phase of this deployment. Gray wanted it to go well, and he prepared his leaders for the challenges ahead. For the first time, U.S. Marine forces would be playing a leading role in NORTHERN WEDDING/BOLD GUARD, this major NATO exercise. My RLT-2 had been reinforced with 80 Amphibious Assault Vehicles, 58 M-60 tanks, and sufficient vehicle transportation to move the more than 6,500 Marines. It was to be the largest Marine Corps deployment into Denmark and West Germany since World War I.

The most challenging training maneuvers were about to begin. The 4th MAB's Marines and Sailors—along with their AAVs, M-60 tanks, hundreds of vehicles, jet aircraft and helicopters, and hundreds of tons of supplies—had to be redeployed over a great distance and into the Schleswig-Holstein region of Northern Germany for the largest NATO exercise during 1978.

The sustained operational tempo and cumulative stress was beginning to test RLT-2 and MAG-36 leadership. After eight days of almost-continuous operations, now circumstances demanded that men, their equipment, and logistical support be moved 80 to 100 miles in 72 hours and then be reassembled and tactically repositioned to defend against the threat of a heavily armored force. It loomed as a most formidable task. The performance standards Gray had set for the 4th MAB were recognized by us all as a uniquely high standard. There were some who hoped he would slow the tempo of operations, but he continued to demand and receive the 4th MAB's best efforts.

Prior to RLT-2's mechanized operations, the initial exercise event in Germany was for the 3rd Battalion, 2nd Marines, under the Command of Lieutenant Colonel Donald R. Gardner, to execute a heliborne assault on Fehmarn Island, off the Baltic Sea Coast. The planned landing zones and troop maneuvering areas were clearly visible from Soviet watchtowers along the coastline and the Iron Curtain separating the two Germanys. Captain James Conway's rifle company led the assault force and clearly demonstrated the highest levels of professional performance. He was later to become the 34th Commandant. The dawn weather broke clear as the 3rd Battalion assaulted into tight landing zones, capturing their objectives in hours. This phase of the NATO exercises was declared successful.[5] The exercise forces then shifted to the decisive phase of mechanized maneuvers against much larger "enemy" armored forces waiting in the Schleswig-Holstein area of the German federation.

In spite of the best-planned schedules, a steady rain delayed truck and train convoys. Field campsites and mess feeding areas quickly became quagmires of mud and prevented the RLT from providing good base-camp support between exercises. The troops would be cold and wet for several more days with no opportunity to rest or clean up. Gray's professional standards had often seemed too high. He was seemingly everywhere, encouraging his Marines on. All recognized that Gray was every bit as wet and miserable as they were. He was his usual self at a challenging moment: always inspiring. One could see other nearby units pointing him out to their drenched troops. His presence seemed to always make a difference, especially during the most difficult of field operations.

In retrospect, he knew each of his subordinate leaders, their professional potential, and the operational capabilities of his air-ground logistics team better than anyone, and he pushed us even harder because of his confidence in us. After four active days of phased withdrawal operations, RLT-2 was finally ordered to take the offensive.

Executing a surprise predawn mechanized attack with Cobra helicopter gunships covering the flanks, the ground forces drove 26 miles against superior armored forces in four hours. The NATO umpire control teams acknowledged that RLT-2's aggressive and impressive maneuvering, and its supporting aviation elements, had the tactical advantage and allowed them to advance forward, with little opposition, for the final exercise objective.

Once there, the exercise was declared a complete success. Gray felt the successful maneuvering of this MAGTF had done much to confirm to the NATO national representatives that U.S. Marine Corps forces could operate as a viable armored mechanized air-ground force on the European continent.

After every major NATO exercise, there is a gathering of all the principal senior commanders to review the training evolution. This is known as the "hot wash-up." During the NORTHERN WEDDING/BOLD GUARD-78 hot wash-up, the senior general of the Federal Republic of Germany included in his exercise review highly favorable remarks on the mobility and anti-armor successes of the 4th MAB. In a follow-on personal discussion with Gray, he stated, "Your ground forces are not like other Marine units who have previously participated in our NATO land exercises. Until now, U.S. Marine units have conducted little land maneuvering, and when they did, it was only at about five miles per hour. We had felt that your forces were limited as our enemy's greater forces would simply plan to encircle your infantry units and isolate them on the battlefield. Your Marines were different, as they conducted mechanized operations and maneuvered at 15 to 20 miles per hour. This has been a very important success for your Marine Corps and our NATO forces."[6]

The German general's special compliment as to the MAB's mechanized capabilities quickly reverberated throughout the 16 amphibious ships already loading for deployment back to the States. Like so many other Gray-led organizations, there was a special bonding of all troops and young officers to their "leader of warriors." He was ubiquitously at every assembly of tired and still-wet Marine units, telling them how extremely proud of them he was and how important their unit's performance was to the Marine Corps and *"The Carolina MAGTF."*

The NORTHERN WEDDING/BOLD GUARD exercise was repeatedly acknowledged as a notable success for the Marine Corps. For the first time, NATO's most senior leaders understood and witnessed the valuable role amphibious forces could play on both flanks of the European continent, should Russian divisions attempt to sweep across the steppes of Poland.

Gray gracefully acknowledged their praise, but for him, the 4th MAB's efforts were far from complete. The immortal words of Yogi Berra, "It ain't over 'til it's over" fit into Gray's plans. For Gray, that meant that a complete review and critique must still be conducted at the earliest opportunity. It was through this particular phase of military training that he excelled. He understood that the size of the exercise force didn't matter; some type of review was necessary, be it a special operations capable (SOC) platoon conducting a hostage takedown, or an infantry company, battalion, or regimental routine training scenario. There were always lessons learned and training techniques to be revisited.

Immediately after the NATO exercise was officially declared "complete," the 4th MAB's 16,000-plus Marines and Sailors began their movements back to the amphibious ships anchored at Kiel, Germany. Once loaded, the ships set their courses back to several North Carolina ports. As the last ship was being offloaded, Gray's headquarters announced the final critique would be held in the base theater at Camp Lejeune. The message also indicated Gray's personal guidance and that a maximum attendance of officers and senior staff NCOs was desired.

Earlier, during the pre-deployment "workup" exercises, each was followed by a brief critique. As these sessions developed, RLT-2 was progressively molding into a well-organized air-ground logistics team. Though it was obvious the unit cohesiveness was improving,

Gray always reminded us that we needed to do a better job integrating our timing schedules to maximize the power of the combined arms maneuver warfare scenarios. We were striving to give each exercise our best shot, but he knew we could improve. We regrouped and pushed on. He had a passion for excellence, and we were getting close to reaching his mandates.

His personal style was cleverly poised as that of a coach and a teacher. He never spoke down to anyone; instead, he reminded all that a career in the Corps must be a continuous learning experience. He reminded his audiences that the world was changing and the Marine Corps had to also change and be prepared to meet new threats. Gray challenged every group to become "smart Marines," to understand their commanders' tactical intent and be prepared to step forward and assume higher leadership responsibilities should their immediate leaders become casualties. At every opportunity, he would remind us of our naval heritage, challenging all Marine officers to set their sights higher—to be more than just a specialist in their primary military skills but to expand their horizon to become a well-versed officer who was also knowledgeable and proficient in naval expeditionary operations. Gray stated that "this was what had been the core that made Marine Corps officers unique," and he was right.

During the almost three-year period, Gray's 4th MAB conducted more than 18 other major amphibious operations along our eastern coastline in the Caribbean, in Africa, in the Mediterranean, and on the northern and southern flanks of Europe, in addition to dozens of smaller specialized training events in other places. The tempo of operations for the 4th MAB's other commitments had also been extremely heavy for units of all sizes, from platoons to regiments. All were involved in an endless cycle of training events. Many were with allied nations, including the first deployment of Marine "Basic Weapons Trainers" for the African continent.

As a commanding general, he always had an active travel schedule and a full plate of important documents, reports, and correspondences waiting for his signature. He remained an unpredictable person and would suddenly appear unannounced for the initial training sessions of routine training evolutions. Gray would not let anyone tie him to a fixed schedule; he was his own person and would remain firmly in control of his daily activities.

Gray had set an unprecedented pace for the conduct of amphibious operations and joint training exercises with Caribbean nations. Like their commander, the 4th MAB staff seemingly was everywhere. In retrospect, Gray brought a new level of intensity of exercises involving his MAB, which would ultimately become the training model for the Navy and Marine Corps as "the place for aspiring professionals to learn the trade of amphibious and expeditionary operations."

As the hundreds of officers and staff NCOs moved into the base theater for the NATO critique, we all realized this was to be our last gathering as RLT-2. When Gray's critique was over, all units' artillery, tanks, engineers, reconnaissance, and engineers would return to their own commands within the 2nd Marine Division. We all recognized that the 4th MAB's rigid training schedules and deployment had enhanced our own professional knowledge and operating experiences.

As Gray entered the theater, we were called to attention. I could sense the feelings of apprehension in the crowded theater. From experience we knew that to be in the audience of a Gray critique was an event few Marines and Sailors ever forgot. Everyone was wondering what his overall assessment of the NATO deployment would be.

The 49-year-old Brigadier General walked briskly down the aisle and bounded up the stairs to the stage like a much younger person. Gray seemed to never tire. He made a few humorous comments to ease the tension that prevailed. During our earlier pre-deployment exercises, each had culminated with some type of review and critique. As our air-ground logistics units were progressively integrating more effectively, he constantly reminded us that we needed to still do a better job with our timing of events to exploit the power of combined arms in the maneuver warfare scenarios. This was not an easy task.

"Okay," he said, "listen up as there are some important lessons learned here that we must not forget." He walked back and forth, catching everyone's eyes as every aspect of the multiple training events were about to be reviewed. Without any notes, but from memory, he began recalling more than 60 days' worth of fast-moving events.

From the MAB's first amphibious landing in the Shetland Islands to the severe weather and high seas conditions to our joint link-up operations with British Commandos, he seemed to have been everywhere observing our maneuvers during the worst of weather conditions. He remembered every detail, reminding the attentive audience of the necessity to be able to execute amphibious operations during marginal weather conditions.

From there, without losing momentum in his critique, he reflected upon the MAB's combined helicopter and amphibious landings on Denmark's western shore. He focused on the Navy and Marine Corps' responsibilities during the ship-to-shore movements. Many in the audience were leaning forward to catch every word while taking copious notes. Since he considered the BOLD GUARD phase of the deployment the most important, his comments reflected heavily on the Marine Corp's future need to conduct more maneuver warfare exercises.

We knew the term "maneuver warfare" was not a popular topic among other more senior General officers. Gray sometimes exposed a bit of his rebel spirit. He remained an unpredictable person. Gray didn't have to exert himself by attending these wrap-up sessions but he did. He would observe an event, stay for the unit's self-critique and then share some of his own thoughts.

His routine for all critiques was simple: assemble the officers and senior staff NCOs so their unit leaders could collectively review and analyze the multiple phases of their pre-deployment training, embarkation, shipboard events, maneuvers ashore, and always their command and control and intelligence measures. When all had spoken, Gray would take the stage—be it on a lonely beach, a scorching day in the California desert, or standing deep in the snows of Norway.

Always in his field utility uniform, he would calmly take center stage and face his audience. It mattered not if this was only 20 to 30 troops or hundreds in a base theater. As he spoke to us, he remained in some type of motion, shifting his body back and forth on his platform as every aspect of the training event was being reviewed.

As I sat there in the front row, I began to see my commander in a more strategic and seminal role for the Marine Corps. First, he was different in so many ways from other Generals I had worked closely with. While listening I began to study him more closely. There was no doubt he was a charismatic, high-energy-prone, dynamic leader. I had quickly learned that he was well experienced in field maneuvers and steeped in his professional knowledge of naval expeditionary operations. He could be hard, persistent, and demanding but would listen and was fair in his personal assessments.

As he continued to speak, I couldn't help but reflect back over the hectic field training scenarios, all of which were necessary to successfully conduct our NATO deployment. I mused over the past year's hundreds of days and nights we had committed to preparing to successfully execute his concept of operations—his "commander's intent." It enabled me to better appreciate his tireless pursuit for perfection. But more significantly, only then did I fully appreciate the magnitude and professional impact these sessions had, not just on our gathering, but on the hundreds of other officers and senior staff NCOs after their exercises. Gray wasn't doing this critique just for RLT-2, he had been doing these operational assessments with hundreds of other units under his command.

There were no time limits on his speaking. A few sessions would last a short time, but most, like NORTHERN WEDDING (Europe) and DISPLAY DETERMINATION (Turkey) could go on for hours. When he foresaw leadership deficiencies, the tone of his voice raised, signaling his displeasure. Many in the audiences took extensive notes. Finally Gray closed out the formal critique by commending the RLT-2 for its professional performance in the NATO arena. And, always, as he closed, he reminded everyone to, "Take care of your Marines and Sailors, and take care of yourselves." Then he would suddenly disappear, probably to attend a forthcoming training deployment. It was a proud moment for all as we recognized Gray had given a "well done."

Without a doubt, during the mid-1970s and in the 1980s there was no other Marine Corps General officer who touched, taught, and imbued more Marines to their profession. There isn't any possible way to ascertain how many thousands of officers, staff NCOs, Marines, and Sailors he tutored or how much he stimulated their awareness of the vital role naval forces play in the nation's security. Though this time period was considered a turbulent but peacetime environment, Gray foresaw the emerging threats of the 21st century and was preparing his audiences for their future wartime challenges. Just before closing his critique, he usually spoke briefly on the growing violence from terrorists, suggesting terrorism would be the greatest threat to world peace and that we, the Marine Corps, must develop counterterrorist measures.

Before we began training under Gray, as a Marine Colonel I felt that my professional knowledge and many years of field and command experiences within the Marine Corps Air-Ground Team (MAGTF) had made me a fairly knowledgeable Marine Corps officer. I was completely wrong about myself. His years of urging me—all of us—to seek greater professional awareness toward becoming more qualified Marine Corps officers was absolutely the right thing to do. He had spurred on many of the RLT-2 officers. This often included a bit of steady harassment, which helped carry us to new professional heights. We became more productive MAGTF officers, and that was far more important to him than any NATO deployment or critique. In the case of RLT-2, 11 of its officers would eventually become General officers. Certainly their operational knowledge gained under Gray affected their maturing as Marine Corps officers. His private goal all along was to make every possible effort to train and educate the Marine Corps' future leaders.

Lastly, he made most officers realize that to be designated a commanding officer was indeed a special privilege. But more significantly, he reminded us that the greater challenge and most lasting reward is to become known as a teacher of your profession. Every Marine officer should strive to become so knowledgeable of the strategic role of the nation's naval services that his contemporaries and seniors would recognize him as achieving the highest level of intellectual and expeditionary professionalism to be recognized as a MAGTF officer. Al Gray was such a person.

Major General Gray's assignment to command the Marine Corps Combat Development Command was an excellent selection as he promptly implemented new programs based upon his own lessons-learned experiences. Now as the leader of the Corps' primary research and development department, it enabled him to test his ideas of maneuver warfare and refine his thoughts about how the Marine Corps needed to change to meet the challenges of remaining relevant in a rapidly changing world. He was particularly fortunate because it gave him the staff position and the funding to officially put many of his concepts and ideas, which had been honed in the 4th MAB exercises, into action.

Three of his immediate concepts were for material solutions to warfighting gaps. The first, and most prominent, emerging concept was in pursuing the acquisition of some type of high-speed warfare vehicle. A second issue was the need to refine tank/anti-tank killing programs within all infantry units. A third and equally important lesson learned was the need to reorganize his surveillance, reconnaissance, and intelligence units into a more cohesive and responsive structure.

The fourth concern—and certainly one of his highest priorities—was a better way to train Marine units to be able to plan and execute several specific special operations missions set in critical shore-time frames. In this regard, it was an increasing requirement to prepare all Marines for new operational missions because of the emerging threats to civilians and military organizations posed by terrorist and radical international organizations. Never content to have the Marine Corps remain status quo, Gray was beginning to expand his thoughts on developing Marine special operations capable (SOC) units. These and other ideas for new capabilities that would make the Marine Corps of the future more useful to the nation would remain firmly fixed in his near-photographic memory and would impact directly on his decisionmaking in the year ahead.

Gray's ideas about the need for greater ground mobility were based on his experiences during his last NATO deployment. The German reconnaissance vehicle was an especially fast eight-wheeled, light armored vehicle that could operate at 60 to 75 miles per hour and, when cornered, could reverse itself with one transmission change by the driver. The Marine Amphibious Brigade had nothing to counter its explosive speed except a Cobra helicopter gunship. Although this vehicle had never penetrated the regiment's front lines, Gray saw the value of such a vehicle for long-range reconnaissance and flank security missions. As a visionary, he also saw the need for the Marine Corps to somehow acquire a similar vehicle. Without any formal announcement, he set his sights on getting a lightly armored vehicle for the Marine Corps.

I was closing in on nearly three years in the 2nd Marine Division when I received a call that General Robert Barrow, the Commandant, had invited me to meet with him at Headquarters Marine Corps (HQMC), in Washington, DC. While the Regimental Landing Team was developing its mechanized and anti-tank killing operations, General Barrow had visited the Division and the 4th MAB training. He observed our use of Amphibious Assault Vehicles (AAVs) as a land maneuver mobile platform for use in mechanized operations. General Barrow and I had spoken several times about the Soviet-made tanks in combat, and he had earlier listened to my 1973 Arab-Israeli War briefing. We had shared a common war experience in combating tanks. Though these two events happened decades apart, it was a special bond between two Marine officers. I felt good about our relationship, and I deeply admired him as our 27th Commandant. Always the Southern gentleman, he was truly admired by all Marines as one the finest of the Corps' Commandants.

An aircraft was arranged to fly me to Andrews Air Force Base, outside Washington, DC, where a vehicle was waiting for me. I had no idea of the purpose of the visit and made light of it to my wife. "We're going to Paris, Bunny, going to Paris, France." All I really knew was that I was to personally meet with the Commandant, General Barrow, and probably get some kind of special assignment. I was deeply honored and eagerly awaiting my next duty assignment.

I received the assignment, but it wasn't what I had ever envisioned. In his soft Southern drawl, General Barrow welcomed me into his office with small talk and coffee. Then he kind of settled back in his leather chair to make himself more comfortable, set his eyes directly on me, and said, "Colonel, I've got a special assignment for you. I'm sending you to Twentynine Palms."

I was devastated. My face unintentionally showed my disappointment. God, I was completely shocked at the thought of being assigned to the Marine Corps' isolated California desert training center! I had been there many times but had never imagined being stationed there. I couldn't help but wonder what I had done wrong.

Noting my surprised response but always in control, General Barrow went on to say he wanted to make major changes in the combined arms training program. He leaned forward with understanding and warmth in his eyes and began to share his thoughts with me. He spoke about how the world's threats had changed over the past decade and said that the Marine Corps "needs to also change, particularly its combined-arms training exercises."

I reluctantly began scribbling his guidance on my ever-ready 3x5 index card. "You'll need to take the mechanized-armor training you gained during BOLD GUARD and institute a similar training program out there. But I want to develop a Marine Corps-wide maneuver warfare and combined arms training program. This will be your top priority." In his soft Southern voice he concluded, "Now, Colonel, y'all get it started right away."

General Barrow also suggested, "You might also change the exercise name, to be sure units know they will have new training objectives." I had scribbled eight "to do" issues on my 3x5 card. With that he shook my hand and closed our session with the comment, "I'll be coming out soon to see how it's going."

I must admit I left his office with mixed emotions. I later learned General Barrow had previously sought advice from his Assistant Commandant (ACMC), Major General Kenneth McLennen, my 2nd Marine Division Commander, and probably Major General Gray as to who should be the designated Colonel to implement the Marine Corps' new combined-arms program. Although I was still a little disappointed, I had to agree my last three years of assignments had made me the most qualified to bring maneuver warfare into the Combined-Arms Exercise (CAX) program.

The task seemed overwhelming, but General Barrow was ever so personal and sincere. I couldn't help but be proud to assist in making the 27th Commandant's visionary guidance become a reality. On December 26, 1979, Bunny and I departed Camp Lejeune and arrived at the Marine Corps Air-Ground Combined Arms Training Center (MCAGTC), Twentynine Palms, California, on New Year's Day. I reported in to Brigadier General Harold Glasgow, the Center's Commander. General Barrow held to his earlier promise, and began coming out and observing about every other combined-arms exercise to see the progress we were making. His frequent presence and obvious concerns to develop creditable training scenarios helped reduce intermediate Headquarters staff resistance when additional training days and resources were needed.

Back in November 1978, Gray reported back to the Marine Corps Combat Development Center at Quantico. Arriving with his usual exuberance and new experiences from his last command, he set himself on an even more demanding schedule to bring forth more changes. Another new chapter in Gray's journey as a warrior leader began, this time as a visionary combat developer.

Gray had the advantage of several tools for use in calling attention to the need for a greater focus on mobile land forces. Several years previously, Retired Lieutenant General Fred E. Haynes had chaired a study on the Marine Corps' long-term needs for ground vehicles. The Mobile Protective Weapons System "Haynes Study Board" issued its recommendations for testing a concept to evaluate Mobile/ Mechanized force operations.[7] All previous evaluations for employing units in mechanized operations had been limited to utilizing only the Marine Corps' current amphibious vehicle track systems.

Gray's NATO exercises had not only convinced him of the need for changes in our ground forces mobility capabilities but it had also reinforced, in tangible exercise lessons, the elevated importance of maneuver warfare operations by expeditionary forces. Accordingly, Gray was able to argue that it was a prudent time for the Marine Corps to review the anti-armor capabilities of MAGTF. At the time the study was undertaken there were high congressional concerns about the U.S. military's capabilities for contesting the Soviet armor threat to the European nations' forces. This high-level interest would be invaluable to the Marine Corps as it moved to create a more mobile and mechanized ground force.

The Haynes Study broke with a long-held tradition of infantry units being strictly foot powered by recommending the establishment of two Mobile Assault Regiments and the evaluation of other types of light armored mechanized vehicles. The Commandant accepted the Board's recommendations and ordered a mechanized test be conducted at Twentynine Palms during fiscal year 1978.

Fate, circumstances, and timing once again seem to place General Al Gray at the right place and at the right time. As the Marine Corps' most experienced General officer on mechanized operations, he was perfectly prepared for the difficult challenges to study and evaluate the

Corps' formal entry into the maneuver warfare environment. When the Commandant issued the Required Operational Capability (ROC) for the Mobile Protective Weapons System (MPWS), Gray, as the Combat Development Center's Director, prepared to act decisively. The ROC stated the need for a highly mobile weapons system that would be helicopter-transportable and capable of providing direct fire support to the land forces.[8]

A field test was then initiated at the Marine Corps Air-Ground Combat Center at Twentynine Palms. The primary objective was to "determine an effective employment concept for ground forces equipped with a MPWS." Gray wanted to avoid the laborious and lethargic process of developing a completely new vehicle from the ground up. He searched for a light armored vehicle suitable from commercial "off-the-shelf" candidates currently operating in other countries. Based upon his earlier experiences in operating against the Federal Republic of Germany's "Lynx" reconnaissance vehicle, he had a fairly clear idea which capabilities were needed to support MAGTF landing forces.

Gray selected General Motors of Canada's Pirana, a rubber-tired vehicle then in use by Canadian Armed Forces. Subsequently, the Canadian government and industry provided the Marine Corps with six vehicles. Three were the six-wheeled Cougar model, and three were the Grizzly model, an eight-wheeled variant.[9] The speed of Gray's initial liaison with the Canadian government and the six vehicles' arrival at Twentynine Palms amazed Headquarters Marine Corps. It could only be attributed to Al Gray's propensity for working outside the normal procurement process. He had the vehicles shipped to the California desert base and ready for field tests before the regulating documents were formally completed.

Almost the same day these "strange to Marines" vehicles arrived at Twentynine Palms base headquarters, Major General Gray (coincidently, perhaps?) also arrived. He was there not just to observe the field tests but to personally orient himself on each vehicle's operational capability. Gray was excited and eager to get behind the wheel and drive each type of vehicle.

As fate would have it, I had earlier transferred from the 2nd Marine Division and been assigned by the Commanding General at Twentynine Palms as Director, Operations and Training. When Gray arrived, it was like old home week, and we shared hours of discussions on mechanized operations. It didn't take long to understand that what Gray was advocating was the acquisition of a highly mobile wheeled vehicle which, if accepted into the Marine Corps inventory, would ultimately change the organizational structure and operating doctrine of the Marine Corps' four divisions. When I began asking a series of questions, Gray wanted to move on and simply said, "We'll work on those questions later." He was not to be distracted from his vision and he knew that concepts and field tests would later answer all my concerns. I was doubtful. He was right.

It didn't take long for Gray to organize a desert test-driving trip. Bringing along the few young Marines responsible for the vehicles, we soon set off for a daylong driving experience. The longer Gray drove the more excited he became about their potential uses. Both in trail and side-by-side, the rubber-tired armored vehicles traveled across sandy alluvial fans and through deep crevices and climbed sharp grades over many miles of desert landscape. Incidentally, they left behind two completely different kinds of tracks. The most obvious tracks were those of the rubber tires; the less obvious tracks were the sporadic spots of "Red Man" tobacco juice as Gray drove and chewed his way throughout the 920 square miles of the base. Upon returning to base headquarters, the young Marines who had held on dearly and uttered a few grunts at Gray's and my driving skills quietly agreed between themselves that "Gray would never have made General on his driving skills." But, all in all, it was a valid driving experience for us, and it was a fun day for everyone.

Although it was a lighthearted day of desert driving, Gray's mind was quietly exploring the possibility of recommending to the

Commandant that the initial Field Analysis Concept Test be further expanded to evaluate conceptual employment of Marine Corps forces in the following areas:

- Infantry Fire Support

- Anti-Mechanized Delay

- Anti-Mechanized Offense

- Mobile Reconnaissance

A series of tests revealed that the rubber-wheeled Mobile Protective Weapons System surrogates, with their demonstrated speed and mobility and potential firepower, would significantly add to the ground elements' capability on the battlefield of the future. The resultant analysis of the MPWS field test would, in the immediate years ahead, influence the Marine Corps to change the organizational structure of every Marine division's infantry battalions as well as their reconnaissance battalions. And it would enable the Marine Corps to expand its operational capability so that its MAGTFs could plan and conduct Division level maneuver warfare.

In April 1979 a Doctrinal White Paper, "Mobile Protective Weapons System (MPWS) Study Organizational Employment Concept" was published. This transitional document couldn't have arrived at a better time. It gave Gray an opportunity to explore his expanding concept for the Marine Corps to adapt to maneuver warfare operations.

Although based at Quantico, Gray spent most of his time traveling. He quickly gathered and reenergized a few of his professional study companions to exchange new ideas on arising issues in a changing world. Fresh from his European and NATO exercises, he spoke extensively on the experiences his Marines encountered across the European theater. This group, like many previous Gray-initiated gatherings was to take a special look at the future of the Corps' concepts and equipment needs. Its membership included a number of highly respected

Colonels: Jim Magee, Tony Wood, Paul Van Riper, and even a future Commandant, Charles Krulak. As the Director of the Development Center, Gray had been formally charged with the responsibility for the research and development for all of the Marine Corps' future equipment acquisitions. And he took full advantages of his charter to ensure the priority projects he felt were most important were always on this working scope.

Now he began a relentless pursuit of the acquisition of new engineering, mine-clearing equipment, and numerous special reconnaissance items. When these and a series of other far-reaching actions were analyzed in their totality, they revealed that Gray was, within the Marine Corps, the leading catalyst in changing the future concept for expeditionary and extended land operations. This would also cause force structure to change. His rapid-fire initiatives over the next two and a half years to procure new equipment and adapt emerging technologies forced the very structure of ground infantry forces to change.

His plan for the acquisition of a fast-moving, eight-wheeled, light reconnaissance vehicle would ultimately provide a major anti-armor advantage on the battlefields of Iraq in 1991. This was because he clearly foresaw the operational need during his experiences in the conduct of many NATO exercises. He was never interested in who was to get the credit for some idea. His only desire was to improve on some issue. It was the way he operated, and it often resulted in his seniors expressing concern about his independent spirit. Indeed, he sent those high mobility vehicles to the vast desert training areas at Twentynine Palms. He took this action in anticipation of a "new" stated requirement for the Light Armored Vehicle (LAV) and Marine Corps doctrine for their use.

During this assignment at the Development Center, Gray became more aware of the cumbersome bureaucratic procedures that had evolved to obtain even the simplest new item of equipment off the drafting board, which had to pass through the milestones of research and development before ever getting into the hands of Marine units in the field. It would be a difficult experience in dealing with the Department of Defense's lethargic and bureaucratic procurement system. He would reflect on the antiquated and cumbersome system for years; a system which, when later selected as the 29th Commandant, he would seek to change.

These changes were destined to have, more than a decade later, a positive impact on the responsiveness of Headquarters Marine Corps and the Combat Development Center to support Fleet Marine Forces during the Persian Gulf War in 1990-91. It would be on the desert battlefields in the Middle East that the Marine Corps would demonstrate to the world its transformation into becoming fully capable of planning and executing large-scale, two-divisional mechanized operations. Once Marine forces crossed their lines of departure, they dashed northward miles into Kuwait and captured its capital, Kuwait City, in fewer than 72 hours. The Marine Corps had demonstrated its newest capability in planning and executing mechanized operation and had done so on a scale never envisioned by Marines, or, perhaps, by the other services.

After two and a half years of heading the Marine Corps Combat Development Center, Gray was alerted that he was to be transferred to Camp Lejeune and would assume command of the 2nd Marine Division. At his change of command ceremony, he was formally cited and credited for multiple developmental projects in coordination with agencies of the other Services, doctrine, tactical techniques and equipment to be employed by landing forces in amphibious operations. In addition, he had streamlined and accelerated studies and doctrinal development. He, personally, was credited with leading to the Department of Defense and congressional approval and acquisition of a Light Armored Vehicle (LAV) for the U.S. Marine Corps. Gray's work schedule at the Development Center only grew in intensity and diversity. The full impact of his tenacious determination to put new equipment and tools into the hands of Marines is yet to be fully appreciated.

Normally, when a new item of equipment, such as a truck, engineer type equipment, a radio, or new artillery piece makes its introduction into a Marine division, it has little impact upon established operating doctrine. Not so, with the arrival of the Light Armored Vehicles (LAVs) at Camp Lejeune. This was a vehicle that provided a new operating capability to the Division. Until receiving the LAVs, Gray's development of armor-mechanized operational concepts was limited in its maneuvering capabilities. What had been needed to advance from basic mechanized operations into fully maneuver warfare concepts was a fast-moving, light armored vehicle that could provide flank security and conduct rapid reconnaissance surveillance missions. The LAV was the ideal vehicle to fill this operational gap. Now with the family of vehicles, tanks, AAVs and the LAV with the 25mm cannon, the Marine Corps had finally achieved a balance of ground combat systems to plan and execute sound maneuver warfare techniques.

Major General Gray took one laudable personal action during his tour at the Development Center, an action he had wanted to take for several years. Upon completion of his special assignment as part of the Holloway Commission reviewing the Iranian Hostage Rescue Operation, he took a weekend off and ended his 52 years of bachelorhood. After more than a decade of courtship, he and Ms. Jan Goss were quietly married on July 27, 1980, in Burlington, Vermont. She had been a longtime employee of the MITRE Corporation in New England and Washington and was assigned to the Defense Special Projects Group when they met in 1969.

Jan was no stranger to the trials and tribulations of military life, since her father was a career Air Force officer. Lieutenant Colonel Goss had joined the Army prior to the outbreak of World War II and served with General Patton as a maintenance officer in Louisiana before being accepted into the Army Air Corps. Serving as a bomber pilot, he was shot down over Sardinia, Italy, and remained a prisoner

of war for three years. After release from the prison camp and reha-
bilitation, he served a full career in the Air Force.

Together, Jan and Al Gray made a great team for the Marine Corps,
and it was the best of times for both of them.

CHAPTER 6
"Papa Bear"

"General Gray is imaginative, innovative, iconoclastic,
articulate, charismatic, and compassionate.
His Marines love him."

Brigadier General Edwin H. Simmons
USMC (Retired)
Marine Corps Historian Emeritus[1]

On June 5, 1981, Major General Al Gray relieved General David Twomey as the Commanding General, 2nd Marine Division. He assumed a command that had on its rolls many of the brightest and most experienced officers in the U.S. Marine Corps. His three infantry regiments were commanded by Colonels Carl Mundy (the second), Jim Joy (the eighth), and Randy Austin (the sixth). In addition, the division was blessed with an array of equally professional senior Colonels such as Harry Jenkins, Tom Stokes, and Jim M. McElroy, and a number of fast-rising young Colonels and Majors who would go on to lead Marines in Lebanon, Grenada, the 1991 Iraq Gulf War and beyond. The latter included such officers as Tim Geraghty, John Grinalds, Dave McCarthy, John Kopka, Tom Campbell, Tony Zinni, and Frank Labutti—all of whom were quick to respond to Gray's challenges—and many others too numerous to mention who were following Gray's lead in studying the tenets of maneuver warfare and fostering a recommitment to warfighting.

Gray now had a much larger role to play than when he was commanding the 4th Marine Amphibious Brigade (MAB). The 4th MAB was an operational command element that had subordinate units assigned as needed for exercises or operational contingencies. Their training readiness prior to assignment was the responsibility of their parent commands. Once assigned to the MAB, Gray's staff coordinated a rigorous training program tailored specifically to mold

119

a Marine Air-Ground Task Force (MAGTF) organization and accomplish specific deployment missions in coordination with the amphibious components of the 2nd Fleet that were to support the MAB's deployment. Once the exercise was completed, these operational units were returned to their permanent commands.

Now, as the division commander, Gray was responsible for the state of readiness of the East Coast ground combat force that supported East Coast MAGTF deployments, and in position to influence virtually all pre-deployment training programs. In keeping with his fundamental focus on fostering a warfighting ethos, one of his first initiatives was to restore Basic Warrior Skills training for all recent recruit depot graduates. This was followed by expanding the infantry squad leaders' course of instruction to 30 days and nights in the field. These and other training programs continued to be a recurrent theme of his innovations.

Gray's efforts built on the foundation established by his predecessor in the 2nd Marine Division. Major General Twomey had instilled a philosophy focused on well-trained fire teams, squads, and platoons as the basis for the division and its units to perform well in combat. His primary concern had been on small units training, and this was where his commanders had placed their emphasis. As Colonel Joy recalls, it paid off.[2] For the first time in the history of the Corps-wide squad competition, the 2nd Division had the winning rifle squad, trained by Major Oliver North, who subsequently served as the operations officer, 3rd Battalion, 8th Marines.

Gray never announced any changes for the division's direction, but during the next few months, his new focus became obvious. He instilled in his staff and commanders that all must become more competent in the employment, command, and control of much larger formations than they had previously focused on.

No longer were his commanders to be of the mindset that everything evolved around the infantry battalion. Under Gray's probing guidance, they started to think of brigades and mechanized armored formations operating in widely separated distances. He made his commanders and their staffs refresh their doctrine so they could walk before they attempted to run. With endless energy and the keen sense of the direction he wanted his transition to take, Gray became more of a teacher and father figure while fostering a greater emphasis on thinking about warfighting. His approach was to get his commanders to think on a grander scale. He repeatedly challenged them to think "outside the box." Gray scheduled his weekly staff and command conference schedules for 1600 hours on Fridays, because "We can all go directly to the Officers Club for Happy Hour after the conference." More often these sessions went long into the evening hours, when there was but a short time to meet at the Officers Club.

Gray's focus on mentorship was evident in his commanders' conferences. Unlike his predecessors', which had been devoted to lengthy assessment of "green ball, yellow ball, and a red ball" measurement processes, Gray quickly reoriented the discussion to a focused effort on key issues that could be dealt with in an expeditious manner. Other staff officers would make brief remarks, and then Gray would take the floor. Typically, there was no announced agenda. Instead, he would hold school on a number of topics designed to get his officers thinking in some new direction. Usually his topics were a precursor to maneuver warfare discussions such as amphibious warfare, fire support, combined arms coordination, principles of command, and joint or coalition operations. It seemed that every session was designed to prepare his leaders to fight in a different mindset heavily oriented on littoral operations in a coalition and joint warfare setting.

Gray often exhorted his commanders to stop thinking of simply taking their battalions to conduct limited exercises, or command post exercises (CPXs). He vigorously charged every officer and staff noncommissioned officer (NCO) to "stop thinking only about commands within the division whose regiments were deployed only several thousand yards apart." They needed to begin thinking about how to talk and operate effectively while separated 50, 60, even 100 miles from each other and from the division headquarters. This was radical thinking at this time, for Marine units had historically operated immediately adjacent to other infantry regiments where they could be mutually supportive, and our forces trained accordingly.

The division communications officer quickly picked up on the general's direction and started experimenting with ways commanders could communicate in such an extended environment. Training cells were established at Fort Bragg and Cherry Point, North Carolina, and Fort Pickett and Norfolk, Virginia. All units began learning how to communicate. Colonel Joy recalls that, "It was difficult and cumbersome, but we made it work." They started with a rudimentary network using airborne relays, messengers, and routine hard-paper message traffic. Together they soon found out the whole family of FM radios would not solve their problems. Next they tried to relay on AM radios, which was slower and also cumbersome. It meant commanders must be able to perform communications within much less frequency mode and much more intuitively, based on their thorough understanding of the commanders' intent and the use of mission-type orders.

His next step was to revise the 2nd Division's Training Exercise and Employment Plan (TEEP). The bulletin laid out an innovative series of new training events and command guidance for all divisional units for an 18-month planning period. Upon receipt, every division unit had to make major changes in previously planned training evolutions. In addition, the training bulletin also contained new training-readiness guidance for his units that had already been deployed to the Mediterranean and were serving with the Sixth Fleet, the Amphibious Readiness Group (ARG), and the Air Alert Force (AAF). This epic document set in motion the greatest change of direction for the 2nd Marine Division since the World War II era. Supporting documents followed to formalize the revised division training exercise and command post exercise (CPX) schedules. There was an intensity and aggressive focus on implementing a comprehensive refocus of the entire command on a new way of operating that was not often exhibited by a General officer.

Just as he had with his previous commands, Gray began impromptu visits throughout the regiments and separate battalions of the division. These visits were usually operational—visiting the forces in the field rather than in garrison—and involved significant interplay with his commanders on not only readiness but on policy issues. For example, while visiting with Colonel Jim Joy at the 8th Marines, Gray alerted Joy that he was to become the Division's Chief of Staff. Jim Joy was caught completely off guard, as he was one of the most junior Colonels. Seemingly prepared for this response, Gray assured him it would never be a problem. It wasn't.[3]

Gray was seemingly everywhere at once, mentoring his commanders, executing command oversight, and talking to his 16,000-plus Marines and Sailors. There was no training event too small to escape his scrutiny. Gray's preferred classroom was always the field environment. He was attempting to introduce a new way of thinking about warfare through his maneuver warfare training exercises. This philosophy of maneuver warfare was built upon the concepts of concentration, speed, surprise, boldness, friction, and disorder. It was a philosophy based upon a commander's intent, aggressive decentralized decisionmaking, a single focus of main effort, an understanding of the necessary actions required to shape the situation, and mission tactics.[4]

His training was designed to make leaders at all levels think, understand the dynamic evolving tactical situations around them, and then take the initiative, based upon understanding the commander's intent. There was an endless array of practical-application exercises, each serving as a teaching tool to acquaint the division units with the maneuver warfare philosophy. A principal goal was getting his officers to understand that by increasing the tempo of operations they could create new opportunities on any battlefield while conducting maneuver warfare.[5] Most exercises were conducted at the battalion and regimental levels. Each exercise varied in scope and focus. Most units began planning from imaginary amphibious ships, and then once projected ashore, became quickly involved in tactical situations that necessitated the forces to maneuver inland. Gray would craft each training evolution by developing the "commander's intent." It was the keystone to his learning process to get unit leaders to move away from the conventional war mindset and operate in an asymmetric warfare environment. No two units ever had the same mission or troop list—such as the same number of supporting tanks, artillery pieces, Amphibious Assault Vehicles (AAVs) or logistical support assets—so there was no set answer. There were MAPEXs (map exercises), CPXs (command post exercises), COMEXs (communications exercises), STXs (situation training exercises), LOGEXs (logistics exercises), TEWTs (Tactical Exercises Without Troops), and always a blend of simulation-supported war games.[6]

Was it easy? No. Were all problems solved? Of course not! Solving problems is the principal purpose of training evolutions! There are so many variables that can come into play—weather, communications breakdowns, timing of events, even the training of new personnel—that every training exercise is unique. To the casual bystander, there is an unappreciated complexity as a major training exercise unfolds, for literally hundreds of leaders must all work in unison for the various evolutions to harmoniously unfold. In contrast to an aviation exercise where there are a finite number of air platforms and a relatively few individuals involved, a ground exercise typically involves literally hundreds, if not thousands, of vehicles, and thousands, if not tens of thousands, of troops maneuvering toward some final objective. The human factor always injects a certain degree of uncertainty in every ground maneuver.

Every exercise, every deployment has unique experiences, and sometimes the memories are not pleasant to recall. Gray was a tireless operational critic, and his detailed critiques of exercises and operations were legendary. When Gray was a force commander during a heavily attended post-deployment briefing given by the 24th Marine Amphibious Unit (MAU) staff at the Camp Lejeune Base Theater, he focused on a multi-nation landing exercise in Turkey with NATO allies. Gray had visited the MAU during the exercise and clearly was upset with the ship-to-shore part of the operation, which had been beset with a number of execution problems. Major Jack Muerdler, the operations officer, had just begun to describe the Turkish endeavor in a reasonably positive fashion when Gray, seated next to the MAU commander in the front row, lit into him. "Some of your forces missed their landing beaches by 500 yards. When an amphibious operation starts out like that, how can you say it was successful?"

The theater grew silent. As it turned out, however, Major Muerdler had acted as an umpire during exercise DISPLAY DETERMINATION in 1977, when then-Brigadier General Gray's 4th MAB landed in Saros Bay, Turkey. Muerdler witnessed the landing of one of the brigade's units at some 1,000 yards from its assigned beach.

Major Muerdler paused and then looked directly at the general. "You're right, sir. We missed the beach. But we got closer than you did in 1977!" The theater went from merely silent to ghostly quiet. The MAU commander twitched uncontrollably. "Lord, help us," he thought. The "master" had been challenged publicly. Gray slowly looked around the theater. After about ten seconds, which seemed somehow like ten minutes, he broke out in a wonderfully loud and raucous laugh. The whole room filled with boisterous laughter as all joined in.

The briefing then continued on for another hour or so to a very relaxed audience. There were many high points in the deployment. But no operational excellence or displays of professionalism could equal the great effect of Gray's response to Major Muerdler's retort. It was the premier topic at the Camp Lejeune Officer Club for weeks.[7]

There were difficult times, even times when everything seemed to go wrong. The constant turnover in officers often made it necessary to repeatedly go back to basics. It was frustrating, but Gray persisted in an effort intended to change such a basic mindset across the entire division. Clearly, he accepted that such a process took time. However, he was quick to anger, and there were times when, once critically focused, he could come down hard when his patience wore thin. This was especially apparent when it was a failure in the conduct of basic leadership steps, or when commanders did not take care of their Marines and Sailors. But once his outburst was over, the incident was typically over. There was no time for prolonging the incident, and Gray was able to rapidly move on to other issues.

Nothing was left to chance. It was Gray's fertile brain crafting what would eventually become his MAGTF campaign plan. Traditional areas, such as combined arms employment, weapons qualifications, and unit amphibious training were drastically revised as new instructions began to creep into all operations. Gray pushed the special capabilities so that his reconnaissance, infantry, and artillery units would be prepared to expand beyond traditional operations to include untested measures to guard against the rising incidents of terrorist activities.

With the basic transitional changes in place, Gray was set to solidify his vision of what and how the Marine division should be prepared to encounter in a rapidly changing world that was being pushed by an unconventional type of threat, emerging new technologies, and the uncertain impact of these and other factors when entering into the Information Age.

His primary tools used to evaluate the effectiveness of his *Division Commander's Guidance* were through command post and field exercises. Gray thrived on the give and take with the junior officers and enlisted personnel as they moved though the mental and operational challenges presented as their units cautiously explored the concept of maneuver warfare.

Each week, different units were scheduled to conduct some type of war game. Once they learned how to communicate—to "talk," no matter how rudimentary it was—they were ready to participate in command post exercises (CPXs). This was a stressful period for all players. Progress was slow, but they were quickly becoming a division, air wing, and logistics team. No longer were his commanders thinking of just the classic amphibious assault-type operations. The steady challenges from Gray were created to make commanders and their staffs think not just beyond the beachhead but deep inland to distances never before advocated in accepted Marine Corps doctrine. CPXs began after the division had arrived in the objective areas from sea and air, and they played these exercises from that point forward. The exercises integrated some type of naval campaign in a littoral setting. As history would later reveal, these early Gray staff training exercises were to serve the division well in DESERT STORM and DESERT SHIELD, and even later, in IRAQI FREEDOM. The terrain picked for these CPXs was most often focused on Iran rather than on Iraq since that area offered more challenging mountainous terrain, a long coastline, few useable air fields, and unique challenges for assembling divisional-level forces, as well as the opportunity to conduct long distance armored/mechanized operations.

Once the division staff and organizational commanders fully grasped the need for an accelerated planning process, Gray undertook a series of war games. He recognized the wide gap between the potential value of tactical exercises and their actual benefits. Always the trainer, and consistently trying to push the readiness envelope, he began introducing computer-assisted tactical command and control tools. Gray believed that by using computer assistance, many of the limitations imposed by manual methods could be overcome.

The Marine Corps had recently purchased the Tactical Warfare Simulations Evaluation Analysis System (TWSEAS) which could be used to simulate certain events such as air strikes and artillery fires. The automated system had additional utility in that it could track unit locations during field maneuvers and then be employed in post-exercise training sessions without troops. However, there were numerous systems and software problems, so delays often discouraged the units from playing a computer-assisted war game. Many leaders quietly wished to go back to the old tried-and-true method of "map exercises," without computer assistance. But Gray was determined to exploit this emerging technology. Upon reflection, he perhaps could have moved a little slower and shared his own vision as to the benefits of computer-supported war games. Logic would also suggest that since Gray participated in nearly every one of his divisional units' separate war games—and thus having been repeatedly exposed to these system difficulties—he would have lowered his expectations. He didn't. Instead, he increased the TWSEAS training tempo for all infantry regiments and their battalions. Gray was using technology to make a quantum leap forward in the conduct of MAGTF training. As discussed in Terry Pierce's *Warfighting and Disruptive Technologies*, it is generally acknowledged that Gray was setting a course designed to transform the division's warfighting philosophy from one based upon attrition to one based on the philosophy of maneuver warfare.[8]

As a result of these war games, a whole generation of commanders and staffs were trained in the intricacies of operating long armored columns over hundreds of miles, and all the problems associated with such operations. The questions that arose were normally about command and control and the maintenance of Marine Corps forces deep inland. The challenges were many, but most significantly, involved learning how to avoid outrunning supporting arms and how to rearm, refuel, and keep on the move. The whole concept of logistics and communications over widely dispersed areas dominated these discussions, which, even though driven by the division commander, were, in fact, Marine expeditionary force-level exercises involving the Marine Aircraft Wing and Force Service Support Group equally in the exercise.

After many iterations of CPXs, Gray determined that they were ready to attempt field operations. Fort Bragg, North Carolina, and Fort Pickett, Virginia, provided "limited opportunities." However, the major training ground was to be at Marine Corps Air Ground Combat

Center Twentynine Palms, California. Gray's mechanized operational concepts were being absorbed into live fire combined arms scenarios. Several of the Fort Pickett deployments proved to be exceptionally successful. When Lieutenant Colonel Ray Smith's 1st Battalion, 8th Marines was executing at Fort Pickett, he received intelligence that the "enemy" had shifted from his earlier reported positions. This move left an opening in the enemy's lines. Smith quickly revised his operations plan and exploited the tactical opportunity, maneuvering his forces toward the final objective without any measurable opposition. This major redirection of his units enabled his mechanized task forces to seize the final objective almost before the exercise was scheduled to begin. Gray was elated, and in later years, would quietly reminisce that this particular deployment by the 1st Battalion, 8th Marines was a pivotal milestone in getting the 2nd Marine Division's leaders to think effectively about maneuver warfare.

Although wargaming was one of his tools to challenge unit planning skills, Gray's primary focus was inspiring unit leaders to understand the concept and theory of maneuver warfare. This involved breaking young leaders away from traditional thought on conventional warf-ighting and refocusing them on exploiting any operational advantage once having arrived ashore. Gray's greatest challenge was to get his maneuver commanders to execute power projection by sending forces 50 to 100 miles inland.

Significant change came slowly, but Gray never relented in the goal of achieving a division/wing team capable of thinking and conducting maneuver warfare. This is not to say that Gray was never frustrated in getting leaders at all levels to accept the maneuver warfare philoso-phy. On occasion, he spoke out firmly when he saw leaders who failed to seize the military advantage when a clear opportunity presented itself. His outbursts were few, calculated, and focused on reinforcing his goals. Everyone who participated in a "Gray war game" never forgot the experience. Gray subsequently strengthened his control of the use of computer-assisted gaming by establishing a maneuver warfare board.[9] Playing the role as both coach-teacher to instill his ideas among the 16,000 men and women in the division to become proficient in employing maneuver warfare techniques, he pressed on.

Colonel Joy reflected back to Gray's vision and direction of training, which was exactly what they later planned and executed in Kuwait and Iraq in 1991. "Under the circumstances, and although we didn't realize it," Colonel Joy said, "we had been training for mechanized desert warfare operations for nearly ten years before the 1991 Iraqi War. There can be no doubt that Gray's vision for maneuver warfare in a changing environment was right on target, and he was largely responsible for much of the Marine Corps success in that conflict."[10]

Gray's sponsorship of maneuver warfare as a doctrinal philosophy for the Marine Corps was well established through his actions as a division commander, even though they did not become established Marine Corps doctrine until he became the 29th Commandant. However, his unrelenting advocacy for maneuver warfare was part of what made his reputation as a visionary. Gray was well aware that he was speaking of Marine Air-Ground Task Force (MAGTF) units operating in strange ways compared to the current thoughts on fighting, and how to fight and win in the next conventional war environment. But he never hesitated to speak out, on all levels, about the need for urgent changes in both training and educational programs. He wasn't advocating change for change's sake, nor was he interested in who should get the credit for doing things right. He often said, "Who gets the credit for some idea isn't important. The only issue is that the Marine Corps will be better for the idea or piece of equipment or training capability acquired."

There was one peculiar style in Gray's field and CPX operations, and that was his unofficial call sign. He was adamant that proper communications procedures always be practiced. However, when voice-radio transmissions came into the division command post announcing his "officially authorized call sign," he seldom responded. However, whenever the informal and unofficial call signal of "Papa Bear" was used, the radio caller almost immediately received a personal response from their division commander. Commanders caught on quickly that if you wanted to make direct radio contact with Gray, you placed a call to "Papa Bear."

Despite the intensity of his new training and education initiatives within the 2nd Division, Gray reactivated his old Camp Lejeune "professional study group." When the word went out that the group was to have a study session, it wasn't uncommon for his disciples to show up from all over the Marine Corps. Most were highly dedicated, much respected, and exceptionally bright individuals who took every opportunity to advance their professional knowledge. A special topic was never announced; it was enough to know the group was meeting. The issues that arose were often spontaneous, whether the subject was combined arms, the need for rapid reaction planning, or maritime strategy, it was always an invigorating, far-reaching session. Gray, the teacher, would always stimulate these gatherings by advocating new concepts and doctrine to stimulate his audiences. He was a master at letting these sessions move forward and then casually shocking everyone with a whole new thought or maneuver option. Most sessions took place on weekends and lasted far into the night. No one complained.

This particular "Gray group" was soon attracting Marines from other bases. Many had become Gray disciples, as they understood his vision for the future and the need to change. Perhaps the most famous character, other than Gray, was Colonel Patrick Collins, USMC (retired in 1989), who had known Gray from their enlisted tours in reconnaissance units. "Paddy," as he was known, was to serve alongside Gray on several occasions, and during each experience their bond tightened. Throughout the early years and into the 1980s, Gray used Collins' expertise extensively and effectively.

Paddy was to become recognized by several Commandants as a "brilliant trainer" and mentor, and perhaps the foremost small unit trainer instructor. General Charles C. Krulak stated that, "Paddy never forgot that the soul of the Corps is the individual Marine, and he never let anyone else forget it either." As a warrior, Collins had been awarded the Silver Star and three Bronze Star medals, and received three Purple Heart medals. While on active duty and even after retirement, he had tremendous credibility with all Marines. Paddy was not atypical of the types of Marines who gravitated to Gray's infectious leadership and vision for molding tomorrow's Marine Corps.

Colonel Collins once said, "There had been 15 to 18 major Marine Corps studies, and Gray was either directly involved or in some way privileged to observe the process or later review the final conclusions."[11] As Gray moved higher in the senior leadership, Paddy was like a yellow Labrador, waiting for his owner's signal to act; Paddy would accept a Gray task and be off on his mission. It was said of Paddy, "There was no national-level office, government doorway, Navy passageway, or pup tent that he hesitated to enter to seek out information, resources, or special insights that would advance the Marine Corps unit and individual training programs."[12] Paddy was but one of approximately 10 to 15 "young Turks" who would often be referred to as "an Al Gray man." No one ever knew how many there were, or how each had been tasked to study, research, or get some new equipment for testing. They all seemed to have ready access to Gray. All these "young Turks" had become masters at bypassing the chain of command to share an insight or make a brief report to Gray. These lone missionaries, on missions known only to Gray, became increasingly visible after he became the Commandant of the Marine Corps. Some would later discover more than one had unknowingly been given the same task by Gray, because he wanted to ensure the gathered information was accurate. Gray usually allowed them into his office for one-on-one sessions but seldom shared the results of these meetings with his Generals or their staffs. Throughout his career, this unusual camaraderie existed between Gray and his disciples and remained unbroken, much to the irritation of the traditionalists who felt everything must be accomplished via the chain of command.

In addition to his advocacy of maneuver warfare was Gray's long-held advocacy for changing the Marine Corps training to better mesh with a changing world. Paddy Collins's comment that Gray had been involved in most long-range studies at Quantico over the preceding 20 years is significant in explaining his appreciation and uncommon knowledge of military affairs. Gray was one of the first to speak out about the military's need to recognize the growing threat of small-scale terrorist activities. As far back as 1964, the Marine Corps had contracted a study that would describe the future world of 1985. This was a major undertaking that encompassed more than 90 scholars from the University of Syracuse, titled "The United States and the World in the 1985 Era." The study resulted in several foreboding declarations that prophesied several trends, which proved to be accurate:

- Urbanization. The large-scale movement of people from the farms and out of the village has already had a profound effect in the developing areas of the world. ... By 1985, many centers of the world would be the most dangerous hotbeds for ambitions, frustrations, and conflict, placing a premium upon knowledge of technologies for contracting and pacifying areas.

- Over the next 21 years, North Africa and the Middle East will continue to be politically volatile, pressed by population and growth, overdrawn economic programs, demands for social and religious reforms and the instability of governments.

The study contained numerous less-important projections. However, the overall study presents a clear nature of the conflicts for the final two decades of the 20th century. Four implications would eventually prove accurate, and each would have a profound impact upon the Marine Corps:

1. The growing urbanization of the world and projected civil unrest in many foreign urban cites—especially in the developing nations—suggested that the Marine Corps must develop both combat and civil affairs teams especially equipped to deal with subversive and revolutionary conflict.

2. Localized and foreign dissidents, subversive or violent in nature in 1985, will call for skills in the maintenance of order. These multinational peacekeeping functions mean soldiers without enemies. The latter has shown implications for the psychological conditioning and training of soldiers.

3. Whether or not disarmament causes a shift in military enemies to civilian-type functions, specialized, highly mobile disciplined units ... will increasingly be used to answer problems of famine, epidemics, disease and natural disasters the world around. Such a unit should include, or have immediately available to it, language officers, observers, and other international humanitarian organizations. The problems of insurgency and counterinsurgency will continue to occur in many allies and neutrals in 1985.

4. The job of the Marine Corps is to be ready for anything. In 1985, we will still see a great deal of distrust in the world. Consideration should be given to nonmilitary functions at home and abroad, which the Marine Corps could undertake in order to keep its skills and organization patterns needed for rapid responses to any crisis.

Al Gray probably reread the Syracuse Study with great care as he formulated his own vision of a new Marine Corps for the 21st century. His early years of reading and absorbing endless bits of information was actually preparing him for a senior command and now, as the Commanding General of the 2nd Marine Division, he was benefiting from his self-education process.

Tenacious in his pursuit for preparing his forces, there were innumerable other smaller unit training exercises he wanted to schedule for the 2nd Division units. To help counter the threats of small terrorist cells, Gray began structuring special operation training programs. Events like amphibious raids, hostage takedown, and the Tactical Recovery of Aircraft and Personnel (TRAP) scenarios would eventually all become standardized training evolutions.[13]

In the latter part of his tour as division commander, his infantry battalions and every deploying MAU headquarters would be examined on a wide series of special operations capable (SOC) abilities before deploying from Camp Lejeune. In Gray's mind, everything was moving in the direction he had set for a reorientation of the 2nd Marine Division's training and readiness to enter the 21st century. It must be assumed he felt exceptionally good at the division's response to his challenges and to his ideas on how to fight future battles.

Gray remained untiring in his informal visits to divisional units and often spoke to groups of any size, especially to the most junior enlisted, on the need to develop the "street-smart" mentality and then be prepared to assume greater leadership roles in future combat operations. Paddy Collins always smiled when he heard Gray reminding all who listened that a new world order was arising and there were unknown challenges ahead.[14] While these planning events were ongoing, Gray was also active in developing even newer training programs for junior NCOs aimed at training young leaders to think about both conventional and special operations missions. He was adamant about the importance of improved training programs to prepare young leaders to fight on future battlefields. Gray realized that there was much more to be done, but the momentum of training readiness and improved NCO training programs was beginning to shift, and that progress was occurring even more rapidly than planned.

The world's battlefields often erupt at unexpected times, and this was to be a time when all Americans were shocked by a distant tragedy involving American servicemen stationed on the very frontier of freedom. Terrorists with worldwide ambitions were about to begin their violent attacks on Americans. The lives of many U.S. Soldiers, Sailors, Marines, and their families would be changed forever when terrorists struck the American Embassy in Beirut, Lebanon.

CHAPTER 7
The Beirut Bombing

*There is a saying that circumstances may not
make the person, but they reveal him.*

Anonymous

On October 23, 1983, a truck laden with the equivalent of more than 12,000 pounds of TNT detonated in the headquarters of a Marine Corps compound at the Beirut International Airport, Lebanon. Early that Sunday morning the suicide bomber drove a large truck through the southern perimeter of the Marine compound, and, speeding past the sentry, detonated the truck loaded with explosives in the lobby of the unit's headquarters. The ensuing explosion killed 241 Marines and Sailors and wounded more than 100. The Marines, from the Second Division and commanded by then-Major General Gray, were part of the peacekeeping multinational force (MNF) in Lebanon.

Forensics and explosives experts from the Federal Bureau of Investigation (FBI) later determined that the compressed gas-enhanced devices caused the largest non-nuclear explosion on record. It resulted in the highest loss of life by the Marine Corps in a single day since D-Day on Iwo Jima in 1945.[1]

Nearly simultaneously, a similar bombing killed 58 French paratroopers from the French multinational force in another part of the city. The coordinated dual suicide attacks—which Iran and Syria publicly supported—achieved their primary objective. Four months later multinational forces were withdrawn from Lebanon, forcing a change in U.S. national policy. The synchronized suicide attacks that Sunday morning resulted in the deaths of 299 American and French peacekeepers and caused scores of wounded. The cost to the Hezbollah, responsible for the attacks, was two suicide bombers.

The bombing was a terrorist act in a country splintered into tribal cells by political and religious conflict. Then-Secretary of Defense Caspar Weinberger wrote, "In many ways, Lebanon is not a real country. Even the borders are artificial, and virtually all the elements of instability are contained in that small, narrow, and unhappy land."[2]

An Israeli invasion set the stage for this act in the nation's history. On June 6, 1982, Israeli ground forces swept northward along the Mediterranean Coast, ignoring and bypassing United Nations observer forces as they sought out Syrian units. Their goal was to destroy the Syrian-backed Palestine Liberation Organization (PLO) scattered throughout southern Lebanon. Their invasion and continued occupation of areas around Beirut would return their closest ally, the United States, to Lebanon as a peacekeeper.[3]

In August 1982, with the full consent of the Lebanese government, a multinational peacekeeping force from the United States, Italy, and France landed in the Beirut area. The Israeli military units encircled the major elements of the PLO, so the multinational force's first task was to supervise the departure of Yasser Arafat, leader of the Palestine Liberation Organization, and his defeated Arab force from Beirut. With the PLO out of Lebanon, the multinational force also withdrew from Lebanon on September 14, 1982. Approximately ten days later, Bashir Gemayel, president-elect and leader of the Maronite Christian militia, was assassinated. It was but a warning of worse things to come. The U.S. Marine Amphibious Unit (MAU) was cruising west near the Italian coastline when a presidential decision ordered the Marines to return to Lebanon to help stabilize the situation.

Following Gemayel's assassination, Israeli forces immediately reentered Beirut. Two days later, Lebanese Phalangist militiamen moved freely through Israeli defense forces into the Sabra and Shaltila refugee centers and massacred more than 700 civilians. The fact that the Israeli defense forces had apparently permitted the massacre to occur was grounds for retaliation against Israel, and, by extension, against the U.S. forces who were assumed to be allied with Israel.

On September 29, the multinational force was back in-country. Its stated operational mission was to "establish a presence," and stand by in a "peacekeeping role."[4] The American forces were repositioned around the Beirut International Airport with the intent of keeping that air terminal operating. It had been assumed by the multinational force that the Israeli and Syrian forces would withdraw from the immediate areas around Beirut. They did not; instead, each side grew stronger in response to a slow but steady escalation of violence on both sides. Ultimately, the multinational force became the target of the various Christian and Muslim factions.

Initially, the MNF, composed of the three nations, was well received by the opposing forces in Lebanon. However, a series of incidents turned Arab radicals against the Americans and led to the April 18, 1983, bombing of the U.S. Embassy in West Beirut where 17 Americans and more than 40 others were killed. Other terrorist activities prevented the Lebanese Armed Forces from achieving a ceasefire. A violent storm was building; tensions were rising while the multinational force was becoming increasingly isolated.

At the heart of the multinational force was a Marine Amphibious Unit (MAU) debarked from the supporting amphibious ready group ships. Each MAU had sailed from the U.S. East Coast, with Marines from Camp Lejeune embarked. The 24th MAU was a Marine Air-Ground Task Force, which included, in addition to a battalion landing team (BLT) from the 2nd Marine Division, a composite helicopter squadron and a logistics support unit. The MAU consisted of about 2,500 Marines and Sailors. The infantry battalion had embarked aboard ships for transit to the eastern Mediterranean early in May, 1982. Most of the 24th MAU's Marine families elected to remain in government quarters on the base or in the local community around Jacksonville, North Carolina. The MAU's six-month deployment was scheduled to be just another routine "Med cruise."

And so it had been for the 1st Battalion, 8th Marines. They had only recently completed a six-month pre-deployment training phase, having joined with other divisional units to form into a battalion landing team. Reinforced with an artillery battery and tanks, it was assigned to the MAU. Commanding the MAU was Colonel Timothy J. Geraghty. Lieutenant Colonel Howard (Larry) Gerlach was the Commanding Officer of the 1st Battalion. [5]

Colonel Geraghty and Gray had known and liked each other for years. Both were former enlisted Marines and had served together in Vietnam. Both had backgrounds in reconnaissance units. Geraghty was specifically selected by Gray to be the commanding officer, 24th MAU. He was recognized by all his contemporaries for his exceptional leadership abilities and rich command experience. Gray realized that the MAU's deployment could be one that demanded the most skilled leadership and professional qualifications, as well as the maturity to operate with more senior officers from other nations. This trusted command assignment can be even better appreciated when one becomes aware that of more than 500 Colonels in the Marine Corps, Colonel Geraghty was selected for this particular command, one of only six MAUs.

On May 30, 1983, the 24th MAU relieved its predecessor, which then re-embarked aboard their amphibious ships offshore and began steaming back to the North Carolina coast. Even before these ships would arrive off Morehead City, North Carolina, the 24th MAU's forces positioned defensively around the Beirut airport were coming under increasing sniper fire. By August 1983, these positions were shelled repeatedly by artillery from the mountains overlooking the airport complex. This led to a command decision to consolidate the headquarters of the BLT in the only reinforced concrete building in the Marines' zone of responsibility.

As September ended, the environment had clearly become more hostile. Two Marines were killed by Arab mortar and artillery fire. From October 14 to 16, two more Marines were killed by sniper fire. Additionally, every day seemed to bring another intelligence report about the possibility of a terrorist bombing. With the increased artillery shellings and more deadly sniper fire raining down on the 1st Battalion's forward positions, the troops felt something big was going to happen but could not put their fingers on what it would be.

The Marine forces had tried to remain neutral to all sides in their peacekeeping role. However, they were ultimately and involuntarily caught up in the political machinations. On September 19th, Druse units backed by the Syrians and Palestinians launched a major artillery and supporting ground attack on a key Lebanese Army position located on a ridgeline overlooking Beirut. If the Druse could seize Souk-el-Ghark, they would be able to direct observed fire on the presidential palace in Baaba, the ministry of defense, and Phalangist-controlled East Beirut. Brigadier General Carl Stiner, then-U.S. Army Military Aide to U.S. Special Middle East Envoy Robert MacFarlane, was in the Lebanese Defense Forces Operations Center when a Lebanese General named Tennous informed him of a "massive" attack on his army at Souk-el-Ghark. Tennous pleaded for immediate U.S. military assistance to keep this most critical terrain safe from his enemies.

General Stiner quickly relayed the situation to MacFarlane at the U.S. Ambassador's residence. MacFarlane, without seeking independent confirmation of Tennous's assessment, ordered Colonel Geraghty to have the Navy ships stationed offshore fire their guns in support of the Lebanese Army. Colonel Geraghty objected to the order, realizing that this would compromise the Marines' neutrality. MacFarlane remained firm even though he had no authority to issue military orders.

Four ships responded, firing 360 rounds at the Druse-Syrian-Palestinian forces.[6] MacFarlane had changed the way the multinational force would be treated by both sides. During the following week, U.S. naval gunfire was applied to a number of Druse targets. These offshore gun platforms continued firing until September 26, when a ceasefire for all forces went into effect. In retrospect, MacFarlane admitted his order to Colonel Geraghty exceeded his authority.

It was less than a month later when, on October 23, a 16-ton construction truck loaded with explosives crashed through the perimeter of the Marine battalion's headquarters compound. Approximately 300 Marines, Sailors, and a few U.S. Army Soldiers had been housed in this four-story building. Most were asleep when the high explosives detonated. The concrete structure essentially imploded, collapsing and killing more than 241.

Initial reports were sent to the amphibious ships offshore. Progressively higher headquarters relayed the limited information available back to the Pentagon and the Joint Chiefs of Staff. From the Joint Staff, reports were passed down to the four military services. As in most crisis situations, early information available was sketchy, certainly incomplete, and of questionable reliability. But there was little doubt that it had all the makings of a major tragedy.

It was 0632 in the morning in Beirut and just past midnight on the East Coast of the United States when Gray received the first telephone call. Once again, that special bond of trust between Gray and his juniors came into play. Gray received an urgent unofficial "early alert" telephone call from Marine Forces Atlantic Norfolk, Virginia. It was the staff duty officer, one of Gray's admirers and a former reconnaissance platoon commander, calling approximately ten minutes after the explosion had occurred.[7] Major Joe Crockett knew Gray needed to be notified as quickly as possible, and without any authority to do so he had called. With a heavy heart, he reported, "It doesn't look good. Looks like maybe 30 or 40 have been killed." Telling his wife, Jan, that, "We have a bad problem in Lebanon," Gray went to division headquarters. He later reflected that his arrival at the division headquarters was 0200, and the following four hours, were critical for the division; it gave him time to think through the initial preparations for the assembly of numerous casualty notification teams.

The bewildered survivors of the blast hurriedly radioed initial reports to the amphibious ships, their conduit back to the United States. It is important to remember that the Marine forces, both embarked and ashore, were no longer under the operational control of the 2nd Marine Division. Once the ships had passed through the Straits of Gibraltar, control of the 24th Marine Amphibious Unit was assumed by the commander, Sixth Fleet. Later, when the MAU and its 1st Battalion, 8th Marines went ashore in Lebanon, their operational control was again changed, and they were under the command of the Commander-in-Chief, Europe (CINCEUR).

This complex chain of command, stressed by the difficulties of first reporting and then describing a major tragedy, lay at the root of innumerable communications problems. Further exacerbating the reporting process was that the bombing incident occurred on a Sunday morning, far distant from CINCEUR Headquarters, which at that time was focused primarily on the Soviet threat from the east. Low on CINCEUR's surveillance and attention level would be the deployment of a small force at the outer limits of the CINCEUR's territorial responsibilities. This helps explain why the Department of Defense (DoD) Commission Report later cited these commanders as partially at fault for not identifying the increasing terrorist threats to the multinational forces positioned in Beirut.

Gray, however, waited until official word came down the chain of command before alerting his division staff officers to come to the headquarters building. It would be about four more hours before further word reached his Division. During that time, he spoke to Lieutenant General John Miller, his immediate superior as Marine Force Commander, in Norfolk, and began receiving the first fragmentary details on the bombing. The reports on casualties continued to flow in. After several additional calls from General Miller, Gray had a fair idea of the situation. At 0500, a local news release went out, and at 0600, the duty officer exercised the Fast Response on Short Transmission (FROST) alert call to key personnel. By this time, Gray had assessed the tragedy and directed that a Casualty Assistance Center be activated.[8]

The terrorist bombing set in motion a Herculean effort to identify, process, transport, and bury the remains of the Marines, Soldiers, and Navy medical personnel killed in the attack. This attack had resulted in the highest number of simultaneous casualties suffered by any Marine Corps unit since the Korean War in the 1950s. As in every such major crisis, there was the inevitable finger-pointing as to why and how the bombing could possibly have happened. This had already begun and only added to the confusion and delays in informing the 2nd Marine Division of the number and identification of casualties. The chaos would eventually cause the assistant division commander to deploy to the Lebanese theater of operations to bring some sense of stability to the scene. But few appreciated the extraordinary humanitarian outpouring, caring, and casualty assistance actions that immediately began taking place for the families of the dead and wounded. What is so often lost at the higher levels of command in an emergency situation is who the survivors are and how they are faring. The survivors were, understandably, a lesser priority for many on senior-level staffs.

When the first report of the bombing reached Headquarters Marine Corps, key personnel were assembled. During the immediate hours that followed, there was no definitive casualty information. However, through the use of modern satellite communication technologies, the international news media became the primary source of information from the bombing scene. The first video coverage began to sweep across American television screens. In Washington and surrounding governmental areas, public affairs offices and congressional liaison officers on Capitol Hill were besieged with inquiries, which obviously could not be answered accurately or quickly. By the end of the day, a huge collection of national media were at Camp Lejeune and actually camped on the lawn in front of the division headquarters.

Meanwhile, at Headquarters, Marine Corps, the public affairs "hotline" number was publicized over the radio and on national and cable television news programs. The United States awakened to news of the bombing and was in an overwhelming state of shock. The flood

144

of telephone calls far exceeded the available lines to properly handle the inquiries, generating further confusion across the country. Many concerned callers with sons and relatives in the 24th MAU waited 12 to 15 hours before getting through on the hotline. At the 2nd Marine Division, the number of calls from distraught wives and parents was equally heavy. The division's representatives could do nothing except to say they were "trying to get more information." It was a lose-lose situation for everyone.

The initial reports back to the States indicated the battalion landing team's headquarters element was decimated and no longer an effective command element. Information was sketchy at best; no senior leaders could be located, and their survival was thus in doubt. At the scene, Lebanese civilian medical personnel had rushed to the collapsed building and began extracting and evacuating the injured and dead to local hospitals. These humanitarian acts providing immediate care for the survivors also resulted in a number of individuals being listed as missing because they were moved from the scene without any record as to who was evacuated or where they had been taken. Casualties were also taken to the five amphibious ships offshore before their names or conditions were accurately recorded. Immediate care was the first priority of the survivors; their identification and notification process could come later.

As an example of how the Lebanese evacuation impacted the reporting process, Lieutenant Colonel Larry Gerlach, commanding Battalion Landing Team (BLT) 1st Battalion, 8th Marines was presumed dead, but he was found two days later in a Lebanese hospital. He, like many others, had been dragged from the debris, picked up by the civilian ambulances, and taken to a Shiite hospital. It was several days after the explosion that a young American reporter, Robin Wright, hearing of Marine casualties at other locations, went to the Shiite hospital and found a semi-conscious Colonel Gerlach and several other Marines. One by one, the BLT's Marines and Sailors were being accounted for.

Back at Camp Lejeune, Gray initially ordered 50 officers and senior staff NCOs, and then 50 more, to serve casualty assistance duties. They were assembled and given a quick course on proper procedures. With these initial decisions made, his staff began to function with its new mission. Gray, true to his character, left his division headquarters and went outside to be alone for a few moments. As he later reflected, he went for a walk, had a chew of "Red Man," and figured out what else needed to be done.

Gray moved a cot into the division command post for the duration of the crisis. His division staff went on a 12-hours-on, 12-hours-off schedule. In spite of the enormity of the bombing, Gray ordered that all units continue with their scheduled training. While all this activity was ongoing, Gray was alerted that the 22nd MAU, which had just deployed for the Mediterranean area, was ordered by the National Command Authority[9] to be diverted to the island of Grenada in the Caribbean to keep a Communist-supported group of rebels from taking over the island's government. Within several days, the island was secured, and the Marine units re-embarked on their amphibious ships and started back on their 12-day movement to the Mediterranean. At the same time, there was an immediate need to deploy more Marine units to Beirut to replace the devastated 1st Battalion, 8th Marines. Gray directed the 2nd Battalion, 6th Marines command element to prepare to mount out, along with one of its rifle companies, as he felt at least one more rifle company might be needed to provide extra security around the demolished area.[10]

More than 24 hours would pass before the first Beirut casualty list from the 24th MAU would arrive at Headquarters, Marine Corps. However, this report included only the names of 18 dead and 63 wounded. Hundreds were still unaccounted for. This partial report was disappointing to everyone. Televisions were projecting a steady coverage of the disaster around the world. This real-time coverage was saturated with pictures of "broken, bent, and dead" Marines. Unfortunately, those reports only aggravated and heightened the tension through the United States, and particularly at Gray's head-quarters. Questions arose across the country, particularly from dependents and families, as to why the Marine Corps was so slow to provide information. The reason was that the Marines wanted to be sure of their facts before they made any definitive calls. A staff officer from the 2nd Division's adjutant and personnel offices later recalled, "The situation on Sunday the 23rd could only be described as chaos. Everyone was highly energized and anxious to get busy on something. All we knew was there were probably numerous casualties, but we didn't have any existing plan for mass casualty notification," let alone solid information. Inaccurate and incomplete information made it difficult to appreciate the scope of the disaster. It would be 52 hours after the bombing before a list of 192 missing personnel was transmitted by the 24th MAU and made its way up the lengthy and cumbersome multiplex chains of command to HQMC.[11] The next day, the initial list was reduced to 170 missing. One can only imagine the confusion and painstaking care with which the two lists were compared.

At Camp Lejeune, three separate major commands had been quickly organized into a mutually supporting team to handle the massive casualty assistance program the situation called for. Gray remained the driving force to establish a common disaster-control center and prepare for the difficult task of notifying local families on the status of their Marines.

There were other areas where Gray's leadership impacted upon his staff. He made several critical decisions even before all the details were in, and in doing so, brought a degree of calm to the situation. One of his first concerns was for the operational mission of the decimated BLT 1st Battalion, 8th Marines. New units would be needed to replace the casualties. The division had long mandated an infantry battalion be prepared to deploy on four-hour notice as the "air alert" force. From this infantry battalion, a headquarters company and one rifle company were ordered to move to the Marine Air Station at Cherry Point, North Carolina, and fly to Lebanon within 24 hours after the bombing. This rapid response was typical of Gray. Historically, he had trained each of his commands to be prepared to "get out of town" on extremely short notice. Following his guidance, the division staff identified and reassigned new personnel to the 8th Marine Regiment to reconstitute BLT 1st Battalion, 8th Marines.

HQMC's Inspector General (IG) had previously scheduled the 2nd Division to undergo a rigorous biannual inspection in the fall. The IG called Gray and offered to postpone or cancel the weeklong event. Gray surprised everyone and elected to proceed as scheduled. His Division passed the inspection with ease. Gray later expressed the thought that, from a leadership point of view, the intensity of the inspection, with literally hundreds of inspectors with all-encompassing agenda, had kept his division fully occupied during this time of tragedy.[12]

General and Mrs. Gray visited the newly organized Casualty Coordination Center early on the 24th. He wanted to review how it had been set up and how it was preparing for the anticipated large number of casualties. It quickly became apparent to the Division's G-1 (Personnel Office) that Gray had envisioned a much larger base of operations and support effort. One of his staff officers recalled, "Within hours, all kinds of support began to materialize. Additional phones were installed, a fleet of commercial vehicles were assigned for casualty notification calls, and our first group of officers, designated for casualty calls, appeared in full dress uniforms, ready for their difficult missions ahead."[13]

Brigadier General Jim Joy recalled, "As the flow of wounded and dead began returning to the United States, it became even more complicated. Every individual in the 24th MAU had to be accounted for. If he was alive, fine. If he was wounded, where was he? Was he aboard a ship? Was he in a hospital in Lebanon, or in an American hospital in Germany? Or was he already in the States? If so, where is he in the States? The Division was desperate for more accurate and timely information on its Marines and Sailors, but little was forthcoming in a timely manner. We needed information for the families, to keep them advised as to what was going on."[14] So the Division's conference room was turned into an information-gathering center. Its walls soon became covered with charts displaying the gruesome toll of the terrorist bomb.

Gray seemed to be everywhere at the same time as he responded to the crisis and he still found the time to spend hours on the phone with families and next of kin across the nation. Now an additional 30 officers and all available chaplains were assembled in a central barracks area. They were directed to bring their dress uniforms and be prepared to remain until called upon, and until all casualty notifications were completed. Once a name was received through the division's Casualty Coordination Center, the officer was notified as to his particular casualty. Then he and a chaplain were directed to deliver the official notification to the family. From that time on, the officer would stay with the family through their personal crisis. In case of a death, the officer would remain assigned with the family until released by the Casualty Coordination Center, which in most cases was not until all death benefits were taken care of and/or the family relocated.

Gray repeatedly met with these officers to stress the need to express their deepest understanding for the bereavement every family was experiencing. Next, Gray set up a program that ensured that he or another senior officer represented the 2nd Marine Division at every funeral throughout the nation. General Gray himself attended more than 140 funerals. General and Mrs. Gray served as the Commandant of the Marine Corps' special representatives. The emotional intensity of these experiences was very high. But when the battered 24th MAU finally returned to the States from Beirut, General Gray stood at the bottom of every ship's ladder, and as each Marine and Sailor debarked, Gray looked him in the eye and shook his hand.

On November 4, President and Mrs. Ronald Reagan visited Camp Lejeune for a solemn memorial service. It was held in a small outdoor amphitheater overlooking New River Inlet behind the 2nd Marine Division Headquarters. The service was for all who had lost their lives in the terrorist attack. It was a profoundly moving scene, captured on television by the national news media. Wives, fathers, mothers, children, grandparents, and relatives from all stations of life who had journeyed to share a painful moment with other strangers were now bound together forever.[15]

Following the memorial service, Gray sent a letter to all the next of kin describing the service and offering his continuing assistance. The letter contained several documents: a videotape of the service, the memorial service program, a copy of the signed presidential proclamation directing the flag be flown at half mast, and a copy of a magazine called "*The Word*," which featured a tasteful pictorial on the members of the 1st Battalion, 8th Marines and the bombing. Months later, the 45 miles of highway from Camp Lejeune to Morehead City would be designated "Freedom's Way," and individual trees were planted to memorialize every American serviceman lost in the Beirut bombing.

Gray's early understanding of the horrific tragedy and its causes would eventually bring about a completely new training program for all Marine Corps units. It was to become formally known as special operations capable (SOC) training and would introduce Marines to aspects of terrorist activity and how best to prevent terrorist attacks. The world's focus was shifting from the fading Soviet threat to worldwide terrorist activity. Gray was initially alone in his quest to better prepare his Marines for this newly prominent unorthodox threat. Ultimately, his newly organized Marine Amphibious Unit (MAU) (SOC) pre-deployment training program was adopted Marine Corps-wide. Amid the varied operational demands in years to follow, this special training was to be repeatedly cited by Marines as the factor that made the difference.

But General Al Gray has never forgotten the human factor. More than three decades have now passed, and Gray has continued to remain in touch with many of the families of the Marines who died in Beirut. On October 23, 2008, Generals P.X. Kelley and Al Gray attended the 25th anniversary memorial service at the Beirut Monument in

Jacksonville, North Carolina. It is interesting to note that General Al Gray, a much respected warrior, has his "finest hours" not on a distant battlefield but on the home front caring for and faithfully responding to the bereaving wives and parents of his dead Marines and Sailors. The journey of life is precious yet filled with uncertainty.

CHAPTER 8
Three Stars and Force Commander

"It is incumbent upon the Marine officer to be constantly teaching his men, his junior officers, and himself."

General Leonard F. Chapman Jr.
24th Commandant, U.S. Marine Corps

It took weeks of burying dead Marines and Sailors before the last bugle sounded its soulful yet calming finality in bringing closure to the Beirut tragedy. It had been an iconic grieving period all across America. Every small community and metropolitan area seemed to have suffered personal losses. The final blessings having been given, graves were now closed, and the hundreds of military escorts returned to their military bases. At Camp Lejeune, the grief continued as the families of the lost were packing their belongings and relocating back to home towns to begin their new lives.

Yet the harsh reality was the men—and now women—of the 2nd Marine Division, the 2nd Marine Aircraft Wing at Cherry Point, North Carolina, and the 2nd Force Logistics Support Group had to chalk up their losses and rebuild as long-planned deployments demanded their units continue to train. Their multiple MAGTF deployments were in various stages of training, and all demanded the highest state of readiness. The young Marines and Sailors knew the Marine Corps' long history of being a force-in-readiness must be sustained. To do anything less would betray their former comrades.

It was here, again, that Al Gray, a survivor of other tragic encounters, played a pivotal role through his understanding leadership to guide all divisional units toward restoring their operational readiness. The challenge was to rise above the personal pains. His style was one of caring, but all understood that the training and readiness standards he demanded would not be lowered. Terrorism had declared open war on the United States and its democratic way of life. Now was the time to begin countering this evil threat.

In 1957, the Eisenhower administration pledged military assistance to any Middle East nation that was invaded and incapable of repelling the aggressor with its own forces.[1] This statement codified the strategic importance of U.S. military deployment to the region—capitalizing on the Sixth Fleet's presence in the Mediterranean Sea that had been a centerpiece of naval deployments since the end of World War II.

What was important to the Marine Corps was the implicit requirement for expeditionary forces that could be rapidly deployed to the theater. Seen in the aftermath of Korea, this was an implementation of the national strategy reflecting changes in the U.S. Code in 1952 that established the Marine Corps' modern role and mission as an expeditionary force-in-readiness. However, even during the late 1940s, in a time the Marine Corps strength had been reduced to fewer than 75,000, the Navy and the Marine Corps were assigned a high priority contingency mission in the Mediterranean. That is why, to this day, two-thirds of the Fleet Marine Forces battalion landing teams (BLTs) and aviation squadrons are stationed on the East Coast at the air station of Cherry Point and at Camp Lejeune.

Initially, the Mediterranean commitment was fulfilled with an infantry battalion, reinforced by a battery of 105mm howitzers, a platoon of amphibious landing vehicles, a platoon of tanks, and small detachments of reconnaissance, engineer, and logistics personnel. The aviation element of helicopters and support teams joined the ground forces at their common embarkation point, Wilmington, North Carolina. Months before a BLT was to deploy, the Marine Amphibious Unit (MAU) assumed operational control of all Marine Corps elements scheduled to deploy at the same time. A full Colonel was designated as the MAU commander. Finally assembled, they formed into an MAU. It was then integrated with an amphibious squadron (PHIBRON) commanded by a Navy Captain.

Together, the MAU and the PHIBRON constituted a naval amphibious task force commonly referred to as the Mediterranean Amphibious Ready Group (MARG). Often the MAU and the PHIBRON commanders literally met for the first time when they embarked aboard their ships. Once in the Mediterranean, the PHIBRON was placed under the operational control of a U.S. three-star Vice Admiral who was the commander, 6th Fleet. His small amphibious task force, commonly and informally referred to as a "gator" task force, usually operated separately from the vast U.S. naval armada of carriers, cruisers, destroyers, submarines, and other support craft that were in constant movement throughout the Mediterranean region. In reality, the amphibious elements were part of a "show of presence" for America's naval might. Secondly, it served as the tip-of-the-arrow of all U.S. forces forward-deployed, alerting all nations that if required it could execute small-scale power projection operations on short notice. The Navy and Marine Corps performed this mission and others throughout several decades while the Sixth Fleet's amphibious task forces steamed the Mediterranean Sea.

Over the years, this became known as the "Med cruise." The Marines often took advantage during the cruise to train with the Navy and Marine forces of the regional countries. It ultimately became a cyclic ritual to conduct joint training exercises with the services of other allied nations. The gray-hulled ships would suddenly appear just off the coastline where helicopters and small craft would fill the horizon with activity. These amphibious landings became major events for each country and received active support from their governments. Once ashore, the Sailors and Marines would join with coalition forces and conduct cross-training on equipment, often capping each deployment with joint live fire, combined arms exercises. It was not uncommon for the Marines to participate in exercises with three or four different countries during each deployment. For the junior officers and young enlisted Marines, it became an opportunity to get to know and better understand each country's customs. It was a "people-to-people" program the Defense Department strongly encouraged. Best of all, it was an exciting and rewarding experience for the troops to join with men of their own station. Lasting bonds were made among military personnel of all the countries participating in these joint training events.

Beginning in 1948, these amphibious task forces continuously rotated on an endless semiannual cycle to sustain their Mediterranean contingency commitment. As each succeeding flotilla steamed through the Straits of Gibraltar, a relief-on-station was executed with the relieved amphibious force immediately setting course for home ports in North Carolina and Norfolk, Virginia.

During their high-visibility commitment, the MARG was a factor in numerous small wars or conflicts, particularly in the eastern Mediterranean region. Examples include Turkey and Greece, over the island of Cyprus; the Arab and Israeli wars of 1956, 1967, and 1973; Egypt and Great Britain over control of the Suez Canal in 1956; and Lebanon interventions in 1956 and 1958.[2] In 1956, Marines landed across Beirut's beaches to calm unrest and violence among religious factions. In addition, there were many "alerts" for the MARG and its Marines, but only a few occasions where they actually went ashore during a crisis. In this period, as in other periods of unrest, the Eisenhower and other administrations utilized America's forward-deployed amphibious task force—with embarked Marines as an instrument of national security policy.

There appears to have been a level of U.S. diplomatic contentment and a lack of appreciation that there were rapid political changes underway in the eastern Mediterranean. Unappreciated by the U.S. national security policymakers, the flames of unrest were being fanned in the urban squalors of large Middle East cities, in ancient Muslim mosques, and in other academic and religious communities. These nondescript, little-known, and seldom studied areas were where only a rare few modern military units were being trained to enter and engage these small disenchanted groups. Every regional country was experiencing unrest within its disenfranchised populace, where little hope existed for better days ahead. The clock of change was running with little attention to the future potential consequences.

In 1971, when then-Lieutenant Colonel Gray deployed his 1st Battalion, 2nd Marines to the Mediterranean, he recognized the need to restructure the MAU and the BLT to adjust to the changing times. There were obvious signs that the Marine units needed to upgrade their equipment and conduct new training concepts with additional mission capabilities before deploying other Mediterranean-bound forces. Perhaps it was his uncommon access to the most sensitive intelligence information that enabled him early on to grasp the magnitude of threat changes that had occurred during the past 20 or more years.

Whenever Gray was exposed to new conditions, he would routinely set in motion a mental process to begin capturing seemingly unrelated facts, lessons learned from his exercise experiences, automatically absorbing other bits of information with his near-photographic memory. He had an endless quest for knowledge, and the Middle East region piqued his curiosity. As Gray closed out his six-month Mediterranean deployment, he began to fully sense the seriousness of the growing tensions throughout the region. He recognized that terrorist incidents were growing in frequency, as was the scale of violence throughout the whole region. Hostage incidents were increasing, as well as car bombings and hijackings throughout the eastern Mediterranean. Unfortunately, these alarm bells were slow to be heard by most U.S. diplomatic and military leaders who were focusing on other priority hotspots.

It is with Gray's "Mediterranean cruise" experiences and keen observations of the different Middle East countries that he began to sense the rising tide of regional changes. Shortly after Gray's return to Camp Lejeune, he assumed command of the 2nd Marine Regiment but continued to closely track events in the eastern Mediterranean. This was coupled with an expanding interest in exploring Marine involvement in the broad military field known as special operations. As a result of these interests, Gray became vocal in expressing his belief that future MAU forces should train to handle non-conventional situations. He became convinced that such additional pre-deployment training of a Marine force could provide the Commander, 6th Fleet, with an ability to make a more immediate response to a broad range of special missions.

The 1983 Beirut tragedy had a far-reaching impact on U.S. military. The security and interest of the United States had been threatened by numerous events and conflicts, which required unconventional responses executed by uniquely capable forces. This perception led to a significant revitalization of special operations forces (SOFs). As a result, in late 1983, the Secretary of Defense directed that each military service and defense agency would review their existing SOF capability that would be required to combat the current and low-intensity conflict threat and provide a report by March 1984.[3] In response to this tasking, the Commandant, General P.X. Kelley, directed the Commanding General, Fleet Marine Force, Atlantic (FMFLANT), to undertake a study and develop a plan that would satisfy the requirement for enhanced special operation capabilities in the Marine Corps. Gray tasked his subordinates to study the terrorist threat issues and develop some initial countermeasures for the deploying MAUs. Then a Major General, Al Gray had been an active member in keeping with his views about the eastern Mediterranean and marine special operations capabilities. His ideas and personal convictions regarding how to begin dealing with the threat of terrorists permeated the study's findings and recommendations.

The study results clearly indicated that "maritime special operations" are readily adaptable to existing Marine Corps roles and missions. Furthermore, Marine Air-Ground Task Forces (MAGTFs) offered the National Command Authority (NCA) a unique asset for conducting maritime special operations with forward-deployed, sea-based forces and were responsive to tactical or strategic mission requirements. The study stated that "any MAGTF appropriately trained and subsequently designated Special Operations Capable offers the National Command Authorities a wide variety of options. Such options extend from establishing a presence close to a strategic trouble area to execution of a tactical mission in a hostile environment."[4] The study further demonstrated the advantage of optimizing these unique qualifications in order to offer the National Command Authorities a complementary capability to the existing service and joint operations capabilities.[5]

As a result of this extensive study, it was revalidated that Marine Air-Ground Task Forces are uniquely qualified to conduct a broad spectrum of special operations in a maritime environment, particularly when a requirement exists for the introduction of helicopter-borne or surface forces from the sea. The study additionally stated the Marine Corps should not establish new organizations that would unnecessarily duplicate special purpose organizations such as Army Special Forces, Navy SEAL teams, etc. Rather, the Marine Corps should work toward ensuring its special operations capabilities are complementary in nature.

As an immediate task, the Corps' objective would be to ensure that MAGTFs that were routinely deployed with the fleet, e.g., Marine Amphibious Units (MAUs), were fully capable of conducting appropriate special operations, either by themselves, or, when mission requirements so dictated, with augmentation by special purpose organizations from Joint Special Operations Command (JSOC) or the other services.

After Gray briefed his final report to the Commandant and the Chief of Naval Operations, he was directed to implement the program for the Atlantic and European regions. It was recognized at that time (1984-85) that the MAGTFs already had a significant capability from the sea, particularly from deployed MAUs. The initial forces assigned to the program became identified as an enhanced forward-deployed MAU trained to conduct appropriate special operations. In the development of this program, Gray utilized a conventional MAU but added specified capabilities inherent within the force, along with its Navy counterpart's Amphibious Ready Group (ARG). The MAU would be designated as special operations capable. Rigid standard operating procedures were required to test and evaluate readiness and performance qualifications.

In subsequent correspondence to the Joint Chiefs of Staff, General Kelley reported that what the Marine Corps was undertaking was "the enhancement of an existing capability within its current unique and proven organization for combat—the Marine Air-Ground Task Force."[6]

Gray's vision for a new special operations capability within the MAU caused him to undertake a second, far-more-epic challenge. The division's maneuver warfare activities would continue, but he would switch his highest priority to developing new and increased MAU capabilities. The diverse complexity of the challenge to construct a plan to implement a special operations capability for the East Coast MAUs was overwhelming in itself. However, he recognized that if successful, the program would likely be extended to the entire Marine Corps MAGTFs worldwide. Gray was also sensitive to the fact that branches within Marine Corps Headquarters, as well as commands throughout the Corps, were closely watching his actions—but with quiet reservations.

It was the kind of challenge that he had prepared for over his years of reading, studying, and reflecting on other military leaders in times of great change. Gray was now everywhere, studying, teaching, holding critiques, and trying out new ideas and concepts. It was a blitzkrieg environment for the Force staff, as well as for all subordinate commands. Changes were being made on a near-daily basis. To those directly involved, it was an exciting but exhausting time. Gray would repeatedly remind his charges, "You have got to do what you have got to do." Wherever he went and spoke to a gathering of Marines, he reminded leaders at all levels how important it was to fully understand the "commander's intent" and repeated that every Marine should be prepared to assume leadership positions two echelons higher than his own. Gray was exhilarated, appearing suddenly, usually with a battered Red Man pouch of chewing tobacco in hand, all the while closely observing any new techniques for defining the Marine Corps special operations training. He thrived on the challenges, and his habit of only three to four hours' sleep a night fit his planning schedules nicely.

Earlier, while still commanding the 2nd Marine Division, Gray issued a new Division Order on training that revised numerous standard operating procedures.[7] In it, he laid out his philosophy for training where centralized management and decentralized execution were to ensure the most efficient utilization of training hours and resources. Gray recognized the value of establishing standardized training concepts. Central within this order was his declaration to stress that unless all unit leaders were tenacious in the pursuit of unit training goals, they would not be achieved.[8]

On a more personal reflection: historically throughout his career as new demands and conditions arose and confronted Gray, there always seemed to be some special individual or small group of dedicated "Gray disciples" who rallied to render support. Such was the case again when a Marine officer, who had frequently joined in his "professional group sessions," joined Gray on a military aircraft flying to Europe. Fortuitously, he was assigned the seat next to Gray. Colonel Michael Myatt had served with Gray in various capacities over the years, culminating with an assignment when Brigadier General Gray commanded the 4th MAB. They had continued an active and close personal and professional relationship. Mike Myatt was an exceptionally bright, personable, visionary individual with highly respected writing skills. He had served with distinction as a staff officer at the highest levels of the government. Mike had also been the lead officer on many of Gray's planning initiatives during their two years together in the MAB.

In the spring of 1984, Colonel Myatt had been working in the Pentagon as a member of the Chairman, Joint Chiefs of Staff (CJCS) staff group. While working directly for the Chairman, one of his responsibilities was to monitor joint training. For this reason, he was en route to Europe for a seminal training conference. He recalled that he was pleasantly surprised to discover that on that aircraft passenger manifest was Major General A.M. Gray's name. It was during this trip that Gray told Myatt of his plans to create special operations capabilities in the MAU deploying to the Mediterranean. During the five- or six-hour flight, the two men were completely absorbed in talking about the challenges ahead, and both recognized how critical it was for the Marine Corps to "get it right." In their in-depth discussions, Gray related some of the issues making this a necessary enhancement step for the MAU. It was one of those memorable moments when Gray became totally comfortable in expressing his deepest concerns.

Myatt was completely captivated by Gray's clear vision of what was possible, and where the potential pitfalls lay. Gray acknowledged that, for various reasons, over the years the capabilities of the MAU had atrophied. He felt that the MAUs were no longer fully trained to do what needed to be done. Gray cited the lack of night helicopter opera-tions as a prime example. "Marine units must never become only a daytime force." Over decades, the "career" concerns by some cautious leaders about personnel safety during regular exercises and live firing sessions had progressively eroded aviation and ground units' opportu-nities to train up to high readiness standards. During this long period, some leaders would rather cancel a risky training event just to ensure "nothing serious" happened on their watch.

A second concern of Gray's was that the U.S. Army, as the main component of the special operations community in 1984, had con-vinced many in the "Joint arena" to change the definition of special operations from specific environmental operations (e.g., arctic opera-tions, jungle operations) to "operations conducted by specially trained forces." When asked by Deputy Secretary of Defense William Taft to give examples of "special operations," the Army representatives listed such things as amphibious raids and noncombat evacuation operations, both historically accomplished by forward-deployed Marines.[9]

Gray had been told that the Special Operations community was "after our platforms" (i.e., our amphibious ships), and that, unless we demonstrated we had the specially trained forces to undertake the mis-sion now being listed as "special operations," the Joint arena might very well put special operations forces on our platforms when those missions were necessary.[10] The key point was that Gray saw the Joint

Special Operations Capabilities (JSOC) force, superb though it may be, as having a single crisis capability. The nation needed to have additional capabilities to complement and execute such missions. Gray countered this issue by telling Colonel Myatt that "We are going to create an organic 'hostage rescue' capability within the MAUs for '*in extremis*' situations."[11]

Gray discussed an example of why the Marine Corps could not afford to be in any situation where it could not immediately protect its Sailors and Marines. Using Camp Lejeune as an example, Gray hypothesized that if hostages were taken on the base and held in the base commanding general's office building, we would have to depend on the JSOC to deploy to Camp Lejeune while the Marines sat idly by, watching the "terrorists throw hostages out the windows. This must never happen."[12]

It was to be a vintage day for Mike Myatt as Gray fervently carried their discussion into a definition of training that would be required for a "special operations capability," and the fact that the units would have to be "certified" after an extensive examination. As Gray talked, he became more at ease, and out came the Red Man chewing tobacco pouch and his search for a paper cup. This was not an unusual situation for Gray, as he often spoke his thoughts aloud as he was formulating his ideas. There was only time to listen, and Mike did. Gray began listing the kinds of missions that he envisioned the MAU must be able to perform, including (1) over-the-horizon amphibious raids, both surface and heliborne, at night under conditions of reduced visibility; (2) non-combat evacuation operations; (3) security operations; (4) extended range raids, exceeding the ranges of the helicopters, so that the MAU would be able to secure and establish forward refueling points clandestinely; (5) mobile training teams capable of working with foreign military forces directly at a site; (6) deception operations; (7) electronic warfare operations; and (8) disaster relief. It was obvious to Colonel Myatt that Gray was totally engaged and professionally committed to making these new special operations capabilities become the deploying MAUs future standard measurements of readiness.

Myatt recalled that Gray touched on other areas that needed to be brought into Marine Corps training. He talked about how a new and more elaborate Military Operations in Urban Terrain (MOUT) training facility was needed at Camp Lejeune. He discussed his relationship with the FBI office in New York that enabled reconnaissance Marines to be trained by New York City's FBI Special Weapons and Tactics (SWAT) personnel, because that office had done more hostage rescues than any other organization in the world. He repeatedly stated that he would seek out any expert organization or individuals who could possibly assist him in creating the best possible SOC capabilities. It made no difference if the individual was a civilian, from a government agency, or from another Service as he sought out only the best sources. Gray expressed the need for training in the urban environment, to include not only direct action and *in extremis* hostage rescue, but instructions on how to do reconnaissance in the urban environment.

Intermixed with the expanding maneuver warfare thought process and the fledgling special operations concept were almost endless small unit activities. Major General Gray was closing in on 33 months of commanding the Division. His vast creativity and range of innovative training ideas had become widely known throughout the Marine Corps and in the other services located on the East Coast. It seemed every possible type of military operation was being conducted in and around the Carolinas. The operations tempo was at its highest pace in a decade.

In addition to regular commitments such as the six-month deployment to the Pacific for one of his infantry battalions, the division was exercising with Landing Force Sixth Fleet, conducting operations at Fort Pickett, Virginia; participating in combined arms exercises (CAXs) at Twentynine Palms, California; deploying units to mountain warfare training at Pickle Meadows, Bridgeport, California; jungle warfare training at the Canal Zone, Panama; and artillery firing at Ft. Bragg, North Carolina; while conducting rapid-response-reinforcement exercises into the U.S. Naval Base at Guantanamo Bay, Cuba. Units and their equipment were constantly on the move. He strived to imbue the "thought process" over and above the planning and execution sequence.

This is but a cursory glance at the division's operating pace as more individuals became aware of the "innovative" training and operating tempo. Senior-level officials from the Department of Defense, Congress, foreign dignitaries, and other U.S. Service representatives requested to visit the 2nd Division to observe training events. Secretary of the Navy John F. Lehman Jr. visited several times to observe amphibious landings for both combat and noncombat operations. Congressmen and their staffers visited, as did leaders of industry and foreign dignitaries. Other visitors came from Canada, the United Kingdom, Thailand, Spain, Germany, and various Latin American nations. All were quickly placed in a field environment. On Gray's signal, helicopters heavily loaded with troops and amphibious tractors launched and headed for the beaches. Simultaneously, tanks and Light Armored Vehicles (LAVs) raced through the pine forests toward mission objectives. It was a bit of showmanship but still realistic and productive training for the units. No one left disappointed.

All of these exercises, including major NATO deployments, were receiving extensive and favorable publicity. Everywhere the units went, multimedia news coverage recorded their training. This only stimulated more interest and more visitors to personally observe "what was really happening down at Camp Lejeune."

It was during the summer of 1984 and shortly after James H. Webb had been appointed as the Assistant Secretary of Defense (Reserve Affairs) that he visited Camp Lejeune to observe a large-scale amphibious exercise. As one of his Deputy Assistant Secretaries (Readiness and Training), I traveled along with Secretary Webb. Gray met us as the approaching amphibious tractors, tanks, and helicopters roared over and above the beach areas. All synchronized to stress a vivid power projection scenario.

Again, Gray was everywhere, gushing with excitement, and Secretary Webb quickly got caught up in the events. Before anyone realized it, Jim Webb had left the viewing area and climbed into an amphibious tractor to talk with the troops. The vehicle had only stopped momentarily before crossing the inter-coastal waterway. When it moved out, the Secretary stayed inside and disappeared for several hours. The more senior officers on the beach pier were suddenly "aghast" and searching for the "missing Assistant Secretary of Defense."[13] But all returned to normal after Webb was located and brought back to the Onslow Beach pier. Webb, scratching a bit from the ever-present sand fleas, appeared upbeat to be reliving some earlier Marine Corps memories, and Gray loved it.

No sooner would one unit deploy than another unit would be preparing to return to Camp Lejeune. All divisional forces were in a cyclic pattern of training; when certified as operationally ready, they embarked on aircraft or ships destined for some distant port or country. Upon their return, there would be a short leave period before the pre-deployment training process would begin again.

Typical to this sequence was the 26th MAU preparing to participate in 84. This exercise provided a unique opportunity for members of the Division to operate in a joint environment with the U.S. Navy, Air Force, and Army, as well as a coalition of our NATO allies. A broad series of events enabled each service to plan and execute their core capabilities. The exercise began with naval operations in the Chesapeake Bay and near Charleston, South Carolina, and then shifted to the Caribbean for more events around Puerto Rico and Guantanamo Bay, Cuba.

Gray encouraged all units to cross-train with other U.S. services and allied nations whenever possible. During one six-month period, from late 1983 into early 1984, his Division's Marines and Sailors deployed on an almost-weekly basis to conduct some type of coalition training. Among the many deployed operations, UNITAS XXV took place in the Latin America/Caribbean regions. It was identified as a medium-scale naval training deployment. A reinforced rifle company had a five-month schedule with plans to conduct 18 joint amphibious landings while visiting 13 ports. After joint operations in Central and South America, the ships traversed across the South Atlantic to West Africa. This latter phase of the deployment was less focused on military operations and more on goodwill, athletics, and social assistance in community welfare projects, and typically served as the high point and most rewarding phase for the troops.

Back at Camp Lejeune during this same period, two new units joined the 2nd Division. The first Remotely Piloted Vehicle (RPV) was assigned to Headquarters Battalion. In February 1984 the unit deployed to support commander, Joint Task Force Lebanon. For the first time ever, the Remotely Piloted Vehicle gave the ground commanders a real-time aerial view of the immediate areas where United Nations (UN) and American forces were positioned. The 2nd Light Armored Vehicle (LAV) Company was also activated at Camp Lejeune. These were the first eight-wheeled reconnaissance vehicles to be placed in a Marine Corps division. The mission of the LAV company was vastly different than that of the infantry units. Their training consisted of long road marches, and a heavy reliance on their .50 caliber heavy machine gun, and 25mm main gun. Heavily used training ranges became even more crowded, and live fire range adjustments were necessary for all units. By spring 1984, LAVs had been assigned to the division. It is interesting to note that while Gray had been at the Marine Corps Development Command, he was the driving force behind getting these two systems added to the Marine Corps inventory. Now he would maximize their use in every possible training event.

It had been more than three long years since Gray had assumed command of the 2nd Division, but he maintained an ever-increasing tempo in honing his Marines and Sailors in their expeditionary trade. In order to keep up with his units, Gray was a world traveler, and he scheduled aircraft flights so he could fly to distant locations and observe each unit at least once during their deployment. It was an exceptionally challenging commitment, but no matter the pace, he kept his promise to "see them in action." The 2nd Marine Division's Command Chronologies during this period are filled with entries of these visits. Between 70 and 80 trips were targeted for this purpose and were recorded during his three-year tenure. Many a weekend was orchestrated to enable Gray to observe the culminating event of each deployment. When it was necessary to fly into the European theater, he would usually be on the ground for less than a day at any one site and then off to another location. On one day he would be in Norway observing winter training, and two days later he would be in Turkey observing an amphibious landing. For those staff officers who traveled with him, it was an exhausting experience. In sharp contrast, Gray would get off the aircraft rejuvenated and ready for the day's events while his staff was still attempting to set their mental clocks back to East Coast time.

Lieutenant General John H. Miller, Commanding General, Fleet Marine Force, Atlantic (FMFLANT), had recommended Al Gray succeed him, and the Commandant nominated him up the chain of command to the President, where it was approved and sent to the Senate, which concurred. On August 29, 1984, Major General Dennis J. Murphy relieved Gray as the Commanding General, 2nd Marine Division. At the same ceremony, Al Gray was promoted to Lieutenant General by the Commandant of the Marine Corps, P.X. Kelley, and had his three stars pinned. Then-Lieutenant General Gray, his wife, his aging mother, and their three dogs climbed into their much-used station wagon and quickly relocated to his new headquarters in Norfolk, Virginia. He had a new and greater charge, and there was much to be done. His new senior flag rank gave him greater clout within the Marine Corps' executive leadership. At the time, there were only seven Lieutenant Generals; five were located at Headquarters Marine Corps in Washington, DC. The other two were commanding Fleet Marine Force, Pacific (FMFPAC), at Camp Smith in Honolulu, Hawaii, and Gray's command, Fleet Marine Force, Atlantic in Norfolk, Virginia. The Commandant and the Assistant Commandant were the only two Marine Generals wearing four stars.

Historically, this small cell of 72 Marine General officers crafted core competency policies and procedures and collectively advised the Commandant on selected issues. This "inner circle" planned and plotted the Corps' direction and sought out the budgetary resources in executing the *Commandant's Planning Guidance*. Gray was recognized by all as the most experienced operational commander among them. Even though the newest member, he often took the lead in discussions on joint, allied, and coalition force planning issues. He contributed, and he proved himself to be a team player.

The advancement to three stars had an additional impact upon Gray. As the Force Commander, Gray also served as a component commander to the Commander-in-Chief, Atlantic (CINCLANT). This placed him as a key decision commander, and he met and worked with his other Service component commanders from the Air Force, Army, and Navy.

Commanding General FMFLANT, he now served as the senior Marine Corps operational commander on the East Coast, and for the U.S. Atlantic command's vast global area of responsibility. Under his control was the 2nd Marine Amphibious Force (II MAF), which included the 2nd Marine Aircraft Wing, 2nd Marine Division (reinforced) and the 2nd Force Service Support Group (2nd FSSG), a combined force of more than 60,000 Marines and Sailors.

When he had commanded the 2nd Marine Division and prepared his units for deployment overseas or for stateside training, he had had to coordinate with the other two MAF subordinate commanders to request support and resources. More times than not, these commands were heavily committed and could not provide the requested support. Now as the overall FMFLANT commander, he began to quickly synergize the diverse and multitude of training and deployments into a more coordinated Training Exercise and Employment Plan (TEEP). This placed a planning strain on all commands, but he knew that this realignment was a critical cornerstone in reengaging the "Carolina MAGTF." The magnitude of this undertaking is better appreciated when one realizes that these three commands make up several hundred deployments a year, with FMFLANT units deploying to Europe, the Middle East, Central and South America, the Caribbean and, increasingly, Africa. The challenge to be more efficient only heightened Gray's intensity to act quickly, and he did.

Gray's arrival at FMFLANT provided him a new dimension for further development of several novel programs. These programs would consume much of Gray's energy and resources, ultimately changing long-established doctrine and the ways Marines would prepare for combat anywhere in the world.

During 1983, when the idea of the civilian maritime prepositioning shipping (MPS) concept originated, there was an internal struggle within the Marine Corps as to the unknown issues that could possibly impact upon the Marine Corps. As with every major doctrinal change the Marine Corps had gone through during its 230-plus years in existence, there were internal perceptions coupled with the traditionalists who want to hold on to old ways, seeking to avoid risks. These internal struggles have always been stressful, as the emotions of traditionalists and visionaries study, verbally spar, and present their perceived solutions. The most vocal dissention in this case was, "If the Marine Corps accepts the maritime prepositioning shipping concept, the Navy will probably want to reduce the total number of its amphibious ships."

There were other concerns, delays and procrastinations. Time was slipping by. The MPS concept was about to be passed to the U.S. Army. A firm decision needed to be made. General Robert Barrow listened patiently, gathering all possible information, and then he made his historic decision: the Marine Corps would accept the Department of Defense's offer and fully commit itself to undertaking the untried concept of establishing and equipping a brigade-sized element of equipment, tanks, trucks, Landing Vehicles Tracked (LVT), ammunitions, supplies, and aviation vans to be embarked on five special type civilian ships. Once the decision was announced, all efforts went into proving the maritime prepositioning shipping could be a valuable asset to both the Navy and Marine Corps. As predicted by the Commandant to the traditional alarmists, the Navy never took any opposing actions to reduce its amphibious fleet.

The Marine Corps had just accepted the concept of the MPS as Lieutenant General John Miller arrived at FMFLANT. It had been a calculated historical break with the past and a bold move to preposition a brigade of equipment afloat on commercial ships manned by civilian crews. The MPS could sail to a preselected designation just in time to meet MAGTF forces that would have been flown into a regional airhead near port facilities. The benefit of the MPS concept was a significant reduction in MAGTFs' deployment time, from the time of alert to arrival in an objective area. Previously, Marine units deploying from the West Coast across the Pacific Ocean would require 15 to 20 days steaming. Closing times to almost any point on the globe could now be achieved in five to seven days from the notice to deploy. As will be seen later, the MPS concept proved so successful during the 1990-91 Iraqi War that other services expanded their prepositioning program to reduce their own closure times. This had been an historic milestone decision by General Barrow while he was the 27th Commandant.

The second seminal project was in accepting that, with the ending of the Cold War and the increase in terrorist threats, there was an expanding requirement that forward-deployed Marine Corps units have special operations capabilities (SOC). Gray was not the sole advocate, but he played a dominant role in implementing this idea, as well as many other revolutionary concepts.

As fate would have it, or perhaps because of a "little bit" of Al Gray's proclivity for behind-the-scenes maneuvering, early in March 1986, Colonel Mike Myatt reappeared. After completing his Pentagon joint duty tour, he was assigned to the II Marine Amphibious Force (II MAF). Gray almost immediately designated Colonel Myatt to be the new Commanding Officer of the 26th Marine Amphibious Unit (MAU) and began to work to make it the first SOC MAU. Even as Mike was reporting, the 24th MAU, then off the coast of Lebanon, had been forced to offload helicopters and Marines from their amphibious ship to make room for a Joint Special Operations Capable (JSOC) team. The offload was necessary because it was felt, by a senior European commander unfamiliar with MAGTFs, that the embarked Marines were not qualified to handle special operation missions. In the ships' crowded spaces, the JSOC was positioned to launch in case of a hostage rescue mission that that high-level leadership believed 24th MAU was not trained to do. Gray quietly vowed this would never happen again on his watch. It never did.

In November 1986, General Kelley, having approved Gray's study and recommendations, issued his command policy guidance for transitioning of the Marine Corps to a special operations capability (SOC) that provided a basic concept for Marine Amphibious Unit (MAU). This was an event of historic proportions. His instructions confirmed the three pillars upon which SOC rested:

- Flawless execution of advance air/ground skills;

- Earliest and continuous integration with the assault Amphibious Squadron (PHIBRON);

- A critical demonstration of the MAU elements' capabilities prior to the award of the designation MAU (SOC).[14]

The overall Amphibious Ready Group (ARG/MARSOC) plan required the execution of 18 tasks as depicted in Figure 2. Equally significant was the edict establishing a 26-week pre-deployment schedule. All 18 operational missions would be evaluated by an independent tactical exercise control group (TECG). At a minimum, the SOC exercise was to include a recovery operation, an amphibious raid, evacuation operation (non-permissive), and the Tactical Recovery of Aircraft and Personnel (TRAP).

SPECIAL OPERATIONS MISSIONS and MARINE CORPS CAPABILITIES MATRIX

Direct Actions

Amphibious Raid *****   Limited Objective Attacks
Hostage Rescue   Non-Combat Evacuation (NEO)
Counter Intelligence Operations   Show of Force Operations
Deception Operations   Security Operations
Mobile Training Teams   Reinforcement Operations
Civil Affairs   Initial Terminal Guidance
Electronic Warfare   Fire Support Control

* Enhanced Raid capabilities (i.e. Clandestine Recovery Operations, Specialized Demolition Operations and MOUT) could be accomplished with enhanced training

---

Figure 2
Special Operations MATRIX defined by HQMC
(Courtesy of Marine Corps Combat Development Command
[MCCDC] briefing charts [1988]).

Gray had earlier predicted that, because just such a special operations mission could arise, all Marine Amphibious Units (MAUs) should have some special operations capabilities. He was emboldened to ensure that, in any future similar situation, his Marines would be fully prepared to quickly plan and execute a number of uncommon missions. Colonel Myatt recalled that Gray had told him to train for the whole spectrum of all possible 18 special operations missions. He added, "You may not be immediately able to be completely proficient in every emergency mission, but you should be capable of planning and executing any assigned task. Be good in performing the most likely special operations missions."[15] With this guidance, Myatt began training the 26th MAU. The special operations missions were over and above the long list of routine pre-deployment training events. It was an intense six-month workup beginning with squad level and platoon tactics and moving up in complexity to combined Navy/Marine Corps amphibious exercises, with every preparatory step being "certified" as ready for deployment. Gray was there watching, ever teaching, ever cajoling in order to reach higher performance levels. There were many miscues. Tempers flared, plans fell short, but as the 26th MAU closed on its 180 days of mandated training, the success of their tireless efforts began to be evident. Confidence grew, and so it was decided to add even more to this intense lock-on training. Additional training scenarios were included for Tactical Recovery of Aircraft and Personnel (TRAP), the hostage takedown, and also boarding commercial ships underway. Even at night!

To prepare for hostage takedowns and rescues, Gray went to the FBI for special training support. He was aware that the FBI was the most experienced organization in dealing with hostage rescues. He contacted the director, who quickly formed a joint planning and coordination team. Special Agent Robert Alderson was assigned on a full-time basis and proved to be the right man at the right time. Through a series of meetings, it was also decided that selected elements of Colonel Myatt's 26th MAU would go to New York City and participate in a series of special operations special weapons and tactics (SWAT) events. Eventually, these training events culminated in a "live fire hostage takedown" in New York. It was the most realistic training the young Marines could get, and they loved every moment of it.

Once the 26th MAU demonstrated its hostage rescue skills, the staff organized and conducted a series of exercises to establish a sequence of steps for a Tactical Recovery of Aircraft and Personnel. This was not an easy mission to plan. Innumerable variables arose: day or night recoveries, urban terrain or open country, weather, distance to the target and, finally, what and where were the most immediate threats? It was a difficult and creative effort, but plowing new ground is always stressful and seldom rewarding to the original planners. Colonel Myatt proved to be the skillful, upbeat professional. Recognizing that Gray's vision of a changing world demanded new thinking and new responses, the MAU began an intense period: an around-the-clock, seven-day-a-week research and implementation effort. Once Colonel Myatt's staff had perfected a complete planning cycle, they executed a number of dress rehearsals. Gray was ever-present, quietly watching the MAU's reactions to "alerts," and then observing the staff's planning process. After months of watching these exercises, Gray nodded and smiled, giving his first sign of approval. The tired staff congratulated themselves and felt their tasking was finally complete. They were wrong.

Unknown to the MAU staff, Gray had also been monitoring the increasing aggressive Iranian patrol boat activities in the Arabian Sea. The Iranian Navy had begun interdicting the commercial oil tankers. Additionally, Iranian military elements with ZU-23 antiaircraft guns were being placed on critical oil rigs along the tanker fleet steaming routes. The threat for direct confrontations was imminent. Without sharing this sensitive classified information, Gray begin to visualize the increasing threat to U.S. Navy ships, and he thought of various uncommon scenarios where Iranian-owned oil rigs would have to be neutralized. After observing the 26th MAU's rescue operations, it didn't take long for him to foresee forward-deployed Marines getting a mission to board, seize, and neutralize an operating oil rig. He felt that with some additional training, a MAU could handle the task, and he was going to prepare for it.

This again was vintage Al Gray. He was a master at raising the bar, so to speak. When he gave Colonel Myatt the guidance to be able to execute all 18 of the special operations capabilities, he already had on his mind that there was much more to be accomplished by the 26th MAU.

FBI Special Agent Robert Aldrich recalls how Gray was always pushing the envelope to increase operational capabilities. Aldrich paraphrased one of Gray's discussions with Colonel Myatt's MAU staff: "We need more urban training for our Marines. Think out of the box, think non-DoD resources, and get me some street-smart police officers, FBI agents with experiences to show us how to take down hostages or even to seize a terrorist. It's not the same old world we're going to be living in; you leaders need to think out of the box. Start learning now."

Gray relished making surprises, always reminding his Marines and Sailors to "think big. Don't ever think your planning or preparations are complete." He gathered the MAU staff and astonished them with a completely new crisis situation: the boarding and takedown of an oil rig platform. Total silence came over his audience. Instead of receiving a "well-done" speech from Gray, they received a new tasking, one that was not only unheard of by those present but was a much more complicated mission. During those initial moments, as individuals were shaking their heads and looking around at the rest of the squirming staff, it seemed like a mission impossible. Furthermore, there were unspoken wondering thoughts whether this was just more busy work. Was it really a potential mission for a MAU? It seemed unreal.

Colonel Myatt, feeling the frustration from his staff, responded to them after Gray had departed. Myatt again thanked his staff for the superb planning efforts his officers and enlisted Marines had produced. He then took a few moments and shared some thoughts about Gray's latest "bombshell." He reminded them of the General's long and rich operational experiences, his special reconnaissance and intelligence background, and his awareness of rapidly changing world threats. "Gray sees things that others don't," he said. After taking a few extra moments to share insights on the general, the staff members shook their heads and agreed that "Gray may be right," and they responded to the new challenge.[16]

A new scramble of creative thinking and planning began. Following the idea of going where real-world conditions are occurring for hostage rescues, they began searching for locations where oil rigs were operating. With the creative support of Special FBI Agent Aldrich, they arranged quiet and effective liaison visits with both the Exxon and Texaco headquarters in the vicinity of New Orleans. Aldrich requested instructions on the technical and engineer aspects of gas/oil rigs. A small group of Marines and Agent Aldrich toured a number of U.S. offshore rigs and working barges. They were apprised of critical areas, power plants, radio control centers, and walkways between rigs. Intelligence and reconnaissance Marines received specialized training, while other Marines met with site managers and conducted inspections of helicopter landing points. Helicopter landings were made on various platforms, all designed to make a Marine unit capable of seizing an offshore platform should such a mission ever be assigned. It would be a complex operation, but they all agreed that, with careful preplanning and lots of rehearsals, such a mission could be successfully accomplished.

But Gray was still not satisfied with just the MAU's ability to plan and execute training in certain special operation capabilities. The bar could be raised higher. He now mandated the seemingly impossible tasking that any "Special Operations 'alert' mission" must be capable of being executed in six hours. Gray related that a well-trained, forward-deployed, and special operations-capable MAU should be able to commence operations on a mission within six hours of receiving a warning order. Gray said, "This will be the time frame. Commanders and staffs simply need to get your heads around what it takes to operate faster." Gray asserted that this was the response the National Command Authorities will expect from MAUs and the "old days of referring to a Fleet Marine Force Manual (FMFM 8-1 [amphibious raids]) that it takes 30 days to plan and conduct a raid are gone."[17]

What Gray advocated was a completely revolutionary response concept. This was particularly true when MAUs are embarked on a three- or five-ship task force. His response concept was that all elements of the MAU—air, ground, and logistics—would, no matter which ship their command element was on, use wireless communications so simultaneous planning could be accomplished. This was light years ahead of the previous process, where men and equipment had to be moved to a central location by boats or helicopters from ship to ship. Further, as the basic plan evolved, all elements could keep abreast and be made aware of any necessary changes. Advanced technologies enabled critical planning time to be reduced from days and hours to minutes. It was not easy, but after numerous rehearsals the six-hour response criteria became possible.

177

But Gray knew the world had changed considerably since such doctrine was written, and he was going to impose his own timeline. The Marine Corps had always prided itself on being the most innovative of the services, yet any change from the current modes of operations caused internal strain. Most often, the resistance to change came from the "traditionalists" who were content with the status quo and wanted no part of special operations tasks. In contrast, Gray understood that new threats were arising, and providing new operational capabilities gave the United States major regional commanders, such as CINCLANT and CINCPAC, greater utility in their forward-deployed forces. He was adamant and declared that all deploying MAU (SOC) forces must demonstrate their "rapid response planning" (RRP) capabilities before deployment. The importance of defining each of the special operations missions, and the unprecedented rapid planning process for the six-hour response to executing every mission proved valid in later events and did, in fact, save the lives of U.S. military personnel.

It is interesting to note that these revolutionary, newly defined special operations missions and Gray's rapid response planning (RRP) mandate would subsequently be executed many times over in the next two decades by forward-deployed MAU (SOC) forces in real-world scenarios. Lives were saved because of this earlier visionary training.

It must be appreciated that when Gray was advocating MAU (SOC)-type operations, there was significant resistance to his ideas. Gray espoused a new concept in that he saw the MAU (SOC) as capable performers in special operations missions that some thought should be performed only by the Delta Force, or by the U.S. Army's Green Berets. He knew and understood that often, when a quick reaction is taken, a potential crisis is prevented. The Carolina MAGTF was thriving and getting the attention of not only the United States but high interest from Allied military commands. Gray was comfortable with his commands' busy tempo of operations. But there was a growing level of a very different interest beginning in Washington. Every four years there is a little-publicized process for selecting the new Marine

Corps Commandant. As 1986 was coming to a close, in Washington, the Pentagon, and particularly within Headquarters Marine Corps, the names of potential candidates began to receive extra attention. The guessing game as to who the 29th Commandant would be had begun in earnest. Al Gray was not among the leaders.

Gray was well aware that he was a long shot, certainly a dark horse at best. He fully understood that his 40-plus years of being a field Marine were fast coming to an end. He had never served as a General officer at Headquarters Marine Corps, and such an assignment was considered an integral step to qualify as a candidate for the Commandant position. Additionally, his age was against him, because, if selected, he would have to serve several months past the mandatory age for active duty officers. He was thankful for having served and achieved the second-highest rank in the Corps. He and his wife, Jan, had quietly begun to discuss where they wanted to settle in retirement, and they were still looking after his mother.

In March 1987, Gray prepared his letter of resignation and request for retirement. He was just weeks short of his 58th birthday. Historically, when a new Commandant is selected, all senior Generals prepare and submit letters offering their retirement. This enables the new Commandant the full freedom to select those he desires to remain on active duty, while approving the retirement of others. It has long been a gentlemanly process. All who attain General officer rank are reminded that they continue to serve at the consent of their Commandant.

The current Commandant compiles a "short list" of nominees whom he recommends and submits it to the Secretary of the Navy. Normally, three individuals are presented as best qualified for the unique position of Commandant of the U.S. Marine Corps. Once in receipt, the Secretary of the Navy interviews each candidate and then makes his recommendation to the Secretary of Defense. Once this selection process is completed, a formal announcement is made. Ultimately, the President of the United States forwards his choice to the Congress, for Senatorial confirmation. When the announcement of who would become the next Commandant was made, Gray knew his tenure as Commanding General, FMFLANT would end around June 30, 1987.

While the guessing game regarding the next Commandant progressed, Gray shifted his operational headquarters from Norfolk to Camp Lejeune, 200 miles south. An annual large-scale amphibious exercise, SOLID SHIELD, was about to begin. This was always his routine, to be where the action was going to take place. He wanted, more now than at any other time, to be with his Marines and Sailors as they practiced their arts of littoral warfare.

CHAPTER 9
U.S. National Security and a Maritime Strategy

*"We must never forget that freedom is never really free;
it is the most costly thing in the world. And freedom
is never paid for in a lump sum. Installments come
due in every generation. All any of us can do is offer
the generations that follow a chance for freedom."*

Ronald Reagan
President of the United States
Report to Congress, April 1988

This particular chapter has a much different focus, and it is presented to briefly highlight the national strategic security objectives. It was written in an attempt to reacquaint the reader with the "geo-econ-social" political world, where the Sailors and Marines travel the world's oceans, and to reflect on the where and why the nation's naval expeditionary forces are often challenged to move into "harm's way." It is in this restless world where Gray and other Commandants must be prepared to respond to natural tragedies and humanitarian and nation-building activities to stabilize regional unrest.

Although the Navy's and Marine Corps' worldwide deployments are often transparent to the vast majority of Americans, the Commandant and other Service Chiefs are increasingly aware of their men and women positioned on the edges of the Free World. With the emerging technical advantages in satellite and other informational systems, they have ready access to systems that can provide updates on arising crises anywhere in the world.

Al Gray served almost his entire military career during the Cold War era. He entered the Marine Corps shortly after the Iron Curtain dropped across Europe, still recovering from World War II. This turbulent 50-year era was one of the most stressful periods in the history of the United

States. The potential of global nuclear war between the Free World and the Communist block caused the United States to continuously redefine its national security policies and national security objectives.

The Cold War was still the reigning paradigm when Gray arrived in Washington in June 1987 as the new Commandant of the Marine Corps. He would ultimately close out his career shortly after the Soviet Union imploded in 1989, thus ending the Cold War. This was an event he had predicted. More than two years earlier, Gray had begun to express his view that the collapse of Communism was not far off—which made him one of the few Americans who felt that the paradigm was about to shift.

Every Service Chief's tenure reflects the time and environment in which he operated. Was the nation at war or at peace? Was the administration of the day strong or soft on national defense? Did the defense budget expand or decline? And were the President and the congressional leaders united in the way they approached national defense policies? Most Service Chiefs aspire to make a lasting contribution to the nation, but sometimes circumstances and stresses overwhelm the officeholder, keeping him focused only on the crisis at hand. This was not true of Gray, who was something of a determined visionary and able to focus on the foreground and the far horizon. He saw a changing world and understood that new unconventional threats, such as terrorism, were emerging. The unexpected violence and shock of terrorist attacks would test his leadership and would forever mark the tenure of the 29th Commandant of the U.S. Marine Corps, General Al Gray.

To understand the office of Commandant, it is useful to look briefly at the structure of the Department of the Navy. From the early days of our republic, it has been organized into three parts: the operating forces of the Navy, the Navy Department, and the shore establishment. The operating forces are comprised of several fleets: the Sixth and Second Fleets in the Mediterranean and Atlantic; and the Third and Seventh in the Pacific. Included in each fleet are surface and air forces, Fleet Marine Forces (FMF), and the supporting vessels of the Military Sealift Command.

What is referred to as the "Navy Department" is different from the Department of the Navy. It contains the executive offices of the Secretary of the Navy, the office of the Chief of Naval Operations (CNO), the headquarters of the naval system commands (air, space, naval warfare, supply, and facilities), and Headquarters Marine Corps. The Secretary of the Navy serves as the civilian head of two separate services, the Navy and the Marine Corps. He is responsible for ensuring compliance with Title 10 USC (Section 5063), which includes the mandate for a Marine Corps of no less than three combat divisions and three aircraft wings. The three divisions and wings, along with various supporting forces, are to be organized, trained, and equipped to provide Fleet Marine Forces of combined arms (that is, air and ground task forces) for service with the fleet "in the seizure of advanced naval bases and for the conduct of land operations as may be essential to the prosecution of a naval campaign."[1] The Title 10 mission, to "organize, train, and equip" the Marine Corps is the Commandant's primary responsibility. As such, he is not directly responsible for leading Marines in combat, a responsibility that falls to the various regional commanders-in-chief around the world (now known as combatant commanders).

The historic cornerstone of our fledgling republic's strategy was America's geographical position in relation to other nations. For the first hundred years, America's "splendid isolation" made an active international strategy unnecessary. The United States was protected by the Atlantic and Pacific Oceans: two broad "moats." This geographical isolation meant that the United States could get by with only a small standing Army.

The beginnings of a force-projection strategy emerged around the turn of the century, not long before the United States entered World War I. The United States acquired overseas possessions during the Spanish-American War, and strategic thinkers called for means to protect the United States' growing overseas trade. Both the Army and the Navy were expanded. In 1916, President Woodrow Wilson proposed and Congress approved the building of a U.S. Navy "bigger" than Great Britain's. This expansion would ultimately change the role of the Marine Corps. There were several long-term advantages to this policy change. First, the United States was becoming a global power and would eventually possess a seapower capability equal to that of the European powers. To maintain the balance of power, the United States would soon send its military force overseas to aid embattled allies. Secondly, in prosecuting a war on another continent, the United States would not experience the destructiveness of war at home. Power projection became a key and lasting element of U.S. strategy.

In the aftermath of World War II, the United States assumed a new burden, that of leadership and defense of the Free World. It was a mantle not easily understood or fully accepted by many American citizens. Included were bold and unprecedented steps to aid the recovery of both allies and defeated foes. When the Iron Curtain fell across a battered Europe shortly after the end of World War II, America committed herself to those nations that shared her values, centering its national security policy on the theme that it was in her best interest to prevent any hostile power from dominating the European land mass. It followed that the United States would station a large standing force of Army and Air Force units in Europe to establish a credible forward defense posture against the Warsaw Pact. A strategy of containment against Soviet expansionism remained the cornerstone of our national strategy through the 1980s.

Another important element of our national strategy has been a commitment to a free and open international economic system. Ours is an island nation. We are separated from Europe and Asia by the Atlantic and Pacific Oceans, and we are fortunate to have friendly nations to our north and south. Many of our closest allies and trading partners are distant from the United States. The oceans saved us from any immediate physical threat of land armies. But these same oceans mandated that our strategic sea lines of communication remain open at all times.

There were also several other major trends that characterized this period of transition in the late 1980s. The first was the revolution in military technologies. New surveillance and accurate targeting systems, new means of destruction, and stealth technology were entering into the Soviet arsenal. Simultaneously, rapid advances in microelectronics would allow the command and control communications, integrated with intelligence sources (C3I), to provide time-critical strategic and tactical direction. All of these technological advancements would cause our military leaders, and adversaries, to rethink military doctrine and force structure.

Throughout the post-World War II period, U.S. forces had equipped, structured, and trained forces to deter aggression and coercion against our government and its allies by persuading potential adversaries that the cost of aggression, whether nuclear or conventional, would exceed any possible gain. To support deterrence, the United States made strong alliances, establishing collective defensive arrangements combining both our economic and military strength and lessening the burden on any one country. The focus of these alliances was to establish a forward defense posture by placing our ground, naval, and air forces in and around Europe, Asia, and the Pacific.

Forward Presence, Crisis & War Since WWII
1945 - 1990

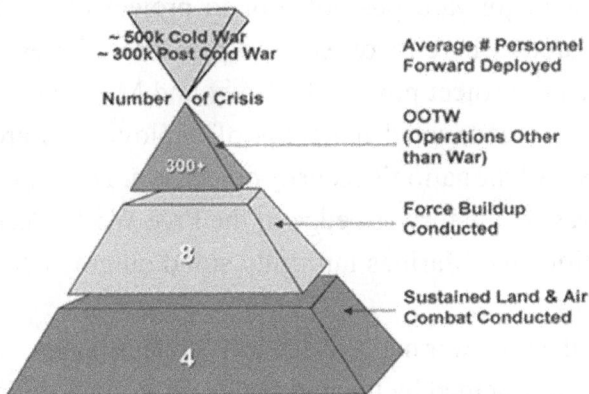

Figure 3
World Crises in Which U.S. Forces Responded During the Period 1945-1990 (Chart developed by Marine Corps in [Navy's] N-85 Branch and courtesy of Marine Corps Archives).

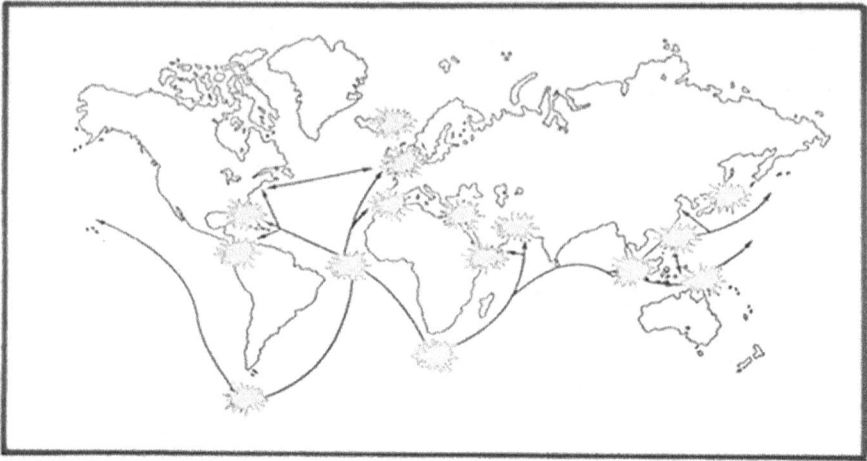

Figure 4
Sea Lines of Communications and Strategic Chokepoints
(Chart developed by Marine Corps in [Navy's] N-85 Branch
and courtesy of Marine Corps Archives).

The final key to the U.S. military strategy was force projection. To best guarantee global security interests, the services maintained ready forces in the United States and the means to move them to reinforce units in forward positions, or to project power from the seas in those areas where there were no permanent bases. The pre-eminent means to project power, the Navy and Marine Corps "blue and green team," conducted hundreds of deployments around the world in support of the nation's security objectives. This Navy/Marine Corps team was on the forward edge of the Free World. As the tip of the spear, Sailors and Marines faithfully stood on gray decks, ready to go into harm's way.

To support the post-war national security strategy, a new U.S. maritime strategy had emerged by the mid-1980s. Since U.S. policy was to enter into alliances, a maritime strategy served many of the needs of the major alliances. It was especially beneficial to the North Atlantic Treaty

Organization (NATO) alliance. But, of equal importance, our maritime strategy also made sense outside the context of the Western Alliance. It enabled the United States to be effective in peacetime operations, or in more limited regional conflicts when acting alone. The U.S. naval air and surface combatants would keep the seas open, with the Marine Corps expeditionary forces providing the power projection capability to control chokepoints, and to conduct surveillance and reconnaissance missions to support the naval campaign.

This was a timely strategy that fitted into Gray's long-term efforts to train and equip a Marine Corps more suitable for the 21st century and to deal with emerging threats.

President Ronald Reagan's 1986 Annual Report to Congress recognized that we were living in a time that historians would characterize as a period of transition in national security affairs. The transition had really begun in the late 1970s, when our policies to rebuild our allies' economies had long been successful, and America no longer had an overwhelming economic position vis-à-vis every Western European and East Asian country. The transitional period was marked by the Soviet Union's massive buildup, which consumed as much as 15 to 17 percent of its annual gross national products. This investment provided the Soviets, by the 1980s, a position of strategic nuclear parity, quantitative conventional superiority in Central Europe, and a modern globally deployed Navy.

In contrast, the U.S. maritime strategy was based on the idea that sea control can most effectively be maintained through the early destruction of the enemy's fleet by projecting seapower into his base areas. This focus on preempting the deployment of an enemy Navy is important because it prevents the enemy from dispersing forces into the open sea. And secondly, it frees up forces to affect the land battle. This aggressive action is predicated on the fact that all application of seapower flows from the sea, the greatest of all highways.[2]

Lastly, a viable U.S. maritime strategy is predicated on scarcity of ships to counter an enemy. Because it requires six to seven years to build most U.S. ships, attrition is not an acceptable approach to prosecuting a naval campaign. During the 1970s and '80s, the U.S. Navy's fleets had been progressively reduced to just more than 400 ships. America's maritime strategy had developed in the short term to serve both national security and economic objectives, yet its unbalanced focus allowed the Navy's operating fleet to dwindle to a size incapable of fulfilling its worldly mission. There were clear inconsistencies between objectives and the nation's capabilities. Gray understood there were no easy, quick course corrections.

The credit for the rebirth of a modern day U.S. maritime strategy must be properly given to John Lehman Jr. He was appointed as the Secretary of the Navy by President Ronald Reagan and confirmed by the Senate in February 1981. Then-candidate Reagan had called for a return to maritime superiority during a campaign speech in March 1980. This was a complete reversal of the nation's most recent military strategy.

During the 1970 President Jimmy Carter administration, Harold Brown served as the Secretary of Defense. Secretary Brown's approach was to perform a series of systems analyses to determine what the military forces needed to contain the growing Soviet threat. John Lehman captured the flaw in this methodology when he wrote that Washington was "a town where systems analysis had been mistaken for strategy itself."[3] Brown began relegating the Navy and Marine Corps to secondary importance in the Carter administration's national defense strategy. The Navy's fleet, which had numbered 950 ships in 1969, dropped to 479 a decade later. At the same time, the Soviet fleet increased by more than 1,600 vessels. The defense doctrine that emerged saw the East-West confrontation in Europe as the central focus of the U.S.-Soviet military balance. In response to this perceived threat, the Carter administration set out to strengthen Army and Air Force capabilities. They deemphasized seapower, wrongly concluding that seapower could contribute little to the defense of Europe. Under the scenario of war, Navy forces were envisioned as "naval resupply forces."[4] Lehman argued that "the Carter team believed that offensive naval operations would be a diversion of resources. Further ... it was certainly true that the defeat of the Soviet Union at sea would not guarantee a successful defense of NATO, but, it was also true—and more important, that the loss of NATO's supremacy at sea would guarantee NATO's defeat."[5]

Like the earlier developers of a maritime strategy, Lehman stated, "The United States is a 'continental island,' tied to its allies, trading partners, and resources by the great seas. The Free World is an oceanic coalition. We must be sure we can use the oceans in peace and war if we are to survive."[6]

John Lehman felt the power of the Secretary of the Navy had atrophied from lack of exercise. He was quick to change course and reenergize maritime strategy. The keystone would be to achieve maritime superiority. He activated the Navy policy board; its functions were to settle the key issues faced by the Navy and Marine Corps. Both Admiral Thomas Hayward, Chief of Naval Operations (CNO), and General Robert Barrow, the Commandant of the Marine Corps, would serve as members, along with a number of Assistant Secretaries of the Navy. It was a new beginning, and through the Navy policy board and other study bodies, eight principles of maritime strategy were defined. These were later codified as fundamental to maritime strategy. Lehman's book *Command of the Seas* lays these principles out in great detail, with supporting rationale. In the book, he states that our maritime strategy is derived from and dependent on overall national security strategy established by the President. Establishing a maritime strategy cannot begin until the President has provided an overall national security strategy for the nation.[7]

Principle I   Maritime strategy is derived from and dependent on the overall national security strategy established by the President.

Principle II   National strategy provides the Department of the Navy with maritime tasks:

1. The Navy is responsible for controlling diverse international crises.

2. The fundamental task of all the armed forces is deterrence to allow our national interests to be preserved in peace.

3. If deterrence fails, prevent the seas from being used against the United States.

Principle III   Maritime tasks assigned to the Navy Department require maritime superiority.

Principle IV   Maritime superiority requires a disciplined maritime strategy.

Principle V   Maritime strategy must be based on a realistic assessment of the threat.

Principle VI   Maritime strategy must be global in concept.

Principle VII   Maritime strategy must fully integrate all U.S. and Free World forces.

Principle VIII   Maritime strategy must be a forward strategy.

From Lehman's principles, the Navy/Marine Corps team was able to establish a modern maritime strategy, and from that strategy project the number, size, and mix of the ships, aircraft, and weapons systems used. The global disposition of the Navy and Marine Corps dictated that these forces must be organized and deployed in peace much as they would operate in war. For purposes of deterrence, crisis management, and diplomacy, the Navy/Marine Corps team must be present in areas where they would have to fight if war broke out. Secretary Lehman's vision and determination proved that one man, even in a bureaucratic world, can still make a difference to a nation.

The goal of a 600-ship Navy grew out of Lehman's initiatives. The size of the fleet was dictated by the maritime strategy and the separate requirements of each of the different geographic theaters— the Atlantic and Pacific Oceans, the Mediterranean Sea, the Indian

Ocean, and the Persian Gulf. Lehman's planning vision and tenacious execution brought to fruition a new U.S. maritime strategy capable of conducting early forward naval operations as a means of dealing with a land-based superpower. Lehman was also committed to the rebuilding of a modern fleet capable of sustained operations in a global war. Additionally, with the numerous changes in national security strategy, the Marine Corps' historic roles and missions were progressively increasing, as reflected in the four major eras of service to the nation:

- Soldiers of the Sea
- Colonial Infantry
- Amphibious Assault Forces
- Force-in-Readiness

Lehman's untiring effort to give this nation a credible naval deterrent was one of few notable achievements within the Department of Defense during the 1980s. He restored institutional confidence to the two services in time for the 1991 Persian Gulf War.

During the critical days in 1990, before the U.S. military and coalition forces launched their ground attack to retake Kuwait from Iraqi invaders, more than 96,000 Marines were positioned ashore and onboard amphibious ships in the Persian Gulf. The stage was set for the land-based forces to move north across the Saudi Arabia-Kuwait border and breach the Iraqi forces' minefields and defensive barriers. There were some congressional estimates that projected more than 45,000 friendly combat casualties. It was a time of great stress across the nation as all realized the decision to launch the attack was only days away. The world was focused on the Persian Gulf War and guessed at the probable success of a multinational force, which included, for the first time, Arab forces side-by-side with American and European armies.

Meanwhile, back in Washington, Gray was doing everything humanly possible to support his deployed forces. As if an impending conventional war was not enough, Gray was also intensively following other naval deployments. New world crises suddenly occurred that caused greater strains on the Navy and Marine Corps Middle East forces. These new world crises arose in the African nations of Liberia and Somalia.

Interestingly, it was just this kind of unstable world situation that had years earlier motivated Gray to increase the operational capabilities of the traditional MAGTF organization to have special operations capabilities (SOC) skills. In response to our nation's maritime strategy, the Marine Corps has had for many decades an important role in the successful prosecution of U.S. foreign policy. These MAGTF forces, deploying from the East and West Coasts, Hawaii, and Okinawa, had become a proven response cell that was, and remains, at every president's fingertips when unexpected events occur. The National Command Authority (NCA) has had to use Navy and Marine Corps forces more often than those of the other services when Americans are endangered.

The three contingencies—Kuwait, Somalia, and Liberia—demonstrated in 1990 and '91 the classic examples of the flexibility and value of forward-deployed Navy/Marine forces. They reflect traditional Marine values, and the influence of the preceding decades, during which maritime and Marine doctrine had evolved. But they also reflect the effect of Gray's leadership and the policies that he put in place. In the first, a deployment of unprecedented size and speed positioned Marine forces at the cutting edge of American national policy in Saudi Arabia preparing for the recapture of the nation of Kuwait. The two later incidents took place on the African continent, where the presence of a naval task meant, for American nationals and others, the difference between life and death, or being captured by unstable insurgent forces.

The first deployment occurred when Saddam Hussein's Iraqi Army invaded Kuwait. Within 72 hours, the Navy sailed one carrier, the USS *Independence* (CV-72), into the north Arabian Sea and began preparing to launch air strikes against any Iraqi forces that attempted to interfere with the American airlifts of men and equipment into Saudi Arabia. Once the decision was made that the United States would provide massive military support to Saudi Arabia, the Navy/Marine Corps team then deployed. Coming halfway around the world, the 18,000 Marines and Sailors of the 7th Marine Expeditionary Brigade were airlifted into northern Saudi Arabia, joined with their equipment, which had been pre-staged on a flotilla of National Command Authority (NCA). Within hours of the ships' docking, the trucks, tanks, and assault amphibian vehicles, ammunition, and supplies were off-loaded. The 7th Marine Expeditionary Brigade's (MEB) M-60 tanks and Light Armored Vehicles (LAVs) armed with anti-tank tube-launched, optically tracked, wire-guided (TOW) missiles would be the U.S. main armor force until other ships brought the Army tanks ashore 30 days later. During the critical early days of the U.S. buildup, this was the only force ready for combat with 60 days of supplies to sustain themselves.

But in other parts of the world, Sailors and Marines were reacting to another series of arising crises. In May 1990, the African nation of Liberia was in a state of unrest, with all indications that rebel forces were about to seize Monrovia, the capital. By early June, those forces, led by Charles Taylor, a former enlisted Soldier, were closing in on the city and were only ten miles from the international airport. The few remaining airlines canceled their flights, and the U.S. government alerted the Department of Defense to send a military task force to evacuate about 1,100 Americans from Liberia if they were threatened by the fighting. The Joint Staff began planning an evacuation mission. The original thinking was to fly elements of the Army's 82nd Airborne Division directly into the besieged airport to rescue the Americans, and possibly other nations' civilians. The operation would be JUST CAUSE II, in reference to the recent successful assault into Panama one year earlier, OPERATION JUST CAUSE. However, when the rebels overran the international airport, the Army air-landed force was no longer a viable option. Another type of response quickly shifted to the nation's Navy and Marine forces.

Weeks earlier, the 22nd Marine Expeditionary Unit had also been alerted to prepare for a possible noncombat evacuation. A small naval task force of four ships carrying 2,000 Marines had arrived off the Liberian Coast and had begun the detailed preparations to evacuate the Americans if necessary. There were justifiable fears that if the rebels took the capital, there would be a bloodbath. As the situation in Liberia worsened, the State Department ordered all nonessential U.S. government personnel and their families to leave.

For the next two months, the 22nd Marine Expeditionary Unit (MEU), commanded by Marine Colonel Granville Amos, would be poised 20 miles offshore. Colonel "Granny" Amos, a protégé of Gray, took advantage of the waiting period to ensure what would be a successful execution of OPERATION SHARP EDGE. As his planning process moved forward, the latest photographs of the American Embassy were reviewed, terrain models of the compound were fabricated, and countless planning sessions and briefings were conducted. As the different units were assigned their tasks in the rescue mission, platoons and squads began to coordinate their tasks, and every phase of the operation was developed into a highly synchronized air-ground team effort. When the evacuation plan was finally set, Colonel Amos demanded that the units repeatedly rehearse until the day before the 22nd MEU was ordered to execute SHARP EDGE.[8]

On June 10, the rebels won control of the international airport. There were attempts at negotiating a ceasefire agreement between the government and the rebel force, but these broke down on July 19th. Prominent Liberians appealed to the United States for a temporary peacekeeping force to prevent further bloodshed. On the 21st, Liberia's ruler expelled the U.S. military attaché, accusing him of supporting the rebels. More than 600 people were killed in five days. The Liberian national government was no longer functioning.

On Saturday, August 4, President George H.W. Bush ordered the evacuation from Monrovia, and word was quickly passed to the amphibious task force off the African coastline. Their mission was to safeguard lives, and draw down the number of Americans at the Embassy to minimum staff and to provide additional security for those who remained. A hundred rehearsals and planning sequences were now to be tested.

A reinforced rifle company of 225 Marines and Navy corpsmen were helicopter-lifted from the USS *Saipan* into Monrovia to evacuate Americans and foreign dependents. In the first lift were 73 Americans from the Embassy compound. Evacuations were also made at two communication sites in Liberia that had the mission to handle diplomatic and intelligence messages in sub-Saharan Africa. Colonel Amos later reported the mission complete and that there had been "no casualties." The Marines would remain in Liberia for another month before withdrawing to their ships offshore. When the situation in Monrovia further stabilized, the amphibious task force sailed away.

But this noncombat humanitarian incident had far greater impact upon the future of MEU (SOC) deployments, for it was the "first" actual test of Gray's vision to train and deploy a MEU with special operations capabilities. Until OPERATION SHARP EDGE demonstrated how the expanded capabilities could provide greater utility to Region Commanders in time of crisis, his concept of MEU (SOC) was just a concept, but untested. The Liberian response proved Gray's demand to train all MAGTFs to be special operations qualified was correct, and even two decades later his mandate to "train up" remains in place.

The second "collateral" use of Navy and Marine forces during OPERATION DESERT SHIELD/DESERT STORM was the rescue of 281 people from war-torn Somalia. At almost any other time, such an operation would have captured the nation's imagination and held it for days. The elements of danger, unexpected obstacles, speed, timing, and sheer courage were all present. The 4th Marine Expeditionary

Brigade (MEB) had been at sea since August 15 and steaming in the Persian Gulf since mid-September. The amphibious task force had spent most of its time in the Gulf of Oman conducting amphibious landing exercises in preparation for what would become the DESERT STORM ground offensive.

The day after Christmas 1990 found the amphibious task force spread over thousands of square miles. They were participating in a maritime interdiction operation in the Gulf of Oman and were widely dispersed to intercept and turn back any ships attempting to return to Iraq. Far to their southwest on the eastern coast of Africa, the nation of Somalia was engulfed in violent civil strife, and American citizens were in danger. On January 2, 1991, Secretary of State James Baker requested that President Bush order an emergency noncombatant evacuation operation to move the U.S. Ambassador and his staff to safety from their Embassy in Mogadishu. Timing again became critical as the rebels began to seek out and kill "the Americans."

The mission was approved and orders were passed down to the Commanding General, 4th MEB, Major General Harry Jenkins, to commence planning for the conduct of the evacuation. Colonel J.J. Doyle, Commanding Officer, 4th Brigade Service Support Group (BSSG), was appointed as the landing force commander. Colonel Doyle was directed to move to the USS *Guam* and take the reins of the Brigade's "Bravo Command Group." Time was of the essence. In the Somalia capital, President Siad Barre was trapped in a bunker at the airport. Anarchy reigned in the city. A decision was made to send two U.S. ships, the USS *Guam* and the USS *Trenton*, on the 1,600-mile voyage to the southwest.

On January 3rd, this small task force was broken out from the large amphibious task force and placed directly under the senior naval commander, U.S. Navy, Central Command (COMUSNAVCENT). Later that day, Colonel Doyle's command elements made non-secure voice communications directly with the besieged Embassy. The contingency planning information on Somalia was badly out-of-date, but the information was corrected with the help of an enlisted man who had served as a Marine Security Guard at the Embassy from 1983-84. It was through him that Colonel Doyle's staff confirmed that the new Embassy had been moved out of the central portion of the city.

During the afternoon of January 4th, the American Ambassador requested immediate evacuation by Army paratroopers or any other force capable of acting before the "slow-moving" task force. The two ships' Captains immediately increased speed to 22 knots, and plans were made to launch a 60-man force in two CH-53E helicopters. The long flight would require aerial refueling and arrangements were made for KC-130 tanker support from the 3rd Marine Air Wing deployed in eastern Saudi Arabia.

Information concerning the threat in Mogadishu was sketchy at best. It would be impossible to distinguish among the government troops, the looters, and the rebel forces. Intelligence revealed that numerous surface-to-air missiles and antiaircraft guns were scattered throughout the capital. Who controlled these air defense weapons and whether they would attack the rescue helicopters was unknown.

The two heavily loaded CH-53s launched at 0600. The plan called for three aerial refuelings, two while inbound and one on the return flight. All knew it was a desperation mission, fraught with danger and uncertainties. As the sun broke over the horizon on the 5th, the two CH-53s roared across the beach just three minutes off their planned arrival time.[9] The pilots saw troop concentrations and numerous antiaircraft guns along their flight paths, but none challenged their progress. At the same time, bands of armed men were attempting to breach the Embassy compound. These forces were firing directly into the compound and were using ladders to scale the walls. The helicopter-borne force arrived at the Embassy compound at 0610. With the arrival of these unexpected reinforcements, the attackers scattered. The Marine security forces quickly formed a defensive perimeter as the evacuation process began.

By the evening of the sixth, USS *Trenton* and USS *Guam* were close enough to begin evacuating the rest of the noncombatants by ten CH-46 helicopters. The helicopters were blacked out, and the pilots flew with night-vision goggles. The evacuation went as planned. The American Ambassador remained until the last wave and then flew out with the last of the Marine security force. When the final tally was taken, 282 people had been evacuated. The list included ambassadors from 12 other nations and citizens from 31 nations. With their rescue mission complete, Colonel Doyle's Marines and Sailors rejoined the main amphibious task force and returned to their preparations for ground operations against the Iraqis.[10]

Gray knew what being a true expeditionary force in support of a viable maritime strategy was all about. It can serve as a naval force, operating just over-the-horizon to provide a combat- ready, sustainable U.S. presence on the littoral of the world's land masses when regional unrest or a natural disaster strikes. These three events reaffirmed the nation's continuing requirements for forward-deployed naval task forces. They also demonstrated the importance of "a presence," of being on the scene as a situation is unfolding. In every one of these crises, Gray involved himself in the planning, deployment, force buildup, and execution of missions by his Marines and Sailors, although he was behind the scenes inside the Washington Beltway. As far back as the 1970s, the Marine Corps leadership recognized that new threats were arising. The Beirut attack in October 1983 demonstrated how terrorism was beginning to replace the conventional warfare patterns developed in World War II and Korea. The more advanced nations were moving into the age of electronic and information warfare, while fanatical groups were preparing to launch worldwide terrorist attacks. The combination of this threat and the reassessment of the possibility of unconventional warfare caused the Marine Corps to begin training its deploying MEUs to be capable of special operations.

The initial stages of this special capability training began under General P.X. Kelley. At that time, Al Gray was commanding the Fleet

Marine Force and the 2nd Marine Expeditionary Force (MEF) and he executed the development of additional mission-capable training for each deploying MEU. This new training syllabus included such events as hostage takedown, raids, tactical recovery of downed aviators, special boat training, and riverine operations. These and other types of special operational events became standard training for all Marine units scheduled for deployment.

Deployments such as the rescue missions cited earlier don't "just happen." They are built upon earlier experiences that evolve from successful or failed missions. As an example, the ability for Marine CH-53 helicopters to refuel in-flight came about from the failure to rescue Americans held hostage by the Iranian government. In an attempt to launch a rescue for them, it was necessary to establish a temporary refueling site in the eastern Iranian desert. Codenamed DESERT ONE, a hastily built landing zone was turned into a roaring fireball of exploding aviation fuel when pilots, blinded by dust storms created by the helicopters landing nearby and by limited vision in the darkness of night, accidentally flew into a KC-130 aircraft loaded with fuel. Pilots and crew were killed. Chaos reigned. The rescue mission had to be aborted. The Iranian government exploited the incident and broadcast the mission's failure to the world.

To ensure that this type of mission failure never happened again, innovative and advanced technologies were fitted into CH-53 helicopters in addition to in-flight refueling capabilities. The point being, the evolution of warfare is constant. The constant dynamics of the military was a basic theme Gray shared with his Marines and Sailors, reminding all to be "smart Marines." There is never a perfect long-term combination of operations doctrine, trained warriors, climatic conditions, and the right equipment to ensure complete success on every battlefield.

At the same time, new challenges to have the Marine Corps infantry become more mobile were proposed, and Gray was in command of the 4th MAB, introducing his mechanized brigade into a series of exercises in the NATO European theater. Although it wasn't readily recognized at the time, these two strands of changes in the Marine Corps represented yet another phase in the transformation of the Marine Corps' "force-in-readiness" capabilities. Unknowingly, the Corps was preparing itself for the kind of challenge that the Iraqi War of 1991 would present, as well as updating its more traditional maritime capabilities.

CHAPTER 10

Commandants of the Marine Corps and Their Roles

"Congress established a Corps of Marines in the 1790s. ... In accordance with the act, William Ward Burrows became the senior officer with the rank of Major but had not used the title Commandant. Thus, for two hundred years the Marine Corps has had a Commandant, and that officer serves as the unquestioned head of service and official leader of the Corps."

Colonel Allan Millet, USMCR (Retired)
Author, *Semper Fidelis: The History of the United States Marine Corps*

With his appointment as the 29th Commandant of the U.S. Marine Corps, Alfred M. Gray assumed a role unique within the armed forces of the United States. Unlike any other Service Chief, the Commandant has no true equal within the other services. This is explicit in his title. He is the Commandant—a derivative of commander. The Army and Air Force have Chiefs of Staff and the Navy has a Chief of Naval Operations (CNO). Their operating forces are explicitly assigned to four-star general or flag officers who command Service components that report to regional joint commanders.

The Commandant position is also unique in that he is the sole titular head of his Service, and, as such, is the primary spokesman and advocate on Capitol Hill with the Congress. As the senior Marine on active duty, he is responsible for the internal leadership climate of his Service, its strategic focus, combat readiness, and future combat development direction. With the exception of the General officers assigned to joint billets, all Marine officers administratively follow chains of command that ultimately report to him. His Lieutenant

Generals owe their nominations to him, serve at his pleasure, and act as his Board of Directors.

Even the Assistant Commandant is clearly a subordinate of the Commandant, and should any other four-star general be appointed exclusively to a Joint assignment—notably General Tony Zinni to US Central Command (CENTCOM), General Peter Pace as Chairman of the Joint Chiefs of Staff, or General James Cartwright as Vice Chairman of the Joint Chiefs of Staff—they are assigned outside the Marine Corps administrative chain of command. As a result, unlike the other services, the Commandant is in a unique position as the sole voice of his Service and empowered like no other Service head to affect the character, ethos, doctrine, and force structure of his Service.

The Commandant also has the advantage over the other services in that the Marine Corps has the smallest Service headquarters support structure, centrally located within Northern Virginia (principally at the Naval Annex, the Pentagon, and in Quantico). This centralization of decisionmaking and a single chain of command ensures that his policies and major decisions can be swiftly acted upon and disseminated throughout the Marine Corps. This is in contrast to the other services, which have their headquarters' elements or support commands widely dispersed across the country, with many key components headed up by rival four-star Generals or Admirals who may or may not fully endorse the direction of their own Service Chiefs.

In addition, the Marine Corps lacks strong internal branches or warfighting communities. In contrast, the Army of the 1980s had at least ten discrete branches (armor, infantry, cavalry, aviation, ordnance, quartermaster, transportation, etc.), each with its own traditions, school- houses, and sense of community. Loyalty in one's branch is reputed to be the surest path to senior leadership. Accordingly, there were times when the intra-branch rivalry meant that the best candidates were not chosen because of the perception that it was not the sponsoring branch's turn to have its candidate appointed to the Service Chief position. In the civilian world, the best comparison is the Roman Catholic Church, where the Jesuits are so notorious in demanding total loyalty to their Order that it can be said "first a Jesuit and then a Catholic."

Within the U.S. Navy, the CNO comes from what are commonly referred to as the aviation, surface warfare, and submarine communities, which, in essence, act as separate "tribes," with their own emblems, distinctive uniforms in some cases (e.g., brown versus black shoes), and specialty specific schools and career paths. Over the past four decades, all CNOs have come from one of these three tribes within the Navy. This is also true in the U.S. Air Force, where the chief of staff has always been a qualified pilot. To enter the Air Force and not become a rated pilot does not restrict an individual from becoming a General officer, but it means that they will never rise to become the Chief of Staff of the U.S. Air Force.

In contrast, any gifted Marine General officer—regardless of occupational specialty—can become Commandant. There is no historical example where the residing leaders of the Marine Corps air-ground logistics team have ever attempted to push or advocate a community choice. For the first time in the history of the Corps, a Marine naval aviator, General James F. Amos, was selected and served as Commandant from October 22, 2010, to October 17, 2014. Further, all Marines attend The Basic School (TBS) for indoctrination as new officers. The Marine Corps credo that "every Marine is a rifleman" captures the ethos that it trains all Marines, regardless of specialty, to first be Marine warriors and then whatever occupational field they are assigned. The result is that all Marines are "Marines" first and aviators, artillerymen, or infantrymen second.

Edgar F. Puryear's book *Marine Corps Generalship* provides a unique insight into the selection and leadership of past Commandants. The Foreword, written by Gray, highlights the similarity of traits of former Commandants. Gray's analysis includes in part:

"The history of the Commandants reveals a variety of similar traits that distinguishes them from others. They have become leaders with broad professional knowledge, not only of the military but also all the elements of national security, including political, economic and social factors. They have understood the value of training and education to include discipline, particularly self-discipline, as essential to develop character, self-control and effectiveness. They stand out as a person who does what must be done."

This is not to say the Commandants have not had their own unique style of leadership, focus, or sense of mission in their role as custodian of the institution that is the Marine Corps. In assessing the records of Commandants before and after Gray, they seem to come from three general categories.[1]

First are those who have proven themselves worthy in battle and have risen to the position of Commandant because they personally exhibit the characteristics most representative of the Marine Corps. These Commandants have thereby assumed a position of reverence that provides even greater morale and actual authority to the position than they might otherwise have had. At times, in the history of the Marine Corps, it has been the heroes who have been able to capture the imagination of our congressional leadership when the Service has been under its most intense attack by those who question why we have a Marine Corps and not simply the traditional Navy, Army, or militia.

The second category is that of the conservers of the traditions and legacy of the Marine Corps. These Commandants might be authentic heroes in their own right, but their focus as Commandant is to preserve and defend the attributes which, over the centuries, have made the United States Marines who they are. This includes not only its customs and ceremonies but its focus on warfighting prowess, discipline, and naval expeditionary character. One example is Medal of Honor recipient General David Shoup, who discarded swagger sticks and other outdated emblems and refocused the Marine Corps of his day on training for combat. These Commandants have proven to be the right choice for the time, preserving the Marine Corps as a fighting force when it might well have followed the lead of society or the other services to reduce standards, eschew training in warfighting skills, or become something less than the nation needed.

The third category of Commandant is the innovator. It has been these Commandants who have either led a major change in direction within the Marine Corps and the Navy or fostered a command climate that enabled others to experiment and innovate without institutional obstacles. In some cases, these too have been war heroes or those interested in preserving our Marine Corps customs and traditions, and through their actions have fostered major changes within the Service. One example is Major General John A. Lejeune, who was not only responsible for codifying the Marine Corps Birthday Celebration but also fostered a command climate of innovation that led to two simultaneously competing doctrinal schools of thought—such as Major General Smedley D. Butler, who believed the Marine Corps should refocus on expeditionary constabulary efforts, culminating in the publication of the seminal *Small Wars Manual;* or the amphibious warfare advocates epitomized by Major Pete Ellis, who thought the nation and the Navy needed a Marine Corps capable of amphibious operations in order to seize advanced naval bases.

Historically, each Commandant's tenure of stewardship was, in many ways, affected by the time of war or peace, an expanding or declining defense budget, the general attitude of the people, and the actions of the President of the United States and congressional leaders. In some cases, however, circumstances overcome Commandants, and few long-term achievements come to fruition.

Every senior commander aspires to make a lasting contribution to the nation during his service career. On most occasions, his leadership, management style, and long-range vision does indeed make a beneficial difference.

Fate and circumstance always play a decisive role in the success of Commandants. However, the characteristics that signal the greatest success seem to center on his recognition of what the nation needed most from its Marine Corps at that time. The best Commandants have exhibited a keen appreciation for the strategic environment of their time and also a conceptual framework for the contributions that the Marine Corps could make to the nation's needs. Lastly, the most successful had universally focused on organizing, equipping, and especially training the force to deliver the warfighting capabilities most needed. Next to opportunistic vision, the one consistent indicator that separates the good from the great is this last focus on fostering warrior skills through challenging and appropriate training on all levels, as well as strong professional education programs. Training and education have universally been the key to accomplishing transformations; even more so than the introduction of new technologies into the operating forces or the crafting of successful new concepts and doctrine.

In every era, as the Marine Corps leaders were crafting their future course and capabilities, there were intense struggles between those who desired to maintain the status quo and the visionaries who were refocusing on the nation's future naval and littoral security interest. During the past two centuries, the Marine Corps has systematically transformed itself to better serve the nation's security objectives. Figure 5 illustrates the four evolutionary phases of the Marine Corps, from its rudimentary beginning as simply "soldiers of the sea" to its existence as the nation's principal "force-in-readiness."

SOLDIERS OF THE SEA	COLONIAL INFANTRY	AMPHIBIOUS ASSAULT FORCE	FORCE IN READINESS
			EXPEDITIONARY TASK FORCES OF COMBINED ARMS
		ADVANCED BASE FORCES/ FLEET MARINE FORCES	ADVANCED BASE FORCES/ FLEET MARINE FORCES
	PROTECT U.S. INTERESTS ABROAD	PROTECTION OF U.S. INTERESTS	PROTECTION OF U.S. INTERESTS
NAVAL SECURITY FORCES	NAVAL SECURITY FORCES	NAVAL SECURITY FORCES	NAVAL SECURITY FORCES
1775 - 1909	1899 - 1921	1921 - 1945	1945 - 20??

Figure 5

U.S. Marine Corps' Progressive Roles and Missions Expansions (Slide adapted from Marine Corps historical eras of service to the nation and courtesy of Marine Corps Archives).

The column headers across the top of the chart describe the warfighting role the Marine Corps provided the nation, which also defined its organization, equipment, and training focus. At the bottom is a range of dates that loosely defines identifiable phases. Of particular note is how the length of the span of years in each phase has seemed to consistently get shorter in the 20th century, reflecting the accelerated rate of change in the nation's strategic role in the world.

The second row from the bottom is a description of the principal naval contribution the Marine Corps made during the period, specifically focused on the contribution to the Navy rather than an amphibious, expeditionary, or a joint role. A steady refocus away from the traditional service as shipboard security is clearly depicted with an implicit increase in a sense of competition for resources within the

Department of the Navy as the Marine Corps identifies a unique service mission separate from that of a supporting naval one.

The third row from the bottom depicts the assumption of a mission ashore outside the traditional soldiers of the sea inherent in providing boarding parties, landing forces, or security forces for advanced naval bases. Inherent in this assumed mission is the implicit separation of the Marine Corps force from command of the Navy's command at sea, with the requisite role of the Commandant in obtaining the necessary resources and force structure to assume this role.[2]

The fifth row from the bottom depicts the formation of the expeditionary task forces of combined arms that were established as Public Law in 1953, which also resulted in the requirement that the Marine Corps consist of three divisions and three aircraft wings and appropriate support forces. This unique identification in law of a service-force structure is tied specifically to the mission header at the top of the column on the right, explicitly assigning the Marine Corps a role as a force-in-readiness stemming from the experience of our armed forces at the outbreak of the Korean War, whereby the nation needed immediately responsive warfighting expeditionary capabilities to act while the nation mobilized.

Each new mission and capability developed to meet the challenges of the mission has taken shape and been institutionalized through the direct or benign support of a Commandant of the Marine Corps. Arguably, no innovation or change has been successfully mandated without the support of the Commandant and, in virtually every case, the innovation has come about only through the vision, leadership, and active advocacy of the Commandant for the change within the Department of the Navy and in the Congress.

Another factor in the successful introduction of top-down change by the Commandant has been the degree of clarity in which the incoming Commandant clearly articulates, early within his command, his vision of the direction of the Service. One of the favored ways some have done this is through publishing a *Commandant's Planning Guidance*. Regardless of the document, the most successful Commandants have universally been able to identify a direction for the Marine Corps and establish a program to progress toward a common goal.

In addition, the great Commandants have been able to capture the support of Congress either to defend the resources of the Marine Corps or to enable the innovative changes needed to transform the Marine Corps for the good of the nation. As the smallest of the armed services, the Marine Corps has survived a series of threats to its very existence, as it has competed with its siblings (the Army, Navy, and Air Force) for scarce resources. In every case, the current Commandant—often supported behind the scenes by former Commandants—have typically been the central figures in establishing congressional support.

The most significant recent challenge to the existence of the Marine Corps occurred almost immediately after World War II, when President Harry S. Truman proposed a reorganization of the Department of Defense along functional lines implicitly eliminating—if not reducing to insignificance—the Marine Corps. Significantly, as it relates to the role of the Commandant, the critical decision point was the May 10, 1946, testimony of then-Commandant General A.A. Vandegrift, who pointedly referred the case for the Marine Corps to the Congress. After illustrating what the Marine Corps had demonstrated to be its values to the country, he concluded with the following:

> "The Marine Corps thus believes it has earned this right to have its future decided by the legislative body which created it—nothing more. … The bended knee is not a tradition of our Corps. If the Marine as a fighting man has not made a case for himself after 170 years, he must go. But I think you will agree with me that he has earned the right to depart with dignity and honor, not by subjugation to the status of usefulness and servility planned for him by the War Department[3]."

Although this intervention by General Vandegrift was successful and staved off the immediate challenge, the Marine Corps remained under ferocious attack up until the opening of the Korean War because it did not fit the perceived needs of the national strategy in the post-war period. After World War II, the focus of our national strategy was the expanding threat of Soviet overwhelming armor and mechanized forces facing Western Europe and NATO.

At the same time, the Bikini Atoll nuclear test made it difficult to envision WWII amphibious operations with emphasis on mass and the concentration of forces. General Vandegrift, a true innovator at heart, recognized the threat and appointed a special board to make a thorough examination of the relationship between nuclear weapons and amphibious operations. It was the board's conclusion that it would be necessary to make radical changes in its ship-to-shore operations. The board believed that the amphibious forces, if widely dispersed, could be successful against an enemy with nuclear weapons. Both the Commandant and the board quickly concluded that the "vertical-envelopment" assault gave new life to amphibious operations. However, there was little interest within the War Department or Congress that such an experiment with vibrating helicopters was taking place, while the national strategy was focused on the European theater and the Russians' ominous threat to the West.

The U.S. Army was to be the centerpiece to America's defense. The single national focus was "NATO first." There was little thought for naval and maritime forces, particularly the Marine Corps. By 1950, as North Korea crossed over the border and marched on Seoul, the Marine Corps had declined to a total force structure of approximately 75,000 Marines.

In the midst of preparations for Korea, the issue of the Commandant's role in the Joint Chiefs of Staff led to President Truman's ill-timed and rapidly rescinded remarks about the Marine Corps' "Stalinesque propaganda apparatus." In any event, the 1st Provisional Marine Brigade's performance at the Pusan perimeter in August 1950, and the 1st Marine Division's participation in the landing at Inchon and recapture of Seoul that September, followed by the Chosin Reservoir campaign of November-December enhanced the Marines' reputation as a ready force. They were acknowledged as adroit practitioners of amphibious warfare and combined arms combat under varied conditions of weather and terrain.

Lemuel C. Shepherd was Commandant when Gray got out of boot camp and shipped out to his first duty station. Shepherd, a distinguished combat commander in World War II, assumed the command, like Vandegrift, of a war-footing Marine Corps with an active strength that had, due to the war, grown rapidly to a total of 235,000 in January 1952. By July 1953, the Korean armistice ended two and a half years of inconclusive, linear warfare reminiscent of World War I. The U.S. Marine Corps would redeploy its third division/wing team, first to Japan and then to US-administered Okinawa in readiness for Far Eastern contingencies without fear of demobilization. The hard-won Marine Corps amphibious expertise from World War II again demonstrated, together with mobilization readiness and versatile combat effectiveness in the first months of Korea, institutional stability with which to face the post-war belt-tightening of the Eisenhower administration's "new look."

Due in no small part to the strong advocacy by the Commandant and former Commandants with the Congress, in 1953, Congress enacted Public Law 416, providing that the Marine Corps "l be organized as to include not less than three combat divisions and three aircraft wings."[4] It is under these provisions that the Marine Corps exists and operates today in this 21st century.

The string of heroic war Commandants came to an end with the appointment of Randolph McCall Pate as Commandant in 1956. Pate was a proven staff officer with service in the 1st Marine Division at Guadalcanal and its commander during the last of the Korean fighting. His team membership was further reinforced by his having graduated from the Virginia Military Institute, as had his predecessor; however, his professional stature was distinctly lessened by not having experienced major combat command in World War II. Unlike his immediate predecessors, he did not have the unquestioned hero stature inside or outside of the Marine Corps.[5]

Pate had been in office less than four months when the most serious institutional challenge to the Marine Corps since the battle for survival in 1947 confronted the new Commandant. In April 1956, in an incident known as "Ribbon Creek," six recruits drowned during an unauthorized night march by a drill instructor (DI) who had been drinking on duty at the Marine Corps Recruit Depot, Parris Island, South Carolina. The DI had been using unofficial but customary means to enhance what he saw as flagging discipline among his recruits, who were well into their training cycle at the rifle range. Pate personally traveled to Parris Island, and in an unexpected but probably wise exercise of institutional openness, put the Marine Corps on trial before the forum of public opinion concurrent with the court-martial proceedings against Staff Sergeant Matthew C. McKeon. Later, Pate initiated a program of sweeping reforms of recruit training that ended broad enlisted drill instructor discretion and latitude and included expanded commissioned-officer supervision of the training process, rigorous screening and training of drill instructor candidates, special training for substandard recruits, and upgraded and systematized physical training.[6]

Pate was a conserver by nature, nostalgic over the legacy of the past. With the permanent tenfold expansion over pre-Pearl Harbor strength, he led an institutional nostalgia for the smaller, familiar Marine Corps of the 1930s and the interwar period with its emphasis on formative schooling, expeditionary commitments, and sea duty. This included many of the revived traditions of this period, such as the enhanced ceremonial role of the Marine Barracks in Washington and the restoration of the old traditional "officers mess night." President Dwight D. Eisenhower reached over nine senior Generals to select Major General David Monroe Shoup as

Commandant in January 1960.[7] Shoup was a veteran of the bloodiest World War II battle at Tarawa, where, as a Colonel, he had exercised immediate command on the beach and earned the Medal of Honor. Moreover, Shoup had been pivotal in the implementation of recent major changes in recruit training and was a recognized hero. However, subordinates remembered prewar peccadilloes, such as the hard-driving command of Quantico's Basic School for new officers during Korea, and all-night high-stakes poker games when he was the Commanding General, 3rd Marine Division, stationed on the island of Okinawa. Shoup's populist Indiana farmboy persona contrasted with those of his urbane, largely southern predecessors. Shoup's assertive approach was complemented by Wallace M. Greene's headquarters savvy, but he still lacked vision and was not a supporter of the nascent vertical assault concept that had been 20 years in development. Like Pate, Shoup never perceived its potential in future naval operations in the littorals of the world. The world about him was entering a new era of warfare, but he hung tightly to conventional warfare doctrine, even while permitting innovative efforts led by others to go on. It would be up to his successors to make dramatic adjustments to new doctrine and operational capabilities. Visionary Marines, led by then-Colonel Keith B. McCutcheon, completed the final development of the use of the helicopter as a viable concept. Without enthusiasm, Shoup assented to the embryonic commitment of Marine helicopters and advisors to South Vietnam. General Shoup did not grasp the full potential of helicopters' mobility on future battlefields. Once Marine units were in South Vietnam and deployed into a counterinsurgency war, he still adamantly resisted the placement of machine guns on helicopters for self-defense use by aircrews.

Wallace M. Greene succeeded Shoup in 1964, and he continued the momentum of innovation within the Marine Corps, even with a change of presidents. However, he was soon involved in the mobilization of the Marine Corps for duty in Vietnam that may well have camouflaged whether he would have turned out to be an innovator. Instead, faced with a vacillating president, it would fall to Greene, in his advisory role as a member of the Joint Chiefs of Staff, to maintain firm and cool professionalism in the face of presidential vectoring and White House micro-management. As the Commandant, Naval Academy graduate Greene would oversee the expansion of the Marine Corps from 1965's 190,000 to a high of 310,000 in 1968—ultimately deploying two divisions and elements of a third, with a major logistical command and an aircraft wing to reach a peak total of 85,000 Marines. These Marines would conduct local pacification, counter-guerilla, and combined arms warfare against indigenous Viet Cong insurgents and North Vietnamese army regular formations in the northern provinces of South Vietnam and the adjacent, misnamed Demilitarized Zone (DMZ). The stateside Marine Corps eroded to a marginally ready base for the manpower demands of an individual rotation policy of initially 13-month and later one-year combat tours, with mounting casualties and no reserve mobilization.

Leonard Fielding Chapman became the 24th Commandant in 1968—at the height of the Vietnam conflict. He was a perfectionist artilleryman, graduated from the University of Florida, and had commanded 1st Marine Division battalions in World War II Pelelieu and Okinawa campaigns. General Chapman was a quiet man from Tennessee. He was a leader all sought to serve under, a man who was comfortable with people from all walks of life, from the rank of private to President of the United States. As President Lyndon B. Johnson's selection for Commandant in January 1968, he was a compromise alternative to dynamic, widely known Lieutenant General Victor Krulak, then commanding Fleet Marine Force, Pacific, who was generally thought to be the natural successor to Greene, but was seen in Washington to have been too closely tied to the President John F. Kennedy administration to be acceptable to the new Johnson administration.

Chapman's command would be characterized by unprecedented internal institutional stress occasioned by the challenge of sustaining

Marine professionalism and high standards in the face of an unpopular war, political and social unrest at home, and the infiltration of society's racial troubles into its uniformed ranks, even within the Marines. Lieutenant Colonel Ronald H. Spector, USMCR (Retired), in his biography of General Chapman, recalled, "A common observation of the times was that there were three types of Marines: those in Vietnam, those recently returned, and those on orders to go." When Chapman became Commandant, the Marine Corps was staffed with more than 300,000, the highest since World War II, and the quality of Marines suffered.[8]

Within six months of Chapman's assuming the command, the Tet Offensive began. The Tet Offensive was one of the largest military campaigns of the Vietnam War, launched on January 30, 1968, by the Viet Cong and North Vietnamese Army against the South Vietnamese Army and U.S. forces throughout South Vietnam. The attacks began on the Tet holiday, the Vietnamese New Year. This began the retreat from what ultimately was seen as a flawed foreign policy. More than a year of combat and heavy casualties followed the Tet Offensive until the beginning of the phased redeployment of Marines to their peacetime bases.

A strong conserver, Chapman fully comprehended the unrest and antimilitary feelings sweeping the nation and the unrelenting pressure mounted on him. To these oppressors, he responded with his edict pronouncement, "Marines don't do that." His mandate to hold the line on its traditional high standards of personal and professional conduct helped quiet the insistent cries for Marines to "go along with the times." With the war's falling manpower demands, redeployment decreased, and casualties dwindled, authority was granted for commanders to expeditiously separate many disciplinary-problem Marines. Through his tenure, Chapman skillfully reduced its strength by more than 100,000.[9]

Chapman's leadership combined bold initiatives of acceptance of minorities' racial and cultural differences with an insistence on adherence to traditional standards of discipline, fitness, and military courtesy among all Marines. In many ways, General Chapman followed the style of General Lejeune when, back in the 1920s, he arrested the downward institutional trend that had threatened the Marine Corps' continued usefulness to the nation. Both had been the right Commandant for the times.

Annapolis-trained Robert Everton Cushman was truly a politically anointed successor in the sense of his special standing with then-President Richard Nixon. Years earlier, Cushman had served as the Military Assistant to Vice President Nixon. From this close association, the President knew that General Cushman's service career had a strong record of combat leadership in World War II, which continued into Vietnam, where, as a Lieutenant General, he commanded the field army-sized III Marine Amphibious Force in the northern provinces of Vietnam. However, he failed to receive acceptance as a hero within the Marine Corps or the gravities to build on his special relationship with the President.

Historically, every Commandant publishes his *Command Guidance,* which lays out his priorities, vision of the future, and how he wants the Marine Corps to be structured and operationally ready for future commitments. On January 1, 1972, General Cushman released a message to all Marines, but it lacked detail. He simply stated the following: "We will continue to take care of our own. To be squared away. To perform outstandingly as our country's number one combat-ready fighting force."

In reflection, this was pretty shallow and fleeting command guidance to a corps of warriors. As the months passed, little additional guidance was provided. His focus was more often centered on White House events and its political and social activities and less often on his operational forces. Cushman retired six months short of his full four-year term because of a quirk in retirement law, after the credibility of the selection process for his successor had been compromised in what was widely perceived as a "Byzantine headquarters" power struggle that had exposed blatant careerism among certain of the Marine Corps senior leadership. The Marine Corps was seemingly searching for direction, and new leadership was needed. As so often happened, the Marine Corps seemed to have several of the right men for the times waiting in the wings.

Cushman was replaced, in turn, by two Southern gentlemen heroes who proved to have strong conservative principles that returned the Marine Corps to its pre-Vietnam disciplined character. The first was Battle for Guam Medal of Honor recipient Louis Wilson, but Robert Barrow was well known as his anointed successor, even as Wilson assumed the role of Commandant in June 1975. Both were firm traditionalists, popular selections as hero Commandants, and both received immediate acceptance within the Marine Corps. We were all looking for leadership, and Wilson and Barrow gave us eight consecutive years of stability and focus.

Wilson began his conserver command with his *Command Guidance* laid out in a very short sentence: "I call upon all Marines to get in step, and to do it smartly." This directive and his highly popular institution, the expeditious discharge program, produced results. The program allowed unit commanders to discharge substandard Marines, those with repeated disciplinary offenses and court-martials, who failed to live up to traditional Marine Corps standards of discipline and excellence. In lieu of the established time-consuming procedure of prosecution, the new process enabled discharges within 48 hours. With this mandate in place, every Marine Corps unit was able to purge its documented troublemakers with less than an Honorable Discharge. It was a new beginning, and almost immediately, the heavy burden of pending judicial actions was removed, stability returned in the barracks, and unit training improved.

General Wilson was a visionary who saw the need for increased combined arms training. To plan and prepare for the future in terms of enhanced readiness and mobility, Generals Wilson and Barrow adjusted the Marine Corps' deployment patterns and refocused our global flexibility to support NATO's defensive mission on the margins including northern Norway. This resulted in a series of amphibious exercises for units based on the East Coast of the United States in which Marine Air-Ground Task Forces (MAGTFs) of increasing size were deployed under a NATO command in a combined allied environment and set the stage for the exercises that, on General Barrow's watch, Major General Gray would show his Generalship in the series of NATO BOLD GUARD exercises discussed in previous chapters.

Wilson also had the profound vision to direct that the vast but little-used desert base at Twentynine Palms in California become the primary site for the live fire training of the Corps' air-ground combined arms teams. These combined arms exercises (CAXs) proved to be so successful they became the premier live fire training evolution for ten MAGTFs and more than 20,000 Marines each year. The CAXs became an invaluable tool in inculcating into every unit leader the uniqueness and operational value of the air-ground team. The historic value of General Wilson's decision to strengthen the training opportunities of the aviation-ground-logistics units has been proven repeatedly over the past three decades.

In a precursor to the clarion call of Al Gray, Wilson called upon the Marine Corps to retain its special competence in amphibious operations while broadening its capabilities as a "general purpose" force. He aimed to prepare the Marine Corps for global missions and to restore its elitist image. In no small part because of this recognized image, it was during Wilson's command that the Commandant of the Marine Corps finally became a full member of the Joint Chiefs of Staff, with authority to advise the President and Secretary of Defense on all matters, not just those affecting the Marine Corps. This had been a long and difficult 35-year battle, and Louis Wilson was the strong, articulate leader who made it happen. Colonel David H. White Jr., USMCR (Retired), in his biography on Wilson, captured his true image when he described General Wilson thus: "As Commandant, Wilson's military professionalism, his leadership style, his tremendous capacity for involvement with people, and his political finesse combined to create a veritable deus ex machine that would retrieve the Marine Corps from its Vietnam legacy, and permit it to survive its organizational crisis of the 1970s."[10]

Succession on June 29, 1979, by General Robert Barrow as the Commandant was a continuation of the same strong conserver command that had marked the Wilson tenure. Like Wilson, Barrow was a Southern gentleman with strong hero credentials from his service in World War II with the Chinese guerillas, Silver Star and Navy Cross awards for his heroism in Korea, and his near-mythic success as a regimental commander in operation Dewey Canyon during Vietnam. During the last two years of General Wilson's tenure, General Barrow was reassigned to Headquarters Marine Corps and assumed the position of Assistant Commandant. Brigadier General Edwin Simmons, USMC (Retired), in writing Barrow's biography, identified how the two had been closely associated for many years and, "To a large extent that they had been formed in the same mold. Both were courtly men whose dignified good manners cloaked firm purpose and iron resolve. Together these two giants created a special era for the Marine Corps."[11]

General Barrow specifically expressed concern at the lack of amphibious ships and the slowness in which obsolescent amphibious ships were being replaced. His efforts meshed nicely with then-Secretary of the Navy John Lehman's goal of a 600-ship Navy. Not surprisingly, General Barrow was present in August 1981 at the keel-laying of the USS *Whidbey Island*, the first new amphibious dock landing ship (LSD 41), and it was during his command that the Marine Corps returned to exercising large-scale amphibious operations.[12]

General Barrow continued General Wilson's personnel programs to rebuild the core of the Corps. Additionally, he foresaw the need for the Marine Corps to prepare for conflicts in which its air-ground units would have to oppose armor and mechanized forces. He expanded the CAX training program from 12 to 19 days of live fire and maneuver operations. This was a historic break with traditional doctrine in that Marine units would no longer be physically linked across the forward battle line. It was the first step toward introducing maneuver warfare inland after an amphibious landing. Had General Barrow not given this his personal and sustained high priority interest, this, like other advances in the Marine Corps' operational capabilities, would probably never have evolved.

Barrow had the gravitas and stature to overpower dissention by the few traditionalists. Their disagreements were never direct but shrouded behind the long-term additional wear on amphibious and wheeled vehicles, and increased operating costs. I saw this firsthand during my assignment running the CAX program. At one point, he listened gravely while staff officers indicated that they would have to shorten the CAX because higher-level headquarters had unknowingly mandated limits on operating hours of all amphibious tractors. Afterward, Barrow looked over at me, Colonel Turley, and quietly said, "You go right ahead and train as you need to." That was the end of traditionally minded staff officers who were quietly attempting to counter his earlier guidance to conduct mechanized and armor maneuvers. This onsite decision reverberated throughout the Corps, confirming that the Amphibious Assault Vehicle (AAV) would be used as the primary troop mobility vehicle for all CAXs. It was the beginning of creating a mobile ground element for the MAGTF.

General Barrow continued his frequent visits to units undergoing CAX training. The live fire exercises made the emphasis clear, ensured that the importance of the CAX to the Marine Corps was reflected by the personal attention and involvement of its leader, and would be precursor to similar hands-on efforts by Gray during his commandancy.

(As a personal note, after my return from the 1973 Arab-Israeli battlefield, I was directed by HQMC to give a briefing throughout the Marine Corps' operating forces on my personal insights on the impact of the Middle East War on Marine Corps operations. General Barrow invited me to his headquarters in Norfolk, Virginia, to brief his Fleet Marine Force (FMF) Atlantic staff. Several years later, in 1976, after I was reassigned to the 2nd Marine Division, General Barrow again invited me to speak at different professional events.

Later, when I took command of the 2nd Marine Regiment, I established a "tank-killer" field training exercise, because I felt infantry units needed to better understand their "close-in" role when contesting enemy armor. Each of the regiment's rifle companies was put through a four-day training period. The tank-killer training captured General Barrow's interest, and he would often visit unexpectedly. When he was a company commander during the Korean War, he had personally battled and destroyed Russian-made T-34 tanks at extremely close range. Barrow expressed solid enthusiasm for this new anti-armor training and wanted to have it expanded to the other two infantry regiments. As a final note, when he became the 27th Commandant, he would later have a direct impact on the future of my military career. Although I never thought about it at the time, I have to assume that this innovative anti-armor training, and my two years of experiences working with Gray on mechanized operations sealed my last duty assignment.)

General "Bob" Barrow's style epitomized a type of quiet professional leadership by an unquestioned warrior. He was a natural unifier, and his tenure was one of the most respected and successful. Where other Commandants aspired to unify their General officers, he styled his leadership to motivate the Corps' Board of Directors. In a manner of speaking, he accomplished this rare achievement with style. Everyone wanted to be on General Barrow's team. He made everyone feel that whatever job or position they held, it was important. His center of gravity for all to follow was well defined, his management style was caring, and he strived to stay in touch with his senior subordinate commanders.

General Barrow's successor in 1983 was Paul X. Kelley, a product of the Villanova Naval Reserve Officer Training Corps, who had commanded the last infantry regiment deployed on the ground in Vietnam. As a junior Colonel on his second tour, he was already identified as a highly competitive fast-tracker in the promotion sweepstakes. As a Lieutenant General, he was selected to command the newly activated Rapid Deployment Joint Task Force, the Florida-based command structure for Middle East operations that would evolve into U.S. Central Command. From this assignment he assumed the command in July 1983 under the supportive civilian leadership of Secretary of Defense Caspar W. Weinberger and Secretary of the Navy John F. Lehman.

Kelley inherited the ongoing commitment of a Marine Expeditionary Unit (MEU) in support of U.S. policy on the ground in violent, faction-torn Lebanon. On October 23, 1983, the truck bombing of the MEU's headquarters building in Beirut occurred, and 241 Americans, mostly Marines, died. As Commandant and a member of the Joint Chiefs of Staff, Kelley had, in fact, not been in the chain of operational command above the lost Marines. His statement was correct, but the manner in which he made his declarative statement to that fact in his congressional testimony led to difficult congressional and public relations for the remainder of his term.

General Kelley's greatest contribution to his Corps was his active pursuit of the Maritime Prepositioning Ships (MPS) program. It envisioned preloaded and regionally positioned flotillas of ships loaded with enough equipment for a Marine Expeditionary Brigade, and it was visionary. This initiative was originally viewed by many Marines as a threat to reduce the number of amphibious ships. But less than a decade later, strategically-placed flotillas of embarked tanks, amphibious assault craft, artillery pieces, trucks, and tons of logistics support validated the MPS program as a decided advantage when the Persian Gulf crisis of 1990 began to evolve into an all-out conflict. MPS was subsequently adopted by the three other services.

During the final year of General Kelley's command, Congress passed the 1986 Goldwater-Nichols Department of Defense Reorganization

Act. This was the largest reorganization of the Department of Defense since 1947 and was a commentary on the growing importance of joint operations as compared to service campaigns. At first, the focus was on strengthening the duties of the Chairman, Joint Chiefs of Staff (CJCS) and curtailing the historic roles of the four Service Chiefs and Service Secretaries. For the first time, the Chairman was given the authority to override the Service Chiefs.[13] In addition, the Goldwater-Nichols Act required that all candidates for promotion to general or flag rank must have served in a joint duty assignment, and all officers recommended for promotion to four stars must first be evaluated by the Chairman, Joint Chiefs of Staff, as to their performance in joint assignments. In case this refocusing on joint capabilities was not already apparent, the Act, as it was further amended, included a restructuring of special operations forces to include establishing both the Office of the Assistant Secretary of Defense for Special Operations/Low-Intensity Conflict and a mandate directing that the Marine Corps develop a special operations force (SOF) capability.

A new age of joint operations was born, enacted by the Congress, and over the objections of the services. It was left to Gray as the incoming Commandant of the Marine Corps to sort out how the Corps would have to adapt to this new strategic context while struggling to obtain the resources for much-needed new capabilities, such as the tiltrotor V-22 replacement for the assault helicopter, the Advanced Amphibious Assault Vehicle (AAAV), and the Landing Craft Air Cushion (LCAC), all thought of as necessary to make amphibious operations viable against the threats of the 21st century.

The stage was set for a Commandant with a vision and a plan that would lead to a new "mission" for the Marine Corps beyond that of a force-in-readiness and task-organized forces of combined arms. The national strategy was changing, with a new appreciation for joint forces and new capabilities.[14] In Gray's journey as the Commandant, he would generate a series of changes that would ultimately effect new concepts, doctrine, operational capabilities, basic and advanced training, and professional educational programs. Gray's energies and intellect would impact the full spectrum of Marine Corps' missions. Gray was to be the leader, in his four years as Commandant, who would direct a major transformation of the Marine Corps and add another revolutionary new phase to our chart of Marine Corps missions, a phase whose significance is only now evident 27 years later.

CHAPTER 11
The Changing of Command

"For over 221 years our Corps has done two things for this great Nation. We make Marines, and we win battles."

General Charles C. Krulak
31st Commandant, U.S. Marine Corps

On July 1, 1987, Alfred M. Gray Jr. relieved General Paul X. Kelley as the Commandant of the U.S. Marine Corps. It was a solemn ceremony enacted on the close-cropped, grass-filled rectangle of the historic Post of the Corps, Marine Barracks at 8th and I Streets, Washington, DC. Kelley and Gray stood side by side during that momentous and silent time in the ceremony when the Marine Corps' colors, heavily shrouded with the ribbons and stars of more than 220 years of service to the nation were to be passed from the 28th to the 29th Commandant.

My wife, Bunny, and I had been seated a few rows up and directly behind the two Commandants and their ladies. In our wildest dreams, we never imagined receiving such an honor. It was the iconic moment in a rich and historic ceremony. The Sergeant Major of the Marine Corps carried the heavily-streamered colors to a point directly in front of General Kelley and presented the colors to the outgoing Commandant. Then, in a solemn moving and hushed moment, when the multicolored battle streamers and hundreds of campaign stars fluttered around the Marine Corps scarlet and gold flag emblazoned with the Marine Corps' eagle, globe, and anchor emblem, General Kelley turned to his left and extended the highly polished flagstaff to Gray. This ritual signaled the precise moment when command passed from one General to the other. Just a second before the transfer, a small breeze caused the flag to flare and extend, fully exposing the proud Marine Corps motto: *Semper Fidelis.*

For all present, it was an emotional moment in the 220-plus year history of the nation's Corps of Marines. Gray was succeeding a tremendous leader of Marines. On this day, General Kelley was closing out his active duty career—a career that began in June 1950 upon graduating from Villanova University and receiving his commission as a Second Lieutenant of Marines. He served as a company grade officer in the North Carolina-based 2nd Marine Division; later, as the executive officer, Marine detachment, cruiser USS *Salem* (CA-139); and then as commanding officer, Marine detachment, when the cruiser served as flagship of the U.S. Navy's 6th Fleet.

After overseas tours in Japan and Hawaii, Kelley returned to Camp Lejeune in December 1957. Shortly thereafter, he completed the U.S. Army's Airborne and Pathfinder Schools at Ft. Benning, Georgia, and was assigned to the newly activated 2nd Force Reconnaissance Company as the executive officer. Later, as the Commanding Officer of the 2nd Force, he actively participated in numerous parachute and SCUBA training operations. As a young professional officer and then as a Captain, he was recognized as one of the Marine Corps' future leaders. He was selected as the U.S. Marine Corps exchange officer with the British Royal Marines. As such, he commanded C Troop, 42nd Commandos in Singapore, Malaysia, Malta, and Borneo.

In 1961, he returned to the States and was assigned to Marine Corps schools at Quantico as tactics instructor at The Basic School for new Marine officers. When the Vietnam conflict expanded to include U.S. combat troops, Major Kelley was assigned as Assistant G-2 III Marine Amphibious Force. Later, he experienced combat as commander of one of the Corps' most famous units, 2nd Battalion, 4th Marine Regiment. Frequently tested, he was found fully capable of handling the demanding rigors of leadership in times of great stress. During this tour as battalion commander, he earned the Silver Star, two Bronze Stars, and the Legion of Merit. In 1970 and 1971, Colonel Kelley commanded the last regiment to see combat in the Vietnam War. Following Vietnam, he served in a pivotal assignment as aide to

General Lewis Walt, who later became the Assistant Commandant of the Marine Corps.

In August 1974, he was promoted to Brigadier General and assigned to command the 4th Marine Division. This was the Marine Corps' only inactive Individual Ready Reserve division. A gifted leader, he was reassigned to the Marine Corps Development and Education Command in Quantico as the Director of the Education Center. He was promoted to Major General and assigned to Headquarters Marine Corps (HQMC) as Deputy Chief of Staff for Requirements and Programs in quick succession, historically a stepping stone to greater responsibilities. In February 1980, he was promoted to Lieutenant General and appointed by President Jimmy Carter as the first Commander of the Rapid Deployment Joint Task Force, where he commanded elements of all four services.

Kelley was promoted to the rank of General and the job of Assistant Commandant of the Marine Corps on July 1, 1981. Two years later, on July 1, 1983, he became the 28th Commandant. General Kelley served his country faithfully for more than 37 years. Now, in July 1987, it was his time to close out his tenure as the Commandant and to pass the stewardship of the Corps on to another Marine General officer.

In the Marine Corps' 220-year history, only 28 other individuals had served as Commandant. Most had served their nation well. Their terms varied from a short year for Brevet Major Anthony Gale to the tenure of Lieutenant Colonel Archibald Henderson, who remained for 38 years. Indeed, Colonel Henderson lived in the Commandant's house so long (from 1820 to 1859) that when he died, it was often rumored, but not true, that he willed the Commandant's government quarters to his heirs. Long known for their judicious use of U.S. government money, it would be the Marine Corps and not Colonel Henderson's heirs who would retain the quarters. Historically, the home of the Commandant is known as the oldest continuously inhabited house in the District of Columbia. It is a stately three-story, white brick, wood-frame house located on the north end of the Marine Barracks rectangle, where all Commandants have lived since 1814.

The date for the changeover of Commandants had been set months earlier, but none of the General officers who were first recommended and who had perhaps been expected to assume the most senior position within the Marine Corps were to be featured on the parade field this day. Instead, an outsider had been chosen by President Ronald Reagan to serve this prestigious four-year assignment. An individual who, four months earlier had submitted the customary letter for permission to retire, was now standing front and center, ready to begin his stewardship as America's leader of the "soldiers of the sea."

In recent times, the established path to the Commandant's house had always included several tours of duty at Headquarters Marine Corps. Then, after selection to the General officer level, additional tours at Headquarters with assignments in the major directorates of manpower, requirements, and programs; plans, policy, and operations; or on congressional liaison matters had proved to be the best assurance for further promotion. In contrast, General Al Gray had never been assigned to the Headquarters staff since his transfer to a field command assignment immediately after receiving his first star as a Brigadier General.

In 1987, the Marine Corps authorized only two positions, the Commandant and the Assistant Commandant, as four-star General officer billets. There were seven three-star Lieutenant General positions. All of these men were qualified for the position of Commandant; however, four stood out as the best of the best. General Thomas Morgan, Assistant Commandant, an aviator, was an exceptionally gifted, insightful, all-around knowledgeable officer who was liked by all Marines. He was a popular nominee.

Second candidate Lieutenant General Earnest Cheatham had been awarded the Navy Cross for his superb leadership in the epic battle for Hue City, Vietnam, during the Tet Offensive of 1968.

Third candidate Lieutenant General Dwayne Gray was assigned to the Headquarters staff in charge of manpower. Initially, the Secretary of the Navy favored Lieutenant General Dwayne Gray, a capable officer with a pattern of repeated, highly successful command and staff assignments at Headquarters Marine Corps (HQMC) and in the Fleet Marine Force.

Lieutenant General Joe Went, the fourth candidate, was then serving as Assistant Chief of Staff, Installations and Logistics, HQMC. A tall, polished New Englander, he had proven himself an exceptional skilled manager during numerous demanding assignments.

At the change of command ceremony, and prominently off to the side of the two Generals, Kelley and Al Gray, stood the recently congressionally-confirmed Secretary of the Navy, James H. Webb Jr. Even before Secretary Webb was confirmed Secretary of the Navy, he had called his predecessor, John Lehman, and requested that he be allowed to select the 29th Commandant, since he would be working with him. Lehman was in the process of reviewing the nominees when he elected to resign. He acquiesced to Webb's request. Webb then began his search for a special type of Marine General officer. He wanted a General from the old school with varied field experiences rather than one who had served in frequent assignments at Headquarters Marine Corps.

Jim Webb, a 1968 U.S. Naval Academy graduate, was a much-decorated veteran Marine officer from the Vietnam War who had been medically retired because of severe multiple wounds received in combat. Based on his personal wartime leadership experiences, plus his Senior Executive Service-level Department of Defense civilian leadership position, Webb had some strong convictions about the kind of leader who should be selected to command a Marine Corps of nearly 200,000 men and women. He set out to find a special Marine officer who was—first and foremost—a "warrior" with extensive combat experience.

Secretary Webb, an internationally recognized and accomplished author, lawyer, and student of history, was serving his country as the Secretary of the Navy only because he could no longer serve as a Marine officer. He set out in his lonely search for a Commandant. With a very select group of veteran Marines, he sought out the names of potential candidates, down to the two-star level. He and I had a series of discussions on this important selection process.

Webb was meticulous and thorough. His motive was to find the best-qualified person not only for the immediate four years but one who could set the stage for a vibrant Marine Corps to enter the 21st century. Secretary Webb invited me to his Pentagon office on several occasions to discuss his views about the future roles and missions of the Marine Corps in the 1990s. He beckoned several highly respected retired Marine Corps Commandants, also other senior Generals, and elicited their views on how the nation's Fleet Marine Forces should be trained and equipped to remain a viable force in the 21st century. Webb's questions would ultimately focus on who would serve the nation best as the next Commandant. Perhaps, just perhaps, it was the special opportunity in which he felt he was personally representing all those young enlisted Marines and corpsmen that he himself had led, bled with, and suffered the loss of during his own Vietnam experiences.

Like many others in the Department of the Navy, Secretary Webb was aware of Gray's reputation as a field commander. At a chance meeting in February after Webb had become the new Secretary, he asked Gray, prior to his forthcoming retirement, to provide him some thoughts on directions for the Marine Corps of the future. Gray understood that it was Webb's intention to use this input as he developed his guidance for the new Commandant after the nomination by the President and confirmation by the Congress. Drawing on the thoughts and experiences of his Atlantic and European commanders and staff personnel as well as colleagues from throughout the Corps, Al Gray quietly put together a comprehensive report to be provided at the Secretary's request.

On May 6, Secretary Webb asked Gray to visit him the next time he was in Washington. Gray replied that he was going to Fort Meade tomorrow in conjunction with the annual National Security Agency Travis Trophy Award to be given to the best Cryptologic Unit of the year. Although Gray did not mention this, his unit had been the first direct support signals intelligence command to win this prestigious award during one of his earlier tours in Vietnam. Webb then told Gray that he had some critical briefings to attend earlier and asked him to meet in his office at 1500 hours. After attending the awards ceremony the following day, Gray skipped the traditional luncheon, telling his aide, Major Bart DeForrest, that he wanted to get out of the Pentagon as soon as possible after the meeting and return to Norfolk because of the current pending crisis in Haiti.

Shortly after 1300, during the trip from Fort Meade, Maryland, to the Pentagon, Secretary of Defense Caspar Weinberger's office called to see if Gray could meet with the Secretary around 1315 hours for about 15 minutes. Gray replied that they were about 15 to 20 minutes away and would be there as quickly as possible. Gray had met with Weinberger during his previous visits to the field, and upon being ushered into his office, was greeted with his usual, "Before we start, tell me how your people are doing." Gray had always had a deep admiration for the Secretary's genuine concern for the country's warriors.

Weinberger then confided that senior civilian and military officials, including certain distinguished retirees, were in disagreement as to who should be recommended for the next commandancy. He went on to say that the three Generals under consideration were General Tom Morgan, Lieutenant General Dwayne Gray and Lieutenant General Ernie Cheatham and that he would appreciate any views that Gray may have. Gray responded that all three Generals would be superb Commandants who would serve the Department of Defense and the nation with distinction. He further elaborated that in the case of Tom

Morgan, he had a wealth of air-ground experience and had performed brilliantly in a variety of command and staff assignments. Further, he was a master of the budgetary process as well as the Washington scene and enjoyed a superb professional reputation among the other services. He also was aware of the Secretary's admiration for Morgan and was able to reinforce Weinberger's view.

With respect to Dwayne Gray, he considered him a consummate and seasoned professional who had performed exceptionally well in every command and staff billet through the years, and they had been good friends since their times as Lieutenants together in Korea. He was Al Gray's counterpart in the Pacific and, as such, commanded all the Marine forces there as part of the Marine Corps' largest field command. Further, Dwayne had held key staff positions of great responsibility at Headquarters and in the Pentagon. His distinguished service in all assignments, combined with his knowledge of Departments of Navy and Defense processes and his facility for maintaining harmonious relationships, made him an outstanding candidate.

However, Al Gray continued, if the Secretary was looking for a highly decorated combat leader with a superb record in command and staff assignments at all levels through the years, then he should look no further than Ernie Cheatham, who was commanding the First Marine Expeditionary Force. Gray related how he was present at the Marine Barracks in Washington in 1967 when Cheatham was presented the Navy Cross for heroism at the Battle of Hue City in Vietnam. Gray recounted this heroic act for the Secretary knowing that he had a special appreciation for these matters. Gray and Cheatham had also worked together to develop and standardize operational procedures among the three Marine expeditionary forces and he was well aware of his broad knowledge. Gray also told the Secretary that the officers and men idolized Ernie Cheatham and would follow him anywhere.

The Secretary then asked for Al Gray's thoughts on future Marine Corps challenges with respect to our national strategy posture. Discussions first covered the NATO and the Soviet-Warsaw Pact, followed by the Middle East and Africa. The conversation then shifted to the Pacific including the Far East and Asia. Naval and maritime strategic concepts were also covered throughout the nearly 90-minute session.

Gray then hustled down the Pentagon's E Ring corridor for his three o'clock meeting with Secretary Webb. This session went pretty much along the lines of the meeting with Secretary Weinberger except that there was much more detail because Jim Webb was not only a Marine but one of the most cerebral persons Gray had ever met. As he did with Secretary Weinberger, Gray recounted his view on all three of the candidates for Commandant as well as his thoughts on the future of the Corps and what should be done. Gray also expressed his views on the national strategy and the role of naval forces within the context of their maritime strategy. After about two hours, Gray thanked the Secretary for the opportunity to express his thoughts and reminded him that he was preparing a document for Secretary Webb to use if he desired. Gray then departed the Pentagon for Norfolk and boarded the amphibious flagship USS *Mount Whitney* that evening in preparation for possible contingency action in Haiti.

Later, and unknown to Gray, after he had departed, Weinberger remarked to Major General Colin Powell, his Senior Military Assistant, and Lieutenant Colonel Rich Higgins that "General Al Gray is the Marine Corps' General Vessey." The search for the 29th Commandant was over. Powell and Higgins both knew how much Weinberger admired U.S. Army General John Vessey, then serving as Chairman of the Joint Chiefs of Staff. He was a true no-nonsense, up-from-the-ranks Soldier. It was immediately obvious to them whose name would be passed on to the White House for the President's approval and then on to the Senate for confirmation.

During the next several weeks, as the search process went on, Gray stayed busy in the field. The Haitian crisis had subsided and his forces were heavily committed for the annual East Coast joint exercise named SOLID SHIELD in which all the armed forces participated.

In early June his helicopter flew to the airfield at Marine Corps Air Station New River where it was refueled. While there, Gray received a phone call from Secretary Webb telling him that he had been picked for nomination to be the next Commandant. On June 16, Secretary Weinberger called in the evening and informed Gray that President Reagan had nominated him to be a member of the Joint Chiefs of Staff and the next Commandant of the Marine Corps.

On June 28, 1987, the Senate Armed Services Committee unanimously approved Lieutenant General Alfred Mason Gray Jr. as the 29th Commandant of the U.S. Marine Corps. Gray was subsequently confirmed by the Senate to the rank of full General and became the Commandant of the Marine Corps effective July 1, 1987.

Beyond the nation's highest level of decisionmakers, Gray's selection for the position of Commandant was completely unexpected. Within the Marine Corps and the Department of the Navy, some compared it to the surprise appointment of Admiral Elmo Zumwalt as the Chief of Naval Operations (CNO) in July 1968. At HQMC, Secretary Webb's announcement was so surprising that no temporary government quarters had been arranged for a new four-star General officer who was not already living in the local area. When Gray arrived in the Washington area, he was temporarily lodged in a local hotel, a situation unheard of for a future Service Chief. What he quickly discovered was that the Commandant's house was undergoing a massive restoration and that it would be months before he and Jan were able to move in. The Grays moved into other quarters within the 8th and I Streets Compound until the Commandant's home was reopened.

The selection of each U.S. military Service Chief is traditionally a much-drawn-out and stressful ritual. Normally appointed for four years, the final year for each potential appointee generates, by its very process, an internal stress among old friends as to who will be picked from the many contenders. Successive tours of duty over three decades had always brought the Corps' small number of senior Generals and their families into an exceptionally close-knit group. This camaraderie historically generates an unfailing alchemy that molds all Marines into a "band of brothers" and creates a uniqueness that does not exist in any other Service. There are no "branch" or occupational specialty groups, e.g., submarine, aviation, or surface warfare designations, which are associated with the other services: just one Corps of Marines. There is a universal recognition and commitment that one Marine Corps must prevail over all other conditions. "To the Corps" is more than just words. It's a way of life. It's a living tradition.

When the decision was finally announced as to who would serve as the 29th Commandant, all Marine Corps General officers understood that, at that historic instant during the change of command ceremony when the colors are passed, they too would render their abiding loyalty to the new man in the corner office.

The greatest example of this loyalty and professionalism would be demonstrated at Headquarters Marine Corps by General Tom Morgan, Assistant Commandant. He never knew it for certain, but he had been a close finalist. General Morgan had never campaigned for the position; however, he was hopeful that he might become the first Marine aviator ever to become Commandant. When informed of Al Gray's appointment, it was he who immediately assembled the Headquarters staff and announced President Reagan's decision. And it was he who reminded everyone present of the critical need to get behind the new Commandant and loyally serve him, and the nation, as all Marines have done for more than two centuries. General Morgan never showed personal disappointment nor did he pause in his service to his Corps. Instead, he drove himself harder, and in doing so was of immeasurable assistance to Gray during his first year of transition.

Hopefully, history will someday better record and illuminate the tremendous contributions General Tom Morgan made during his nearly 40 years as a Marine officer. Tom Morgan was the epitome of a professional Marine officer as demonstrated by his exemplary military service to his country. What will certainly stand out among his many achievements will be his extremely loyal and dedicated service to two Commandants.

Imaginative by nature—"Al," as he called himself—Gray had long been recognized for his innovative thinking, keen intellect, and sheer tenacious stamina to complete the difficult missions assigned. "He is good," it was often said, "but not seasoned in the arena of Washington or of the high visibility that is woven into every aspect of the day-to-day business for a Service Chief."

Most of his contemporaries thought, and several prominent retired General officers spoke out, that Gray should not be the next Commandant. The position of Commandant was physically demanding, and he was too old, they said. He would be past the mandatory retirement age before his four years as Commandant were completed. They thought he had the wrong image for the Corps at that time of a rapidly declining defense budget. As a General, he had neither served at Headquarters Marine Corps nor in the Pentagon's Joint arena. Many believed that he had almost no association or testimonial experience with Members of Congress. This rumor was incorrect, as Gray had repeatedly been called to testify on a number of major acquisition programs.

Further, it was perceived that his lack of recognition on Capitol Hill would seriously impact his effectiveness in dealing with key congressional committees. There were also serious questions as to his executive management skills. The critics didn't really know Al Gray. His impatience with routine administrative paperwork was well known. The unspoken concern that was foremost in the minds of many observing the ceremony was "could Al Gray, a short, rough-cut, 'hard-as-nails' field Marine be an effective Commandant of the U.S. Marine Corps?"

The U.S. Marine Band brought everyone's attention back to the ceremony as the Barracks Commander called the formation to "Attention! Present arms!" The Marine Barracks ceremonial companies, smartly dressed in white caps, deep blue blouses with shining brass, and white trousers and all carrying rifles or swords stood facing the grandstands while the Marine Corps Band and Drum and Bugle Corps, positioned at one end of the parade field, responded to the Commanding Officer of the Barracks' clear commands.

With full pomp and precision, the ceremonial troop units stood ramrod straight as the flowing colors were brought forward and presented to General Kelley, who then passed the flag to Gray. They exchanged positions, Gray moving to the more senior right side. The Marine Corps had its 29th Commandant. After the Sergeant Major returned the Marine Corps colors to the Color Guard, both Generals made brief remarks.

During the 1980s, Gray had spoken to this nation many times about the unique role of the U.S. Marine Corps. He was not the first to do so: Lieutenant General Victor Krulak brilliantly described the Marine Corps' role in his seminal book *First to Fight*. Years earlier, Colonel Robert Heinl also wrote and spoke about the role of the Marine Corps in supporting our national security objectives. So too did Dr. Allen Millett, a USMC Reserve Colonel, in his classic book *Semper Fidelis*. More recently, Brigadier General Edwin Simmons, USMC (Retired), published numerous writings on the past and future role of the nation's "soldiers of the sea," prior to his death in 2007.

When the time came for Gray to speak, his thoughts reaffirmed the historic role of the Marine Corps as the nation's force-in-readiness. But at the same time, he injected a more personal mandate for every Marine to better appreciate their individual responsibilities to Corps and country. On June 30, 1987, Gray said, in part:

"This great nation loves her Corps of Marines. They pray for us. They support us. They fund us. They demand that you and I and all others like us be a little special. The nation demands that we are the best led, the best trained, the best disciplined, particularly self-disciplined, force on Earth. The nation demands that we teach nothing but winning in battle and in life. And, by God, you are going to make it happen in the years to come."

Many individuals attending the ceremony thought his insightful challenge was only words to fit the occasion. In the months and years to come, they would come to realize that their perception was wrong. His words came straight from the heart and expressed his beliefs that the U.S. Marine Corps must re-examine itself, and if it was found wanting, change was needed to better support the nation. Years earlier, Gray had related to a few close friends that the world was beginning to undergo eruptive and unprecedented changes and that the Corps must also change to deal with new threats to the United States. His words were not meant to criticize others but to lay out the tasks he saw as fulfilling the responsibilities of the 29th Commandant. He had recognized and personally accepted the greatest challenge of all—to change an institution steeped in tradition, doctrine, disciplined thought, regimentation, and long-established standard procedures.

The Marine Corps as an institution was functioning well at a peacetime pace, but the speed of world changes and the increasing threats from terrorists and expanding worldwide drug cartels would soon demand a realignment of the nation's national security priorities. Time would reveal how the unknown challenges that lay ahead during the next four years would measure the success of General Alfred M. Gray Jr. as the 29th Commandant. What was known on that historic day was that the world was erupting with unprecedented changes.

Of the world's three great superpowers, China was seething. The voices of their young were gathering and demanding a more democratic form of government. The Soviet Union's Communist-controlled society and economic system was in a visible state of collapse. Only the United States had a stable government, but its economy was slowing, and economists forecast a mild recession. The Third World nations were in economic and social unrest—rife with regional conflicts.

It was a period of great uncertainty as the immediate road ahead lay awash with rising issues for the world's leaders. It was an unstable world, where historic events such as the Berlin Wall tumbling and the ongoing dismantling of the Soviet Union were occurring at a record-setting pace. In the Soviet Bloc the world was erupting with religious and tribal fractionalizations. It was into this world that an individual, who was controversial within his own Corps of Marines, was to take the reins of leadership and begin reaffirming the role of the U.S. Marine Corps as the nation's force-in-readiness.

At the ceremony that day, no one could have foreseen that within three years the United States would mobilize more than 600,000 men and women from its active and reserve forces, go to war against Iraq, and win a lopsided military victory. History often records how one individual's appointment to a high-level position reveals that he was "the right man at the right time."

As the change of command ceremony concluded, it was readily apparent to all attending that General Al Gray was a different kind of leader than most other General officers present. In the months and years ahead, the 29th Commandant would become inherently involved in the post-Cold War's emerging world threats. Gray's extensive experience in the most secretive intelligence-gathering programs enabled him to have a leg up on many other senior General officers serving in the Department of Defense in the mid-1980s. His insight and in-depth knowledge of the world and its leaders would be recognized at the highest levels of government. Gray was often called upon to help develop national security policy and support military objectives. His stewardship and stalwart leadership would affect the Marine Corps and have considerable impact on how the U.S. forces would serve this great nation.

During the next four years, time and unanticipated events would record how Al Gray would perform as the 29th Commandant of the United States Marine Corps.

General Alfred M. Gray
29th Commandant of the U.S. Marine Corps.

Secretary of Defense Caspar W. Weinberger swearing-in General Alfred Gray as the 29th Marine Corps Commandant while Mrs. Gray holds the family Bible (Source: Marine Corps Photographic Archives).

President Ronald Reagan meeting with General Gray (Source: Marine Corps Photographic Archives).

Change of Marine Corps Commandants at Marine
Barracks, Washington, DC General Paul X. Kelley,
President George H.W. Bush, and General Gray
(Source: Marine Corps Photographic Archives).

Secretary of the Navy James Webb Jr. and his
wife, Mrs. Gray and General Gray at Marine
Corps Scholarship Foundation (Source:
Marine Corps Photographic Archives).

Former Commandants of the Marine Corps, Generals
Leonard Chapman, Louis Wilson, Robert Barrow,
Wallace Green and Paul X. Kelley with General Gray
(Source: Marine Corps Photographic Archives).

General Gray with Gerry and Bunny Turley in
the Commandant's Quarters in Washington, DC
(Source: Marine Corps Photographic Archives).

Groundbreaking ceremony at the General Alfred M. Gray
Marine Corps Research Center, Marine Base Quantico with
Brigadier General James Davis, Marine Corps University
President, Lieutenant General Paul Van Riper, Commanding
General, Marine Corps Combat Development Command and
General Gray (Source: Marine Corps Photographic Archives).

The General Alfred M. Gray Marine Corps Research
Center, Marine Corps Base, Quantico (Source:
Marine Corps Photographic Archives).

Entrenching tool used by General Gray in the groundbreaking ceremony of the General Alfred M. Gray Marine Corps Research Center, June 20, 1991 (Source: Marine Corps Research Center Archives).

General Gray with Beirut Commanders, Lieutenant Colonel Howard Gerlach, 1st Battalion, 8th Marine Regiment and Colonel Timothy Geraghty, 24th Marine Expeditionary Unit Commander at the Beirut Memorial, Jacksonville, NC (Source: Marine Corps Photographic Archives).

General Gray with the senior Marine Corps Generals in Saudi
Arabia (Source: Marine Corps Photographic Archives).

General Gray, on a tank, reenlisting Marines in Saudi
Arabia (Source: Marine Corps Photographic Archives).

General Gray, Secretary of the Navy "Larry" Garrett
and Lieutenant General Carl Mundy (Source:
Marine Corps photographic Archives).

Light Armored Vehicle (LAV) used in the Marine Corps
field test at Marine Corps Base Twentynine Palms, CA
(Source: Marine Corps Photographic Archives).

General Norman Schwarzkopf, Commander U.S. Forces in
Iraq War, with his assigned 15 Marine Corps Generals.
(Source: Marine Corps Photographic Archives).

Burning Iranian oil rig in the Persian Gulf during OPERATION
PRAYING MANTIS (April 1988) (Personal photograph by raid
commander Lieutenant Colonel Sam Brinkley, USMC [Retired]).

General Gray,
in his utility
uniform,
discussing
his Corps
of Marines
(Source:
Marine Corps
Photographic
Archives).

President George H.W. Bush, Chairman of the Joint
Chiefs of Staff Admiral William J. Crowe, U.S. Navy,
General and Mrs. Gray at Commandant's Garden
Party (Source: Marine Corps Photographic Archives).

General Alfred Mason Gray and Mrs. Jan Gray
in the Home of the Commandants (Source:
Marine Corps Photographic Archives).

CHAPTER 12
The First Year

"Never before have armies been challenged to assimilate the combined weight of so much change so rapidly. In this environment, the payoff will go to organizations which are versatile, flexible, and strategically agile, and to leaders who are bold, creative, innovative, and inventive. Conversely, there is an enormous risk in hesitation, undue precision, and a quest for certainty."

General Gordon R. Sullivan
U.S. Army Chief of Staff

There is no record of the exact time Gray arrived at his new office. What is known is that long before the sun's rays touched the roof of the Pentagon just half a mile away, Gray had already completed his move into the Commandant's corner office on the second deck of the Navy Annex, Henderson Hall. He was almost exploding with ideas and energy as he began reviewing his initial plans for action. Although Gray wanted to put his immediate attention on new warfighting concepts, integrating special operational capabilities, expanding the role of the Marine Corps in joint doctrine, and other operational issues, there were more pressing bureaucratic matters that demanded his full attention.

Assuming the position of Commandant greatly expanded Gray's scope of responsibilities. As a force commander, he was primarily responsible for the training of approximately 190,000 Marines and Sailors. His new responsibilities would now encompass all aspects of Title 10 U.S. Code to recruit, train, equip, and advance the operational readiness of more than 175,000 active duty personnel, 43,000 reservists, and more than 23,000 civilian employees. And he had now become the key decisionmaker for manpower issues and for the quality of the force. It was a gargantuan leap in responsibilities that would demand his close scrutiny of all matters relating to Marine Corps logistics and support structure of the Corps' widely dispersed bases, air stations, and maintenance depots.

Historically, a new Commandant is quietly selected at least 90 days before his assumption of command. He assembles a transition team that organizes the multiple briefings necessary to acquaint him with all Marine Corps matters, current and programmed for future years. In the case of Gray, he did not take any such preparatory steps because of his total commitment to his demanding duties and because he was not a candidate for selection to Commandant. The delay in selecting a successor to General Paul X. Kelley caused an extended period of unusual stress within Headquarters Marine Corps. The prevailing question was who was to be the next Commandant? In contrast to the normal process of early selection and a long period of preparatory time, fewer than three weeks now remained before the change in Commandants was to occur. This was an unheard-of situation.

Earlier in May, Gray had met with Secretary of Defense Caspar Weinberger. At that time, the Secretary was probably making his own assessment of the leading candidates to be the next Commandant. However, this topic was never broached; instead, the exchange centered on global strategic issues. Gray's special interest in intelligence and his long interest in potential worldwide threats enabled him to share his deep knowledge of strategic issues. Later, the Secretary shifted his focus to the Pacific region specifically, and here, too, Gray skillfully articulated his professional insights and thorough understanding of Asia. As Gray later recalled, Secretary Weinberger was surprised at the breadth of his global assignments and ability to recall specific details concerning geographical characteristics, social and economic factors, and rising threats to regional stability in Asia. It was a typical example of Gray's photographic recall and his tireless pursuit of information. Their long, informal chat was rewarding to both individuals and added immensely to their mutual respect and professional confidence.[1]

On June 12, 1987, the White House Press Secretary issued a news release stating that Lieutenant General Alfred M. Gray was nominated to be the next Commandant of the Marine Corps. More time passed until the Senate's Armed Services Committee met on June 23 and unanimously approved the appointment and passed it to the full Senate for confirmation on June 25. Following the Senate's confirmation, Lieutenant General Gray turned over his FMFLANT Command in Norfolk to Major General Clayton L. Comfort on June 26, 1987.[2] Once relieved as the Commanding General, FMFLANT, Gray drove up to the Washington-Virginia area and registered in a large hotel immediately adjacent to Headquarters Marine Corps. On June 30, the Secretary of Defense formally swore Gray in as the new Commandant. Gray was sworn in just six hours before his mandatory retirement date as a Major General. He and his wife, Jan, were invited to Secretary Weinberger's office, where Gray raised his hand and took his oath of office on his mother's well-used family Bible.[3]

The arrival of Gray on the scene happened so quickly that there was not time to assemble a transition team to function within his inner office. Colonel Harvey Barnum, recipient of the Medal of Honor, who was serving as the Director, Special Projects Office, was relocated to act as the Military Secretary to the Commandant. Colonel "Barney" Barnum, several officers and newly enlisted Marines picked up the challenge and adjusted to the increased pace. A few months later, in August, then-Lieutenant Colonel James L. Jones relinquished command of the 3rd Battalion, 9th Marines, returned to Washington Headquarters Marine Corps, and became the Senior Aide to the Commandant. The following April, Jim Jones was selected for Colonel and was assigned duties as Military Secretary to the Commandant. Colonel Barnum remained close by as Director of the Commandant's Special Projects office. Colonel Jones had previously served as the Marine Corps liaison officer to the U.S. Senate, and his congressional experience proved to be of invaluable assistance to Gray. They formed an unusually close team in dealing with both the House of Representatives and the Senate.[4] Jim Jones would later become the 32nd Commandant of the Marine Corps.

When Gray was finally situated at Headquarters Marine Corps in the first few days of July 1987, the Marine Corps had already completed its annual budget submission for fiscal years 1988 and 1989. As prescribed by the Congress, each Service and the total Defense Department had prepared and submitted their proposed budget requests for the next five years. The first two years were highly specific submissions; the three "out years" were more generally depicted.

In essence, when a new Commandant assumes office, he must operate inside the constraints of the vision and budget submitted by his predecessor. Except for some limited flexibility in reallocating funds from one budgeted program to another, he must live within another Commandant's previous submissions for the first two years of his tenure. To implement the kinds of changes he envisioned, Gray understood that some supplementary funding was needed from the Congress, and Gray immediately set his staff to preparing such documentation.

There were pressing issues in the supporting establishments for expanding family housing, logistics management, and support measures. There were also complex environmental issues that were adversely impacting field training, as well as the need to somehow correct the near $150 million in backlogged maintenance requirements to bases and family quarters. These were difficult, seemingly mundane burdens to plan and manage but critical to the vitality of the Marine Corps' supporting establishments.

Although earlier Commandants had all requested additional funding to overcome these perplexing problems, there were never enough dollars allocated, so it was a difficult struggle each year to plead to Defense and congressional leadership the need to resolve the money issues. The bottom line in any new initiative was a lack of funded resources. Gray realized that his vision of how he planned to take the Marine Corps into the 21st century could not be implemented without the addition of a sizeable new allocation of funds. He directed his staff to prepare the necessary paperwork, and he prepared to personally go through channels to justify the need for funding.

There were other important matters that affected the most senior General officers. Within months of Gray's ascendancy, four of the eight active duty Lieutenant Generals were retired. Lieutenant General Edwin J. Godfrey replaced Dwayne Gray as the Commanding General FMF, Pacific, located with the CINCPAC Fleet at Camp Smith, Honolulu, Hawaii. At HQMC, John Phillips retired from the Plans, Programs and Operations (PP&O) billet and Carl Mundy was advanced to Lieutenant General. Mundy was an exceptionally gifted General officer who would be challenged many times over in fulfilling his responsibilities interacting with the Joint Staff and other government agencies. Carl Mundy made a second move later when he succeeded Lieutenant General Ernest T. Cook Jr. at FMFLANT.

Within Gray's immediate Headquarters Marine Corps staff, Ernest C. Cheatham was succeeded by John I. Hudson, a distinguished naval aviator, as the Assistant Chief of Staff for Manpower and Reserve Affairs. In the Aviation Branch, Keith A. Smith, an absolutely superb officer admired by all Marine officers, was replaced by Charles H. Pitman. The colorful Pitman came into this important position with all the enthusiasm, visionary vigor, and aviation expertise that Gray could have hoped for to assist in changing the Marine Corps' aviation community. The successor to Lieutenant General Clyde D. Dean, Chief of Staff, HQMC, was Louis R. Buehl III—a gifted and much respected, can-do officer, a person with a stable personality who would become the driving force behind the multitude of actions and coordinate the various actions. Buehl was the perfect match for orchestrating Gray's immediate efforts to transition the Marine Corps into the 21st century. Lieutenant General Buehl served his Corps and its Commandant exceptionally well but tragically he would lose his sudden fight with cancer only 15 months later.

With these pivotal senior leadership positions filled, Gray's team was in place. Over the next three years there would be other Lieutenant General retirements, and the loss of one personality and entrance of another always caused a few ripples in the effective management and span of control from the Headquarters to the most distant field commands.

One of the most significant tasks of any new Commandant is articulation of his priorities during his tenure in his *Commandant's Planning Guidance*. It becomes the cornerstone document that presents his professional vision and philosophy as to how he perceives his responsibilities to the nation and to his Corps of Marines and Sailors. He puts forth his focus of efforts, and in general, his "center of gravity" for the "way ahead." Over the past 50 years of Marine Corps history, only one Commandant chose not to publish a Commandant's guide. When General P.X. Kelley assumed the role as the 28th Commandant, he felt that since he had served the previous two years as the Assistant Commandant to General Barrow, no new guidance was necessary.

When Gray became the 29th Commandant, he had no time to undertake the deliberate process of developing positions and direction on the most urgent issues. Since the interval between his nomination and his appointment was such a short period, Gray opted not to publish any guidance. Instead, he elected to be his own messenger. He sought to share his "warrior philosophy" and spread his thoughts and guidance through a whirlwind of personal visits.

In a flurry of trips, he scheduled up to three and four sessions with different commands each day. It was an exhausting tempo that wore out his supporting staff, but he only became more energized after each meeting with units and their leaders. There was no stage too small. He would charismatically capture his audience as he spoke to "his" Marines. The theme was the same from East Coast to West Coast, in Hawaii, Okinawa, Japan, and Korea. Gray seemed to immediately connect with roaring crowds of Marines and Sailors. He invited me to travel with him on this 14-day trip. He was vibrant and fully energized as he imparted his warrior philosophy, reminding everyone that they must recommit themselves to serving his or her Corps above personal wants. These were strange words to some senior career-minded individuals now serving in a peacetime setting. For the junior Marines, his easygoing style and pragmatic and humorous thoughts brought roaring approvals as he challenged them to become "street smart." He sought to warn his audiences that they must be alert to new threats on the horizon.

A common theme in these initial presentations was Gray's reminder to all that the Beirut bombing marked a new era where terrorists had entered the global arena. He was comically clever but effective in declaring that the tactical skills you learned growing up in the hypothetical small town of "East Cupcake, Nebraska," won't keep you safe in the far corners of the Third World where Marines are deployed overseas. Gray warned them that "just getting your high school diploma doesn't make you a warrior, it doesn't make you a leader, it doesn't make you a gunslinger—but Marine training can." He liked to use the East Cupcake, Nebraska, example because it always made his audiences laugh, but all understood what he meant. "Be on the alert, take care of your buddies and yourself," he would say, reminding them that "Marines are priority targets for terrorists or fanatics who hate the United States."

Over the immediate months after assuming the position of Commandant, Gray crafted a series of informal papers addressing special topics. These were not widely distributed but were cited innumerable times as his position on deliberated issues. Gray's basic culture and his long-known warrior philosophy helped him effect his first mandate: that every Marine would be trained first as a rifleman. When he took office, he had a vision of what the Marine Corps needed to concentrate on to get back to basics and return to an emphasis on the warrior ethos. He felt the Corps had strayed from its traditional focus.[5]

Secretary of the Navy James H. "Jim" Webb Jr. had a similar feeling about how the Marine Corps had steered away from its mission of being an organization marked with a warrior's prowess. It was largely for this reason that Gray had become Webb's nominee to Secretary Weinberger.[6]

Even without the more formal *Command Guidance* document, all Marines knew their feisty Commandant was reestablishing the historic ethos that every Marine is first and foremost a warrior, a rifleman. To formalize his warrior philosophy, Gray directed the publishing of

Fleet Marine Force Manual 1, Warfighting, (FMFM-1). He played an active and direct coordinating role in the drafting and publication of this historic manual. It had an immediate and significant impact inside and outside the Marine Corps. The manual was to actually change the way Marines would think about warfare. General Charles Krulak, the 32nd Commandant, would later state, "It has caused energetic debate and has been translated into several foreign languages. The Corps' current naval doctrine is based on the tenets of maneuver warfare as described in *FMFM-1*. The publication describes the philosophy which distinguishes the U.S. Marine Corps from the other services. It provides broad guidance in the form of concepts and values. It requires judgment in application."[7]

Gray's preface to the manual succinctly reveals his understanding of warfare and the importance of sharing that insight with all Marines and Sailors when he stated:

> War is both timeless and ever changing. While the basic nature of war is constant, the means and methods we use evolve continuously. Like war itself, our approach to warfighting must evolve. If we cease to refine, expand, and improve our profession, we risk becoming outdated, stagnant, and defeated. ... MCDP #1 refines and expands our philosophy about the nature of war ... read it, study it, and take it to heart.

The arrival of Gray at Headquarters Marine Corps was in essence the beginning of an internal and often-turbulent revolution focused on transforming the Marine Corps in preparation for its entry into the 21st century. His approach was typically an action-oriented promulgation followed by a short deadline to the staff to implement. Not to detract from how his predecessor managed day-to-day activities, Gray was intent on immediately imposing his own unorthodox methods of management upon the HQMC staff. In his view, they had, for a decade, performed through well-established administrative procedures that were encrusted with standardized formats, where all staff officers were accustomed to a deliberate sequential evolution from the initiation of any correspondence to the culmination of an approving signature. His staff wanted him to prioritize his new initiatives, but he wouldn't. Instead, Gray knew that to do this would cause other projects to stagnate. He was mindful that he was creating more projects than his staff could handle, knowing that only some would be fully accomplished.

Most often an Action Officer (normally a Major or Lieutenant Colonel) researched the circumstances and prepared an initial draft paper. This was subsequently passed to his senior officer, such as a Colonel, who patiently waited with a sharpened pencil for the opportunity to substantiate and inject his detailed knowledge of Headquarters policies and his own perceived writing skills. The paper was then returned to the Action Officer, who noted the proposed revisions and the miscellaneous penciled editorial scratches often found along the borders of the pages. He then incorporated all comments into the new "revised" paper. Now the correspondence was passed back to the Colonel branch head, who reviewed it again before passing it up to a General officer for possible signature or making his own revisions before finally signing off and letting the paper enter into the holistic arena of the Headquarters for final staffing. It is here that the "infamous" pink route sheet is placed over the basic correspondence and routed to from one to a dozen other staff officers to receive their approval before being released from the Headquarters. However, should any branch propose changes, it goes back to the original Action Officer to coordinate and resolve the remaining issues. Processing every paper in a timely manner was deemed very important. "Format, gentlemen, please use the proper format" was an important issue to satisfy. It was into this smooth but convoluted and slow-functioning climate that Gray arrived, and he knew he must confront the self-importance of the almighty empowered branch heads and the lethargic administrative process.

To say this was a shock in management style would be a classic understatement. Where branch heads systematically controlled oversight of their staff sections, now Gray was to inject his own conceptual

"Task Force" committee approach. In essence, it neutralized much of the previous administrative processes. Over the years as a distant commander far removed from the Washington arena, Gray had experienced repeated occasions where HQMC staff officers systematically delayed and even worked to oppose his priority requests for new training programs or for new items of equipment for his operating forces. Having always been a bit of the rebel to subjecting himself to inefficient laborious administrative procedures, Gray had learned early on to work around perceived opponents. His approach was simple and direct: to cut the multilayered and pink routing sheet process, he devised the task force team concept. As issues were brought up to the staff, he would personally appoint a responsible officer and would often identify just who could be the members of his committees. They, the task force teams, made up of Marines from all relevant branches, were then directed to take all necessary actions to accomplish their task and report directly back to him. The more Gray was briefed, the more task force committees he appointed, and this plunged the Headquarters staff into a sea of confusion. Gray became deeply involved with all his taskings and monitored them closely. He recognized that these emerging special task force teams were unsettling to some, so he directed team members to "keep their senior directly informed of their actions." They were urged to use "their proper chain of command."

There were seemingly a hundred or more disparate actions that Gray immediately started. He changed current procedures while canceling others. Headquarters Marine Corps was experiencing a surge of actions coupled with short deadlines, placing the staff on a 24/7 routine. Changes were occurring, followed by even more changes to the recent day-to-day routine. It was his aggressive holistic approach to revise or replace the prevailing business-as-usual attitude of some senior officers. The air of uncertainty reigned in every hallway and on the four decks of Henderson Hall. Gray was definitely aboard and taking charge. It was not an uncommon occurrence for Gray to pick up a staffing paper, note the Action Officer's name and his room location, and then walk down to his office to answer some question. Many a HQMC staff officer was surprised to look up from their busy efforts to discover Gray standing there looking at him. But it did wonders for the morale of many Action Officers. The younger officers welcomed the change as a technique to make the Headquarters more responsive to the operating forces. Action Officers were also good for many more long days of paper pushing when one of their actions came back with a bold felt-tip pen notation: "Good job, G."

There was a second action Gray took that affected every General officer. When he saw the need to issue guidance to the staff, it was in the form of a broad mission statement. Once the issue was announced, it was as if it was written in granite. Unless someone directly appealed to Gray, the guidance held firm. It was difficult for some senior officers to accept the broad tasking and step aside. For those who were hesitant and more comfortable in slowly approaching each phase of a project before presenting it to his seniors, the Gray "take it and run" approach for the timid or cautious career-oriented officers was foreign and difficult to cope with. Some slid back to the previously established administrative procedures, and submitted their route sheets with "interim status reports," which Gray considered an inefficient time-consuming approach to conducting business. He had a long and personal unspoken level of mistrust in the HQMC bureaucratic administrative processes, and he was not going to become tethered to its inefficiencies. The failure of several senior officers to adjust to his way of handling administrative matters disturbed Gray, although it did help him to evaluate all his Headquarters department heads in the way they responded to his instructions. Gray knew he was being disruptive to the HQMC staff, but he never blinked as he settled in as the 29th Commandant. He chose the road less traveled; it was his style.

From the beginning, Gray was faced with the need to revitalize his senior leadership, either through retirement or reassignment of many of the General officers he'd inherited. In 1987 the Marine Corps had 72 General officers on active duty and eight in the organized reserve. The Commandant and his Assistant Commandant were the only four-star Generals currently assigned to the Marine Corps. General George Christ was outside the Marine Corps officer structure in a unified assignment heading the U.S. Central Command. There were eight three-star Lieutenant Generals, 26 Major Generals, and 36 Brigadier Generals. Gray knew each of them, some for the entirety of his military career and others for shorter periods. He knew their previous assignments, commands, and performance histories and had observed that several of the more senior Major Generals had begun to slow down. Perhaps worn by time and career demands, the "fire in the belly" of his most senior leadership had begun to fade over the past 25 to 30 years of service. The Directors, his Board, had each successfully competed against hundreds of his classmates to become a General Officer of Marines. As a generalization, it can be said that out of every hundred newly commissioned officers, only one ever reaches the rank of Brigadier General. So at the core of his General officers were exceptional Marines. The only unknown was, "Would all his Generals fully dedicate themselves in assisting their Commandant's move in new directions?" Time would tell.

Many of the Major Generals were nearing "five years in grade, or 35 years" of service, and most knew their own advancement was unlikely. Additionally, there was a significant backlog of newly selected Major Generals who could not be promoted because there were no vacancies. There were even more newly selected Brigadier Generals who were also caught up in the "no vacancy" problem. Colonels who had been selected were still waiting to be promoted and receive their first star after more than a year. Additionally, several of these newly selected Brigadiers had been "frocked," meaning they could wear the star because of the position they were holding but were still receiving a Colonel's pay. The problem trickled down to the promotion from Colonel to Captains selected for Major. Drastic action would be needed, and Gray set about it in a deliberate manner. Using the official Marine Corps lineal list, "The Blue Book," he determined that the dividing line for those to retire would be those commissioned in 1953. I felt privileged that he shared this decision with me during one of our offsite meetings.

The Lieutenant Generals had previously prepared their letters of resignation and presented them to Gray. In this way, he could have the full freedom to select any one, or more, to remain on active duty. Gray accepted several of these resignations, and early retirements were established. He devoted careful thought to selecting his most senior operational commanders. Like every other previous Commandant, he was putting his team in place. However, he wanted his selections to not only reflect his opinions but also those of his senior Generals. Accordingly, he convened a special selection board made up of Assistant Commandant General Morgan and all seven of the serving Lieutenant Generals. He directed this board to review the records of all 26 Major Generals and then "identify those who were best quali-fied for future promotion and/or a major command assignment." The selection board's protocol was to provide by "unanimous" vote their recommendation as to the best qualified to continue on active duty.[8] This "unanimous" agreement by the selection board was a deliberate initiative by Gray to avoid the perception of "team building."

With the results in hand, Gray began his self-appointed mission to meet with and inform each Major General of his decision and dis-cuss their options for continued service. This was no easy task. Gray pointed out that he hoped they would volunteer to retire early for the good of the Marine Corps. Each encounter was personal and filled with professional emotion. But it had to be done, and quickly. In the case of Major Generals, Public Law 96-513, paragraph 636 was specific as to the duration or limits of their period of service: "Retirement for years of service … Marine Corps … who holds the regular grade of Major General shall if not retired earlier then on the first day of the first month beginning after the date of the fifth anniversary of his appoint-ment to that grade or on the first day of the month which completes 35 years of active commissioned service, whichever is later."[9]

In keeping with the public law, Gray could not direct the retirement of many of his Major Generals, even though they were not recommended for continued service by his board. Instead, he was in the unenviable position of having to request their voluntary retirement. During Gray's first year in office, more than 20 Generals would retire.

At the Colonel level, there had also been a progressive buildup of officers who had not been selected for promotion to Brigadier General but remained on active duty. Gray authorized a special early-retirement board to review the records of these Colonels and select a large number for early retirement. This became an emotional issue for those in the selection zone, but it was the only measure to select individuals for early retirement. The board was diligent, fair, and produced a credible list, which included several of Gray's longtime members of his professional groups. He, however, made no exceptions to the proposed list, and all were eventually retired earlier than their mandatory retirement dates.

Over the past several decades, the Marine Corps had held its annual General Officers Symposium in the fall before the Thanksgiving holiday. It had progressively moved from strategic thoughts, maritime issues, and operational and training concerns to a more administratively oriented executive management focus. Much of this originated during the Vietnam War because of the President Lyndon B. Johnson administration's endless demands for information.

Gray felt this first gathering of his Board of Directors could be better served with a completely different approach. As he reflected on former Secretary of Defense Robert McNamara's excessive overarching and total control of low-level operational matters, Gray saw a lingering flaw in his past approach to managing the military services. He realized that the Secretary demanded military leaders adapt civilian management procedures to achieve improved executive management skills. Warfighting skills and operational commands were relegated to a secondary position. McNamara's unrelenting demand for vast quantities of information and data was actually eroding the military's traditional decisionmaking process. The Secretary rebelled against such leaders and instead openly praised those "enlightened" individuals who responded as the military's future leaders. The military's treasured class of operational commanders, who knew how to fight and win wars, were relegated to a lower status. The resultant impact of this executive management versus warrior skill was still lingering in the Pentagon and within Service headquarters years after McNamara left the Defense Department.

Gray set out to change this threatening trend in the professional effectiveness of his Marine Corps General officers. He was deeply concerned with the lack of strategic thinking that existed among many Marine General officers and most Colonels. In his view, they were not studying their craft and were not sufficiently conversant in areas of national policy, strategy, and emerging joint doctrine to be able to effectively command warfighting in an increasingly complex and rapidly changing world.

His solution was typical of Gray. His early assessment of his Generals proved to be accurate. The war game struggled through a series of events and maneuvers, in which only a small number of the Generals actively participated. Most remained silent, perhaps hoping not to be called upon. Gray gracefully accepted this situation, but the message to all was crystal clear: "Change your strategic focus from being a successful manager to warfighting in the world's littorals, where the wars of the 21st century are going to be fought." In his closing remarks, he encouraged all to be prepared to fully participate in future war games.

There was one unusual personnel situation Gray injected into his Commandant's office routine. Within the more junior officer ranks, Gray allowed a small group of individuals to continue to informally meet with him after he became Commandant. This caused consternation and confusion within the HQMC staff, as these individuals walked routinely into the Commandant's outer office for unscheduled meetings to report personal observations to Gray. These few civilians and a small group of Marines, ranging in grade from Captain to Colonel, both retired and on active duty, had developed and maintained a personal and professional relationship with the Commandant over a period of years. Gray encouraged these individuals to "come and see me," and they took full advantage of his offer. Most were credible professionals who had special, often unique, skills Gray was deeply interested in. Gray was seeking information to help make his vision of the new Marine Corps a reality. He didn't limit his queries to just his own Marines but sought out any individuals who had special knowledge and field experiences. Rarely would these officers willingly share the purpose or subject to be discussed with the Commandant's staff. Instead, when the Commandant was informed that "Major So-and-So" or "Retired Marine So-and-So" was here to see him, they were quickly ushered in for private sessions. This was a major break in military protocol and made it impossible for Gray's staff to efficiently schedule his time. Military visitors normally provided a brief summary of any topics discussed, and if follow-up actions were assigned by the Commandant, someone of authority in his office made a note of the event. This was not the case for these favored few. However, as Gray became more comfortable with his staff, the frequency of such visits and their influence eventually declined. It is interesting to note that although Gray never wavered in his loyalty to these individuals, none ever received a major command position.

Within six months, only Colonel Pat Collins, a true warrior and a loyal friend remained a frequent visitor and confidant, continuing to meet privately with the Commandant without any kind of remuneration. All knew that "Paddy" simply loved his Corps and had no personal motive but to serve his Commandant. It became known after his untimely death in 1994 that there were no contractual funds available for his services as he freely gave his time, intellect, and energy at a personal cost to himself and his family.

As Gray continued down his initial priorities list, it became necessary to further define some issues on an even higher "most urgent priorities" list. Warfighting and professional education programs were first and foremost on his mind, but other areas of deep concern had to be attended to quickly. Training and education programs were constantly on his daily agenda, and he set his mind and actions to making changes. Gray made this abrupt change in focus in such a manner as to never criticize or blame others for the condition of the Marine Corps. He only wanted "to move forward" without criticizing its leaders. He felt that each had done his best with what he had been given. He implanted his philosophy that "you take what you get and you make what you want."[10]

He additionally expressed concern about how the Marine Corps was applying the "zero defect" mentality that was not only stifling younger Marines in a climate that forbade mistakes but was having a particularly crippling effect on the initiatives of junior leaders. It was leading to obstruct by-the-rules command climates that all too often fostered a "when in doubt, make no decision" mentality. Gray felt that the zero defect concept was a cancer on leadership and needed to be approached differently, in alignment with his warrior philosophy where individuals were encouraged to assume greater responsibilities and to take charge and act without guidance when opportunities to accomplish the commander's intent became apparent.

Within the first four months, Gray directed changes that would affect every Marine's career. Gray understood that the basic Marine Corps premise "every Marine a rifleman" was as much a part of Corps ethos as were the core values of honor, courage, and commitment. These were uniquely Marine characteristics dating to the founding of the Corps. The traditional ability to use non-infantry Marines in critical combat situations allows infantry units to focus on operations at the very "point of the spear."[11]

The 1947 congressional revision to the National Security Act directed the Marine Corps to become the nation's force-in-readiness ("most ready when the nation is the least ready"). To revitalize this historic responsibility, Gray undertook a number of major changes to training, from the recruit's initial exposure to the Corps, to the smallest of tactical units. The most immediate impact was to develop Basic Warrior Training (BWT), in which all recruits would receive the rudiments of individual combat training. At an earlier time, exceptions were made for some new recruits to pass basic infantry training and proceed directly to some special skills schooling. Gray eliminated this "exception rule." His view of a rapidly changing world and the emergence of irregular warfare threats demanded that early training of all Marines be revisited. He understood that these "so-called low-intensity conflicts" would make his Marines vulnerable to guerrilla warfare and terrorist attacks. Such a vision was uncommon to most Marine leaders who remained focused on Russia's massive armor threat to Western Europe. In spite of his minority view, he persisted in his preparations of the Marine Corps for a less conventional future.[12]

In such a conflict, he said, there would be no front lines and rear areas. In his mind, all Marines must be able to fight. Because of this conviction, he felt that combat skills were critical for all Marines, regardless of gender or military occupational specialty (MOS), and that all must be capable of serving as "rifleman first." William Vaughn, in his Masters thesis, captured this core belief when he wrote that Gray wanted to stress physical and mental toughness. "Besides," he noted, "Gray said, 'Youngsters come in the Marine Corps to be warriors, to be fighters, and there is no reason why we shouldn't give the training to them.'"[13]

To this end, the Basic Warrior Training was to be 160 hours of combat training that included hand-to-hand combat and boxing training; the introduction to all weapons organic to the infantry battalion; how to operate in a field environment; and the experience of throwing a live hand grenade. He was particularly upset by one briefing he received about recruit training at Parris Island, South Carolina, that verified his concerns about the attitude toward combat training. Apparently, the base's grenade throwing range had become only marginally safe; therefore, someone in a leadership position must have quietly decided just to eliminate all grenade throwing. Evidently, the decision was made to not expend the funds required and to expend little effort to refurbish the range to make it safe, but to simply close the range and eliminate the training. He wondered how this could happen. His direction had been specific. Action commenced immediately to upgrade and reopen the grenade range. Deep down, he couldn't help wondering if some officer was more concerned about a possible recruit accident—or his personal career—rather than properly training Marines under his direction.

Recruit training was extended three weeks to a total of 13. Grenade throwing was identified specifically in this revised curriculum. The extended training would cost millions of additional dollars and therefore was not automatically accepted by the bureaucracy in Washington. However, through numerous personal trips to Capitol Hill, he convinced congressional leaders of the importance of the training. It was an important milestone for Gray for setting the course of his tenure.

Later, in 1989, Basic Warrior Training for all Marines was further supplemented with additional combat training. The infantry training regiment had been disestablished in the early 1970s. Gray brought this idea back by establishing the School of Infantry. One of the main changes was a new period of schooling called Marine Combat Training. This four-week course was designed to hone those skills previously presented during recruit training. The instructors for this training would focus on hands-on opportunities for recruits to gain greater knowledge of all weapons while being in a field environment. Later, the Marine battle skills training program would be focused on the development of combat skills for all Marines. Gray felt that the single most important early training element was to "ensure that all Marines are capable of effectively serving in a rifle squad." To this end, he instituted annual testing and examinations to sustain earlier combat training. In addition to placing more emphasis on better training, he directed that the fleet service support groups (FSSG) be given the responsibility in doctrine for their own security during movement and operations in the field instead of relying on supporting infantry units to do so.[14] But these new training events were only the beginning that sparked other training improvements.

The next important change Gray made was to institute a complete evaluation and subsequent overhauling of the Marine Corps Professional Military Education (PME) system. His years of being stationed at Quantico made him aware that Marine Corps education and training needed to be standardized. He had early visions of a single facility for Marines to study, learn, think, and grow to their potential regardless of where they were deployed, and regardless of rank or grade. His intent for the PME program was to teach military judgment rather than knowledge. Knowledge, being important for developing sound judgment, was taught in the context of teaching military judgment, but not as material to be memorized.[15]

To support the renewed emphasis on PME, Gray had a preliminary review made of the Breckenridge Library, a facility constructed in the 1930s that lacked any type of modern electronic enhancements. The much-worn traditional Dewey Decimal card catalogue system—long ago phased out as obsolete in most libraries—was a testimony to the absence of emphasis on professional educational support to military students. Discussions over the years mentioned the need to upgrade the library but nothing was done to implement upgrades. Gray developed an increasing interest in building a completely new research facility. There were several specific benefits to constructing a more powerful research facility for the Marines and other U.S. and foreign students within Marine Corps schools. The single greatest impediment to obtaining certification of a Marine Corps University at Quantico was the lack of a credible library and research center. It was Gray's vision that the Marine Corps should consolidate "all of the educational type institutions in the Marine Corps under the broad umbrella of such a Marine Corps University."

The words "Marine Corps University" seemed foreign to most Marine Corps senior leaders. Such a dream seemed unlikely to become a reality. At the Marine Corps Command and Staff College the course, primarily focused on Majors and Lieutenant Colonels, was thought of as the pinnacle of Marine Corps professional schooling. Establishing a war college and thus a true university of professional education across a Marine's entire career seemed beyond the means of the Marine Corps. To the disbelievers, they didn't know or appreciate Gray's determination and tenacity once he made up his mind.

Just months after he returned from his first western Pacific trip, Gray called me to explore the idea on his "new library" project. First he told me he had no money for a new building. Then he instructed me, along with one Marine officer, Captain Robert Campbell, to go visit the other service libraries to see what they had in place. Our mission was to study each facility's layout, its management procedures, and its automated support services, and then make recommendations for constructing a new library facility near the Command and Staff School. These initial instructions were verbal, much in the same way he initiated other new projects. Our small, two-man advisory team visited the other services' military libraries and their war colleges and returned with a proposal as to which capabilities, and more specifically, best features, could be incorporated into any new construction at Quantico.

Unknown to Captain Campbell and me at the time, Gray had previously visited most of the other services' libraries long before we began our search for information. As a General officer, Gray spoke several times about the Marine Corps' capabilities and issues to the students of the Air University at Maxwell Air Force Base in Montgomery, Alabama. Colonel Charles J. Goode, Marine Corps Liaison Officer at the Air War College recalled that "Gray was always impressed with the organization and infrastructure of their library." Gray felt it was specifically designed and laid out to best serve its student population. All levels of Air Force professional military education were located at Maxwell and in close proximity of a world-class library and research facility. It was staffed with exceptionally qualified military and civilian instructors who, in turn, were responsible to a credible university president. Colonel Goode felt that Gray's frequent visits and tour of the Air Warfare Library probably played some role in bringing forth his vision for a Marine Corps library.

In late October 1987, our preliminary report was presented to Gray. He had dictated the meeting be held in the current Breckenridge Library so that he could observe the library's current capabilities and internal management procedures. It was to be one of those rare occasions where Mrs. Gray accompanied him during a briefing.

With the support of the Breckenridge Chief Librarian, we set up our briefing charts in the center of the library so that the current staff could listen to the briefing and any follow-up discussion. It was a solemn hour for them, and they quietly wondered about their own futures. Our team felt that the Air Force's Air War College in Montgomery, Alabama, best suited the Marine Corps. It was first class in every way. (It was the Air Force, after all, so what else would one expect?) Its internal arrangements, with librarians directly in the center to assist students and serious researchers, would be the ideal setup for students who needed assistance and fast answers between classes.

Gray listened, asked several questions, and then remained silent for a few minutes as he gazed around at the many tired old bookshelves. Then he looked at me and approved the concept of a new library for the Marine Corps, saying the new facility must have a first-class computer system so that Marines from all over the world could access and use the library. He was specific in insisting that Marine units deploying to the Mediterranean or the far Pacific regions would be able to search out the latest "lessons learned" on any earlier exercise or event. The challenge of such an undertaking caused many a skeptic's eyebrows to rise as few foresaw the scope of the pending revolution in information technology. Without a budget or funding of any kind, Gray approached Congress with the urgent need for such an educational center. Among the first to support Gray's initiative was Congressman Ike Skelton from Missouri. Others from both the House and the Senate were enlisted to provide swift and strong support to Gray's request for supplementary funding to begin construction.

Gray felt so strongly about the project that he directed his Assistant Commandant, General Thomas Morgan, to personally assume responsibility for it. His advice to Morgan was "don't worry about the funding." Morgan was a superb choice, because over time, there would be numerous unforeseen obstacles to overcome. But Morgan was able to follow Gray's guidance to "go first class and have it electronically networked with all creditable library systems." Tom Morgan, Gray's quiet and loyal partner, made it happen. His personal attention and tireless oversight in constructing a first-rate facility would result in the development of a significant Marine Corps' educational asset. I was placed on the Marine Corps Research Center's planning committee as the project coordinator and it was truly a pleasant experience to work directly for General Morgan. It was a noble cause and an honor for each of us to serve on a project that would benefit the Corps for decades to come.

On short notice, Congress approved the establishment of a National Marine Corps Research Center at Quantico. With this initial outlay of government funding, Gray then received several proposals for funding from the private sector. This resulted in a "third party" funding arrangement with the Command and Staff College Foundation. The Command and Staff Foundation was established in 1980 as a private, nonprofit foundation to provide private funding for the Marine Corps' professional education programs when government funding was unavailable. Led by General Leonard F. Chapman, 24th Commandant of the Marine Corps, the Foundation's Board of Trustees committed to raising $9,000,000 toward the library's projected cost of $18,000,000. Colonel Charles Goode had that special knack for being able to meet with diverse audiences of potential large investors and quickly gain their confidence, and their commitment to build a Marine Corps Research Center grew. The Command and Staff Foundation actually raised more than $11,000,000. The Command and Staff College Foundation was later renamed The Marine Corps University Foundation. Ground was broken in May 1991, with Gray shoveling the first scoop of dirt with an entrenching tool emblazoned with four stars on the back. The Marine Corps Research Center opened in 1992.

This exceptionally short period of time from dream to reality was immeasurably helped by the always cheerful demeanor and professionalism of Retired Colonel Goode—CJ, as he was known. As the Executive Director of the Marine Corps University Foundation, he organized its first capital campaign. When General Jim Jones became the 32nd Commandant, the Marine Corps Research Center was renamed the "General Alfred M. Gray Marine Corps Research Center." The library archive continues to display Colonel Goode's photograph in respect for his creative capital fund campaign. Colonel Goode was an extraordinary Marine officer who made a lasting contribution to the Marine Corp's professional military education programs.

Another factor that influenced Gray's emphasis on professional military education was the fact that only about 25 percent of Marines were able to attend Marine Corps resident courses. Gray recognized the need to provide professional education for the other 75 percent. Historically, this was done through the completion of non-resident courses offered by the Marine Corps Institute (MCI). Through a series of different subjects that encompass much of the knowledge offered in the classrooms of Quantico, a Marine is required to read, learn, and apply the knowledge and information presented in a written test at the end of each booklet. It was a system based solely on the individual Marine's desire to seek self-improvement. Gray directed major revisions of the MCI curriculum, requiring upgrade of many courses and the development of promotion incentives to those who pursued scholastic and professional education. In 1989, Gray further demonstrated the emphasis he wanted placed on Marine enlisted education and training with the introduction of a Professional Noncommissioned and Staff Noncommissioned Officers Education Training System.

In addition to innumerable revisions and upgrades to individual warfighting skills and unit training programs, Gray launched several studies that would ultimately cause institutional changes within the Marine Corps. Recognizing a window of opportunity that existed as the "new" Commandant, he assembled some of the best and brightest and charged them to study the Marine Corps' structure and to identify the changes needed to improve the Marine Corps. The principal members of this study group were Colonels Clifford Stanley, Marty Brandtner, Larry Livingston, David Richwine, Paul Van Riper, and Tony Zinni. This battle-hardened assemblage of exceptional Colonels didn't just happen; Gray handpicked these selections from across the Marine Corps. All had been longtime Gray disciples, and all would eventually become General officers. After completing their research, the resulting findings were passed to a team of General officers who validated the ideas and confirmed the specific recommendations. Within four months, Gray was prepared to implement the recommendations of this team by directing the reorganization of the Marine Corps Development and Education Command (MCDEC).

It was not surprising that Gray's first strategic target was the complex of development, training, and education commands at Quantico. During Gray's first 37-plus years of military service, he would spend more than 12 years in assignments at Quantico, first as a Lieutenant in the Basic School and in the Communication Officer's course. Later he would return at different times while serving as a Major, a Lieutenant Colonel, and finally as a General officer. These intermittent tours in a variety of related assignments exposed him to the complex functions and responsibilities of the base's different organizations. Gray released an "all Marines" directive that stated, "Effective November 10, 1987, the Marine Corps Development and Education Command (MCDEC) will become the Marine Corps Combat Development Command (MCCDC)."

MCCDC was given a much broader charter than MCDEC had previously enjoyed. It was designed to have a direct interface with the Fleet Marine Forces (FMFs) to provide a more effective means for meeting the needs of the operating forces.[16] This action would enable MCCDC to better identify requirements, make changes to organizations, develop doctrine, and improve warfighting capabilities. Within three months, a second proposal emerged to execute the major reorganization and activation of the Research Development and Acquisitions Command (RD&A). This directed the consolidation of all Marine Corps technology research, development, and acquisition efforts into a single command, eliminating bureaucratic layering and streamlining procedures and providing a capability development companion organization in Quantico to MCCDC.

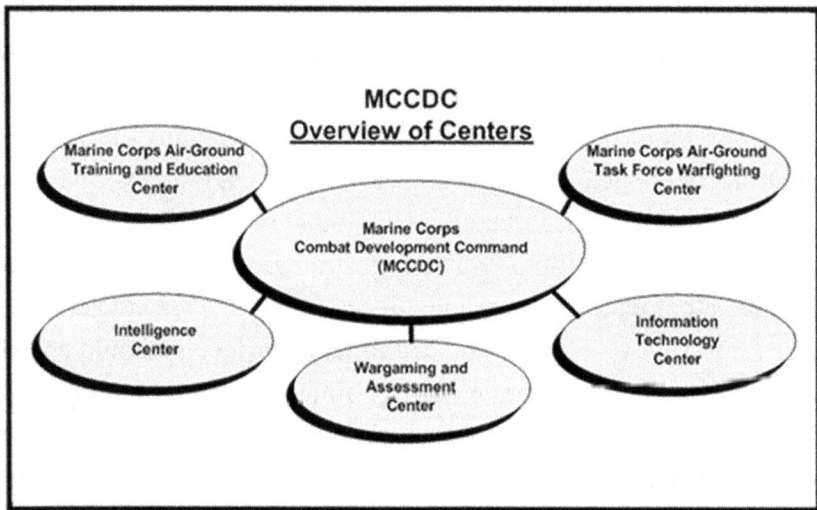

MCCDC
Overview of Centers

- Marine Corps Air-Ground Training and Education Center
- Marine Corps Air-Ground Task Force Warfighting Center
- Marine Corps Combat Development Command (MCCDC)
- Intelligence Center
- Information Technology Center
- Wargaming and Assessment Center

Figure 6
The Five Warfighting Centers at
Marine Corps Combat Development Command (MCCDC)
(Chart developed to support MCCDC reorganization
as directed by the 29th Marine Corps Commandant in 1988).

The creation of MCCDC was a major undertaking. The new command would be responsible for the development, assessment, and promulgation of operational concepts, plans, and future operations in the 21st century. Further, Gray directed that MCCDC was to be reorganized around five centers, as shown in the figure above. The critical functions previously divided between several locations were combined to link doctrine, combat development, and training. This was to be the organization Gray would use to address, plan and transition Marine Corps' doctrine, force structure and material requirements in addition to the development and implementation of policy and programs for the training and education of all regular and reserve Marine Corps personnel, units, and schools.[17]

The tempo of activities only increased as Gray settled in. Simultaneous to the multitude of projects he had initiated, he continued to travel at every opportunity. This was a difficult issue with many within HQMC, as they felt he was spending an unusual amount of his time traveling out of the Washington area. There was merit in this thought, because he had placed so many projects in action and seemed to be gone an inordinate amount of time. The impetus driving Gray to maintain an intense schedule of visits to the operating forces was concern that he would lose contact with his field commanders' concerns while focusing on major changes to the supporting establishment in Quantico. His senior leadership discussed the subject of his travels with him. He noted their concerns but continued to travel and accept a growing number of invitations to speak about his vision and the role of his Marine Corps in the future. Gray simply would not accept anyone restricting his daily schedule. He viewed interference in his schedule and protocol as a means of controlling him, and he refused to subordinate himself. Gray reveled in unpredictability and was always in search of the levels of professionalism to enhance the operational capabilities for Marines.

In late August 1987, Gray made his first trip to the western Pacific region. This particular extended trip was one which his predecessors always made shortly after assuming their Commandant position. But it was special for Gray as he selected the newly appointed Sergeant Major David W. Summers; Lieutenant Colonel James L. Jones; Mr. Peter Murphy, the Commandant's counsel; and me, Colonel Gerald Turley USMCR (Retired), to travel with him. My invitation came as a surprise. General and Mrs. Gray, my wife, Bunny, and I had been out to dinner, and as we were leaving the Commandant's home, he told me of the western Pacific (WESTPAC) trip and then indicated I would be going. Initially I wasn't too excited about a two-week period of living out of a suitcase, but he restated his desire that I accompany him.

Several days later I received a telephone call from a young Marine asking for my service number. I responded by telling the Marine I had decided not to go on the trip. He paused for a moment, said, "Thank you, sir," and hung up. A few moments later, the young Marine called back, again asking for my service number. When I repeated my decision, he stopped me and said, "Sir, my mission is only to get your service number. I don't know about anything else." He had me! So I gave him the information requested.

Days later, I received a copy of the flight manifest and saw my name and rank (Colonel Gerald Turley, USMCR [Retired]) designator. This situation could have easily been solved because HQMC could have provided any information the Commandant's office required. It was a learning process for me, but I understood completely that when Gray made decisions, they were to be followed. Once on the flight, I enjoyed every minute. It was a most enlightening and insightful experience. I began to better understand the man and his determination to change his Marine Corps.

Again, Gray was as energized as ever as he visited numerous units from the 3rd Marine Division and 1st Marine Aircraft Wing, logistical support, and joint commands in Okinawa, Japan, and Korea. He gathered with his Marines and Sailors at every possible location to share with them his "warrior philosophy" and stress their need to subordinate themselves "first to the Corps and then to their personal needs." He spoke of a changing world and their responsibility to prepare themselves for new, emerging threats. He rallied around and talked to small groups, especially to the junior enlisted. He touched them. They cheered his demands that they prepare themselves to be "smarter Marines."

The flights across the vast Pacific Ocean provided quiet moments as Gray was able to sit back with his four traveling companions to reflect and enter into long meditations concerning the complex issues that would face the Marine Corps in the years ahead. His Gulfstream C-20 jet aircraft was designed with a forward cabin with an executive desk and cushioned seats across the aisle. The typical seating included Gray sitting alone in the forward cabin with his pouch of Red Man chewing tobacco on the desk in front of him, along with a Styrofoam cup for his discarded "chew" and another holding his coffee. We, his traveling companions, rotated into the other seat across the table as he explored new areas and new ideas. We became fully aware of how little sleep Gray needed to sustain his intense activity levels. He just never seemed to stop and rest.

It was during the second segment of the westward flight, from Alaska to Japan, that Gray suddenly opened up and began to discuss a broad series of concerns. New topics were coming fast. It was his personal style to think out loud. As he talked, he also listened to himself—stopping to correct or expand on his previous comments—and then continuing on with his monologue. For the next eight hours, we passengers mostly listened, astounded at his broad knowledge on a range of subjects and his ability to precisely recall events, long-forgotten studies, correspondence, and the previous actions of the Navy and the Marine Corps' most senior leadership.

During the few breaks on the westward flight to Okinawa and Japan, Lieutenant Colonel Jim Jones and Sergeant Major Summers recognized the urgency to begin recording his ideas and future plans. Over the next 12 to 14 days, they filled several legal pads with notes on his articulated thoughts. The topics were diverse and ranged from the imminent future implosion of the Soviet Union—which raised his listeners' skeptical eyebrows—from creating a Marine Corps University, to the need to raise the bar on enlisted training and education programs, to enlisted promotion issues. Whatever Gray spoke about was hurriedly written down. When the group finally returned to the States and HQMC, the notes were delivered to Lieutenant General Louis H. Buehl's Chief of Staff office. It covered nearly 100 different topics. Within a few weeks, the various topics and subjects were transcribed into multiple taskings among the departments of the headquarters. The HQMC staff went into another surge effort.

One encounter during this trip had long-term repercussions to the Marine Corps. It depicted Gray's action-oriented decision process. He was introduced to the last "Marine Gunner," a special type Warrant Officer, on active duty. The Marine Corps had previously progressively phased out this special designation. Gunner Gilbert H. Bolton and I had previously served in the same infantry battalion during the Vietnam War, so there was a brief moment of reminiscing between us. Gray moved in closer; he became very interested. I believe Gray was mesmerized as the Gunner related his career as a former staff NCO, his appointment to the commissioned ranks, and his pride in being the last of his "Marine Gunner" breed. Gray listened and turned to his traveling companions, saying, "We need to correct this. I want a new, expanded Marine Gunners program."

Our flight back to Hawaii called for a refueling stop on the Island of Guam, but because of severe weather conditions in the region, our aircraft was diverted to Wake Island, 2,300 miles west of Hawaii. We arrived about three a.m. Gray decided to get off and walk around, and he asked me if I wanted to go. Honestly, his fast-paced schedule had simply worn me out. I declined, and he left. Moments later, the crew chief shook me awake and said that Gray wanted me to come over and meet him in the north beach area. I struggled into my dress shoes, grudgingly stumbling down the aircraft ladder. As the crew chief pointed into the darkness, indicating "he's over there about a hundred yards away," I wasn't too excited.

I found him standing near the water's edge. As I approached he just started talking, as if I had already been following beside him, about the defense of Wake Island during the bleak days immediately following the December 7, 1941, Pearl Harbor attack. He pointed toward different parts of the island—where the guns had been positioned, where the Japanese fleet had approached from, and where their assault forces landed across the beach. He pointed to a small mound a short distance away, saying, "That's where Marine Major James Devereux's command bunker was located."

To say the least, I was astounded at his detailed knowledge of one of America's first battles of World War II. We walked along the water's edge as he retold the story of the island finally being captured. When I questioned how he was so certain of his details and positions, he mumbled about being on the island for 60 to 90 days "at an earlier time." I realized then that I had known my friend Gray for nearly two decades, yet I barely knew him at all. His special intelligence world, and his total silence regarding those varied duties would prevent me, and all his closest acquaintances, from ever completely "knowing" Al Gray.

During the remainder of the trip, Gray continued to discuss the importance of the Marine Gunners and their historic role in Marine Corps units. The Gunner designation had been part of the Marine Corps for more than 75 years. The actions of this small group of Warrant Officers is replete in the historic chronicles of the Marines in battle from World War I through Haiti, Nicaragua, all the Caribbean campaigns of the 1920-30s, World War II, and Korea. It had a history of unusual professional achievement by a special breed of men, and Gray wanted more of such men. We discussed it for hours on the flight to Hawaii. Informal notes were taken, and during the flight back to Marine Corps Air Station Kaneohe, Hawaii, a draft concept was presented to him. With minor changes re-emphasizing his role as the "weapons expert" in every infantry battalion, he approved the restoration of the Marine Gunner Program for Warrant Officers.

His intent was to find older enlisted Marines who possessed combat-arms skills, combat experience, and expertise to a degree so rich that their contribution to warfighting would be out of proportion to their small numbers. After several drafts, we crafted a basic letter from him to the HQMC staff. When we arrived in Kaneohe, Hawaii, I carried our draft to the brigade headquarters and had a Master Sergeant type one copy of our draft. Gray reviewed it and scribbled on it, "Approved. A.M. Gray." Upon returning to Washington, it was passed to the Deputy Chief of Staff for Manpower for implementation. There was staffing resistance to restarting the Gunner program, but Gray ignored the distant grumbling of a few staff officers and directed the immediate implementation of a commissioning and training program.[18]

This would be no small undertaking, and numerous members of the HQMC staff did not initially support this initiative. However, staffing began immediately, and within months, the first class of Marine Gunners underwent training at Quantico. Upon graduation they would be authorized to wear the unique "bursting bomb" insignia. It was determined there would ultimately be 54 Marine Gunners, enough for each infantry battalion and some support units. The Gunner's position on the battalion staff would be within the S-3 Operations Section focused on assisting overall training management.

This was to be Gray's first highly visible initiative, designed to focus the Marine Corps on warfighting and professional excellence. Since the reinvigoration of the Gunner program, hundreds of exceptional senior staff NCOs have been selected to serve as recognized experts in training and weapons skills. During the 1991 Iraqi War, the Marine were repeatedly cited for exceptional training prowess and their applications of all infantry weapons. At the infantry battalion level, the Marine Gunner contributed immeasurably to the combat successes of both Marine divisions as these mechanized forces rolled into . As the complexity of weapons and multiple support accessories increased, the value of the Gunner program became even more beneficial to all Marines. They would repeat their contributions as the recognized experts in infantry warrior skills in the second Iraqi War. Gray's vision for needing such special Marines held true.

As his earlier reorganizations were being implemented in Quantico, another study group was being formed. It would determine the direction of the Corps in what Gray considered an uncommon occurrence of situations that could quickly change the international environment. At a time when most Defense Department leaders were focused on the Russian massive armor threat to the NATO community, this study group ascertained that the most likely future threat to the United States would be low- to mid-intensity conflicts. Accordingly, this study determined that in order for the Marine Corps to remain the nation's premier force-in-readiness, its active force must be structured and equipped to react immediately and decisively to these emerging threats without relying on mobilization of Marine Reserves. The study concluded that in an era of constrained budgets, the nation could not afford to maintain large forces that did not have general utility in a wide range of potential conflicts.[19] Gray was adamant in his belief that regional commanders, with Marine forces forward-deployed—such as the Commander-in-Chief of U.S. Forces in the Pacific (USCINCPAC)—needed smaller, more nimble forces that exhibited capabilities then associated with special operations. This finding was not only consistent with Gray's vision of future conflicts but was in keeping with his previous efforts to expand the range of capabilities resident in the Marine Amphibious Units (MAUs).

In addition, he saw a need to increase the ground mobility of Marine forces. Years earlier, while serving as the Commanding General, Marine Corps Development Command, he orchestrated the introduction of the Light Armored Vehicle (LAV) into the Marine Corps inventory. Although it was not apparent to most senior Generals at that time, the acceptance of a highly mobile armored vehicle would eventually cause reorganization of the Marine division into a lighter, more flexible force. Now, as the Commandant, he was able to complete that prophecy. He took no special pride in the accomplishment; few even knew him as the instrument of the change.

Gray had still more initiatives in mind for Quantico. He recognized that, in addition to the School of Infantry and Basic Warrior Training during recruit training, other changes had to be accomplished in order to meet the emerging demand of an eroding international security environment. In mid-1988, as part of his overall reorganization at Quantico, Gray established the Marine Air-Group Training and Education Center, which was charged with overseeing all training and education throughout the Marine Corps. Gray's charter to every study group was to ensure that "Marines at every grade will be more proficient in their primary duties as warriors."

Well read, Gray knew that Marines historically were the most innovative of the U.S. military services, and the changing times would require significant change. He realized that the multitude of reorganizations and studies he was directing would drastically change the "institution" forever. But mandating changes is the easier part of any issue; getting approval and then achieving the intended objectives, perpetuated by the paucity of fiscal resources, becomes the greater challenge. Gray would be challenged every day to lower his expectations. Though often alone in his convictions, he remained firmly convinced that each initiative needed to be pursued vigorously. He would not lower his sights no matter how difficult the challenge.

It was from these studies and various other planning documents that Gray developed the concept for a Marine Corps Campaign Plan (MCCP) that he directed be drafted to document and chart the direction of the Corps so that it would enter the 21st century as the nation's most viable force-in-readiness. Other critical planning documents were also to be written. The Marine Corps Long-Range Plan would establish future goals. The Marine Corps Air-Ground Task Force (MAGTF) master plan would serve as the impetus for all planning and budgetary programming efforts. The MAGTF Master Plan would provide implementing measures in future doctrine, training, education, and equipment changes needed to attain the necessary capabilities Gray envisioned.

Gray's 1988 Annual Report to Congress about the Marine Corps' progress summed up testimony, stating:

The ability of our operating forces to fight has been enhanced, and our ... supporting establishment has been streamlined for our total force-in-readiness. We are leaner, more mobile, and more expeditionary. If asked, we could go to war now.

Gray honestly believed this to be true.

Shortly after James H. "Jim" Webb became the Secretary of the Navy, he made it known that he opposed the procurement of the Marine Corps' experimental tiltrotor V-22 replacement for the medium lift helicopter. Instead, Secretary Webb felt the H-60 Army helicopter would better serve the needs of the Navy and Marine Corps. A senior-level meeting was held at HQMC in which plans were made to formally brief Secretary Webb on why the V-22 Osprey was vital to the Marine Corps' "from the sea and over-the-horizon" capabilities. HQMC was fully aware that I had served as one of Secretary Webb's Deputy Assistant Secretaries of Defense when he was the Assistant Secretary of Defense for Reserve Affairs. General Tom Morgan invited me to participate in the workup sessions. I quickly accepted, as General Morgan had been of immense assistance to me as I transitioned into the DoD's Senior Executive Service (SES) and Pentagon working relationships with General and flag-rank officers. Initially, a three- to four-hour technical briefing was proposed, but understanding Webb's preference for short decision briefs, I pushed instead for a 20- to 30-minute operational presentation. We could then always expand the presentation into more technical areas should the Secretary seek more detailed information.

The meeting was held in the Commandant's conference room in Henderson Hall, Room 2213. Gray assembled his key aviation and ground Generals. All were aware of Secretary Webb's earlier statements to the press that he opposed the further development of the Osprey. It was a long and deeply discussed session. Gray, sitting beside Secretary Webb at the end of the long table, seldom spoke. Instead, the seven to nine Generals carefully laid out their future operational needs, and the 1980s technology of the V-22 far exceeded the 1960s era technology of the H-60. Throughout the discussion, Lieutenant General Joseph W. Went, an aviator—but also the senior logistician then serving in the Marine Corps—remained silent until concluding comments around the table were requested. General Went, a New Englander, in a clear but unemotional assessment, skillfully summarized the future value of the V-22 to a future Marine Corps. It was a compelling summary and validation.

After a long silence, as he considered what had been said, Secretary Webb glanced at Gray and then back at me sitting a few feet directly behind the Commandant. Then, looking around the conference table, he said that he had been convinced that the Marine Corps couldn't accept the high cost of each individual V-22 aircraft and the demand for highly technical maintenance support. But, based upon the testimony that he had received at this briefing, he would change his mind and support the continued development of the Osprey. With that decision, Secretary Webb authorized more than $200,000,000 in long lead-time tooling requirements. It would be one of Jim Webb's most significant decisions during his tenure as the Secretary of the Navy.[20] The Osprey had survived another critical milestone, and as future years would unfold, the V-22 began its first combat service in the Iraqi and Afghanistan wars. Another important link in Gray's vision became a reality.

For every Service Chief, the flow of data and information into his or her office contains the broadest spectrum of interest and issues that must, in some manner, be addressed. The quantity of correspondence that arrives on his or her desk is beyond the wildest grasp of most individuals. Personal letters, often handwritten in pencil, are received from people from every walk and station of life, and each requires close personal attention. From within every Service organization there are requests for decisions, speaking engagements, or to simply respond to a request for an autographed picture; or all too often, letters from anguished families seeking information on a wayward son or daughter are received.

Additionally from within the Defense Department and the legislative branches are demands for enacting new policy, and taskings for endless responses on the broadest spectrum of miscellaneous reports. A classic example of such a situation was concerns about the actions and welfare of women in the military.

Women in the military had long been a sensitive issue and had resulted in Congress needing to continually amend and broaden the role of women to achieve "equal player" status with their male counterparts. It would be this delicate issue that Gray and the Department of Defense's Advisory Committee on Women in the Services (DACOWITS) would have strong differences that led to direct exchanges on the limits of women in the military. What this politically oriented women's organization wanted was for women to have total equality with men, which included placing women in combat situations. Along with the much-politicized environment was the fast exploding interest in the "exclusion rule," which had historically prevented women from combat. The DACOWITS agenda was focused on three issues:

- Is the present policy valid and correctly implemented?
- Is the present policy valid but not correctly implemented?
- Is the present policy invalid?

In late 1986 through 1987, all the services had experienced unfavorable notoriety because of the widespread incidents of sexual harassment against women and the exposure of a series of lesbian cells within all the services, a clear violation of the military's uniform judicial code. There was a progressively vocal clamoring of emotion from women's organizations demanding corrective actions be taken at all levels. Unlisted, but high on their agenda, was an attempt to erode the "exclusion rule," which was the cornerstone preventing women from combat. The newspapers and television medias were well primed and kept the issues of women in the military in the headlines for months.

Only weeks after Gray took office, the issue of women in the military resurfaced with an emotional outpouring from women's groups demanding "fair treatment and total equality." In September 1987, the Secretary of the Navy tasked the Commandant with undertaking a comprehensive examination of the progress of women in the Marine Corps. Gray handled this task personally and assembled a task force study group. Further, he directed there would be no limiting protocol measures on the study, just a thorough and completely studied assessment. On October 5, 1987, his task force convened. It consisted of a General officer steering committee and a working group of 29 Marines of various grades and experience levels, from different geographic locations. There was a wide variety of military occupational specialties (MOSs) whose members were single, married, or divorced; some were single parents; and there was an even split between men and women. Their guidance from Gray was manifest and direct: "To thoroughly explore the role of women in the Corps today."

The task force was specifically challenged to look at the long legislative history of women's role in the military and review the "combat exclusion rule." The task force fully documented its research, which reaffirmed that, after World War II, Congress recognized that retaining women in the armed forces would be of great value to the nation. As a result, Congress passed the first piece of legislation to authorize the admission of women to regular, peacetime military duty. Section 6015 Title 10 U.S. Code of the 1956 Act authorized the enlistment and appointment of women into the regular and reserve components of the Army, Navy, Air Force, and Marine Corps. However, it also placed "no combat" restrictions on all female assignments. For the Navy and Marine Corps, this precluded women from duty on naval vessels, except hospital ships and transports, and duty on aircraft serving combat missions.

The task force also confirmed that in 1978, the constitutionality of Section 6015 was successfully challenged in a federal district court, which invalidated some aspects of Section 6015 based upon absolute prohibition against women assignments to sea duty, left the "exclusion rule" intact. Later, during hearings in 1979 and 1980, Congress conducted other reviews on women in combat and again rejected proposed legislation to placing women in close combat situations.[21] Congress, faced with other legal matters, amended Section 6015 for the purpose of broadening the Secretary of the Navy's authority to have greater discretion in prescribing the type of duty women assigned to temporary duty on vessels not engaged in combat missions would receive.

The issue of women's role in the military arose again in 1980 when President Jimmy Carter decided to reactivate registration for the draft under the Military Selective Service Act and recommended that Congress amend the Act to permit the registration and conscription of women along with men.[22]

Congress rejected the proposal after discussing the proper role of women in combat. The 1980 amendment was adopted by both Houses, stating:

> The principle that women should not be intentionally and routinely engaged in combat is fundamental and enjoys wide support among our people. ... Through history, women have not regularly participated in combat, and no society has ever relied upon conscription of women primarily for combat roles.[23]

It was with this historic background of the legislation chain of events and the affirmation that women could not be placed in a combat role that the Marine Corps women in the military task force meticulously pursued their study. Their in-depth review early on revealed substantial advances within the Corps in the utilization of its women Marines. It was noted there was a fourfold increase in the end strength for women Marines since 1970. The task force validated that there was a 429 percent increase in end strength from 2,339 to almost 9,800 women in 1987.

It was noted, in 1990, largely as a result of the performance of women in the Panama Invasion, that the debate concerning the role of women in combat resurfaced. Many of the women in uniform who were summoned before a House subcommittee testified that they did not desire to have their duties expanded to include more combat-oriented tasks. It became apparent that in spite of the outcries from women's political activist groups, women in the services were in basic disagreement with the agenda of the Department of Defense's Advisory Committee on Women in the Services (DACOWITS). A revised amendment on "women in combat" before the 101st Congress was again rejected, reaffirming the historic policy of precluding women from being placed in high-risk areas.

In December 1987, the task force submitted their study on "Women in the Marine Corps" to the Commandant. Their research revealed significant advances for the Corps in the utilization of women during the past 15 years. Before 1975, separate women Marine units existed throughout the Marine Corps. Command opportunities for women were generally restricted to units that were predominately women. Since that time, women have been fully integrated into operational units. They are currently assigned to numerous challenging and important positions. They serve at Headquarters Marine Corps, and on Joint staffs, serve as instructors, and in key billets. In 1979, women officers were integrated into the previously all-male company of Lieutenants at The Basic School. The basic training of enlisted women was expanded in 1985 to a position that, except for offensive combat training, mirrored the training of their male Marine counterparts.

Despite these advances, issues were raised that prompted recom-mendations for a renewed emphasis on sustaining the current policy. It was considered by the study members as a fair and balanced policy at the time. In looking at the recommendations regarding policy affecting accession, training, and utilization, the task force ultimately focused on how it related to women in time of war. The study members looked carefully at sexual harassment incidents, as well as the nature of entertainment in military clubs, adequate recreational facilities, and the availability of quality childcare and any special support necessary for women Marines. Quality of life concerns received much attention, including those raised by a DACOWITS team, which had previously toured the western Pacific region, and had highlighted a number of concerns. Many -related issues were explored as they related to quality of life as well as viewing the need for any limiting assignments.

A list consisting of 46 issues, from which 83 recommendations were drawn, was presented to Gray. The issue of physical risk and its relationship to the direct combat exclusion was a premium issue in the area of policy, utilization, and implementation. Another issue presented was whether or not women were being allowed to participate in deployment exercises.

These were paramount areas for the Commandant to consider. The study recognized that training of women was currently proscribed by two concepts: physiological difference and restriction from offensive combat. Pertinent combat exclusion had been widely interpreted to exclude women Marines from participating in certain types of field training. It was further noted that all Marines within a given military occupational specialty were expected to perform to the same standard but women were precluded from receiving basic-level combat training.

In reviewing the study report, and even before, the Commandant submitted his overview assessment to the Secretary of the Navy. He took corrective actions and directed women Marines to undergo Basic Warrior Training upon completion of recruit training. Gray's decision to require women to attend Basic Warrior Training was based on the premise that women Marines will contribute to unit defense during unexpected times of crises and will be present in some areas of the combat zone.

Performance requirements and deployment concepts required all Marines to receive the same training, from entry level through completion of their MOS schools. He released a "White Paper" (the Commandant's administrative procedure to pass along his immediate command guidance) notifying all commanding officers and officers-in-charge:

> It is apparent to me that commanders have denied many train-
> ing opportunities for their Marines. Not allowing women this
> opportunity to participate in training exercise deployments
> fosters negative attitudes in the women who are excluded, and
> in the men who must bear the brunt of increased deployments.
> … Commanders must seek to utilize women in training exer-
> cises at every opportunity.[24]

This command guidance eliminated the concept of physical risk as a criterion for exclusion of women. Additionally, it expanded the utilization of women in the MAGTF deployments to serve in command and aviation control elements of the Marine Amphibious Brigade (MAB) and on the Marine Amphibious Force (MAF) at headquarters level.

The task force members also identified one issue, or its full and adverse impact, few individuals were completely aware of: the naval services restriction to embark only male Sailors and Marine personnel on ships for overseas deployments. This restriction was a constant strain on junior enlisted Marines. For the naval services, particularly the Marine Corps, exclusion of women from being placed on amphibious ships had an adverse impact on the morale of young male Marines and Sailors. When women were finally authorized to serve and deploy within the Marine Corps air-ground logistics, they could do so only during land-based stateside deployments. The exclusion policy had become divisive. Woman could train and did train well, right up to the day their unit embarked aboard ships, but they could only stand on the dock and wave goodbye. Yet the critical positions these women had filled now needed to be refilled by male Marines. In essence, it was a festering issue that continued to grow as the male Marines, who in many cases had completed previous deployments, were again called upon to replace all women Marines. It was a "Catch 22" and needed a better solution. It was an unworkable situation, and Gray sensed the disruptive nature of the "no women on ships rule" and was determined to somehow correct the double standard policy created by conflicting congressional mandates. It would take time.

In mid-December 1987, Gray submitted his "Report on Women in the Marine Corps" to Secretary of the Navy Webb. He highlighted that little, except the "combat exclusion rule," remained the same as it was ten years ago. In his executive summary, Gray acknowledged the task force study that confirmed sexual harassment and fraternization existed and both were anathema to good leadership. He reported that he had taken action to correct this serious deficiency. Gray addressed the quality of life issues and reported that there was much improvement over the past five years, but more would be done. Closing his letter-report to the Secretary, he shared the revelation that "the work of the task force prompted energetic and searching debate that was healthy for the Corps." Gray reported that he received a quality study document that contained many constructive recommendations. Secretary Webb later was supportive of almost all recommendations, except the politically sensitive issue of placing women in combat or at locations that presented uncommon risks. To this complex issue, he believed placing women Marines now serving in the Marine Security Battalion and down to the assignment to an embassy was too high a risk to ensure their safety.

Gray would subsequently appear before the subcommittee with responsibilities and oversight for women, where he testified in part as follows:

> As you know well, the terrorist threat to American diplomatic missions has grown significantly over the last several years. There is no indication now that the global situation will improve. In fact, we view the assignment to this duty as assignment to which Marines may become engaged in actual combat at any moment. Since 1978, eight Marines have been

killed, 11 wounded, and 14 were taken prisoner while serving on Marine security guard duty. Security of our posts is dependent upon the ability of a combat-trained Marine to respond to a variety of physically demanding highly stressful and dangerous contingencies, to include offensive action necessary. ... I said before, this deterrence is based on the sure knowledge that these guards are truly combat-trained Marines.[25]

Several weeks later, then-Acting Secretary of the Navy Henry L. "Larry" Garrett III complimented Gray on the thoroughness of the study and the timeliness of corrective actions.

Often, individuals and officers within the Washington, DC area are so focused on their own areas of responsibilities that when changes occur, they do not appreciate the scope of the cascading effects the interrelated changes have on the institution. As the multiple Gray initiatives began to have their effect, few Marines were aware of the resulting close relationship that was emerging between Gray and Secretary Webb. Gray and Webb were fast becoming close friends and professional allies. The Marine Corps rarely, if ever, had enjoyed such a relationship with the Secretary of the Navy.

Then, just months after Gray became the Commandant, Caspar Weinberger resigned on November 5, 1988, as the Secretary of Defense. He was replaced by Frank Carlucci, an individual who did not have the current global awareness of his predecessor. Because of previous commitments to international conferences and national events, Secretary Carlucci had little time to be in the Pentagon, to adjust and understand the intricacies of the military and the civilian Title 10, U.S. Code interface. Small problems arose, often more from his own perceptions than long-established policies or procedures. His new style of management required adjustments and caused some level of turbulence but the changeover was taking hold. One of the first unintended consequences impacted Secretary of the Navy Webb. The Department of Defense was struggling to implement a mandated $33,000,000,000 reduction in the fiscal year '89 budget. The Navy was directed to absorb approximately $12,000,000,000. Webb expressed serious concerns regarding the budget reduction process. He believed that the many defense reductions had been made in the wrong areas and without clear strategic thought. On three occasions, the uniformed and civilian leadership of the Navy Department provided the Secretary of Defense with proposed cuts totaling the amount required to meet the budget reduction. In each case, the advice of the Navy's senior leadership was ignored. Webb revolted against the warped politics in the Defense Secretary's unexplained action and stated he would resign rather than support unwise decisions.

Secretary Webb's letter of resignation sent directly to President Reagan stated, "Since my recommendations to that effect were rejected by your Secretary of Defense, I am unable to support him personally, or to defend these amended budget deliberations. Consequently, I find it necessary to resign from my position as Secretary of the Navy."[26]

Although I was startled by the announcement, especially after serving with him for more than two years, it didn't surprise me, as Secretary Webb was a man of strong convictions. There were no "gray areas" with him.

The nation was shocked as the media flashed the news. Most of the media praised Secretary Webb for standing by his convictions.[27] Jim Webb was still carrying much love for the Marines he had fought and bled with and watched die, so every decision he made while serving in the Pentagon was a personal payback to his comrades. He was personally restoring, where he could, the political integrity within the Department of Defense. Those who knew Webb as a Marine Corps officer would have predicted his steadfast rebellion against compromising his personal integrity.

Assistant Secretary of the Navy Henry L. "Larry" Garrett III assumed the role as "acting" Secretary of the Navy, pending confirmation of a replacement. To the unskilled eye, these changes made no apparent impact on senior leadership. However, in a matter of weeks, two of the Defense Department's leaders had been replaced, and all previous agreements were placed on hold. Months of planning came to a halt as both new Secretaries reset their organizations' priorities. It was a disruptive, difficult period as unintended consequences of these changes began to directly impact the Marine Corps. The road ahead was unclear.

CHAPTER 13
The Second and Third Critical Years

*"Every Marine is, first and foremost, a rifleman.
All other conditions are secondary."*

General Alfred M. Gray
29th Commandant, U.S. Marine Corps

Even as Gray focused internally on his changes to Quantico, and on promoting a focus on warfighting and training during his first year as Commandant; he was faced with an immensely difficult external battle of ideas with the Navy. During his second and third years as Commandant, this issue of future strategic vision of the naval services dominated his command.

Both the Navy and the Marine Corps have long recognized that to maintain a viable readiness posture, there is a continuous requirement to adjust to the changing world situations and new technologies. The evolution of ship-to-shore movement has been progressive over the past half-century. In the late 1960s, the Marine Corps focus was on integrating helicopters in a vertical assault maneuver to enhance the traditional surface phase. The aging landing craft of Korean War vintage, characterized by their high, blunt forward ramp, were being phased out as obsolete just as more capable helicopters were routinely being brought onboard the amphibious ships. Embarking aviation units, along with infantry units, put a new meaning to the aviation "A" in Marine Air-Ground Task Force (MAGTF), providing a third dimension to the Amphibious Ready Group/Marine Expeditionary Unit's (ARG/MEU's) operating spaces. Furthermore, these new troop transport helicopters could launch from ships over-the-horizon directly into inland destinations, maneuvering over or around suspected enemy troop concentrations defending a beach or port area. This expanded the operational flexibility and speed of movement and denied any defender the opportunity to mass his forces at a single location in order to contest an amphibious assault. Accordingly, the vertical assault became the preferred method of amphibious entry for MAGTF forces. After more than a decade of deployments, and literally hundreds of operations, a multi-air-ground assault evolved into a proven process that could fit most scenarios, from power projection and personnel rescues to security assistance and other nation-building measures.

The development of new amphibious assault ships during the 1970s also complemented the force-in-readiness posture of the Marine Corps. The LHA-class, multipurpose amphibious assault ship, which could launch helicopters from its flight deck and amphibious vehicles from its well deck simultaneously, made its debut with the USS *Tarawa* (LHA-1) in 1975.[1] These ships became important to the nation's security policies and were of great value during the 1990-1991 DESERT STORM Iraqi War. The Navy's shipbuilding also included a revolutionary high-speed, air-cushioned water craft. Known as the Landing Craft Air Cushioned (LCAC) and designed to operate out of the well decks of amphibious ships, their purpose was to move large quantities of tanks, trucks, and engineer equipment over the horizon to distant coastal regions. Moving at speeds of more than 40 knots, the LCACs cruised inches above the surface of the ocean and could cross the beach and move inland before disgorging their cargo. In minutes, the craft could then be unloaded and reenter the surf to return to the flotilla steaming miles out at sea. The Navy/Marine Corps team visualized that the combination of large troop-carrying helicopters— to include the long-range development of the tiltrotor V-22 Osprey helicopter, the LCAC to ferry vehicles rapidly from ships to shore, and the Advanced Amphibious Assault Vehicle (AAAV)—with the speed to travel from ships over the horizon and still assault through the beach zone and inland, would ultimately create the most balanced and powerful expeditionary amphibious combat force in the nation's history. By the close of the 1980s, the "Gator Fleet," as the amphibious ships were called, was well on its way to becoming a force well suited for the rapidly changing world, where insurgency and terrorism was becoming the primary threat.

Gray, a longtime and ardent student of military history, appreciated that with the implosion of the Union of Soviet Socialist Republics (USSR), the post-World War II strategy of containment had succeeded. The international strategic environment was transitioning from a bipolar to a multi-polar world. Long-held alliances aimed at a single common foe were evolving, and the previously acknowledged super powers were losing their influence in a world heavily dominated by economic considerations via security concerns. The growing dependence on scarce resources would require a focus upon the traditional maritime nature of the United States. Further, in consonance with a new strategic policy, national military strategy could no longer be viewed as two distinct complementary strategies, but rather as a single integrated policy—a strategy based on the maritime nature and the future global force of military efforts.[2]

There was also the immediate requirement to implement the Goldwater-Nichols Defense Reorganization Act of 1986. Section 106 of the Act provided for restructuring of the DoD components involved in Special Operations (SO) and Low-Intensity Conflict (LIC).[3] When Gray studied Section 106 of the Act, directing the services to refocus on SO/LIC, he couldn't have helped but ponder in amazement at the timing of this Act in view of his own areas of special concern. For more than a decade, he had advocated for the Marine Corps to increase its special operations capabilities to better contend with the rising global threat of insurgent groups and terrorists. The new congressional mandate came at a most fortuitous time, giving Gray the policy tools to energize his vision of where the Marine Corps should place its intellectual energies and allocate its limited resources. In January 1988 he addressed his General officers and the members of his force structure study group. He shared his conceptual framework and emphasized several key points. First, he recognized the major shift in defense policy inherent in the expansion of special operations and indicated that we should all recognize that the world was entering a SO/LIC era that presented "a unique window of opportunity that seldom comes along." He expressed his conviction that "we hold destiny in our hand and can make the kind of Corps we need tonight, and for tomorrow's crises." His guidance to all in attendance was to help define the Marine Corps structure for a seapower strategy to exploit future small war scenarios. To this end, MAGTFs must be good at both mid-intensity and low-intensity conflict.

Further, he indicated the following guidance for the Marine Corps:

- Must get there as the nation's force of choice;

- Must make the Marine Corps to be in the best interests of the nation;

- Must have special operations capability in every MAGTF; and

- No one can come from the sea except us, and we have to be there first.[4]

Gray was aware many credible thinkers from diverse quarters had embraced the concept of the need to prepare primarily to contest low- or mid-intensity situations, and he felt it was time to act. Other individuals were beginning to speak out. James Webb, former Secretary of the Navy, wrote in the 1988 winter issue of the *Naval War College Review* that the most difficult current strategic question may be how the nation can deter low- or mid-intensity conflict. Or, if deterrence does not work, when do we fight and to what extent? He, like others, did not see any easy solution to a growing threat.

In late 1986, Secretary of Defense Weinberger had appointed a commission to review long-term strategy. In January 1988, the commission, which included the country's most distinguished military and foreign affairs experts, published the report *Discriminate Deterrence*. Even without a contributing Marine Corps advocate among its writers, the report called for MAGTF-type forces. Among its recommendations were the following:

- Need to fit together our plans and forces for a wide range of conflicts, from the lowest intensity to the highest;

- To defend its interests properly in the Third World, the United States will have to take low-intensity conflict much more seriously;

- Increasingly well-equipped small powers as well as new major military powers are likely to give us still stronger incentives to develop a more versatile and discriminate force.[5]

It was into this strategic climate that Gray injected his insights and operations-oriented influence. As the Commandant, he was particularly concerned about the growing threats of regional insurgencies and terrorism in the less developed nations. He saw a need to reassess the Navy and Marine Corps' roles in a changing world. He was quick to become the leading voice on the issue of sustaining America's already limited seapower capabilities. This would become one of Gray's most challenging actions. Historically, when Congress mandates reductions in the defense budget, the size of the fleet becomes a major issue of contention. Gray saw the ominous signs of this happening even before he became the Commandant and he knew the total number of amphibious ships had become the most sensitive unsolved issue between the Navy and the Marine Corps' senior leadership. Their opposing views had evolved into innumerable clashes of wills. There was no definitive solution, as each Service presented different perspectives: the Navy view was for a "deep blue water war" and the Marine Corps was for "combat in the littorals."

Gray's actions to avoid peacetime reduction of the amphibious fleet were counter to the Navy's resource priorities. Throughout the nearly continuous discussions about the long-term size of the total fleet, the Chief of Naval Operations (CNO) and his Navy staff would present a continuous perplexing problem, a mystifying impediment in bureaucratic terms, in their intransigence in accepting a new strategic climate. The Navy staff apparently did not grasp the potential impact of changing worldly threats Gray was using to justify his convictions as to the growing importance of the nation's seapower capabilities.

By 1989, the inter-service conflict within the Navy and Marine Corps had been stretched to near breaking point. This festering issue was more than the different opinions. It had escalated to the seminal level of discussion as to the future role of seapower in support of a maritime nation. With the collapse of Russia and Communism and the peaceful resolution of the Cold War, national leaders and the Congress sought to drastically reduce the Defense Department's annual budget. The Navy saw the opportunity to transfer 15 amphibious ships to inactive status over a two- to three-year period. Gray rebelled against the Navy's nearly unilateral decision to reduce the numbers of active amphibious fleet. It was rare for Gray to take his felt-tip pen and write a lengthy letter, particularly to his seniors, but the issue had reached a crisis requiring immediate corrective action. He prepared a memorandum on the need to maintain the nation's seapower.[6] He also penned a personal letter to the Secretary of the Navy.[7] These two documents remain as seminal arguments for the important role of seapower to the nation's security and economic well-being. Presented in great detail, they reflect back over 44 years, on how naval forces—ships, aircraft, Sailors, and Marines—had responded to significant crises on more than 180 occasions, and how Marines embarked on amphibious ships responded more than 100 times. Equally important in his argument was the increasing trend in the use of forward-deployed amphibious forces to respond to crises around the world.

Gray predicted that, as the world entered a new and uncertain post-Cold War era characterized by increasing numbers of terrorist activities, violence in drug trafficking, and the use of coercive tactics such as hostage-taking, amphibious forces with their evolved special operations capabilities would emerge increasingly as the force of choice.

This far-reaching and forward-looking memorandum captures the breadth and scope of Gray's vision as to the role of the Navy/Marine Corps amphibious forces in the 21st century as exemplified in the following excerpt:

> The United States is a maritime nation. It has always and will always rely upon the seas for commerce with its friends and allies far from our shores, for on-scene response to crises where we have no access rights or permissive facilities, and for simply representing our national interest around the world. ... It is abundantly clear that the ability of adversarial states and groups to openly flourish and aggressively sponsor activities which threaten us across the spectrum of conflict has not diminished, nor can we afford to speculate that it will. ... If we agree that our peacetime presence has contributed to whatever stability has existed in the world to date, then it follows that our absence will increase instability and encourage a power vacuum that could increase our vulnerability.[8]

In the Navy's view, low- and mid-intensity conflicts would continue but would have no appreciable impact on the total fleet. In sharp contrast, the Marine Corps' view was a forecast for a high probability of increased low- to mid-levels of violence, suggesting that the nation should have a force especially configured as its "force of choice" to respond to these "contingency response" issues. Gray's thrust was to bring to the fore the naval forces' inherent flexibility that makes them especially well suited for the contingency response requirements along the likely conflict spectrum. This view put Gray in conflict, not only with the submarine-centered Navy, but also with the Army and the Air Force, which were focused on redesigning forces for high-intensity conflict, such as superpower confrontations in Europe and Asia.

Each Service has a primary focus. The Navy's role in general war is obvious and essential: keep the sea lanes open; project amphibious forces ashore; keep the sea-based leg of the nuclear triad ready and use it if necessary. In all deliberations, Gray carefully articulated that "the nation cannot afford two land armies or two Marine Corps. The concentration of the right forces on the right task just makes good sense and makes the application of limited resources more productive to the nation."[9]

In at least two respects, Gray combined characteristics of the defense intellectual and the strategist warrior. He was keenly aware of the capabilities of his various-sized Marine Air-Ground Task Forces (MAGTFs), and he enjoyed taking the offensive to stimulate even more thinking at the highest administrative and congressional levels. During his many invitations to speak, his common theme was that "the nation's Navy/Marine Corps team has in place the task organizations appropriate to small war situations as they are forward-deployed or can be deployed on amphibious ships or other means, without mobilization, to respond to crises throughout the world."

Later in his congressional testimony, he declared, "While we are fully prepared for the most challenging conflict, your Marine Corps must also stand ready for the most likely conflict—and that is in the Third World. Our amphibious capability, our seaborne mobility, and our expeditionary nature make us uniquely suited for the task; this is the major contribution we provide the nation."

He reminded all that "The Marine Corps is the only military organization in the world that can commit a potent, integrated and balanced air-ground logistics force on short notice without mobilizing a single person."[10]

In spite of Gray's almost solitary effort to paint the changing world's threats as something other than global war, the "blue" side of the team held firm. The Navy's senior leadership did not fully appreciate the immense contributions naval forces could make in supporting low-intensity combat operations and in a naval campaign with extended operations ashore. Few Navy officers were seriously interested in low-intensity conflicts, characterized as they were as both a political-military struggle between contending states or groups and below the level of conventional wars. They saw no naval relationship to the Third World, where unrest prevailed, and the real conflict was waged for the minds through a combination of means employing political, economic, informational, and military instruments.[11]

There would be repeated planning sessions where the Navy and Marine Corps interactive staff exchanges were explosive, with little give on either side. Even after the publication of the DoD's *Discriminate Deterrence* study, the Navy's leadership would not bridge the mental gap that a dynamically changing world also mandated major changes in its operational readiness and warfighting capabilities. The Navy maintained its sense of direction that the super carriers with their aviation components, surface warfare ships focused on fleet defense, and an expanding fleet of nuclear submarines would remain their highest budgetary priorities. This constantly made the already limited number of amphibious ships even more vulnerable to fleet reductions. This basic disagreement would consume much of Gray's time and energy throughout his four-year term as Commandant. With no resolution to their differences, Gray, in late 1989, composed both a personal letter and a seminal memorandum on the critical role seapower provided to the safety and security of the United States.

In spite of the Navy's fixation on a status quo when it came to global threat, Gray changed the focus within the Marine Corps to studies on the possibility of conflicts other than major conventional wars. The whole topic of unconventional warfare, rising insurgency, and terrorist threats had been a matter of deep concern to Gray as far back as the 1970s. As he advanced in rank from Lieutenant Colonel to General officer, he constantly alerted his commands to the rising unconventional threats. After the October 1983 Beirut bombing, he became even more assertive in adapting the operational readiness of the MAGTF to prepare for counterinsurgency scenarios. Gray frequently and deliberately used the terms mid-intensity conflict and low-intensity conflict to clarify several "small war" conditions that could confront American forces in the future. Such an emphasis on irregular warfare made little headway with the Navy, but within the Marine Corps, his independent actions started an internal shift to a new intellectual course. Embracing his own guidance to "turn on the brain power," Gray assigned several study groups to examine specific issues.

Both before and after becoming the 29th Commandant, Gray recognized the constant need to inform and educate the public and foreign nations on the vital role the Marine Corps plays in the international scene. In his rustic and charismatic style, he would often begin his speeches and briefings with the statement, "There is no military formation in the world like the Marine Air-Ground Task Force: the MAGTF." It would consistently cause his surprised audiences to raise eyebrows, and it piqued their interest as he began to clarify that statement. It was a compelling declaration. He shared his insights, dispelling myths and misunderstandings as to why the MAGTF commander and staff were spending so much time and effort before exercises and prior to any deployment orders. Gray explained how he hypothetically issued "trust me" certificates to his audiences and asked for their trust. He said that because of its uniqueness, planning for deployment of a MAGTF is misunderstood by many in the joint and combined arms arenas. He went on to relate that "to understand the MAGTF, one must first understand why the MAGTF exists as it is."

Key to that understanding of the MAGTF is recognizing that Marines are inherently naval forces. They come from the seas. Together with the Navy, they comprise the naval services of the United States. Both services are within the Department of the Navy and take their organization direction from the Secretary of the Navy. Marines serve in key billets on Navy staffs in ships' companies; help in the design and development of amphibious ships, training craft, and aircraft; and participate in the formation of naval strategy.

Ships are designed to handle Marine Corps equipment, and Marine Corps equipment is designed to fit on and operate from Navy ships. Marine pilots are naval aviators, fly naval aircraft with tail hooks and folding wings or rotors, and are trained to operate from either aircraft carriers or from airfields ashore. Navy officers and Sailors serve on Marine staffs—not in a liaison capacity but as permanently assigned members of every Marine tactical organization. It is this Navy/Marine Corps team relationship that is far deeper and more interdependent than simply the necessary association of two organizations assigned to operate jointly on a temporary basis. Thus the MAGTF is not just an organizational association of arms; it is more of grassroots kinship of men and women who employ their skills and weapons when and where needed.

On every occasion where Gray appeared and spoke, he reaffirmed that the historic MAGTF structure "is, and remains, the centerpiece of Marine Corps competencies into the 21st century." In almost every instance, the payoff came in the final praise and at least grudging acknowledgment that he was right, especially after an ensuing successful operation.

Although the Navy/Marine Corps discussion of the reduction in seapower remained "front and center" for Gray, he was actively pursuing a number of other complex issues. His staff was also intensely active in 15 to 20 additional hallmark issues that would have long-range impact upon the future of the Marine Corps. The broad array of these issues and new project proposals seemed endless and almost overwhelming to his Headquarters staff and subordinate field commanders. Letters and naval wireless messages were dispatching the latest command guidance while seeking more information to make the soundest possible decisions. It was uniformly recognized, even to the far corners of the world wherever Marines were deployed, that Gray was in the driver's seat, and that he was driving hard and fast. There was little time to pause, to plan, to think, as most officers were focused on confronting their most immediate problems. The tempo made all aware that major changes would be forthcoming—and soon. Long-range solutions would have to wait. Yet, Gray seemed to consider almost every issue as "one of my highest priorities." There was a wide variety of projects underway, e.g., restructuring the Fleet Marine Forces (FMFs); a DoD base closure and realignment (BRAC) study; the new Maritime Prepositioning Ships (MPS) program; professional education initiatives; and women's roles in the military during combat conditions.

Intermingled with routine day-to-day matters was the persistent scarcity of budgetary resources. The Marine Corps' funding posture was running on a near-empty tank. At the same time there was a constant need to monitor certain programs almost on a daily basis because the DoD, often without warning, would recall large sums of monies that had originally been assigned to the Marine Corps. Every unspent dollar was at risk. In direct contrast, the Corps' experimental funding needs were rising fast to support the experimental tiltrotor V-22 Osprey, the new M1 main battle tank, the upgrading of the Light Armored Vehicle (LAV-25) with a 25mm gun, a new artillery weapon with a complex automated fire-control system, and the latest advancements in night-vision technologies for all infantry units.

Also, in Gray's opinion, there were no "unimportant" developmental programs, and he managed to interact with his Requirements and Programs departments at the Pentagon and the Development Center at Quantico. He took particular note as to the status and progress of developmental programs he had personally approved years earlier (1978-1980) when he had commanded the Development Center. His innate ability to instantly recall many of these projects constantly amazed the Center's project officers. He would frequently share a colorful story or two on why a particular experimental program was initiated, and then wonder aloud why it had not progressed or, unbeknownst to him, had been canceled. In such cases there was always an awkward silence as individuals quickly launched out to get the latest information. Often he would casually point to someone, telling him to go down to the Center's basement, look in such-and-such storage room, and find a specific dust-covered file cabinet holding the results of an important decision briefing. "I want to review that final report again."

Interrupting what appeared to be a full plate of all-consuming issues would frequently emerge an unexpected real-world crisis—which seemed to always explode late on a Friday night or on the afternoon preceding a holiday weekend—that required immediate action by his staff. Too often, the result was a late phone call by work-weary staff officers notifying their families that planned family outings would have to be delayed. Often the situation had a security classification, so the reason they were needed could not be shared with their families.

There were two especially notable crisis situations. The first occurred when Colonel William (Rich) Higgins, USMC, was seized by the Hezbollah while serving with the United Nations Truce Team in Israel, triggering several weeks of fruitless, frantic staff planning efforts. The second was when a specially trained MAGTF was directed to takedown an Iranian oil rig in the Persian Gulf. It was to be a special operations combat event such as had never before been undertaken by the U.S. military. The risks to this venture were extremely high. If the mission failed, it would adversely impact the nation's Middle East long-term commitments. This historic tasking will be discussed later in this chapter.

As Gray approached the midpoint of his four years as Commandant, there was a series of retirements and promotions among his most senior Generals. However, even more significant was the turbulence within the Department of the Navy caused by Secretary Jim Webb's sudden resignation and replacement as Secretary of the Navy by William Ball. Then Ball too resigned after only serving 13 months. His successor was Henry L. "Larry" Garrett III, who moved up from the number two position as Under Secretary of the Navy to become the Secretary of the Navy in May 1989. There was also a change in the Secretary of Defense during this same period in that Secretary Frank Carlucci made a decision to resign from his position in January 1989 and was replaced by Richard B. Cheney, who assumed the office in March 1989. Accordingly, Gray would, over a two-year period, serve three different Secretaries of the Navy and three Secretaries of Defense.

Within the Marine Corps there is a fairly continuous and routine changing of positions at the higher levels. This process and annual rotation of senior officers is more than just name changes. Routinely, each of the individuals involved has more than 30 years of service in the Marine Corps, each with his own areas of expertise, strengths, and views of where the Corps should focus its long-term innovative spirit. Personnel changes in any major institution always cause turbulence as newly positioned leaders adjust to their increased responsibilities. However, in view of the fast tempo of actions and operations occurring under Gray's watch at the midpoint of his tenure as Commandant, each newly appointed person was challenged to his fullest to rapidly assume his new responsibilities and keep up.

General Thomas Morgan, the only other four-star General in the Marine Corps at the time, had been serving as the Assistant Commandant and elected to retire on June 30, 1988. He was a designated naval aviator, an exceptionally bright officer, intellectually quick, steady under pressure, and keenly knowledgeable as to the ways and sensitivities when operating in the Washington arena. He had been a valuable asset to Gray as he transitioned into his Commandant position. Lieutenant General Joseph J. Went, a New Englander and also a naval aviator, was nominated for a fourth star and assumed the position as the new Assistant Commandant on July 1, 1988. General Went was a gifted logistician, with broad experiences as a commander of all types of Marine Corps units, who would prove to be a steady influence in a sea of chaos.

Lieutenant General Ernest C. Cheatham, a much-decorated warrior, had been serving at Headquarters Marine Corps as the Deputy Chief of Staff for Manpower. In January 1988, he elected to retire after faithfully serving the Corps for more than 36 years. His successor was Lieutenant General John I. Hudson, a naval aviator with a commendable combat record and numerous command and important staff assignments.

Within HQMC, the staff's activity directions and tempo were most often set by the Plans, Policy and Operations Department. It was this Department that had the primary responsibility to interact with the Joint Staff and the other services on the broadest aspects of military operational matters. The incumbent, the soft-spoken and brilliant Lieutenant General John Phillips, elected to retire in January 1988. His nominated successor was Major General Carl E. Mundy, who was advanced to Lieutenant General and assumed the full responsibilities as Deputy Chief of Staff for Plans, Policy, and Operations in March 1988. After a year in this position, Carl Mundy would assume command of Fleet Marine Force, Atlantic (FMFLANT) in Norfolk, Virginia. He would serve in this important position until June 1991, when he became the 30th Commandant of the Marine Corps. General Mundy was a Southern gentleman in the finest sense. He performed exceptionally well in Washington's "give and take" activities and was recognized as a person who could smoothly interact within the "joint arena" and bring closure to difficult issues.

Lieutenant General Keith A. Smith, a naval aviator, was ending his career as the Deputy Chief of Staff for Aviation. He was much respected as a true professional by all Marines. Wherever he served, he consistently performed superbly. General Smith's military assignments encompassed all aspects of the Marine Corps U.S. Code Title 10 responsibilities. A quiet man, Smith was consistently cognizant and vigilant to the care and welfare of his Marines and Sailors. A Marine's Marine. Though deeply hurt by the loss of his son, Vincent, a Marine Corps Captain who was killed in Beirut, Keith Smith and his family never hesitated in faithful service to their Corps. He retired in April 1988.

Smith's replacement was Lieutenant General Charles H. Pitman, an exceptional pilot who could and did fly about every aircraft in the military's inventory. Pitman was one of those few individuals who were truly at home in the air. On the ground, General Pitman was noted for his social graces, but when flying there was never a more focused or safer pilot. An individual without fear, he braved repeated incidents of enemy fire as he led troop-carrying helicopter assaults and rescue missions during the Vietnam War and was involved in the ill-fated Iranian hostage rescue. General Pitman proved to be an innovative and creative Deputy Chief of Staff, Aviation, and a valuable asset to Gray's efforts to transition the Marine Corps into the 21st century.

Another key Lieutenant General position, located 30 miles south of Headquarters Marine Corps, was the Commanding General, Marine Corps Development and Education Command (MCDEC) at Quantico. Lieutenant General Frank E. Peterson, also a naval aviator and much-decorated combat veteran, was nearing the end of his colorful career. General Peterson was the first black General officer in the Marine Corps, and there could not have been a better role model for all Marines. After 36 years of service, he retired on August 1, 1988.

His successor was Lieutenant General William R. Etnyre, a former enlisted Marine who had been commissioned as a Second Lieutenant in August 1953. General Bill Etnyre was a talented, soft-spoken person who never sought the spotlight but just performed well wherever he was assigned. His duty assignments varied greatly. From being a Special Assistant to the Secretary of the Navy to multiple commands and challenging staff assignments, he proved to have those special skills and talents to become a General officer. Later, after his service as the Commanding General, Marine Corps Combat Development Command (formerly MCDEC), Gray would remark on the extraordinary performance and forward-looking visions that General Etnyre had shown in supporting the preparations for and during the 1990 Gulf DESERT SHIELD and DESERT STORM conflict.

During the tenure of every national leader, or in the appointments of the Chiefs of Services of our military forces, unpredictable events occur. Such unforeseen events, be they a procurement scandal, a family pleading for assistance and requesting information on a wayward son or daughter, or an operational situation that ends in tragedy, impact these leaders in a variety of ways. Each Service Chief often stands alone during such occurrences because he is the single spokesman and symbolic head of the particular Service. Often, the event can be dealt with in a purely procedural manner, because when leading a Service of between 200,000 and a million men and women, that Service's leader neither knows the individuals involved personally nor their families. Though the grief is felt for his charges and communicated to the bereaved families, it is a distant type of response.

Colonel William Richard "Rich" Higgins, USMC, vanished while serving as the Chief, Observer Group (Lebanon), and as the Senior U.S. Military Observer (Palestine). Colonel Higgins had a personal relationship with Gray that spanned a decade of service together. They first met when Captain Higgins was serving as infantry company commander. They shared intermittent duty assignments in the operating forces and during staff assignments in the Pentagon throughout the next ten years. The military world provides everyone with many acquaintances, and, over the long haul, with few really close friends. However, a true friendship developed between Higgins and Gray. As Colonel Higgins was closing out his duties as the Military Assistant to Secretary of Defense Caspar Weinberger, he and his wife, Robin, made a departing call on Gray. Gray knew Rich had been personally selected for duty as Chief of the prestigious U.S. Military Observer Group, Truce Supervision Organization (Palestine). But Gray was apprehensive about Colonel Higgins taking this Middle East assignment. His finely tuned intelligence monitoring alerted him to the high risk and possible threat to the safety of Colonel Higgins during his forthcoming Middle East assignment.

Colonel Higgins and Robin—a Marine Corps Major—had earlier found a sketch of the Commandant's historic quarters at Marine Barracks at 8th and I Streets in Washington, DC. Not content with just a copy of the sketch, they searched and located the original 29th signed copy, which they felt was a most appropriate Christmas gift to the Marine Corps' 29th Commandant. Gray was surprised and delighted with the gift.

Rich Higgins and I, Gerry Turley, had also served together several times. First, when he was a Captain, we were both assigned as Marine advisors to the South Vietnamese Marine Corps. Later he served as a company commander in the 2nd regiment, and when promoted to Major, I reassigned him to my regimental staff as the S-4, Logistics Officer. He performed superbly during our NATO deployment in BOLD GUARD-78. Even later, when I was appointed as an Assistant Deputy Secretary of Defense, Rich was assigned to Secretary of Defense Caspar Weinberger's office. We were in near-daily contact, often running the Washington, DC trails from the Pentagon gym together.

On July 6, 1988, Colonel Higgins arrived in Israel and assumed command of the U.S. Military Observer Group, Truce Supervision Organization. He was serving as a direct representative of the United Nations, donning the blue beret that distinguished all UN personnel. He immediately began meeting the different national components while visiting all the observer checkpoint positions. Colonel Higgins was a skilled military professional who quickly bonded with the 75 to 80 multinational peace observers. On February 17, 1989, he was on his way to a UN observer position near the Lebanese border when he was captured by a Hezbollah terrorist group.

A search was made of the area, but it was only a halfhearted gesture after a lengthy delay with little planning to accomplish an effective effort. Shortly thereafter, a statement was issued by the Organization of the Oppressed of the World declaring that it would put Colonel Higgins on trial for crimes committed against the Lebanese and Palestinian people. Colonel Higgins was declared a spy with no rights. The Marine Corps had no choice but to declare Colonel Higgins "missing." On April 21, the Hezbollah, following terrorist standards, released a photograph of Colonel Higgins to the Western news agencies. He was later executed by Iranian terrorists. Although the exact date of his death is uncertain, he was declared dead on July 6, 1990.[12]

The apparent indifference to the Higgins hostage situation by the United Nations was perhaps the most shocking aspect of the affair. Regrettably, the UN Secretary-General did not see the long-term consequences of Higgins's captivity on other UN employees. More than a week passed before the Secretary-General even issued a simple statement, in which he said, "I have regretfully come to the conclusion that it is almost certain that Colonel Higgins is dead." That was, in substance, his only response to Higgins's "probable" death.[13] Over the next few months, the passive inactions by the UN Secretary-General led to the implication that the United Nations would not counter the kidnapping, illegal incarceration, or murder of its staff by other terrorist organizations.

It was this type of multi-bureaucratic passivity that frustrated the efforts of Gray to get Colonel Higgins released. Throughout the hostage ordeal, Gray had sought out innumerable individuals and agencies, even foreign contacts, to explore every possible avenue to obtain Higgins' release and return to the United States. Members of the Congress also appealed to the UN Secretary-General, declaring, "Whenever we order a member of our armed forces to hazardous assignments, we—and they—must have every assurance that those who direct them will abide by the same tenets held by their brothers in arms … and that when they die fighting for peace and freedom, we will do all that is right and fitting to honor their service and sacrifice. This includes putting them to rest properly."[14]

On July 31, 1990, Hezbollah terrorists released a grisly image of a hostage, bound and gagged, dangling from a scaffold. The man was later identified as Colonel Higgins. The brutality of this act, as well as the epic decision by the Hezbollah terrorist organizations to videotape this tragedy, seemed incomprehensible to any civilized society. Most

Americans were aghast at the insensitivity of the terrorists. It was a clear display of brinkmanship by the captors: "a war of nerves." It was also a clear forerunner of other terrorist actions to be perpetrated against the United States at some future date.

The terrorists claimed they killed Colonel Higgins in retaliation for Israel's seizure of Sheik Abdul Karim Obeid, in southern Lebanon. Gray's anguish was very deep, because he felt a personal responsibility for his fellow Marine officer's death. It was obviously not his doing, but in the months that followed, he silently reflected and mulled over what else could have been done. Tragically, like Presidents Carter, Reagan, and Bush, he also realized how elusive terrorist groups are, and, accordingly, how difficult it is to take meaningful action against them.

Finally, on December 24, 1991, the bodies of Colonel Higgins and American hostage William Buckley, CIA Station Chief in Beirut, and also a close friend of Gray, were returned to the United States. The Air Force C-141 cargo jet carrying their bodies arrived at Andrews Air Force Base on a cold, dreary, and windy afternoon. A solemn crowd of several hundred remained watchful and silent as the two flag-draped coffins were removed and placed in waiting hearses. There was a special area set aside for diplomats and dignitaries, and Gray would clearly have been one of the luminaries, but he chose not to join them. He came to pay homage to a fellow Marine, not to be seen. Bunny and I were also there, and we noticed how Gray moved to the general viewing area and stood several rows back in the crowd, in civilian clothes, unknown to the group around him. He came to pay his final respects as Colonel Higgins's loyal friend and, incidentally, also as his former Commandant. General Al Gray, USMC, was retired by then.

Colonel William Richard Higgins, USMC, was buried with full military honors on December 30, 1991, in the National Cemetery at Quantico. A small brass plaque placed on his gravesite reads:

HE DIED FAR AWAY, BEFORE HIS TIME,
BUT AS A SOLDIER AND FOR HIS COUNTRY.[15]

The graveside service finally brought closure, but the hurt remained with Gray and the small group of Colonel Higgins's closest friends.

By the time Gray was closing on his second year as the Commandant, there were so many new projects and programs under way it was difficult to distinguish between the more important initiatives. There was expanded recruit training, more hands-on opportunities for weapons skill refinements, improved schooling for junior enlisted Marines, improved education programs for senior staff noncommissioned officers, and advanced training within all educational facilities. What is most interesting with all these programs is that Gray recognized the vital need to increase the educational opportunities for his Marines. The second aspect of this focus was making "smarter Marines." Many other leaders had previously recognized the increasing requirement mandated by the acquisition of advanced information and weapons systems entering the operating forces. The difference is that Gray took the lead and demanded that changes be implemented. He made it happen.

Years from now, historians will recognize Gray's many important milestones that were triggered to begin the Corps' transition into a viable force-in-readiness for the early 21st century. He will be known for many achievements, but most prominent will be his title as "The Professional Education Commandant."

In July 1988, he established the Marine Corps Professional Reading Program and issued these instructions: "I firmly believe that professional reading is essential to the growth of all Marines. In the profession of Arms in particular, reading is a demanding personal chore to continually remain militarily proficient. Marines fight better when they fight smarter."[16]

He also stated, "The reading program will be used to provide a continuum of study for all Marine leaders. Whether serving in the FMF, the supporting establishment, or attending resident formal schools, as in the past, commanders will continue to be responsible for the professional development of the Marines under his charge."

On November 10, 1988, Gray established new mandatory continuing professional military education (PME) requirements for all Marine leaders, Corporal through General. The initial Professional Reading List contained 100 books that provided commanders with the framework to use to implement their PME program.[17] In order to implement and manage the new PME program, a new organization would be established to serve as the focal point for PME with the Marine Corps. This organization became the Marine Corps University (MCU).

The MCU was established to strengthen and enhance the PME process by providing a professional military education system designed to impart a common base of professional knowledge throughout the Marine Corps. This system provided a progressive and sequential process that included the analysis and development of PME competence appropriate to grade and responsibilities of the individual Marine. The MCU provided an integrated, worldwide PME network and integrated the Marine Corps Institute and the Marine Corps Research Library under a common commander.[18]

The Marine Corps University was founded on August 1, 1989, by Gray. However, the Marine Corps schools claim a much longer history, beginning in 1891 with 29 company grade officers attending the School of Application. This school became the Officers Training School in 1909 and eventually relocated from Philadelphia to Quantico, immediately following America's entry into World War I. Beginning in 1930, special groups were formed from selected Field Officer School graduates and students to work on amphibious doctrine and requirements. To reflect the importance of the Marine Corps' new mission: "To seize advanced bases for naval operations," two schools were designated Amphibious Warfare Senior and Junior Courses for field grade and company grade, respectively.

In 1946, the Marine Corps reestablished the three-tiered, professional military education system. Lessons learned from World War II and new concepts based upon atomic warfare theory were quickly added to the curriculum of the Amphibious Warfare course. In 1965, shortly after the Corps introduced vertical envelopment, the curriculum at both schools was again modified to include the helicopter in amphibious warfare.

In 1964, the Senior Course was re-designated Command and Staff College and the Junior Course became Amphibious Warfare School. Amphibious warfare remained the core theme in both courses. The Corps' professional educations were further expanded in February 1971 when the first course of the Staff NCO Academy was convened. Later, in 1981, the NCO Basic Course was established at 18 widely dispersed sites, and the Senior Course for Staff Sergeants was activated in 1982, adjacent to the Advanced Course for First Sergeants and Master Sergeants at Quantico. All of these modifications to the Marine Corps education were deemed necessary to stay abreast of changes in national security strategy, worldly threats, and the progressive advancement in new operational concepts, doctrine, and emerging technologies.

Shortly after Gray became the Commandant, maneuver warfare theory was more formally introduced, and a renewed focus on Marine Air-Ground Task Force (MAGTF) operations was implemented. He was bringing the concept of asymmetrical warfare into the Marine Corps education process, an unprecedented step toward transitioning its forces for greater utility to regional commanders in the 21st century. In 1989, Gray directed the five independent Marine Corps schools at Quantico be organized into the Marine Corps University. And in 1990, the Art of War Studies, which he visualized, was created, and a year later it matured into the Marine Corps War College as the Corps' senior-level officer professional military education school.

Even though Gray was stationed at Quantico during the 1970s and 1980s, his professional activities enabled him to have a profound impact upon the developments and accomplishments of the Marine Corps War College.

Unappreciated by many, his broader vision and ultimate goal was to eventually have the Marine Corps University accredited to award a Masters of Military Science Degree by the Commission on Colleges of the Southern Association of Colleges. This was not to be an easy task. It would take years for the commission's deliberation process to grant accreditation. In 1999, long after Gray's retirement, the MCU was formally accredited to award a Masters of Military Science Degree and, by 2003, MCU was further accredited to award a Masters of Strategic Studies and a Masters of Operational Studies to professional warfighters. After more than 220 years of rudimentary and progressively demanding educational programs, the Marine Corps had finally reached a professional level equal that of the other military Service schools.

Two frequent questions prevailed throughout Gray's tenure as the Commandant: "Where is Gray?" and "Has anyone seen Gray?" He was the type of individual who revolted against all measures to hold him to a rigid daily schedule. Historically, as a regiment, brigade, and 2nd Marine Division and Force Commander, it was not uncommon for him to be off schedule because someone or some event arose that became more important to him. He also had an irregular pattern of simply disappearing with no one having the slightest idea where he was. When Gray became the Commandant, any sudden disappearance would cause many a staff officer to scurry to locate him.

Gray enjoyed showing up unannounced in unexpected places. A classic example of trying to monitor his exact location took place on the Quantico Marine Corps base. In this case, he unexpectedly entered the main gate and, as ordered, the sentries quickly notified the commanding general's office that the Commandant had just entered the base proper. However, since Gray was not on an official schedule to visit any specific location, the word was quickly passed to subordinate commands to "be alert, but don't disturb him—wherever he is."

Almost an hour went by with no one reporting to have sighted him. There was a rising question as to his whereabouts. The Base Commander became concerned about the many questions: "Where is Gray?" He asked then-Colonel Anthony "Tony" Zinni to try to locate him. Zinni took his personal car and drove all over the mainside areas in search of Gray's Jeep station wagon, to no avail. Finally, he drove into the small town of Quantico, across the railroad tracks, down the main street, and then turned to reenter the base via the back gate. Colonel Zinni knew Gray was an avid reader, so he drove by the Marine Corps Association Book Store, but his Jeep wasn't there. Tony recalls glancing across the street toward an active and noisy softball game being enjoyed by young Marines. A familiar-looking Jeep station wagon parked near the ballpark fence caught his eye. Zinni assumed Gray must have stopped to watch the game. He was wrong.

Somehow, Gray had borrowed a glove and managed to get himself in the "pickup" game as the shortstop. Crouched over, beating his fist into his glove, he was totally absorbed in the game. He was chattering at the batter as though he had been there all day. Zinni initially couldn't believe his eyes. Nor could Gray's teammates believe they were playing ball with the Commandant of the Marine Corps.[19] Finally discovered, Gray returned the glove and, grinning broadly, trotted off the field. The players and the spectators in the stands cheered wildly, and Gray gleefully chastised Colonel Zinni for interrupting his ballgame. Perhaps, just for a few moments, Gray was recalling his own high school teammates from another time and another place. It was a good release mechanism for him.

There would be other sudden disappearances by Gray over the years. These were not disappearances "getting away" from his responsibilities. On the contrary; knowing the intensity of his focus on difficult and complex issues, his stepping back by getting out of the immediate arena provided opportunities to refresh himself. It was important for him to take time out to gauge the environment and the road ahead and thereby review the direction the Corps was moving and quietly reassess his vision.

Among the endless evolving activities within the Virginia and Maryland Beltway circling Washington, the priority of focus is often jarred by real-world happenings. Most often, those unexpected, to the general public, emerging crises have been under the Defense Department's scrutiny for some time, and preliminary responses have been covertly planned, "Just in case." One example was a contingency response plan being carefully monitored for months before the U.S. military would take any direct action.

At an earlier time, November 17, 1987, Lieutenant General Ernest Cook, Commanding General, Fleet Marine Force Atlantic in Norfolk directed that a contingency Marine Air-Ground Task Force be activated and deployed to the Persian Gulf in January 1988. As Colonel William "Bill" Rakow, the MAGTF commander, recalled, the mission was quite vague; simply to report to the commander, Joint Task Force Middle East (JTFME) in Bahrain in support of OPERATION EARNEST WILL (American military protection of Kuwaiti-owned tankers from Iranian attacks), and the escort of re-flagged (Kuwaiti to U.S.) oil tankers passing through the Gulf from the Strait of Hormuz to Kuwait. There were no amplifying instructions or actual mission tasking given at that time. Bill Rakow had to assume that any mission would entail direct action against an armed force. But the "who, what, and when" remained unknown.[20]

On his return to Camp Lejeune, Rakow met with Colonel Mike Myatt, Officer-in-Charge of II MEF's Special Operations Training Group. Colonel Myatt had also made a recent visit to the Joint Task Force Middle East operations area, and the two Colonels formed a small planning cell. With little to go on, they decided to base all their planning action on the MAGTF organizational structure, with special operations capable (SOC) abilities. Next, they assessed different potential missions for each of the 18 tasks identified as special operations missions. It was the only effective methodology in which they could explore the broadest variety of probable, or possible, missions. It became obvious that they would need additional support and technical assistance to plan and execute many different type missions, so on November 10, 1987, a meeting was held to inform other II MEF Commanders of the arising contingency mission. Support was immediately offered, and a special contingency MAGTF task organization was organized. It consisted of more than 400 Marines and Sailors, the vast majority of them with Marine Expeditionary Unit (Special Operations Capable) MEU (SOC) experience.

Intense training began in mid-November, with deployment in late January 1988. The time in transit was devoted to preparing standard operating procedures that were progressively expanded into separate annexes on each of the potential SOC contingency missions. Much like all Marines and Sailors, while aboard ships, they conducted situational training exercises (STXs), using what they believed could be real-world targets: oil rigs, islands, ships, takedowns, etc. Each was continually refined by the battle staff's composite rapid planning techniques, including execution checklists and prepackaged ammunition and equipments lists.[21] The Navy staff and the other Services, such as special operations forces (SOFs), were continuously sought out to provide their professional expertise.

As they continued to mold their teaming efforts, they were able to run audible unplanned situations depending upon different scenarios thrust upon the MAGTF planners by the ever-present "red cell." To ensure every leader was completely knowledgeable, all key participants were active players in the near-daily situational training exercises.

With the increased tension in the Middle East, anti-American propaganda activities by Iran were progressively challenging the presence of U.S. ships in the Persian Gulf. On April 14, 1988, the guided missile frigate USS *Samuel B. Roberts* struck a naval mine, suffering extensive damage and personnel casualties. It was subsequently determined that Iran was responsible for the hostile act of laying the mines. The Commander, Joint Task Force Middle East was directed to execute a proportional retaliatory operation.

A number of potential targets were examined, including the capture and destruction of an offshore oil rig complex. After extensive examination, it was decided that the preferred means of neutralization would be by helicopter insertion of a Special Operations Capable Marine Air-Ground Task Force.[22] The mission was designated as OPERATION PRAYING MANTIS. The target was dead center in a massive Iranian oil field known as the Sassan Region.

Within 72 hours of the USS *Samuel B. Roberts* striking the mine, the JTFME Commander ordered Colonel Rakow's Contingency MAGTF 2-88 to take down a particular Iranian oil rig complex. (Interestingly, the Rakow planning team had actually used this oil rig with multiple well heads for rehearsal during their training sessions.) It was an enormous complex, with multiple platforms linked together by catwalks. One of the buildings had seven levels that would need detailed searching. There was a separate large living quarters for the oil rig crew, indicating a sizeable Iranian complement. One Russian-made ZU-23 twin-machine gun was located on one of the helicopter landing pads, showing that the crew had a limited defensive capability. The unknown factor was whether or not they would fight.

In addition to the MAGTF, the Navy assigned four surface warfare ships to provide preliminary fires and, later, on-call supporting fires to the assault element. The risk to the helicopter assault mission success was carefully supported with well-developed deception plans. The Task Commanders' *Rules of Engagement* were distributed to all hands. The decision to execute the raid was given to the MAGTF on the 17th of April. Colonel Rakow and his two immediate leaders, Lieutenant Colonel Larry Outlaw, the Airborne Commander, and Lieutenant Colonel Sam Brinkley, the raid commander, began their final preparations.

At precisely 0803 the next morning, Global Oil Separation Plant in Iran was engaged by naval gunfire from the USS *Merrill* and the USS *McCormick*. Their fire was selectively placed on the southern half of the oil platform using air-burst in order to demonstrate to the Iranians that the United States "meant business" and was taking direct combat action. The enemy responded with the ZU-23, but all rounds fell short of the ships. After a short period, U.S. naval gunfire was halted. The Iranians were notified that they had ten minutes to evacuate the oil platform. They complied, scrambling down to a small boat dock and into a rusty old tug that quickly steered away from the oil rig.

Two CH-46 helicopters, each with 20 combat-loaded troops, lifted off the USS *Trenton* and were placed under the control of the raid and air commanders who were already airborne in a Huey near the Global Oil Separation Plant (GOSP) target. Following another short period of naval preparatory gunfire, at 0936, the two CH-46s moved in and hovered directly over the oil plant's landing pads. The troops quickly rappelled down by "fast-roping" onto the oil rig. The barracks had caught fire and were burning, creating heavy smoke and limiting visibilities. A systematic search was carried out on all platforms, at all levels. A number of small 7.62mm weapons were recovered. No enemy personnel were found. As the troops searched, there was a continuing series of secondary explosions caused by the earlier naval gunfire, but there were no injuries to personnel on either side.

The second phase of the raid began when the critical role of the seizure team gave an all-clear. A special explosive ordnance demolition team then landed by helicopter on the oil rig's small helo-landing pads. Their mission was to destroy the GOSP by placing charges on the catwalks, ammunition storage areas, generator sheds, lifting cranes, and communications facilities. *Mission Guidance* stated, "No charges are to be placed on storage tanks or directly on well heads, to avoid causing a major environmental oil spill."[23]

Once on the platform, Gunnery Sergeant David F. Goley, with his seven-man infantry support team, began placing more than 1,300 pounds of various types of explosive charges in key locations. As this phase began, the planned withdrawal of the assault force began. Within an hour and a half, all charges were set. Colonel Rakow then ordered the complete withdrawal of U.S. personnel from the rig by 1300. With the last Marines being lifted from the oil rig landing pads, Gunnery Sergeant Goley set the explosive timing switches and the rig was completely neutralized by the multiple explosions that followed. For his heroic actions, "Gunny" Sergeant Goley was recommended for a Bronze Star with Combat V.[24]

The planning and complete success of this unique raid mission could not have happened without years of earlier planning and training. Unknowingly, this mission was conceptualized back in the mid-1980s. The basic idea originated when General Al Gray was the Commanding General II MEF "in the Carolinas." It was a time when most Marine units were keying on amphibious and mechanized operations. It was a time of "Cold War" peace when Gray, on his own, insisted upon the inclusion of special operations capabilities in the operational readiness of all units under his command. This initiative, one of many, was considered by other officers as moving in an unpopular direction, and it troubled many tradition-minded Marine leaders. Gray had created further exasperations when he began to join with several agents of the Federal Bureau of Investigation (FBI) who had been requested to assist in his Marines' training for special operations missions. He ordered more emphasis placed on raids, to include the seizure of oil rigs. To many, it had sounded like "mission impossible," an extreme crisis situation many suspected would never happen. They rationalized that Gray's tempo of training operations was already high, and this tasking seemed unrealistic and unnecessary.

In quiet response, there was a consensus among some Marine officers that Gray was attempting to mimic the British Royal Marine Commandos. Gray knew of these distant comments. He perhaps felt some resentment, but, as a visionary, was not deterred. He firmly believed the world was changing, and new thoughts, ideas, and

capabilities should be integrated into every deploying unit. The boldness of his vision, and his tenacious determination to move forward
and raise the capabilities of MAGTFs was subsequently validated
when Colonel Rakow summarized the success of OPERATION
PRAYING MANTIS:

> The procedures we used during the workups, deployment,
> and employment of Contingency MAGTF 2-88 were taken
> directly from those learned from the MEU/SOC program. Our
> success can be attributed to the knowledge, attitude, skill, and
> habits learned from the programs placed into being by Gray.
> He was one of those rare leaders whose influence dominated
> our thinking and our approach to mission accomplishment.

Reflectively, this event validated the concept that any MAGTF-
sized force, with additional "certified" training, would be able to
conduct special operations missions. The success of PRAYING
MANTIS did much to accelerate the Marine Corps' initial transition
in preparation for the growing threat of insurgencies and terrorism in
the littorals of the world. More real-world special operations missions
would follow in other parts of the world, reaffirming that the Marine
Corps remained the nation's force-in-readiness. Parts of Gray's vision
of developing future operational capabilities of the Marine Corps
were falling into place.

As Gray closed out each year in office, he prepared a personal letter
and sent it to all the Marine Corps' General officers. He appreciated
the fact that many from his Board of Directors were on joint, or perhaps, distant overseas assignments and did not have the opportunity
to stay in close touch with Headquarters, Marine Corps. His initiative was to keep his Generals informed of the series of changes that
occurred during the year, and set forth the anticipated plans for the
coming year. *The Commandant's Report to the Officer Corps,* dated
May 1989, begins, "The young Marine of today wants to understand
his Corps. He wants to know where we are heading, and he wants to

know why. … This report to the Corps' officers is intended to assist you in understanding what my vision of the future for our Corps is in terms of what we have accomplished so far and where we still have to go." Gray then proceeded to present the following broad categories:

- How we will train and fight;
- Marine battle skills training;
- MAGTF Structure and manning initiatives;
- Major ground and aviation programs;
- Our role in supporting national security; and
- Marine Corps role in the maritime strategy.

He closed his letter on a more personal note. Written with his felt-tip pen was the following:

> We should understand and use the thoughts contained here—
> in everything we do—in or out of combat situations. In other
> words, a way of life and career-long thought process.[25]

Just when most Marine officers, who had been watching and reading of Gray's multitude of activities and new projects, assumed he had finally identified all his major projects, they were surprised with his decision to study and activate a riverine capability. It was a bewildering declaration, and openly deliberated by all officers. The general consensus was, Gray was trying to turn the Marine Corps into something like the British Royal Marines. This was not the case at all, because, as in all new activities, Gray would turn to recognized experts. We see this type of response from Gray time and time again. A classic example was his unusually close alignment with the FBI when he saw the need for experienced experts in hostage takedown or special weapons and tactics (SWAT) and raid activities.

Historically, U.S. forces had been involved in a number of riverine environments from the river campaigns of the Civil War, to the pre-World War II China River patrols, and on to the various actions in the Mekong Delta during the Vietnam era. From the late 1980s through the '90s, U.S. Atlantic Command played a significant role in the government's efforts to stem the flow of illegal drugs into the United States. The initial commitment was in support of Columbia, with the objective of conducting riverine operations with the Columbian Marines to deny the narco-guerrillas longitudinal use of specific waterways within Columbia. The goal was to achieve complete control of the waterways "at and inside Columbia's borders."[26]

While Gray was the Commanding General at FMFLANT, he continued to advance the special operations capability of the Marine Amphibious Unit (MAU). He saw the need for small water craft that could be employed during amphibious raids.

Actually as early as 1987, while commanding Fleet Marine Force Atlantic, then- Lieutenant General Gray directed Colonel D.N. Noble, Officer-in-Charge, Special Operations Training Group (SOTG), to procure watercraft capable of providing battalion landing teams with an improved over-the-horizon surface amphibious raid capability. After extensive research, the SOTG purchased from Boston Whaler Corporation 36 Rigid Raiding Craft. This craft and the Zodiac Combat Rigid Raiding Craft were selected to provide a dependable long-range means for landing a large raid force on almost any coastline.[27] Shortly thereafter, the 3rd Battalion, 6th Marines began training at Little Creek in Virginia.

In May 1988, Gray testified before the Senate Armed Services Committee. In his closing remarks, he stated:

> It is in the Third World regions where many of our vital interest live, and where conflicts are going on right now. And, where I would say that the sea services should be the predominant service, the service of choice in meeting most of these contingency requirements. This is because with the capabilities that the nation needs to protect its sea lanes of commerce also live the capabilities needed in the Third World.[28]

What concerned Gray was that more than 90 percent of the U.S. riverine craft had been deactivated after the Vietnam War. He saw a growing need for such craft to be utilized to both conduct drug interdiction and suppress terrorist use of the Third World's waterways.

The Marine Corps actually began deploying detachments to Panama in 1995 and maintained a presence there through 1999. In August 2000, a detachment of a Small Craft Company deployed to Argentina, Paraguay, and Bolivia to conduct bilateral training with riverine forces. Their mission was to conduct drug interdiction on the nations' three major rivers. Much later, the Marine Corps' small riverine force would play a significant role in addressing the river-borne insurgents during the Iraq War.[29] Although the eventual use of riverine craft was never envisioned for service in the waterways of Iraq, Gray saw the future potential need.

As Gray moved past his 1,000th day of tenure as the 29th Commandant, the results of his efforts to transition the Marine Corps into the 21st century portrayed his determination to push the operating forces into a more flexible and "most ready" force when the nation was least ready. It had been three years of dynamic efforts that spanned the full spectrum of the Corps' mission responsibilities. So many new initiatives had been undertaken since June 30, 1987, time to reflect on which lasting transitions were actually achieved became necessary.

Although there was a nearly endless expansion of programs and training scenarios, Gray achieved immediate and long-range benefits from a number of notable initiatives. The expanded recruit training was showing favorable trends. The recruits' follow-on Marine battle skills and the School of Infantry Training were well established and produced a more qualified, expeditionary-oriented Marine. Gray's initiative to upgrade more advanced educational courses for junior NCOs, staff NCOs, and commissioned officers was showing measurable change. His conviction that every Marine must subordinate himself to the betterment of the Corps was being universally recognized. Additionally, that every Marine must enter into a lifetime of learning through self-education and professional experiences had energized their reading and searching for military knowledge. Gray's Professional Reading List had become an intellectual stimulant for Marines of all ranks as readers were encouraged to read selected books that focused on their particular ranks and skills.

To foster greater attention of field exercises, particularly MAGTF maneuver warfare operations, Gray frequently scheduled his travels to arrive at the culminating events. He showed personal interest in the various special operations events that commanders had included in their training. His continuous interest in all types of operational exercises further stimulated his fellow General officers and senior unit commanders to be more creative in their planning and execution of littoral-warfare-related operations. All commanders soon discovered there was no field exercise that escaped his attention. Surprise visits were common, with the commanders usually receiving his personal encouragement. They also learned that "there is always room for improvement." This was just Gray's way of continually pushing young leaders to "raise the bar" to achieve even greater things.

When new equipment, radios, Unmanned Aircraft Vehicles (UAVs), or weapons were brought in to the various MAGTFs, Gray would ensure the Marines programmed to use the systems received proper preliminary training to maximize the benefits. Surveillance, reconnaissance, and intelligence (SRI) activities were sought out during every visit. When found, he would stress their increasing role of SRI units that must be anticipated in a rapidly changing world where small wars and terrorist threats are rising.

During the past three years, Gray's two premier items of equipment had advanced through critical developmental milestones. The tiltrotor V-22 Osprey had experienced some technical problems, but nothing to hinder its movement into the Marine Air Wings. The V-22 was a vital aviation system to support the Corps' Over-the-Horizon concept for Navy and Marine Corps operations in the world's littorals during the early years of the 21st century. For the Corps' ground forces, the Advanced Amphibious Assault Vehicle (AAAV) had also experienced the normal amount of technical problems as it continued to pass through its developmental milestones. Collectively, these two air-ground systems, when included with the Navy's Landing Craft Air Cushion (LCAC), would culminate with the nation having the most advanced expeditionary capabilities ever. These would be the major tools that would best fulfill the need for a naval expeditionary force to serve the nation during a potentially violent and restless era where future enemy forces would prepare for small wars and terrorist aggression.

The final dimension to the true readiness of the Marine Corps warriors to do battle on a distant desert was the intangible and always transparent assessment of its warriors. New equipment and new doctrine doesn't ensure success on the battlefield. The Marine Corps hadn't been in a major combat situation since the last battles of the Vietnam War, in the 1970s. This was a new breed of men and women. In contrast to the prevalent low educational levels of the Service members enlisted in that war, almost all the enlisted were now high school graduates. They were not openly patriotic, but deep down, they were proud to wear the title Marine. They had earned it, and much more, as they advanced their professional knowledge and military skills. The advanced training programs Gray had put in place gave them the confidence to know that if tested, they and their immediate comrades could take on any enemy and win. They had become the warriors Gray had challenged them to be. In retrospect, one of the most important and timely situations was the Secretary of Defense's 1986 decision directing the Marine Corps to expand its mission activities by activating a new force of special operations force (SOF) units. This was a milestone for the Marine Corps. In the previous 220-plus years of history, the Corps had experienced four eras of mission expansion. Figure 7 presents the expanded SOF mission and the Corps' focus on small wars and its renewed counter-insurgency training within all MAGTF operations.

SOLDIERS OF THE SEA	COLONIAL INFANTRY	AMPHIBIOUS ASSAULT FORCE	FORCE IN READINESS	SMALL WARS (GWOT)
				DISTRIBUTED OPERATIONS (STABILITY OPERATIONS)
				JOINT FORCE CAPABILITIES
			EXPEDITIONARY TASK FORCES OF COMBINED ARMS	SPECIAL OPERATIONS FORCES (SOF)
		ADVANCED BASE FORCES/ FLEET MARINE FORCES	FLEET MARINE FORCES	EXPEDITIONARY FORCES (MAGTFs MEU(SOC) INCREASED CULTURAL SITUATION AWARENESS
	PROTECT U.S. INTERESTS ABROAD	PROTECTION OF U.S. INTERESTS	PROTECTION OF U.S. INTERESTS	PROTECTION OF U.S. INTERESTS
NAVY SHIP DETACHMENTS	SHIP DETACHMENTS AND NAVAL BASE SECURITY	NAVAL SECURITY FORCES	NAVAL SECURITY FORCES	FLEET ANTI-TERRORISM SECURITY TEAMS (FAST)
1775 - 1909	1899 - 1934	1921 - 1951	1951 - PRESENT	1983 - 2020

HISTORICAL EXPANSION OF THE MARINE CORPS MISSIONS

Figure 7
Five Historic Major Eras of Marine Corps Service
(Chart developed by author from historic sources).

This new "Small Wars" mission would impact every facet of Marine Corps expeditionary doctrine and MAGTF training. Gray was quick to take action to get the Marine Corps special operations forces activated. All other MAGTFs were instructed to be prepared for small war encounters and militant terrorist actions during their deployments. Gray realized that his efforts were just beginning to lay out the latest foundation for small wars concepts and doctrine but with new advanced technology capabilities. He reminded commanders to "think smarter, not harder." The next Commandant, who would follow in less than a year, would further solidify the Corps' posture and advance its capabilities to be fully prepared when the nation calls.

However, as Gray was completing his third year, he was becoming even more concerned about the suddenly increased level of terrorist violence around the world. He cautioned his Marines on every occasion to be ready to counter the world's increasing terrorist threats. His concerns became fact the day Saddam Hussein made an unprovoked attack on his neighbor, the small nation of Kuwait. All of Gray's visions and preparatory efforts to transition the Marine Corps into a viable force for the 21st century were about to be tested.

CHAPTER 14
The Final Year and Moving "Into Harm's Way"

"Gray ... instilled the wisdom of maneuver warfare on generations of Marines even when enthusiastic endorsement of the imbedded concepts was likely to face stiff opposition ... taught us the importance of knowing how to operate and fight and win in a changing world. He taught us to manage risk."[1]

Martin R. Berndt
Lieutenant General, USMC (Retired)

Gray's final year as Commandant was to be an intense period of momentous happenings. The Iraqi War, DESERT SHIELD/DESERT STORM, would capture the world's media, but as his Marines and Sailors deployed to the Middle East, other rising situations would soon place Americans in harm's way. The imminent Gulf War was to be the ultimate test of Gray's vision and demanding actions to transition the Corps to the uncertainties of 21st century emerging threats to confront the United States' superpower status.

Iraq's invasion of Kuwait in August 1990 caught most nations in the Middle East and Europe by surprise. Without warning, Saddam Hussein's armies invaded and overran Kuwait's capital city and rapidly captured the vast Kuwaiti oil fields before consolidating on the Saudi Arabian border. By this action, Hussein had captured—or now threatened—oil fields that held more than half of the world's known oil supply.

President George H.W. Bush, the 41st President of the United States, was the first world leader to condemn and demand the immediate withdrawal of Iraqi forces out of Kuwait. While declaring "This shall not stand," he immediately placed U.S. military forces on alert for deployment to the Middle East. His call for assistance quickly resulted in the assembly of a multinational military coalition of forces that was composed of Western countries and friendly Arab nations.[2]

The Marine Corps had been alerted to prepare a Marine Air-Ground Task Force (MAGTF) consisting of two Marine divisions with appropriate aviation and service support organizations for movement into Southwest Asia. At the time the alert was received, Gray was holding one of his General officer war games at Quantico. In attendance were the majority of the 74 Marine Corps Generals, including his reserve component Generals from the 4th Marine Division/Wing team. The war game couldn't have been timelier. Serendipitously, the war game's scenario focused on the Middle East and was designed to explore the anticipated challenges of multiple MAGTF operations operating in a harsh desert environment.

At the conclusion of the war game, Gray commended the players for their innovative thinking. He then requested all personnel except his General officers leave the conference room. I was the one exception who was permitted to remain. Gray proceeded to share the latest information from the Defense Department and Joint Chiefs of Staff (JCS) strategic plans. He then added his own insights as to where and when the Marine Corps forces, as well as other friendly countries in the region, would be staged in Saudi Arabia. He exhibited a solemn, professional confidence in his comments. The nation was again calling upon its Corps of Marines to go to war. As I surveyed the audience, I was struck by the close attention and the obvious recognition of the awesome responsibilities being placed on their shoulders. As he closed his remarks, looking specifically at the seven or eight reserve component Generals present, he said, "This is your warning order, gentlemen. Be prepared to mobilize in 30 days or less."

In response to the President's alert, Gray began to shuffle his General officers in preparation for combat in the Middle East. Major General Walter E. Boomer was nominated to take command of the 1st Marine Expeditionary Force (I MEF) located in Southern California.

The newly-promoted Major General Michael M. Myatt was assigned to command the 1st Marine Division. Gray decided he would officiate at their respective change of command ceremonies. He invited me and several others to accompany him on the flight out to the West Coast. It was to be a memorable occasion.

Major General John Phillip Monahan had been simultaneously commanding the 1st Marine Division and I MEF for about two years and was now being rotated to his next assignment. I knew Phil Monahan well. He was a stylish leader who was much respected by his Marines. When I commanded the 2nd Marine Regiment, Phil Monahan had been one of my infantry battalion commanders. Even as a Lieutenant Colonel, he had appeared to me to be destined for General officer rank.

On the morning of August 8, 1990, Gray requested those Generals present for the change of command to assemble in the 1st Marine Division headquarters conference room. After a brief overview of the planning and deployment schedules, Gray promoted Boomer to Lieutenant General in preparation for assuming command of I MEF. Major General Myatt was confirmed as the new Commanding General, 1st Marine Division. Moments later, these two future battle commanders walked out onto the Quantico parade grounds where more than 10,000 members of I MEF's air-ground logistics team were in parade formations. The atmosphere was electric, heightened by the hundreds of unit guidons, its organizational colors with battle streamers fluttering in the soft ocean breeze sweeping across the silent mass formations. An unusual calm fell across the growing crowd of spectators as the three Generals took their positions for the ceremony to begin.

Major General Monahan passed the Division's colors to Major General Myatt and then passed the I MEF colors to Lieutenant General Boomer. As the two changes of command occurred, appropriate honors were rendered, and an artillery battery fired the customary ceremonial salutes. Shortly afterward, the I MEF Parade Adjutant ordered "Pass in Review." This would be their last assembly before their individual units began embarking on ships and aircraft. All present understood that at that moment, I MEF forces had begun their long journey to war. For those of us who had been in combat, the scene was especially poignant, for we knew from experience that some in these formations before us would undoubtedly be wounded or killed on a distant desert battlefield. Marines and Sailors, men and women, were once again moving "into harm's way." Within 96 hours, the first elements of the MEF began transitioning from Southern California air bases. The first troops landed in Dharhan, Saudi Arabia, on August 14, 1990. The buildup of American forces had begun.

There was growing certainty that a multinational force was moving into their initial assembly positions with the mission to restore the nation of Kuwait's borders and push back Saddam Hussein's invading Iraqi Army. Saudi Arabia was fast becoming the central staging area for more than 550,000 American, European, and Arab troops. The 18,000 U.S. Navy and Marine troops, on amphibious ships steaming in the Persian Gulf, were at their battle stations. Ashore, as a vital part of the multinational force were another 75,000 Marines consisting of two infantry divisions, a reinforced air wing, and hardworking logistics support groups. They were organized as 1st Marine Expeditionary Force (I MEF) under the command of Lieutenant General Walter E. Boomer. Boomer and his staff were deeply involved in the continuous planning as the buildup in units and equipment arrived. All units quickly transitioned into their severe desert environmental training and live fire exercises. Boomer would command the largest assembly of Marine air-ground and logistics forces in more than 30 years.

Although Marine forces had come from all over the globe, including the U.S. East and West Coasts, Hawaii, Okinawa, and Japan, they had all undergone common training. They spoke a common operational language. Although not envisioned in the decade before the coming Iraq War, the combined arms air-ground live fire and mechanized maneuver training provided all the Corps' operating forces with the most realistic and ideal unit training for a desert war. The commonality of planned Combined-Arms Exercise (CAX) tasks in each of these exercises at Twentynine Palms culminated in a newly discovered expertise of maneuver warfare. This ensured that, through a decade of maneuver and live fire experiences, the common planning and execution process every MAGTF unit experienced unknowingly raised the Corps' high standards. Though the exercise units had deployed to Twentynine Palms separately, all were required to plan and execute similar combined arms events. Therefore, when these widely dispersed units arrived in Saudi Arabia, all they had to do was set up their Combat Operation Centers (COCs) and turn on their radios to be immediately integrated into I MEF's Order of Battle plan. As Lieutenant General Boomer would later state, "The CAX and mechanized training exercises, which all units had gone through back at Twentynine Palms, was the best pre-deployment training they could have had."[3]

During the critical days before the U.S. military and coalition forces launched their ground attack to retake Kuwait from the Iraqi invaders, more than 95,000 Marines were positioned ashore and onboard amphibious ships in the Persian Gulf. The stage was set for the land-based forces to move north across the Saudi Arabia-Kuwait border and breach the Iraqi forces' minefields and defensive barriers

It was a time of great stress and emotion as all realized that the decision to launch the multinational attack was only weeks away. The world was focused on the Persian Gulf and guessed at the probable success of a multinational force that included, for the first time, Arab (Muslim) forces side-by-side with American and European Christian armies. It was an unprecedented situation where Egypt, Kuwait, and Saudi Arabia aligned with the nominally Christian world to fight an Arab aggressor.

SOLID SHIELD—The Buildup

As the U.S. military was deploying to the Gulf, there was a stridency of politically oriented outcries from several prominent Senators predicting that any war with Iraq would cost the United States as many as 45,000 combat casualties. The potential for the United States to suffer thousands was very much in the press. Media newscasters guessed at the probable success of the multinational force. There was also media focus on how the Arab (Muslim) forces would function within the multinational force (MNF) coalition. It was an unprecedented situation where Egypt, Kuwait, and Saudi Arabia aligned with the nominally Christian world in a common cause.

Additionally, leading military historians and the ever-ready "instant analyst experts" repeatedly appeared on the nation's televisions. All were quick to develop their own specially crafted score sheets to determine the number of tanks, aircraft, artillery weapons, etc., within each opposing force, and they then used these numbers to justify their dire predictions. The Center of Naval Analysis (CNA) used a casualty prediction model to estimate that a seven-day ground campaign would result in more than 10,500 casualties based on current planning figures.[4] Credible defense analysis organizations conducted studies that resulted in the declaration that on paper, the Iraqi Army was the fourth largest in the world. In addition to Iraq's three special armored Republican Guard divisions, there were more than 40 additional divisions. Most were equipped with aging Russian-made T-54, T-55, and T-72 tanks. Saddam Hussein's armored brigades were estimated to have a total of more than 4,000 tanks. Such a huge armor-versus-armor potential confrontation hadn't occurred since the European campaigns of World War II.

Comparing numbers of like weapons seemed to be the prognosticators' magic formula for predicting battle outcome. From a pure numbers point of view, Iraq was a formidable enemy, and time was initially on the invader's side pending the arrival and integration of the coalition's widely disparate forces into a cohesive combat force. There were many conditions that determined the outcome of the pending battles. Some factors tangible, others intangible, would ultimately impact on predicting the outcome of any battle. The weather, terrain, readiness of units, cohesiveness of command and control, and the willingness of the individual soldier to fight and possibly die are often unpredictable. Time would soon reveal who would win and why. In every case, the noted analysts' approach failed to equate the qualitative differences in the opposing forces' respective technologies.

Much of the MNF was equipped with new thermal and other night-vision sights, as well as laser designators for guided munitions. These systems would give the MNF unprecedented levels of 24/7 precision anti-armor killing capabilities. In addition, the effective range of the latest American anti-armor weapons far exceeded that of the obsolete T-54, T-55, and T-72 tanks. This clearly presented the U.S. tank crews with a huge battlefield advantage. The various other coalition forces also had limited numbers of precision-guided, anti-tank missiles. Also often overlooked by the analysts was the impact of the newest advanced "Cobra" attack helicopter, which would be providing unprecedented levels of direct close-in air support to II MEF's ground and mechanized units. The helicopters were equipped with the most modern anti-tank missiles and day/night weapon sights.

The Light Armored Vehicles (LAVs) that Gray had nearly single-handedly brought into the Marine Corps were now equipped with a turret-mounted 25mm gun and/or a precision-guided, tube-launched, optically tracked, wireless-guided (TOW) weapon system. The MEFs' infantry battalions were also equipped with a smaller, short-range, precision-guided anti-tank missile. For the first time in combat, individual riflemen would be equipped with the latest night-vision devices on their helmets to have around-the-clock combat capabilities. From a technological assessment, the United States and allied forces appeared to have a far better capability to fight under any desert conditions. The war was shaping up as a contest between old aging weapons against advanced technology weapons systems.

Among the other high technology systems that were placed on a battlefield for the first time was the use of the Global Positioning System (GPS), which eliminated the major problem in desert warfare: becoming lost in a nondescript landscape. The ten-meter accuracy of the GPS and its real-time position reporting could significantly reduce the potential for fratricide incidents. All units and vehicles equipped with the GPS were quick to discover the devices would become the cornerstone of positional reports by ground units. Electronic signals from each GPS device were automatically passed to higher headquarters forcing all MAGTF combat operations centers (COCs) to transition from the long-established routine of having paper maps hung along tent flaps to large screen electronic data displays of real-time unit positions.

Additionally, the newest capability for U.S. ground forces was the employment of unmanned aerial vehicles (UAVs), which were to be operated and controlled by the frontline units to provide aerial surveillance over their areas of operation. Gray was an early visionary in the use of invaluable unmanned airborne surveillance systems to track his real-time movements of both friendly and enemy forces. Such airborne surveillance systems could provide timely information that could prevent the Iraqi forces from conducting surprise attacks. This system would not be perfect, as signals were often lost, but it clearly revealed a future technology that would change the methods of warfare reporting. Even with its initial faults, it still enabled a commander to observe his more-distant units and any enemy movement in the alleys or built-up sites in his area.

The only real question that remained as to the use and employment of all this Information Age technology was whether the multinational force (MNF) personnel were sufficiently trained to employ their technology advantage, and if they were mentally prepared to win.

Though the Iraqi forces did not actively posture to continue the attack into the Saudi Arabian northern oil fields, their proximity clearly demonstrated a threat. To show the world how determined he was to roll back this unwarranted invasion, President Bush immediately directed the U.S. military to stage forces in the Gulf. Additionally, to booster the shaky confidence of Saudi Arabia's leaders, he felt it was necessary to direct an immediate movement of units in that country to present a strong show of force.[5]

Within 72 hours the Navy sailed one carrier battle group, the USS *Independence*, into the north Arabian Sea and began preparing to launch air strikes against any Iraqi forces that attempted to interfere with the American airlifts of men, women, and equipment into Saudi Arabia. Close on its heels was the Air Force deploying fighter aircraft directly into the International Airport in Riyadh, Saudi Arabia.

As the Navy began positioning its carrier forces into the eastern Mediterranean Sea and the Persian Gulf, elements of the Army's 82nd Airborne Division were flown into Al Jubail Airport near the Saudi Arabian coastline. This small force then moved into initial forward staging areas as a *de facto* blocking force. They arrived with a supply of only several days of food and water, as well as limited amounts of ammunition. Placing light-infantry units forward with limited anti-armor capabilities to confront the Iraqis' armor divisions was fraught with risk if the Iraqi armored divisions should continue the attack. Though they might appear to be nothing more than a "speed bump" against a determined attack, they were seen as a necessary symbol of our national resolve to halt any future Iraqi advance.

Coming halfway around the world, the Seventh MEB's 18,000 Marines and Sailors were airlifted into northern Saudi Arabia and linked up with their brigades' equipment, which had been pre-staged on a Maritime Prepositioning Ship (MPS) flotilla. Within hours of the ships' docking, the trucks and Amphibious Assault Vehicles (AAVs), equipment, supplies, and ammunition were being offloaded and distributed to waiting drivers and unit supply sergeants. The MEB's M-60 tanks, artillery, and Light Armored Vehicles (LAVs) armed with anti-tank missiles would be the main armor force until other ships leaving the States could bring the Army's M1A2 heavy tanks ashore days later. During the critical early days of U.S. buildup, this was the only viable combined-arms force ready for combat with 60 days of supplies on hand with which to sustain it. Within 48 hours after receiving their MPS equipment, Major General John I. Hopkins, Commanding the 7th MEB, pronounced his forces "operationally ready."[6]

This was the first-ever combat deployment of a MAGTF to a distant site, where personnel were also separately flown into a forward airfield, and quickly married with their prime conditioned equipment. Until this "real-world" massive buildup, the whole MPS program had been an untested concept, with many skeptics questioning the feasibility of a floating flotilla of Marine Corps wares. Additionally, the vast array of MPS equipment of supplies were used to logistically support the 82nd Airborne Division elements that arrived in the desert with little more than what they could carry. Had the Iraqi Army attacked these lightly equipped airborne units in a flat desert terrain, they would have been at a critical combat disadvantage, lacking adequate anti-armor weapons.

The records also show Gray's avid support for the radical concept of Marines flying to some distant country and meeting preloaded ships with their equipment and supplies. As far back as 1978, during the NATO exercise BOLD GUARD, his 4th MEBs quietly embarked excessive amounts of equipment and supplies that would later be recognized as the initial field test in developing the MPS's required supplies to support a fly-in MEB. Historical records state that such a concept for the rapid buildup of the 7th MEB's combat capabilities was sufficient to make the Iraqi Army withhold any immediate invasion from captured Kuwait into Saudi Arabia territory.

Major General John I. Hopkins' 7th MEB was composed of the 7th Marine Regiment as the ground combat element (GCE), Marine Air Group 70 as the Aviation Combat Element (ACE), and Seventh Brigade Support Group (BSG) for combat support. All were from bases located in Southern California. Marine Aircraft Group 70 (MAG-70) had fixed-wing aircraft, helicopters, and air defense missile units. Hopkins' desert-trained units were predominantly from the installation at Twentynine Palms, California, and were an exceptionally well-trained MAGTF. Due to their immediate proximity to Marine Corps premier live fire maneuver ranges, they had become especially well versed in fire support coordination skills. General Hopkins was a hard taskmaster, maintaining his Marine Expeditionary Brigade (MEB) in a high state of readiness, ready to go on a moment's notice.

The 7th MEB's first alert came from General H. Norman Schwarzkopf's Central Command (CENTCOM) on August 4. After three days of around-the-clock planning in Tampa, Florida, Hopkins and his staff received their official alert to deploy. The Joint Chiefs of Staff designated August 7 as the day to begin deploying U.S. forces to the Middle East. Within 72 hours the Seventh Marine Expeditionary Brigade (7th MEB) began deployment from Southern California air bases.

As the 7th MEB's lead elements flew into Saudi Arabia, the untested flotilla of Maritime Prepositioning Ships (MPS) Squadron #2 with the MEB's equipment and supplies was transiting the North Arabian Sea from Diego Garcia north toward the port city of Jubail, Saudi Arabia. The initial flight of Seventh MEB landed at Dhahran, Saudi Arabia, on August 15, 1990. From the airport, the Marines then shifted 100 kilometers north and staged in an unused warehouse located in the industrial port city of Jubail. The nearby Al Jubail naval air facility soon became the main arrival port of entry for Marines and marshalling yards for the arriving Marines with the equipment and supplies offloading from the MPS squadron. General Hopkins' MEB arrived so quickly—and was becoming combat-ready with the rapid offload of the embarked equipment—that the local Saudi government and military authorities were taken by surprise. At first, they refused to allow the Marines to deploy tactically away from the port. "John I" Hopkins as he was known, was not used to unexplainable delays. Hopkins fumed as his troops sweltered in 120 degree heat in the port's huge, unsanitary metal warehouses. It was difficult to hold his patience, but he managed.[7]

I MEF would eventually deploy its major air-ground logistics teams into the Gulf in a four-phased process that would last 40 days. On August 17, 1990, Lieutenant General Walt Boomer and his staff arrived in Riyadh, Saudi Arabia, where they established relations with General Schwarzkopf's Central Command staff. Lieutenant General Boomer held two command responsibilities. As the Commander, Marine Forces Central Command (COMMARFORCENT), he served as one of the U.S. Services Component Commands under General Schwarzkopf. In addition, he served as the Commanding General, I MEF. To support these two commands, he would activate two separate staffs. He subsequently established his command post in an unused building at the port city of Al Jubail with the Seventh MEB. All Seventh MEB units were directed to reactivate their tactical radio communications nets and integrate into the MEF's secure command and control communications systems.

The follow-on Marine forces also began deploying to the Gulf. From the East Coast, the 4th MEB, embarked aboard amphibious ships, had sailed from Morehead City, North Carolina, on August 17. Fourth MEB, with Major General Harry W. Jenkins Jr. commanding, joined with the carrier strike force already in the Gulf. His MEB would later play a vital role in causing the Iraqi Army to keep two key armored and up to five infantry divisions dispersed along the coast to counter the anticipated amphibious landing by Marines across the beaches near Kuwait's capital city. The 5th MEB, commanded by Brigadier General Peter Rowe, and the 13th MEU were also embarked into amphibious ships from the West Coast and would eventually arrive in the Gulf to reinforce the 4th MEB in the role of both amphibious assault force and the MNF's strategic reserve. There were high expectations that the 18,000 Marines and Sailors afloat would be conducting a major amphibious operation.

By September 6 the 1st Marine Division's major elements had arrived in Saudi Arabia. The 1st and 7th MEBs were fused into the division under Major General Myatt. Myatt had a long and close personal and professional relationship with Gray. As previously discussed, he was an early proponent of Gray's maneuver warfare concept. It wasn't too surprising that General Myatt set aside a traditional conventional warfare organizational structure in favor of a mechanized and armored task force structure conducive to implementing an asymmetrical warfare operational concept.[8] Accordingly, he reorganized his three infantry regiments into three mechanized task forces to counter the immediate Iraqi threat just miles to his north.

The 2nd Marine Division at Camp Lejeune, North Carolina, was put on alert and began arriving in December. Major General William "Bill" Keys, commanding the 2nd Marine Division, recipient of the Navy Cross, and the Silver Star in Vietnam, was a much respected warrior. He had previously "looked the elephant in the eye" on several occasions. During the last year of the Vietnam War, then-Major Keys and I had also served as advisors to the South Vietnamese Marine Corps (VNMC). In late summer of 1972, his VNMC brigade came under a series of armor attacks by the North Vietnamese Army. For the VNMC brigade, there were a few hectic moments when the North Vietnamese Army made their surprise tank attack. When the Soviet-made T-54s and T-55s roared toward the South Vietnamese marines' front lines, Major Keys observed the oncoming dust clouds and heard the increasing roar of engines and the clattering of tank tracks. He quickly called in U.S. supporting arms to contain the attack. He later reported the young enlisted Vietnamese marines were moving forward to destroy and damage tanks with Light Anti-Armor Weapons (LAWs). In a matter of several hours, between 18 and 22 tanks were destroyed, and a number of surviving crewmen were captured. This was to be the last North Vietnamese Army (NVA) armored attack before the January 1973 Ceasefire Agreement. However, for Major Keys, this rare battlefield experience was just a precursor to the forthcoming large-scale maneuver warfare his division was about to launch. Now, as a commanding general, Bill Keys was fully prepared to go back to a distant battlefield. He would be an inspiration to all his units.

With the arrival of these follow-on forces, the MEF was finally reformed. Boomer would now command the largest assembly of Marine aviation, ground, and logistics forces since World War II. It had been more than 45 years since a Marine General had commanded a Corps-sized unit with two or more maneuver divisions.[9] Throughout the Vietnam War, the Marine Corps had two divisions in-country, but it never conducted any joint or multiple division maneuvers. One would have to reflect back to the final stages of World War II to the battles for Iwo Jima and Okinawa to find where two Marine divisions had last been maneuvered abreast of one another in a multi-division assault.

The MEF's aviation squadrons and support elements would scramble from air bases on both the East and West Coasts, Okinawa, Japan, and Hawaii, and from Marine Corps Reserve Squadrons and air groups home-stationed in local air facilities across the country. Several fighter squadrons would actually arrive in Saudi Arabia before the major ground forces. On September 3, Major General Royal Moore established his 3rd Marine Air Wing (MAW) headquarters at Shaikh Isa in Bahrain. Subsequently, their headquarters would relocate to Jubail, Saudi Arabia.

It would take time to rally and then preposition the total multinational coalition force. Once the assembly of the multinational and coalition forces began, massive airlifts and sealifts were launched from Europe, the Balkans, Asia, South America, and small African countries. Their units came in all sizes and specialties to join in a common cause. The control and coordination of the arriving ships, aircraft, and personnel, and attending to each nation's special cultural needs and operational requirements became a nightmare of unexpected issues all demanding the greatest patience by Christian and Islamic nations. Once in Saudi Arabia, there were even more complex issues of assembly and unit movements into assigned initial training and staging areas throughout the region. In a matter of weeks, the coalition forces were close to reaching a total of half a million men and women in theater, all focused on preparations for an attack to restore Kuwait's national integrity and reduce the threat to the Saudi Arabian oil field.

From the moment the I MEF command element arrived, Lieutenant General Walt Boomer and his staff were deeply involved in continuous planning for the pending attack as the buildup in units and equipment arrived and began desert environmental training, and later live fire exercises. There were no established training areas or live ordnance ranges in the region. There were immediate requests for land areas where infantry units could maneuver and conduct live fire exercise for their machine guns and mortars. It would be the first opportunity for Marine tankers to actually fire the highly vaunted "Sabor" anti-armor killing round. For the artillery and tank units, their equipment recently removed from the Maritime Prepositioning Ships (MPS), there was a prudent safety requirement to test fire and "bore-sight" the main guns. It would take time—too much time—but a series of infantry and artillery ranges were marked in different sections of the desert, and initial live firing began. The whole idea of a variety of training and impact areas had never been envisioned by the Saudis. The Marines and Soldiers simply took the initiative and improvised whatever type of training facility was needed. "Just improvise" became a daily situation. These same ranges were later made available to the coalition nations and actually served as an important element in generating a working bond between all the Muslim and Christian nations. An uncommon grouping of nations was slowly blending into a viable military force.

Though Marine forces would come from all over the globe (East and West Coasts, Hawaii, Okinawa, and Japan, and mobilized Marine reserve units from most of the United States), they all had previously undergone a common training experience, and spoke a common operational language. During Gray's tenure as the Commandant, he continued to raise the bar on the live fire and maneuver warfare exercises at Twentynine Palms. He saw it as the most realistic combat exercise any MAGTF could experience during peacetime. Consistent with General Barrow's earlier vision of combined arms training, Gray was a firm supporter of mechanized operations. Serendipitously, in the decade before the Iraq War, the Marines' premier combined arms exercise (CAX), with its live fire, mechanized, and maneuver warfare focus, provided Marine operating forces with a realistic and ideal unit preparation for desert maneuver warfare. Every MAGTF experienced, and unknowingly acquired, common universal standards for fire and maneuver. Though each exercise unit may have deployed to Twentynine Palms separately, the tactical exercise control group (TECG) at Twentynine Palms required each force to plan and execute similar combined-arms events. Therefore, when these widely dispersed units arrived in Saudi Arabia, all they had to do was set up their Combat Operation Centers, turn on their radios, receive the latest intelligence briefings, and be immediately integrated into I MEF order of battle.

Maritime Operations and Marines Afloat

The strategic role of naval expeditionary forces is often misunderstood. For example, Norman Friedman, in his book *Desert Victory*, did not take into consideration the sort of operational flexibility the U.S. circumstances demanded. The central issue, as naval officers viewed the vastness of the oceans, was the key to their mobility. In contrast, Marine commanders think in terms of key terrain and the effects of terrain on mobility of both friendly and enemy forces. Naval forces at sea use their mobility to provide unrestricted maneuver and thus can influence the Marine's and Army's mission ashore through their presence offshore. The potential for amphibious landings is a vital element of what makes naval forces a credible threat. Accordingly, credible naval forces, when operating in littoral areas, maintain a closely coordinated relationship between the Navy and embarked landing forces. Friedman captured the seminal impact of the U.S.'s domination of the world's oceans and its resulting ability to influence events when he wrote, "Seapower tends to act invisibly but powerfully."[10]

General Schwarzkopf was Commander, USCENTCOM. General Schwarzkopf then passed operational control of the 4th MEB to Marine Forces Afloat (MFA) under Rear Admiral LaPlante, who then reported to Vice Admiral Henry H. Mauz, Commander, U.S. Navy Central Command (COMNAVCENT). This "multilayered chain of command" was to pose problems, since both the MFA afloat (which would eventually include the 4th and 5th MEBs) and the I MEF staff ashore would have to work through NAVCENT aboard the 7th Fleet flagship in order to conduct any serious planning for amphibious operations in support of the MEF ashore. From the very beginning of the Middle East deployment, the Marine Corps had anticipated executing several types of amphibious operations. Such a multilayered chain of command was fast becoming a major problem to the Marines Afloat.

The NAVCENT flagship, the amphibious Command Ship USS *Blue Ridge* (LCC-19) was stationed for much of DESERT SHIELD in the north Arabian Sea more than 400 miles from the MFA generally stationed inside the Gulf. This made face-to-face contact between the various commanders difficult. To further hinder any amphibious planning, there was also no "three-star equivalent" Marine presence in Riyadh serving as Commander, Marine Forces Central Command and providing input on the use of all Marine forces collectively. Instead, Lieutenant General Boomer wore dual hats as both Marine Corps Forces Central Command (MARCENT) and I MEF and was seldom able to be present in his Riyadh headquarters because of his principal responsibilities: getting the MEF ready for combat. This presented a similar situation for the Navy with Vice Admiral Mauz at sea and a Deputy located in Riyadh, who when pressed, would both represent amphibious options to the CENTCOM staff's planning efforts. This issue was later singled out by senior planners as a key factor in the limited combat employment of Marine Forces Afloat in the emerging war.

During most of DESERT SHIELD and all of DESERT STORM, the Marine forces ashore remained under the operational control of Lieutenant General Boomer, whereas the embarked Marines—collectively known as MFA—remained under the operational control of COMNAVCENT (Vice Admiral Mauz initially but later replaced by Vice Admiral Stanley R. Arthur). As a result, the MFA and I MEF were operating under completely separate chains of command. The principal responsibility for amphibious planning and their employment would necessarily be the responsibility of MFA and NAVCENT. It was confusing to all and hampered any serious plans to undertake a major amphibious operation.

With the commitment of 4th MEB and the 13th MEU to CENTCOM, amphibious planning had begun even before the task force arrived in Southwest Asia. A special planning cell, formed in the Pentagon, included Rear Admiral Stephen S. Clary, Commander Amphibious Group 3, and Brigadier General Russell H. Sutton, Director of Operations within Headquarters Marine Corps. Because Saddam Hussein had refused to allow more than 12,000 Westerners living in Iraq and Kuwait to leave, the 4th MEB had to be ready to conduct noncombatant evacuation *in extremis* hostage rescues upon short notice. This initial plan for the employment of the MFA was quickly overcome by events and follow-on taskings. Upon the 4th MEB's arrival in theater, General Schwarzkopf visited the staff aboard the USS *Blue Ridge* and redirected planning toward raising the profile of potential amphibious operations aimed at Iraq's vulnerable beaches. Clearly, Schwarzkopf was thinking strategically and intending to pose an additional strategic dilemma for the defending Iraqi forces in Kuwait as part of his multinational force (MNF) campaign.

Throughout the DESERT SHIELD preparatory buildup phase, Gray pushed the concept of the Navy and Marine Forces Afloat (MFA) to plan a series of options for executing some type of amphibious operations in concert with the future land battles. On September 19, a planning conference between Vice Admiral Mauz and Lieutenant General Boomer resulted in agreement that the basic concept for amphibious operation needed to provide a wide variety of options that would include noncombatant evacuations, amphibious demonstrations, raids, support for special operations, and a possible MEB-level amphibious assault. Although Major General Jenkins, with Gray's assistance, continued to advocate his MFA amphibious capabilities, there was little interest displayed at either the higher naval command levels nor within the CENTCOM staff beyond the level of amphibious force demonstration and presence. Vice Admiral Mauz felt the pressure from the Marines to pursue a greater role, as he later stated, "I wanted to see an amphibious operation as much as anyone, but there was no good place to do a landing."[11]

The Defense Reorganization Act of 1986 profoundly changed the duties of the Joint Chiefs of Staff. Instead of being "one among equals" the Chairman became the principal military advisor to the President. The new rules were not relished by an activist like Gray. Gray did not limit his activities in support of a greater Marine Corps force in the Gulf to just Washington's corridors of power. He went to the Gulf in October and met with senior Navy and Marine officers. The tour convinced Gray that there should be a Marine-generated amphibious campaign plan similar to the "Instant Thunder" air campaign created by the U.S. Air Force "Checkmate" planners. Accordingly, Major General Matthew P. Caulfield was ordered to have the Marine Corps Combat Development Command make recommendations for more effective uses of amphibious forces in the Gulf. An ad hoc study group was quickly assembled at Quantico to look at the amphibious options, and the Warfighting Center conducted a series of war games to test the study team's recommendations for a major amphibious assault into Iraq, codenamed OPERATION TIGER. A series of amphibious raids proved to be far more practical and were accepted by Gray in November. One of the first priorities for Admiral Mauz was to develop a Naval Strategic Campaign Plan. This was to include a theater tactical plan focused on a seaward plan, an ashore deception plan, and the synchronized employment of the MFA with General Schwarzkopf's theater-level battle plans. A wide range of potential employments would necessitate developing a generic amphibious plan with broad options. The resulting initial plan would serve as the basis for a series of future plans which could be quickly amended to fit into emerging combat situations. Furthermore, these plans must include a wide variety of amphibious operations by a brigade-sized force, and for special operations such as raids, noncombatant evacuation operations (NEOs), and demonstrations by smaller units.[12]

During Gray's late September visit, he inquired as to NAVCENT's contingency plans and discovered there were few preparations underway for any large-scale amphibious operations. Thereafter, he "nudged" Major General Jenkins to aggressively raise the interest in the potential employment of amphibious operations. The 4th MEB began revising their ten-option generic amphibious contingency plan. At that time, the NAVCENT and Amphibious Task Force (ATF) relationship was still emerging, and staff coordination was far from functioning smoothly. Major General Harry Jenkins felt "NAVCENT displayed little interest in what went beyond the level of 'presence.'"[13]

This was only the first of three visits by Gray to the Persian Gulf. In addition to meeting with General Schwarzkopf, he typically met with Marine and Navy commanders afloat to explore the concept of conducting amphibious operations. During his September visit, Gray discovered that the LAVs did not have the thermal sights, so vital for effective night targeting. Upon returning to the States, he contacted the Marine Corps Supply Activity, in Albany, Georgia, and directed the technicians to develop hardware to place a thermosight on every LAV in the Middle East. Fortunately, the new night-vision sights arrived and were installed on each LAV just days before the ground war began. This timely action by Gray to provide the LAV crews with a 24/7 capability would later make a major difference on the battlefields.

Gray held firm for the MFA to be fully prepared to conduct amphibious operations as a viable means to respond to any unexpected delays in the conduct of ground operations by the MNF in general, but specifically by the MEF ashore. In addition, Gray was cognizant of the strategic value of the amphibious force in conducting supporting operations to include raids, demonstrations, and assaults. This included during the DESERT SHIELD pre-assault phase, as well as in support of the offensive during the follow-on DESERT STORM phase of the Gulf War. But to be able to be effective in this role, he recognized that it required not only credible planning by the combined Navy/Marine Corps staffs afloat but agreement by Navy and Marine Corps commanders that the amphibious force could credibly execute amphibious operations at an acceptable risk to ships and the landing force.

Gray thought this task was too important to leave only to the Marine and Navy staffs afloat. Accordingly, he tasked then-Brigadier General Matthew Caulfield, director, Marine Corps Warfighting Center at Quantico, to assemble a select group of Marine officers and explore all possibilities. This small planning cell, led by Caulfield and notably involving his Chief of Staff Colonel Marty Steele, rapidly developed a series of amphibious options linked to the strategic situation in the region. This was a unique situation in which a Service Chief, without the tasking from the operational commanders involved, convened a planning effort in the U.S. focused on developing operational plans for Navy and Marine staffs in a combat theater. Notably, the similar effort involving the "Jedi Knights" from the Army's School for Advanced Warfighting in Fort Leavenworth was commissioned not by the chief of staff of the Army but specifically requested by General Schwarzkopf and supported by the Army.

Historically, it is important to inject here the increased role of the senior U.S. commander. In 1986, the Goldwater Nichols Act was designed to ensure the military services work jointly through a single overall commander when waging any future wars. The Chairman,

Joint Chiefs of Staff (CJCS), and a series of regional commanders would, for the first time, have the full authority to form and conduct operations under the geographical commander. Before the 1986 Act, the senior U.S. commanders in a particular region of conflict usually had their own warfare priorities, and mutual agreement was sought to conduct a multi-service campaign. The 1991 Gulf War would be the first armed conflict prosecuted under this law. General Schwarzkopf fully understood his new charter to have the complete freedom to employ the services as he saw fit. He did not hesitate to fend off the Air Force when it wanted to delay the timing of the Air War. For the Army, he notified them his G-Day would go as planned. When the Special Operation Command (SOCOM) wanted to conduct pre-Ground day operations, and when the U.S. Army wanted to conduct an airborne operation, he disapproved. Later, when the Marine Corps proposed a series of amphibious options to General Schwarzkopf, he placed a "hold" on their conducting any amphibious landings or raids prior to the ground campaign DESERT STORM.[14]

General Schwarzkopf felt that any amphibious operations posed potential risk of losses either from mines or to the landing forces during the assault and might actually distract forces from ensuring the success of the principal elements of the ground war as he envisioned it. General Schwarzkopf's primary focus remained on first achieving success in the ground war, based on fixing attacks by the MEF on the east, and a decisive main attack, by the U.S. Army and other allied forces, sweeping far out to the west to encircle and ensure annihilation of the Iraqi forces in Kuwait. The Goldwater-Nichols Act clearly mandated that General Schwarzkopf's control was complete on all theater operation matters. The Act, yet untested, hopefully would soon confirm that when a single commander was fully in charge, joint and combined operations would be conducted more effectively.

On December 30 and 31, Admiral Stanley R. Arthur held an amphibious planning conference aboard the USS *Blue Ridge*. General Matthew P. Caulfield and Colonel Marty Steele had flown to the Persian Gulf and presented the results of their planning efforts to the Navy and Marine Corps commanders and staffs to specifically include Vice Admiral Arthur and Lieutenant General Boomer personally. Most of the Navy and Marine flag officers in the theater attended. The flag officers were discussing only a landing to reinforce and sustain the coalition's ground offensive, however, not an operation to strike the enemy flank or cut their lines of communication as at Inchon, Korea. The Quantico stateside plan received a cool reception from the Navy and CENTCOM staff, and it was obvious that OPERATION TIGER was not going to be implemented.[15] Gray and other Marine Corps leaders, who had consistently pressed for a major amphibious operation, redoubled their efforts.

Finally, on February 2, 1991, General Schwarzkopf made it clear to his chief subordinates that he would not order an amphibious landing on the coast of Kuwait. Brigadier General Tom Draude recalled that once Schwarzkopf issued his order, the Marine commanders were once again able to direct all their planning on the coming ground battle. Major General Robert B. Johnston, who was General Schwarzkopf's chief of staff, and Brigadier General Richard L. on the CENTCOM staff were both Marines, and they kept a watchful eye within the CENTCOM staff deliberations on the amphibious issue. But the nature of their joint responsibilities kept them from becoming outspoken advocates for amphibious operations. Later Brigadier General Neal asserted that "it became apparent there was no spokesman for Marine Forces Afloat (MFA)." The bottom line was that amphibious planning at CENTCOM took a back seat in Riyadh to the primary mission, and there was no one whose primary mission was to oversee a brief amphibious option. The mining of the USS *Princeton* (CG-59) and USS *Tripoli* (LPH-10) a few days before the ground assault began caused the Navy's leadership to be even less enthusiastic about any naval vessels entering the northern Persian Gulf, near the major port of Basra at the mouth of the Euphrates River, along the Iranian border.[16]

Navy/Marine Corps' Deception Planning

As the Air War commenced, 18,000 Marines and Sailors from the 4th MEB, 5th MEB, and the 13th MEU deployed 31 amphibious ships constituting three Amphibious Ready Groups (ARGs) and were threatening the coastline of Kuwait with assaults from the sea. Early in the planning for the ground war, allied intelligence detected that the Iraqis had committed heavy infantry forces to beach defense. Early on General Schwarzkopf had directed the Marine Corps' amphibious presence to be put on a high profile to cause Iraqi forces to hold along the beaches, preventing their employment in the mainland battle. Schwarzkopf was, in essence, beginning to shape his tactical campaign plan.

Throughout the SOLID SHIELD buildup, there were two separate areas of high Navy and Marine Corps interest. In support of the MNF's guidance to include deceptive measures in all DESERT SHIELD/ DESERT STORM preparations, the Navy and Marine Corps components began their "at sea" and later "ashore" deceptive plans. Their initial task was the development of an overall deceptive naval plan to ensure a cohesive, well-integrated, and well-timed series of events to confuse the Iraqi forces. This included the requirements for I MEF and its Afloat MEBs to exploit and demonstrate to the Iraqi leadership the power projection capabilities of the naval task force immediately offshore. A series of landings known as SEA SOLDIER were conducted along the shores of Saudi Arabia, Oman, and the United Emirates. On January 21, elements of the three Marine shipboard units conducted OPERATION SEA SOLDIER IV, an amphibious exercise that employed the largest amphibious force since the 1950 Inchon landing. The signal to the Iraqi leadership was unmistakable as the Navy began clearing the mines from the Kuwaiti coast and the simultaneous destruction of all Iraqi naval craft. On the same day as SEA SOLDIER IV, the island of Jazirat Qurah was recaptured, with 50 prisoners of war (POWs) taken. On January 29th, elements of the 13th MEU landed on the island of Umm Al Monida, 12 miles off the coast of Kuwait. The Marines raised the Kuwaiti flag and destroyed Iraqi antiaircraft and artillery positions.

The intent of I MEF's "ashore" deception plan was to convince the Iraqis that two "mythical" Marine divisions were still occupying the coastal areas. The clever plan was primarily the brainchild of Brigadier General Thomas V. Draude, Deputy Commander, 1st Marine Division. Draude assembled a nondescript group of fewer than 200 people into Task Force "Troy." Draude understood the importance of continuing to deceive the Iraqis along the most forward edge of the Marines' positions, so a series of noisy, combined arms raids were continued against the Iraqis several weeks before G-Day.[17] For two weeks before the allied forces stormed into Kuwait and Iraq, Troy, the phantom Marine task force, conducted artillery attacks on Iraqi targets and used small reconnaissance patrols stalking the border while armed with loudspeakers and blaring tank noises. They also filled sandbags and placed dummy tanks and artillery pieces partially hidden behind earthen berms. General Draude stated, "We wanted to create the illusion of force where there was none. We hoped no one would counterattack across the border!"[18]

Additionally, to strengthen the I MEF's desert-oriented deception plan's effectiveness, on G-Day, General Draude reassembled his units into small-sized radio teams, which activated a multitude of radios to generate multiple radio transmissions that would be typical of several divisions preparing to conduct an amphibious landing near Kuwait City. On G-Day, the Iraqi radio intercept units operating in the area picked up the radio traffic and reported to their higher headquarters that an amphibious landing was happening.[19]

It would be later assessed that there were many reasons not to conduct any amphibious operations. The most obvious reason was that it was unnecessary, given the huge success of the ground war. It seemed worth the opportunity to avoid the casualties the Marines might have taken going through mine-filled waters and well defended beaches. However, the desire to engage in a fake amphibious landing further confused the Iraqi leadership and caused several Republican Guard divisions to "stay by the beaches and out of the battle." It would later be verified that when coupled with the western flanking movement and operational deception, these activities completely unbuckled the already sagging Iraqi defenses.[20] The immediate offshore presence of Navy and Marine amphibious forces did much to convince the Iraqi forces to look seaward until it was too late. When they found it was a deceitful ploy, it was ultimately too late to reposition the two Republican Guard divisions against the allied flanking movements.

Arising Crises and MAGTF Contingency Operations

Between August 1990 and January 1991, three classic examples of the flexibility of Navy/Marine forces occurred. Each situation demanded the highest degree of preparedness, urgent complex planning, critical timing, and expert execution. As America's emerging national policy toward the Middle East evolved, the first near-immediate response was for massive deployments of divisional, aviation, and logistics support units of unprecedented sizes to the Middle East. The other two incidents, both on the African continent, required the presence of an American naval task force to prevent the capture or death of American nationals and others by unstable insurgent forces.

It all began with DESERT SHIELD, when the United States committed to an unprecedented massive deployment in response to Saddam Hussein's army invasion of Kuwait. Within 72 hours, the Navy sailed one carrier, the USS *Independence*, into the north Arabian Sea and began preparing to launch air strikes against any Iraqi forces that attempted to interfere with the American airlifts of men and equipment into Saudi Arabia. Once the decision was made for the United States to provide massive military support to Saudi Arabia, a large armada of Sailors and Marines deployed to the region. Coming halfway around the world, an MEB's 18,000 Marines and Sailors were airlifted into northern Saudi Arabia and linked up with their brigades' equipment, which had been pre-staged on a flotilla of Maritime Prepositioned Ships (MPSs).

Within hours of the ships' docking, the trucks and Amphibious Assault Vehicles (AAVs), equipment, supplies, and ammunition were being offloaded and distributed to waiting drivers and unit supply sergeants. The MEB's M-60 tanks, artillery, and Light Armored Vehicles (LAVs) armed with anti-tank missiles would be the main armor force until other ships leaving the States would bring the Army's M1 heavy tanks ashore days later. During the critical early days of U.S. buildup, this was the only viable combined arms force ready for combat with 60 days of supplies to sustain itself. This was the first-ever combat deployment of a MAGTF to a distant site, where personnel were also separately flown in to a forward airfield, and then quickly married up with their prime conditioned equipment. Until this "real-world" massive buildup, the whole MPS program had been an untested concept, with many skeptics questioning the feasibility of a floating flotilla of Marine Corps wares. Additionally, the vast array of MPS equipment and supplies were used to logistically support the U.S. Army assault units which arrived in the desert with little more than what they could carry. Had the Iraqi Army attacked these lightly equipped airborne units in a flat desert terrain, they would have been at a critical combat disadvantage, lacking adequate anti-armor weapons. Historical records state that the rapid buildup of the Seventh MEB's combat capabilities were sufficient to make the Iraqi Army withhold any immediate invasion from captured Kuwait into Saudi Arabian territory.

Maritime Contingency Operations

There were other hotspots in the world and although the focus was on the Middle East, Sailors and Marines already forward-deployed were alerted for new contingency operations. The following brief segment may seemingly be a distracter to the reader who is focusing on the forthcoming battles; however, two "real-world" unanticipated situations were occurring at a most stressful time.

One of the Marine Corps' basic core competencies has long been responding to contingencies operations. It is what forward-deployed Sailors and Marine MAGTFs are routinely called upon to do. Serving as the nation's naval forces, they plan and help sustain our national maritime strategy. While cruising the world's sea lanes, they can provide a "presence" and be directed into any region where unrest or a natural disaster has occurred. They come from the sea, when needed, and return to their offshore ships when their mission is complete. During the past four decades, Marine units have responded more than 100 times to bring a quick response and stability to a rising social unrest, helping to stabilize a troubled government, or conducting humanitarian and nation-building missions. This is what seaborne MAGTFs do, in times of peace and war.

OPERATION SHARP EDGE

In May 1990, the African nation of Liberia was in civil revolt, with all indications that rebel forces were about to seize Monrovia, the capital. By early June, rebel forces led by the rebellious Sergeant Charles Taylor were closing in on the city and were only ten miles from the international airport. The few remaining airlines canceled their flights. The U.S. government alerted the Defense Department to send a military task force to evacuate about 1,100 Americans from Liberia if they were threatened by the fighting. The Joint Staff in the Pentagon began planning an evacuation mission. The original thinking was to fly elements of the Army's 82nd Airborne Division directly into the besieged airport to rescue the Americans and possibly other nations' civilians. The operations would be called JUST CAUSE II. However, when the rebels overran the airport, the Army's air-landed force was no longer a viable option.

On June 10, 1990, the rebels won control of the international airport. Attempts by several other nations at negotiating a ceasefire agreement between the government and the rebel force broke down on July 19. Prominent Liberians appealed to the United States for a temporary peacekeeping force to prevent further bloodshed. On the 21st, Liberia's ruling strongman expelled the U.S. military attaché, accusing him of supporting the rebels. More than 600 Liberian civilians were killed in five days. The rebel leader, Prince Johnson, had ordered his forces to start arresting Americans and other foreigners to force foreign intervention. The Liberian national government was no longer functioning. It was time to act.

Weeks earlier the 22nd MEU had been alerted to prepare for a possible noncombat evacuation. A small naval task force of four ships carrying 2,000 Marines arrived on the Liberian Coast and began the detailed preparations to evacuate the Americans, if necessary. There were justifiable fears that if the rebels took the capital, there would be a bloodbath. As the threat of war in Monrovia increased, the State Department ordered all nonessential U.S. government personnel and their families to leave. The MEU conscientiously reviewed its contingency plans one more time.

For the next two months, the 22nd MEU, commanded by Marine Colonel Granville Amos, would be poised 20 miles offshore. Colonel "Granny" Amos, a protégé of Gray, took advantage of the waiting period to ensure a successful execution of OPERATION SHARP EDGE.[21] As his planning progressed, the latest photographs of the American Embassy were reviewed, terrain models of the compound were fabricated, and countless planning sessions and briefings were conducted for all possible scenarios. As the different units were assigned their tasks in the rescue mission, platoons and squads began to coordinate their tasks, and every phase of the potential rescue operation was developed into a highly synchronized air-ground team effort. Even after the evacuation plan was finally set, Colonel Amos demanded that the units repeatedly rehearse until the day before the 22nd MEU was ordered to execute SHARP EDGE.[22]

On Saturday, August 4th, President Bush ordered the evacuation of Americans from Liberia. The order was quickly passed to the amphibious task force off the African coastline. Their mission was to safeguard lives, to draw down the number of Americans at the Embassy to a minimum staff and provide additional security for those who remained. One hundred rehearsals and planning sequences were now to be tested. A rifle company of 225 Marines and Sailors from the MEU were flown by helicopter from the USS *Saipan* into Monrovia to evacuate American and foreign dependents. The first flight included 73 civilians hastily lifted to the ships offshore. The operation continued as troop helicopters were used for evacuations at two isolated communications sites with the mission of handling diplomatic and intelligence messages in sub-Saharan Africa.

Once the evacuations began, there was no letup until more than 2,700 men, women, and children were rescued. Though the immediate crisis was over, the Marines remained in Liberia for another month before withdrawing to their waiting ships. It was a routine commitment for the Marines. There would be stories to tell when they returned to Camp Lejeune and Cherry Point.

But this noncombat humanitarian incident had a far greater impact upon the future of Marine Expeditionary Unit (Special Operations Capable) MEU (SOC) deployments. For it was the "first" actual test of Gray's vision to train and deploy MEUs with limited special operations capabilities. The MEU's infantry units were effectively playing the role of the Embassy's Marine Security Guards. Until OPERATION SHARP EDGE demonstrated how the expanded capabilities could provide greater utility in times of crisis, his concept of MEU (SOC) was just that: a concept, but untried. The Liberian response proved Gray's demand to train all MAGTFs to be special operations-qualified was correct, and even two decades later his mandate to "train up" remains in place.[23]

When the situation in Monrovia stabilized, the amphibious task force sailed away. Colonel Amos later reported the mission "complete" and "with no casualties." Although the evacuation received national media attention, the Pentagon again, in its customary response regarding a noncombat operation by the Navy/Marine Corps team, issued a simple statement. "No hostile actions taken against the OPERATION SHARP EDGE forces, which was conducted smoothly and without incident."

Major General Robert H. Scales Jr. masterfully summed up this noncombatant evacuation operations (NEO) humanitarian response when he wrote, "Even with their total focus on Saudi Arabia, the Marines had to divert their attention when a bloody revolt in Liberia required them to deploy a force to that African country to protect and evacuate U.S. citizens trapped by violence there. The Marines pulled it off flawlessly and then went right back into preparations for the defense of Saudi Arabia and the liberation of Kuwait."[24]

Actions such as this could not have been effectively executed had the 22nd MEU not undergone Gray's mandate and demanding requirements to demonstrate and be certified for special operations capability (SOC) missions before embarking for their deployment. An interesting footnote to Operation Sharp Edge was that the rifle companies that subsequently went ashore to perform the embassy reinforcement mission found themselves performing the traditional roles of the Marine Security Guard. OPERATION SHARP EDGE was as successful as it was because of the innovativeness that MEU (SOC) training breeds at all levels of leadership; the MEU (SOC) program adds a sizeable capability to the overall effectiveness of the Navy/Marine Corps team. What Gray had earlier envisioned was that future operating environments would place a premium on adaptable expeditionary forces, able to act with unprecedented speed and operate in austere environments from sea bases against a wide range of adversaries. He saw that the Corps' skill sets and posture would need to shift to meet these challenges better. Initially, his was a lone voice toward developing the special operations capabilities but this situation and a whole series of other emergency incidents have shown that Gray's early vision was on target.

Crisis in Somalia

The second "collateral" use of the Navy and Marine forces during OPERATIONS DESERT SHIELD/DESERT STORM was the rescue of 281 people from war-torn Somalia. At almost any other time, such an operation would have captured the nation's imagination and held it for days. The elements of danger, unexpected obstacles, speed, timing, and sheer courage were all present. However, for the Navy and Marine commanders ordered to execute an unplanned noncombat evacuation operation, the mission proved to be "one-of-a-kind." A bloody insurrection against the government of Said Barre, the president of Somalia, caught the diplomatic community by surprise. The Embassy in the capital city of Mogadishu was one of the more primitive American diplomatic posts and lacked the sophisticated security and perimeter defense systems emplaced at other embassies. Americans were under the extreme risk of being taken hostage or killed.

On January 2, 1991, a naval task force was formed and ordered to conduct an evacuation from the U.S. Embassy in Mogadishu. It was designated EASTERN EXIT. Timing became critical as the rebels began to seek out "the Americans." In a desperate effort to forestall the insurgents, a landing force of Marines was directed to be launched from their ships in a night helicopter operation while still 500 miles at sea.

Several critical factors must be appreciated to understand the significance of the Marine Corps' role as a forward-deployed force and its utility to the nation in time of peace and war. First was the Marine Corps' recently resurrected policy that every Marine is basically a rifleman, or "warrior." Second, leaders at all levels and skills must be prepared to respond to any and all unexpected situations. Whether logistician, aviation mechanic, or infantryman, they must step forward and take charge when leadership is called for. OPERATION EASTERN EXIT is a classic example of embarked Marines and Sailors suddenly being called upon to plan and execute a time-sensitive humanitarian rescue mission.

The mission was to be conducted over a vast distance, taking the aircraft to the absolute edge of their operating envelope. There was a myriad of opportunities for the rescue mission to turn into a disaster. The 4th MEB had been at sea since August 15, steaming in the Gulf of Oman and conducting amphibious landing exercises in preparation for what would become OPERATION DESERT STORM. In preparation for the forthcoming battles, occasional sorties of the task force were being made in the Persian Gulf to conduct feints along the Kuwaiti coastal areas. This forced Saddam Hussein to place a large contingent of his forces along the Kuwaiti coastline.

However, the day after Christmas 1990 found the amphibious task force spread over thousands of square miles. They were participating in a maritime exercise and were widely dispersed to intercept and turn back any ships attempting to return to Iraq. The task force had only recently intercepted and boarded the Iraqi ship *Ibn Khaldoon*, south of the Straits of Hormuz. It was a supply ship carrying medical and food supplies, 250 women and children of various nationalities, and a few journalists. The purpose of the voyage was to run the blockade, and failing that, to garner unfavorable press coverage of the multinational naval force for refusing to allow the "women of the world" to bring food and medicine to Iraq. After a series of naval maneuvers, the *Ibn Khaldoon* was boarded and escorted out of the immediate entrance to the Straits of Hormuz. With this accomplished, the Marines turned their attention back to possible amphibious landings to support the Iraqi ground war.

Far to their southwest on the eastern coast of Africa, the nation of Somalia was engulfed in a violent civil uprising. American citizens were again in danger. On January 2, 1991, Secretary of State James Baker requested that President Bush order an emergency noncombat evacuation operation to remove the U.S. Ambassador and his staff from their Embassy in Mogadishu, Somalia, to safety.

The mission was approved and orders passed down to Commanding General, 4th MEB Major General Harry Jenkins to commence planning for the conduct of the evacuation. Colonel James J. Doyle, commanding the 4th Brigade's Service Support Group, was appointed as the landing force commander. Colonel James J. Doyle was directed to relocate to the USS *Guam* and take the reins of the brigade's Bravo Command Group. Time was of the essence, for in the Somalia capital, President Barre was trapped in a bunker at the airport. Anarchy reigned in the city. A decision was made to send two ships, USS *Guam* and USS *Trenton,* on a 1,600-mile voyage to the southwest.

On the third, this small task force was broken out from the large amphibious task force and placed directly under COMUSNAVCENT, the senior naval commander. Later that day, Colonel Doyle's command elements made non-secure voice communications directly with the besieged Embassy. The contingency planning information on Somalia's Embassy layout was found to be badly out-of-date. But, as good fortunate often unfolds at the most unexpected moment, this was corrected with the help of a young sergeant who had previously served in the Somalia Embassy Security Guard from 1983-84. Through him, Colonel Doyle's staff confirmed that the Embassy had been moved to the center of the city. The few maps they had were woefully outdated. Plans for new extraction tasks were prepared for the landing of the force.

During the afternoon of January 4, the American Ambassador requested immediate evacuation by Army paratroopers or any other force capable of acting before the "slow-moving" task force. The two ships' Captains immediately increased speed to 22 knots, and plans were made to launch a 60-man force in two CH-53E helicopters. The long flight would require multiple aerial refuelings. Arrangements were made for KC-130 tanker support from the 3rd Marine Air Wing deployed in eastern Saudi Arabia. It was a precarious commitment of resources from seemingly everywhere. There was no other choice. Timing became more critical by the hour. The two heavily loaded CH-53s were launched.

This plan called for three aerial refuelings—two while inbound and one on the return flight. The challenge of the two flights of aircraft finding one another over such a distance was enormous, yet it was crucial if the Marines were to reach the Embassy in time. Both aircrafts' Omega Navigation systems were degraded due to the extreme distance from any ground transmitting station. Under increasing stress, the pilots continued using dead-reckoning navigational information that they had previously calculated. The KC-130s had flown more than a thousand miles before linking up to begin their refueling mission. Four hours after takeoff and two nighttime refueling operations, the CH-53s neared the Somalia coastline and descended to an altitude of 100 feet.[25] The onboard Marines made their last-minute equipment checks and loaded their weapons.

Information concerning the insurgency threat in Mogadishu was sketchy as best. It would be impossible to clearly distinguish among the government troops, the looters, and the rebel forces. Intelligence revealed that numerous surface-to-air missiles and antiaircraft guns were scattered throughout the capital. Who controlled these air defense weapons and whether they would attack the rescue helicopters was unknown.

All knew it was a desperate mission fraught with danger and uncertainties. As the sun broke over the horizon on January 5, the two CH-53s roared across the beach just three minutes off their planned arrival time. The pilots saw troop concentrations and numerous antiaircraft guns along their flight, but none challenged their progress. At the same time, bands of armed men were attempting to breach the Embassy compound. These forces were firing directly into the compound and using ladders to scale the walls. The helicopter-borne force arrived at the Embassy compound at 0610. With the arrival of these unexpected forces, the attackers scattered. Marine security forces quickly formed a defensive perimeter as the first 61 evacuees were marshaled, loaded onto the waiting helicopters, and the evacuation process began.

Once the evacuation operation force arrived, the Ambassador's main concern was to ensure that evacuees located elsewhere in the city were escorted to the compound. Among those escorted to the American compound were the Soviet Ambassador, his wife, and 37 Soviet Embassy personnel.

By the evening of the sixth, the USS *Trenton* and USS *Guam* were close enough to bring the rest of the noncombatants by ten CH-46 helicopters. The helicopters were blacked out, and the pilots flew with night-vision goggles. The evacuation went as planned. The American Ambassador remained until the last wave. Then he climbed aboard a CH-46 and flew out with the last of the Marine Security Force. When the tally was taken, 282 people had been evacuated. The list included ambassadors from 12 different nations and citizens from 31 nations.[26] With their rescue mission complete, Colonel Doyle's Marines and Sailors rejoined the main amphibious task force and returned to their preparations for ground operations against the Iraqis.

There can be no doubt that the 282 evacuees, including a baby boy born during the five-day transit to Muscat, were plucked from near death in Mogadishu. The whole operation was a shining example of the capabilities of the Navy/Marine Corps team when operating from the sea. History reminds us that many similar noncombatant evacu-ations operations have been conducted in every region of the world, and for this nation's force-in-readiness, there is every likelihood that they will continue. Naval forces, such as cited here, are constantly rotating in and out of U.S. ports on both coasts, traveling the oceans of the world to demonstrate both presence and the U.S. desire for stability in all regions. Often they are operating just over the horizon. A powerful and sustainable U.S. presence on the distant littorals of the world is structured to respond to civil unrest or when a natural disaster strikes. With the Somalia rescue mission completed, the ships turned and steamed for the Arabian Sea. The embarked Marines and Sailors immediately began replenishing their basic ammunition and supply loads so that they could conduct amphibious air and land assaults "on order" into Kuwait and potentially, Iraq.

These three situations confirmed the nation's continuing requirement for forward-deployed naval task forces. They also demonstrated the importance of "a presence," or being on the scene as a situation is unfolding. For the primary goal of any naval task force dispatched to a trouble spot is to deter the outbreak of hostilities and guarantee the safety of American citizens.

The role which the most junior officers, enlisted Marines, and Navy corpsmen play in rescue missions is often unappreciated. Gray freely referred to the need to be "smart Marines." He emphasized that small unit leaders in an arising crisis must make life and death decisions. This awareness would become particularly significant when General Charles Krulak, the 31st Commandant, brought forth his "three block" war scenario, as presented below.

One moment a Marine is rendering humanitarian or nation-building assistance, and in a matter of seconds, he is exposed to close and dangerous combat conditions. Planning is often done on an accelerated basis by senior officers, and when the order is received to execute the actual landing, the assembly, security measures, and the rescue itself are accomplished by Lieutenants, Sergeants, and other Marines in their late teens or early twenties. At the point of action, the execution of our national security policy and maritime strategy is accomplished by the very young men of an expeditionary task force. History has repeatedly recorded that their caring and military performances have heaped credit upon our nation. This doesn't just happen. It is the direct result of dedicated training, teamwork, and actions by confident young leaders who are fully aware of the risks and the great responsibilities on their shoulders. In every situation presented above, Gray was, although behind the scenes to the Washington Defense and Joint Chiefs of Staff leadership inside the Beltway, continuously monitoring the planning, deployment, force building, and execution of missions by his Marines and Sailors.

OPERATION DESERT SHIELD Buildup Continues

The original plan of the multinational force (MNF) had placed the MEF's 1st and 2nd Marine Divisions in a zone of action along Kuwait's Gulf coastline. This Tactical Area of Responsibility (TAOR) would enable them to maximize the use of their expertise in naval aviation close air and naval gunfire support. However, because of a breach in security at the highest levels, major revisions were made to the entire MNF combined arms organization. The Saudi Arabian National Guard, and a small contingent of the Kuwaiti military, Qatar and Moroccan units would replace I MEF units and would "on order" attack straight up the coastline. The new secret battle plan would shift the Marine Corps zone of action into a more western locale, while also strengthening I MEF forces to include reassigning the U.S. Army's Eighth Division, plus two British and a French division. This was a gargantuan increase in operational responsibilities for the Marines and would necessitate a dramatic shift in their planning, and, ultimately, an expanded command and control process. Time was short; there was much to do—for all.

In early October, Lieutenant General Boomer's staff made an assessment that the Iraqi opportunity to successfully invade Saudi Arabia had passed. He shifted the MEF's focus for a defensive posture and increased the planning for future offensive operations. Boomer's battle staff planning group went into a surge planning cycle to develop the MEF's basic plan. General Schwarzkopf concurred with this initiative as his CENTCOM staff was already developing a concept of operations to employ the MEF as if it was an Army Corps maneuver force.

He assigned MARFORCENT the following mission: "Conduct supporting attack to fix and destroy Iraqi operational reserves in southeastern Kuwait, to preclude their employment against the CENTCOM main attack in the west. The MEF will isolate Kuwait City for military operations in Urban Terrain."[27]

This initial plan called for a single breach of the Iraqi mine-fields. This would have required thousands of vehicles trucks, tanks, LAVs, artillery pieces, and other specialized equipment to enter Kuwait territory single file. It was too high an operational risk. This decision had been made because of the limited engineer equipment available to the MEF and the brief time for the 2nd Marine Division to conduct training

When Gray became aware of the shortage of minefield breach-ing equipment, he too directed action to acquire the most advanced engineer equipment. Working with Lieutenant General Bill Etnyne, then Commanding General, Marine Corps Combat Development Command at Quantico, they approached the Israeli military, bypass-ing numerous peacetime procurement protocols. They purchased the critically needed systems and had them flown to I MEF. Now, with sufficient breaching assets, the two divisions began preparing their final attack plans.

During the second week in November, the Marine Corps Forces Central Command (MARCENT) battle staff began developing courses of action and rough estimates of supportability. Most of these involved a single penetration of the Kuwaiti border, and a link up with an amphibious assault along the Kuwaiti coast by the 4th and 5th MEBs. With the arrival of the 2nd Marine Division, a renewed effort was undertaken to formalize the initial attack plans.

Lieutenant General Walter Boomer and his staff were deeply involved in continuous planning as the buildup in units and equipment arrived and all quickly transitioned to their new desert environmental training, and later, live fire exercises. Throughout the Vietnam War, the Marine Corps had two divisions in-country, but never conducted any joint division-sized maneuvers. One would have to reflect further back to the final stages of World War II to the battles for Iwo Jima and Okinawa to confirm where two Marine divisions had last been abreast of one another and maneuvered against the Japanese.

By December 10, the main body of I MEF reinforcements began arriving in the Al Jubail naval port and adjacent airfield. As doctrinally planned, the 7th MEB was deactivated and its staff and personnel integrated into the MEF's Divisions and Air Wings. Major General Hopkins was moved to I MEF as the Deputy Commanding General. It was a timely move as the pace of staff planning was so intense that senior staff officers had cots placed beside their desks. Later he was rotated back to the States, and Major General Richard D. Hearney assumed this important position. General Hearney was a no-nonsense aviator and was exceptionally gifted, mentally and professionally. He proved to be the perfect Deputy to direct the two Marine Corps staffs and effectively serve and respond to General Schwarzkopf's staff.

General Norman Schwarzkopf, the MNF Commander, subsequently developed an audacious attack plan with the primary attack consisting of massive armor and mechanized helicopter gunship attacks from the far western Saudi Arabian desert. Simultaneously, I MEF, operating under Lieutenant General Boomer, would launch a supporting "holding force" attack in the east. This was to be an attack into and through the Al Burqan oil field, toward the Al Jaber Air Base, and toward Kuwait City. The Marine divisions began moving into their final staging areas. To the immediate front of the Marines' assembly areas and eight miles inside Kuwait were two deep lines of minefield barriers.

As the final dispositions of I MEF forces were taken, Gray, just before Christmas, was again in Saudi Arabia visiting his Marines and Sailors before the actual jump-off. In a style similar to General Eisenhower's the day before the Normandy Invasion, he sought to reflect a casualness and upbeat image. For Gray, it was a natural characteristic. He was with his troops again, which further motivated him to want to shake hands and grasp the open hands of the youngest of his warriors. The word was out, and those units searching for Gray were quick to identify his swagger within the milling crowd following him across the desert. Cheers erupted as he crawled up on the nearest tank or truck so he could be better seen and heard as he encouraged them to "be smart Marines. Be prepared to assume more senior leadership positions if your commanders become casualties and always take care of your men." This was his theme. His footprints zigzagged across the desert from one assembly of Marines to the next. Then he was off to meet with other elements of the air-ground logistics team. Before this flight home, he was flown out to the embarked 4th and 5th MEB units. Again, he moved from ship to ship. He wanted them to know he was with them in spirit and in his prayers. Finally, he had to return to Washington. As his plane lifted off the runway, the MEF's forces were passing out the basic allowances of ammunition to the eager and confident assaulting divisions. The pre-battle stress was felt by everyone, including those officers and staff NCOs assigned back in Headquarters Marine Corps. They were monitoring every request for assistance or receiving the latest status reports from the MEF. Gray was continuously being updated on all matters of logistics and readiness. For him, it was a personally challenging experience to be playing a distant coaching role at a time when his MAGTFs were going to war.

During the DESERT SHIELD fast-expanding buildup phase, Gray made his final trip into Saudi Arabia. In addition to meeting with General Schwarzkopf, he met with Marine and Navy leaders offshore who had continued examining the idea of conducting some type of amphibious landing. Gray, long recognized as a notable global military strategist, felt there could be an active option for the naval forces to plan for either an amphibious landing or amphibious raids. He saw this as a viable option if there were unexpected delays in the land-based flanking maneuvers. He felt strongly about exploring the concept of conducting some type of amphibious maneuver during the DESERT STORM phase of the Gulf War. However, by its very nature, such an undertaking would involve both the Navy and the Marine Corps planning staffs to conceptualize a plan and assess the risks to ships and personnel. Because of the danger of mines, the Navy staff was less than enthusiastic about venturing into the northernmost part of the Gulf.

As Commandant, Gray had much earlier tasked then-Brigadier General Matthew Caulfield, Director of the Marine Corps Warfighting Laboratory at Quantico, to assemble a select group of Marine officers to explore all possibilities. General Caulfield and Colonel Martin Steel, his chief of staff, were exceptionally qualified to lead this special group. They explored a series of issues relevant to the Marine Corps forces in the Gulf, a number of amphibious landing options. It was recognized by all that Gray's initiative was a rather uncommon staffing process. An innovative plan was developed back stateside by a Service Chief and was carried forward to the Navy and Marine component commanders, who, if they accepted the plan, would have to brief the theater commander and receive his approval to execute any type of amphibious operation.

In November 1990, General Caulfield and Colonel Steele flew to the Gulf and presented several options for conducting amphibious operations to Vice Admiral Arthur and Lieutenant General Boomer. Although Arthur and Boomer made no final commitment to conduct any amphibious landing or raids, they agreed to take the issue to General Schwarzkopf. Later, Schwarzkopf received the joint Navy/Marine Corps' latest conceptual briefing for conducting amphibious landings or raids, before the outcome of the ground campaign of OPERATION DESERT STORM. General Schwarzkopf studied the Marine Corps' and Navy's plan but eventually rejected it, because he believed it would take from his basic principle to "mass" all his forces in a single but massive maneuver.[28]

There were a number of other reasons it was not needed, given the huge success of the ground war and the opportunity to avoid the casualties the Marines might have taken going through the mine-filled waters and over defended beaches. It was a disheartening decision for the Commandant and his afloat Marines, who were eager to storm "any" Iraqi beach. Intelligence sources also indicated that

Saddam Hussein made it a high priority to track Marine Corps forces' movements. Lieutenant General Boomer considered his potentially greatest threat to be from the indirect fires from Iraqi artillery. Their artillery brigades were considered the most experienced in the world because of their sheer numbers and previous use of chemical fires on troops and civilians.

Walt Boomer was no stranger to the violent destructive capabilities from Soviet-made 122mm and 130mm weapons. In March 1972, while serving as an Advisor to the South Vietnamese Marine Corps (VNMC), the Third VNMC Infantry Battalion came under extremely accurate artillery fire. After 36 hours of constant shelling, their fire base was physically overrun. Boomer, along with his Assistant Marine Advisor, Captain Ray Smith, the VNMC battalion commander, and a very small group of survivors abandoned their positions, evaded the enemy, and were eventually recovered after a harrowing escape. Boomer clearly understood the violence of war and the importance of his leadership responsibilities. He kept an open mind and listened to all deliberations before announcing his planning decisions.

Major General William "Bill" Keys almost never spoke loudly, but when he did, all listened as he showed an exceptionally high level of combat maturity and a keen sense for the coming battles. Once he arrived in the MEF's new area of responsibility (AOR), he pushed to change the initial attack plan from a single breach of the minefields to two simultaneous breachings. He noted that even with two cleared lanes, the division-support trains would extend back more than 25 miles. General Keys' recommendation for two separate breachings was approved and the MEF's final attack formations began to solidify.[29]

On January 1, 1991, Lieutenant General Boomer signed the Marine Corps Forces Central Command (MARCENT) Operations Plan for DESERT STORM. On January 16, 1991, President Bush authorized the ground attack and OPERATION DESERT STORM began. The poised massive assault had been preceded by 32 days and nights of an aerial campaign. What few Iraqi aircraft flew to counter the allied forces air attacks were quickly destroyed. By Ground Day (G-Day), all Iraqi air threats to the ground forces had been completely eliminated. Not only were hundreds of Iraqi armored vehicles and troop concentrations destroyed but, more significantly, their lateral command and control communications were neutralized. This would later inhibit the Iraqi commanders from obtaining a clear understanding of what was happening across the hundreds of miles of battle space. Additionally, without receiving reliable battle reports from their commanders on the ground, their situational awareness from the highest military levels down was essentially nonexistent. But the Iraqi ground troops still remained a formidable force-in-waiting.

The Iraqi Threat to I MEF
As the II MEF forces moved closer to the Kuwaiti border, their search for more detailed information on their opposing enemy became even more intense. Within the multinational MNF staffs, which were focused on the theater-of-operations level, a fairly accurate image was being developed. However, this information was slow in being passed down to the tactical levels, where it was needed. Much of this information, however, did not reach the MEF—particularly the warfighters—in a timely manner.[30] It was difficult for the MEF to accurately define the boundaries of the Iraqi divisions directly opposing them and also to make any comparative assessment of their residual combat capabilities. It was apparent that the Iraqi forces, which were spread across 200 miles of desert, were in disarray.

The MEF was aggressive in using its organic intelligence to create a fairly accurate image of the Iraqi's lay-down of forces which included divisional boundaries, but they still did not have a firm portrayal of the damage inflicted during the preparatory air campaign or its overall effectiveness. The MEF persistently updated its intelligence estimate and continued to adjust its schemes of maneuver.[31] There was intense concern that their two divisions, reinforced by the

U.S. Army Stryker Brigade, would still be attacking a significantly larger entrenched enemy in terms of sheer numbers.

Furthermore, there was the ever-present Iraqi threat to employ chemical weapons. The use of weapons of mass destruction (WMDs) was repeatedly deliberated in every planning session at every command. This was truly the great unknown: Would Saddam Hussein unleash such weapons on the advancing maneuvering forces? In addition, there were thousands of Soviet-made artillery weapons pointed straight at them, defying the MEF to attack. And if all these artillery pieces were synchronized and massed, they could effectively neutralize large areas of the battlefield and annihilate any units in the impact areas. There were so many unknowns that needed to be answered, and time was running out. Every commander, from platoon leader to division and Corps commander, silently felt awesome responsibilities on their shoulders. They had all trained to the fullest, and they could do no more but launch and lead their units in the attacks. There were no options.

Equally significant in the MEF's intelligence assessment was the greater number of Iraqis staged to counter any attacking force. Military doctrine outlines the benefits of the attacking force when they possess at least a 3 to 1 numerical superiority. In sharp contrast, which the MEF gleaned from their intelligence reports, was that the combined armor and mechanized force they were facing posed a serious numerical disadvantage of a 6 to 1 ratio.[32] This was common knowledge at the highest levels resulting in projections of extreme battle casualty assessments. Several of these studies that included II MEF could suffer the loss of the combat effectiveness of both Marine divisions. Brigadier General Thomas Draude, Deputy Commander, 2nd Marine Division, recalled that there was great sensitivity to these discouraging ratio assessments. Considering several of the extreme predictions and, if the Iraqis staged a determined defense, Draude felt it was possible that both Marine divisions might have to be completely reconstituted because of their battle losses.[33]

By any manner in which the ratio of opposing forces were viewed and studied, these high casualties forecast were frightening to all leaders. Intelligence agencies indicated that behind the minefields were Iraqi infantry and armored units waiting to engage any attacking forces. It was obvious that the intent of the Iraqi defense forces was to restrict and channelize any attackers attempting to penetrate the barriers. The intent was that once the MNF attacks were blunted by Iraqi armor, their artillery would neutralize the attackers with artillery fire. To counter this strategy, the I MEF general concept was to breach the wire barriers as rapidly as possible, defeat the immediate forces in the zone, and seize their assigned objectives in and around Kuwait City. Their goal was to deceive the Iraqi commanders as to the real focus of their efforts using continuous fire support—both air and artillery—to cause the Iraqis to take cover and reduce their fighting capabilities. The two Marine divisions would then attack, emphasizing speed and concentration of forces. The 1st Marine Division's final battle instructions read, "Exploit, Exploit, and Exploit." [34]

When viewed in its entirety, Boomer's Commander's Guidance was like none ever received by Marine divisions waiting to launch their attacks. The Gray doctrine of the Marine Corps' MAGTF forces executing maneuver warfare operations was about to be fully tested. Boomer set the final stage for his planning staff when he directed that all planning be conducted using the principles for maneuver warfare versus traditional attrition warfare methods. He reminded his commanders that maneuver warfare's characteristics included high tempo of operations, speed, and decentralized control, with the objective of shattering the enemy's cohesion, organization, and command structure. To accomplish this, Boomer directed that every commander, down to the lowest level, understand exactly what his intent and objectives were. Each commander on the battlefield would receive "mission-type orders" that empowered him to make decisive tactical decisions necessary to accomplish his mission. The directive stated, "If unseen circumstances arise, such as a sudden opportunity or a counterattack, each commander is to deal with this situation immediately rather than pass the information back to the chain of command."

This directive surely must have been the strangest ever published for a Marine Corps commander whose forces were staged to launch a massive armor-mechanized attack against a numerically superior force.[35]

The effect of the deception plan was undoubtedly aided by the massive air campaign that preceded its implementation with 32 days and nights of air bombardment. What few Iraqi aircraft flew to counter the air attacks were quickly destroyed. By G-Day, all Iraqi air threat to the ground forces had been completely eliminated. Not only were hundreds of Iraqi armored vehicles and troop concentrations destroyed but, more significantly, their lateral command and control was seriously degraded. This inhibited the Iraqi commanders from obtaining a clear understanding of what was happening across the main battle lines. Additionally, without a reliable aerial view (to add a three-dimensional view of the battlefield) and receiving unreliable battle reports from the Iraqi commanders on the ground, their situation awareness, from the highest military levels down to the tactical commanders on the ground, was essentially nonexistent.

In complete contrast, the coalition forces had developed an incredibly accurate view of the battle space and of the Iraqi forces through intensive aerial reconnaissance and from small reconnaissance teams that both divisions had sent forward covertly to examine and fix the exact locations of the two barriers and covering defenses. The clocks were fast ticking toward G-Day.

Throughout these final weeks of staging and preparations for DESERT STORM, I was in frequent satellite telephone contact with Lieutenant General Boomer. From the tone of his voice, it was possible to sense the growing stress he was under. Yet during every phone call, he praised his staff and commanders. He was well aware that among his 75,000-plus men and women were the finest leaders the Marine Corps had. Just a few days before DESERT STORM began, I received a short note from him that said, "Gerry, I don't believe they will put up a fight." I prayed he was right. Time would soon tell the fate of his men and women.

CHAPTER 15

DESERT STORM: "The 100-Hour War"

*"No matter how frantically soldiers prepare for
combat, at some point they can do nothing more than
wait for it to begin. Time, that precious commodity
always in short supply, as last minute orders are
issued, inspection completed, and adjustment made,
seems to stop as the moment of truth approaches."*[1]

Robert H. Scales
Brigadier General, U.S. Army (Retired)

When it became apparent to Saddam Hussein that the ground campaign was just days, possibly hours away, he directed the Kuwaiti oil fields to be set afire. The result was an environmental catastrophe. The whole region was affected as the belching black smoke turned day into night and night into a strange, pitch-black world. The soft desert wind slowly spread smoke in all directions, in most cases hugging the ground and blotting out aerial observation of the desert below. There would be no way for the troops, now in their pre-assault positions, to remain clear of the smoke and vapors, and many would complain later of the effects of inhaling the resulting dangerous contaminants.

Several days before G-Day, Lieutenant General Walter Boomer held his final coordination meeting with his division and task force commanders. A carefully planned agenda was laid out to ensure that whatever the Iraqi response was to be, the Marine expeditionary force (MEF) was fully prepared to meet any challenge decisively. It was an upbeat session, but with little idle chatter, as each leader sensed G-Day and H-Hour was upon them. All were seeking the latest information on the enemy waiting just north of the minefields. There were no complete answers, as there were still many unknown factors. One unanswered question stood out above all others: "Would Iraqi military leaders employ weapons of mass destruction (WMDs) from their huge stock of chemical and biological gases against the multinational force (MNF) units?" All MEF personnel would be carrying their gas masks—just in case the unthinkable happened. Units had repeatedly conducted "gas attack" drills. The guidance was that should the Iraqis release WMDs, the MEF would continue their ground attacks and fight "dirty" as long as possible before performing any decontamination efforts.[2]

As Lieutenant General Boomer's meeting closed, his leaders shuffled around, talking and sharing firm handshakes indicative of their long years of camaraderie. A close look into each other's eyes and a soft-spoken "good luck" between commanders ended the session. They picked up their helmets, gas masks, and gear and shuffled out of the briefing tent into the waiting desert and the war.

DESERT STORM: G-Day of the Ground Offensive

At 0100 on February 24, 1991, aging battleships USS *Wisconsin* and USS *Missouri* initiated the Navy's planned amphibious demonstration by launching a series of Harpoon missiles. Their nearly half a decade of unused 16-inch guns also began thundering just off the Kuwaiti coastline, convincing the six Iraqi divisions defending the beaches that the long awaited amphibious landing by U.S. Marines was but moments away. Ashore, the Marines' deception plan, crafted under the supervision of Brigadier General Tom Draude, was being fully energized with small illusionary teams from the 1st Marine Division roaring into action with loudspeakers and false radio signals to further confuse the Iraqi leadership. DESERT STORM was under way, and the coalition forces were at war with Iraq. It was a cold, rainy Monday. The desert sand had turned into a gritty mud.

The ground attack began at 0400 on February 26, with the 1st Marine Division attacking in its zone. The MEF's armor assets were composed of 190 M-60 and 74 M1A2 tanks.[3] The initial attack did not begin at the nominal forward edge of the battle area. Instead, it had begun from concealed forward attack positions established 30 hours earlier, when two regimental task forces—Ripper (7th Marines) and Papa Bear (1st Marines)—crossed covertly into Kuwaiti territories and began the infiltration of the area up to the first Iraqi defensive belt.

Risking occasional contact with the enemy, the 1st Division's infiltration task forces had crept into no-man's land with selected small reconnaissance Marines carefully mapping out paths through the poorly maintained minefields.[4] Farther to the northeast, Major General William "Bill" Keys' 2nd Marine Division reconnaissance teams had similarly covertly crept into Kuwait and began marking safe routes through the first minefield barrier belt.[5]

For the MEF's air-ground logistics team, this would be a history-making event, as the Marine Corps had not conducted a coordinated two-division attack since the 1945 World War II battles on Iwo Jima and Okinawa. This was to be the largest Marine Air-Ground Task Force (MAGTF) combat operation conducted since World War II.

The 2nd Division cautiously launched its attack at 0530, several hours ahead of schedule due to the rapid advances of the probing and marking teams. They experienced little incoming fire from Iraqi artillery. The 6th Marines, commanded by Colonel Larry Livingston (awarded the Navy Cross in Vietnam), plowed through both Iraqi minefield barriers within a matter of hours, encountering only light resistance and taking few casualties.

For the Marines, the twin breachings were accomplished with little enemy opposition as M-60 and M1A2 tanks with specially designed bulldozer blades led the way. Engineer crews following close behind erected wire and emplaced stakes to mark the safe lanes. Within the two cleared passage lanes, tanks and Light Armored Vehicles (LAVs) followed by hundreds of trucks loaded with troops moved forward as the windswept desert uncovered hundreds of anti-tank mines. Every mine stood like a silent sentry armed to destroy the unwary.

The attacking Marine and Army Stryker Brigade Task Forces were quick to discover that the Iraqis had half buried their tanks behind sand berms, reducing their mobility to maneuver. Once their positions were identified, they were taken under fire and destroyed, typically before the Iraqis were able to fire back. The U.S. advanced technological tank sights were clearly far superior to the Soviet-made 1960 and 1979 gun systems with our increased range accuracy and laser designator systems.

General Schwarzkopf's primary MNF attack was heavily weighted to support the huge Army and coalition armor and mechanized forces on the far western flank. It was his intent to have the MEF's divisional attacks fix the Iraqi defensive forces and hold them in place while the main attack circled and struck deep into the rear. However, the main attack failed to gather momentum and developed much slower than anticipated. So when the Marine forces reported successful breaching, they reported they were entering into their breakout engagements, and General Schwarzkopf and staff were surprised the MEF's breaching and breakout was accomplished so quickly. Without waiting, II MEF forces continued their attacks to the north toward the Ahmed Al Jaber Air Base.

Later, during his February 27th news briefing, Schwarzkopf stated, "I can't say enough about the two Marine divisions breaching the barriers. It was an absolutely superb job they did in breaching the so-called impenetrable barrier. It was a classic, absolutely classic, military breaching of a very tough minefield, barbed wire, fire trenches-type barrier. They went across the second barrier line even under artillery fire at that time. They continued to open up the breach. ... Classic superb operation, a textbook case."[6]

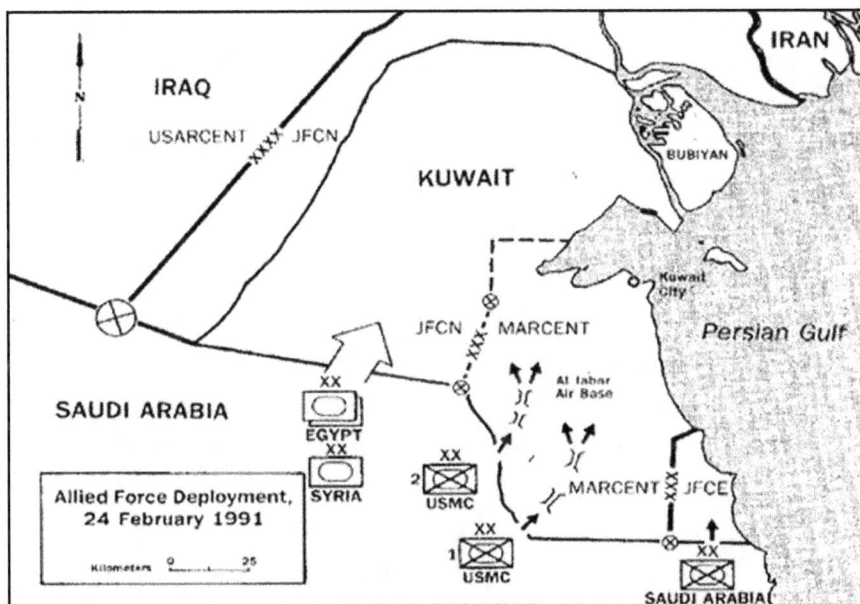

Figure 8. Allied Force Initial Deployment on February 24, 1991 (Courtesy of Marine Corps Monographs from OPERATION DESERT STORM).

While the encircling main attack continued to move in a deliberate manner, the MEF began a rapid advance toward the Al Burqan oil field at a much faster speed than scheduled. Their attached U.S. Army Tiger Brigade, with M1A2 main battle tanks, met only sporadic artillery and organized resistance from Iraqi armor units. The MEF's six task forces began exploiting the penetration, thus creating an even more confusing tactical situation for the Iraqis.

Task Force Shepherd, comprised of the 1st LAV Battalion, was assigned a screening operation in the Al Wakrah and Al Burqan oilfields and engaged enemy tanks south of Ahmed Al Jaber Air Base. As the sun was setting and darkness was fast approaching, the 1st Marine Division's four regimental task forces, organized into combined arms teams, breached the obstacle belts and captured the Ahmed Al Jaber Air Base, MEF Objective A. The division reported its first day's encounters as 21 enemy tanks destroyed and more than 4,000 prisoners of war taken at the cost of three damaged tanks, with one Marine killed in action (KIA) and nine Marines wounded in action (WIA).

Once the 2nd Division broke through the last obstacle belt, the 6th and 8th Marine Regiments, and the First Brigade, Second Armored Division temporarily consolidated their positions to defend against a "possible" enemy armor column moving south out of Kuwait City. Close air support was called in to attack the moving column which, in short order, was completely destroyed. The division then continued its attacks, capturing an entire enemy tank battalion including 35 T-55 tanks and more than 5,000 prisoners, at the cost of one Marine KIA and eight WIA.

The Marine Corps air-ground logistics forces were performing well, as the 3rd Marine Aircraft Wing flew more than 650 sorties, striking elements of six Iraqi divisions and destroying 40 tanks, three armored personnel carriers, and more than 100 trucks and miscellaneous vehicles. The 1st Force Service Support Group (FSSG) pushed supplies forward, moving thousands of gallons of water and fuel by roads and airlifts. They quickly adjusted their resupply plans to use available southbound traffic to move the growing number of POWs to the rear. Brigadier Generals Charles (Chuck) Krulak and James Brabham were vigilant to every opportunity to use their scarce assets to adjust to every unexpected situation and immeasurably aid the warfighters.

G-Day+1

On the second day of ground combat, the MEF continued attacking northward, advancing in the face of moderate resistance. The 1st Division began the day on a line forward of the Al Burqan oilfield. Earlier intelligence anticipated that once the two Marine divisions were through the barriers they could be subjected to a heavy armor counterattack by the enemy. To counter this threat, the Division massed its artillery and fired a regimental-sized time-on-target fire mission on suspected enemy assembly areas. The fragmentary battlefield intelligence proved to be very real, as a large enemy armor force roared out of the impacted areas and executed a counterattack that almost overran Major General Myatt's 1st Division's forward command post. It was a hectic and violent close-in fight, but the enemy force was systematically destroyed and prisoners taken. As Brigadier General Richard Lake, then the Assistant G-2 Intelligence Officer recalled, "It was an Intelligence success story." At the end of the day, the Division consolidated and prepared to clear out the last of the enemy around the Ahmed Al Jaber Air Base.

The 2nd Division began the second day of the ground offensive south of Al Abdaliyah by attacking north toward a hard-surface road complex nicknamed the "ice cube tray." Following the division's heavy artillery prep fires, scores of enemy soldiers began streaming toward the division's front lines as the Iraqi forces were losing their will to put up any serious fight. During the day, 248 tanks were destroyed and 4,500 prisoners taken. It was a most successful day of heavy combat. More prisoners drifted into the MEF's task forces during the night.

The Marine expeditionary force (MEF) encountered its heaviest concentration of Iraqi tanks and mechanized forces as they moved through the oil field. The roads to the Ahmed Al Jaber Air Base and Kuwait City appeared open. There were few prepared enemy positions, and fewer organized ground units in sight. By the second day, the Iraqi forces had suffered unprecedented losses of high numbers of tanks, combat vehicles, and personnel. Organized resistance dwindled as the MEF's task forces continued to capture thousands of Iraqi troops. Initially, only small groups vigorously waved white flags. As the Iraqi resistance faltered, they began surrendering in battalion-sized units, waving white flags, hands in the air, and walking straight toward the advancing Marines. They all gestured wildly to show they did not intend to resist and often, upon initial contact, they pleaded for mercy and for water. To keep the MEF's attacks moving, only a handful of Marine riflemen were often assigned to march 100 or more prisoners of war back to pre-designated POW compounds. These sparsely erected campsites were quickly overflowing as the number of prisoners rose into the thousands.

By the close of the second day, the Iraqi forces were retreating even before they came under fire. In one brief encounter, a Marine Reserve Tank Company, equipped with the Army's latest M1A2 tanks, destroyed 59 tanks and 32 armored personnel carriers without incurring any casualties. For the Marines, it was almost like a one-sided "turkey shoot" as they destroyed 20 tanks in the first 90 seconds, while the engagement lasted only seven minutes. As suddenly as it started, it was over, before higher headquarters had received the initial contact report.

With a collapsing enemy, both Divisions' maneuvering task forces became increasingly confident in their maneuver warfare techniques. They were repeatedly witnessing how the speed of attack and deadly accuracy of their tanks and wire-guided anti-tank missiles, supported by Cobra attack helicopters armed with anti-tank missiles, were rapidly destroying enemy positions and vehicles even before the enemy was able to engage their weapons. The combined arms team was working very well.

The 3rd Marine Aircraft Wing flew 480 sorties against the six defending Iraqi divisions, destroying 522 tanks, nine armored personnel carriers, and six artillery pieces. Their most surprising success occurred the day enemy soldiers began waving white cloths of surrender to a Remotely Piloted Vehicle (RPV) orbiting overhead. Throughout the battle area, Force Service Support Group (FSSG) units worked around the clock conducting sustainment operations and resupplying ammunition as well as water, fuel, and missiles.

At sea, the 4th MEB forces conducted a series of well-organized demonstrations using a combination of naval gunfire and troop-carrying helicopters. Ships offloaded amphibious vehicles into the waters of the Persian Gulf to further convince the Iraqi leadership that some type of amphibious landing was to be launched. The deception plans were working. To further confuse the enemy, the 5th

MEB began flying ashore elements of Regimental Landing Team-5, commanded by Colonel Randy Gangle, to assume the role as the MEF's reserve force.

A historic milestone was achieved during this phase of the attack. Although the two divisions had a common boundary for fire-control purposes, they did not maintain a physical linkage during their attacks. On several occasions, they were separated and were miles apart. First, one division was ahead of the other, and then back and forth as they each encountered different enemy units. This was the first "real combat" venture in conducting large-scale maneuver war- fare operations as envisioned by Gray years earlier. Not only were the divisions operating on mission-type orders but within the divisions various task forces were similarly operating using maneuver warfare tenets (especially within Major General Myatt's 1st Marine Division). They did experience control and reporting problems, partly because of the unexpected rapidity of their advances, but flexible command and control measures were employed that maximized the speed and shock of the armored and mechanized task forces as they searched for and continued to destroy their bewildered and dissolving enemy. It was to be a day of many enemy kills, thousands of prisoners taken and, fortuitously, few Marine and Army casualties.

G-Day+2
The third day of OPERATION DESERT STORM's ground offensive operations found the MEF continuing the attacks in zone, advancing against a clearly disorganized defense. The 1st Marine Division's Objective (MEF Objective C) was to take the Kuwait International Airport. The final assault began at 1600 and immediately encountered armored resistance. General Myatt was aggressive in his tactics and continued to press the attack until the enemy surrendered northwest of the airport. In seizing the airport, the division destroyed 250 aging T-55 and T-62 tanks and more than 70 of the newer T-72 tanks with only minimal casualties and equipment losses. The M1A2 advanced

tank gunsights were superior in every way against the enemy. Most enemy vehicles were destroyed even before they could locate the Marine and Army gunners. It was often a one-sided firefight.

The 2nd Division advanced to the MEF's final objective, the city of Al Jahra, with only moderate opposition. It had become routine to sight and destroy enemy armor and other fighting vehicles before the Marines would receive any counter fire. At 1600 on February 27, the 2nd Division continued through the city to secure blocking positions to include the high ground known as Mutla Ridge, northwest of Al Jahra. Again, the 2nd Division's casualties and equipment losses were minimal, while numerous enemy tanks and vehicles were destroyed.

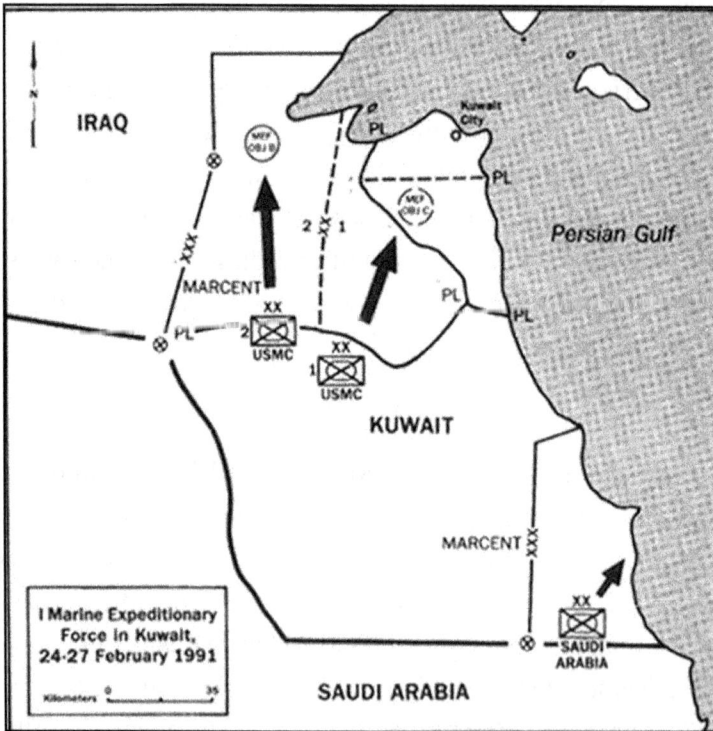

Figure 9. I MEF Forces Tactical Advancements into Kuwait February 24-27, 1991 (Courtesy of Marine Corps Monographs from OPERATION DESERT STORM).

The 3rd Marine Aircraft Wing continued to support the MEF's advance, striking targets throughout both divisions' zones, and concentrating on any remaining Iraqi artillery or armor in the vicinity of MEF Objectives B and C. The Air Wing's damage assessments identified 16 tanks and more than 50 vehicles destroyed.

So it was with the logistics support teams, spread across the vast desert battle areas—they continued their vital support while moving more enemy POWs to the rear. At sea, the 4th MEB conducted a pre-dawn demonstration toward the Bubiyan and Faylaka islands.

G-Day+3

On February 27, the fourth day of the ground combat operations, I MEF continued the ground attack in support of DESERT STORM. To maintain effective operational control over his advancing divisions, Lieutenant General Boomer continually moved his mobile Forward Command Element northward toward Kuwait City. He had positioned has mobile command post group just outside Kuwait City and waited for Kuwaiti armor brigades so they could be the first units to officially reenter the captured capital.

The 1st Marine Division completed the consolidation and securing of Kuwait International Airport by 0900 and began clearing operations, preparing to receive elements of Special Operations Command and Kuwaiti officials. The Division also coordinated passage of lines for the Arab forces Joint Command East to enter Kuwait City. The 2nd Marine Division remained in the vicinity of Al Jahra in blocking positions on Mutla Ridge while linking up with Kuwaiti resistance forces. The remaining enemy units in their battle area were inactive.

The 3rd Marine Aircraft Wing flew more than 200 sorties in support of the divisions in striking the withdrawing elements of the Iraqi forces in northern Kuwait. By late afternoon, airborne forward air controllers reported that it was difficult to find any targets along the main roadways because so many Iraqis were waving something white. All indications were that the major battles were over and some type of ceasefire agreement would soon be announced.

There was one small unit incident that confirmed how strongly the Iraqi military leadership was convinced that amphibious forces were going to make some type of assault landing. The platoon leader, First Platoon, 2nd Force Reconnaissance Company established an observation post within the U.S. Embassy in Kuwait City. On February 27, they discovered an enormous "sand table" in a Kuwaiti school adjacent to the Embassy. This sand table depicted the extensive Iraqi defensive fortifications prepared in anticipation of any amphibious assault, including many bunkers, obstacles, and minefields. The numerous amphibious exercises and demonstrations conducted by Major General Harry Jenkins' 4th MEB had clearly served their purpose and saved many lives with the successful exploitation of their deception plans.

G-Day+4 (Victory Day)

On February 28, offensive combat operations ceased at 0800 at the direction of President George H.W. Bush. I MEF prepared to assist the Kuwaiti government in clearing operations and civil affairs matters. Both the 1st and 2nd Marine divisions had reached the limit of their advance with substantial combat power forward in position to block any Iraqi retreat. A preliminary statistical review provided by Lieutenant General Boomer's staff indicated that in the 100 hours of ground combat, the MEF had destroyed or captured 1,040 enemy tanks, destroyed more than 600 armored personnel carriers, destroyed hundreds of artillery pieces, destroyed five short-range unguided Free Rocket Over Ground launchers, killed more than 1,510 enemy soldiers, and taken more than 20,000 enemy prisoners of war. Marine casualties resulting from ground action during this period were reported as five killed and 48 wounded in action. Marine aviation losses from the initiation of the ground war on February 24 amounted to two fixed-wing aircraft and one helicopter lost in action, and two lost in non-battle mishaps.

On the day after the ceasefire, I MEF continued operations in support of DESERT STORM. The 1st Marine Division remained in their defensive positions near Kuwait International Airport and Ahmed Al Jaber Air Base and prepared for retrograde operations. The division units remained vigilant as they continued searching for enemy soldiers and covering the Iraqi weapons, ammunition and equipment in their zone. The 2nd Marine Division, in defensive positions in the vicinity of Al Jahra, continued to process enemy prisoners and to destroy enemy equipment while preparing to retrograde. The 5th MEB ground combat element was relieved of its MEF Reserve mission and was directed to retrograde back to the coastline and re-embark aboard amphibious ships. The 3rd Marine Aircraft Wing, the MEF Aviation Combat Element (ACE), entered an extended period of maintenance stand-down while continuing to provide resupply and medical evacuation support. The 1st Force Service Support Group continued its resupply and enemy prisoner transport effort, while explosive ordnance disposal personnel continued to destroy enemy ammunition, clear bunkers, and neutralize weapons.

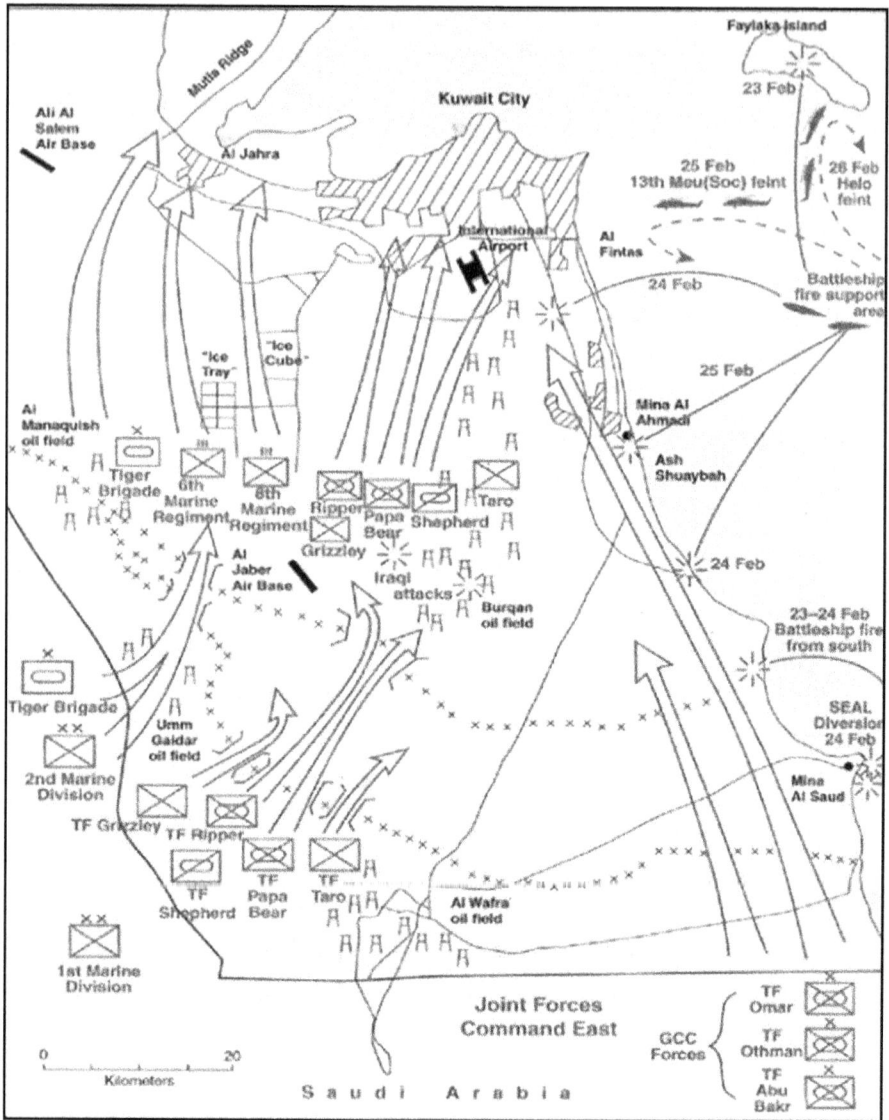

Figure 10. Ground Assault on Southern Kuwait, 24-28 February 1991. (Courtesy of *Shield and Sword:* Edward J. Marolda and Robert J. Schneller Jr., Naval Historical Center [1998]).

The Retrograde of Forces Begins

Marine forces come from the sea, and when their mission is complete, they return to their amphibious ships and set sail to steam the ocean's highways and await their next call. From the Corps' earliest years to the present, the Navy/Marine Corps team has been charged by the nation's leadership to respond to most arising crises. Whether it is to project combat power ashore, conduct a noncombatant evacuation operation (NEO), or assist other nations during times of crises, the team serves as the nation's force of choice and has executed hundreds of noncombat missions in the world's littorals. From Lebanon to Somali to Liberia, or racing to the Indian Ocean to the impoverished Muslim country of Bangladesh, they go in peace. When a devastating typhoon in the western Pacific region killed more than 100,000 people, the Navy/Marine team was first on the scene. They came to help. Sailors and Marines embarked on amphibious ships landed and brought desperately needed medical supplies and equipment to help restore a floundering nation. Whatever the mission or the size of the forces involved, all Marines afloat know that when the mission is complete, their last and most important task is to prepare to re-embark to offshore ships and refurbish their equipment to be prepared for the next call. It's a way of life.

On March 7, 1991, General Schwarzkopf announced his "Retrograde Plan." For the Marines, this retrograde and re-embarkation from the Persian Gulf would be different in many ways. For the ground and logistics elements of the MEF, most units would be flown home while their heavy equipment would be returned via available shipping. Other Marine units re-embarked all their personnel and equipment to Navy ships and sailed back to their homeports in Japan, Hawaii, and the States.

Just before the I MEF Headquarters was to depart, General Schwarzkopf gathered its major commanders and gave Lieutenant General Boomer and his staff generous praise to his Marines, saying, "You absolutely executed superbly. You did everything I thought you would do and more." By assigning I MEF the supporting attack,

[Schwarzkopf] had given them the 'toughest mission on the battle-field.' Schwarzkopf continued, "We had to throw somebody in against the toughest barriers. [We] had to throw you in where the enemy thought we were coming because that's the only way we could pin down the enemy." On a personal level, Schwarzkopf told them, "How very, very proud you've made me to be your commander." The feeling was undeniably mutual.[7]

Until the Middle East Iraqi War, the Maritime Prepositioned Ships (MPS) program was an untested concept. The MPS immediate response to support arriving units proved to be an overwhelming success. With the announcement of the multinational force's retrograde plan, the MPS ships quietly moved back into the Saudi Arabian ports in preparation for reloading their assigned equipment. This would be no small task as indicated by the magnitude of the loading list of some of the major equipment and stores in the backload operation:

- 30 M1A2 tanks

- 24 Light Armored Vehicles (LAVs)

- 105 Amphibious Assault Vehicles (AAVs)

- 282 Five-ton trucks

- 530 High Mobility Multipurpose Wheeled Vehicles (HMMWVs or Humvees)

- 45 Dump trucks

- 206 Cargo trailers

- 22 Wreckers

- Millions of gallons of water and gasoline

- Hundreds of thousands of rounds of ammunition

- 30 days' worth of all classes of supplies.

As the two Divisions, the 3rd Air Wing and Logistics organizations began their long retrograde march from Kuwait to Saudi Arabia, they marked all their equipment for staging in selected port area assembly areas. All hands knew their equipment had to be refurbished and placed in the best possible condition before it could be repositioned aboard the ships. It was to be a difficult, dirty, and dusty task, and care had to be taken at every phase of their reconditioning actions. But it was also an exhausting and joyful labor of love, but equally important, it was providing the Marines the fastest ticket home.

It took almost a week for the first elements of I MEF to begin the long trip back to the States. The Marine Corps' retrograde policy was to give priority to the "first units in," as they would be the first units rotated home. As the various units began arriving in the States, they were welcomed home by hundreds of proud citizens who gathered at airports and dockside to greet their returning warriors. Gray was often there at the foot of the ships' ladder, or at airports to personally greet his warriors. As even larger units began arriving at home stations, a fervent feeling of euphoria emerged across the nation. A war had been won with minimum loss of life. The troops were home again. Spontaneous parades and small local ceremonies occurred from the smallest communities to major cities. On March 12, President Bush signed an Executive Order establishing a Southwest Asia Service Medal for members of the U.S. Armed Forces who participated in Operations DESERT SHIELD and DESERT STORM. On June 8, Operation WELCOME HOME paid tribute to every member who had served in the recapture of Kuwait and the destruction of the Iraqi Army. There was a DESERT STORM National Victory Parade in Washington, DC that was led by General Schwarzkopf. Marines from I MEF marched in the parade reviewed by Commander-in-Chief President Bush. Two days later, more than 1,700 Marines, including more than 650 Reservists, marched down Broadway in New York City's ticker tape parade.

Months later, after returning to the States, Lieutenant General Boomer would share how he based his earlier note to me, saying, "Gerry, I don't think they are going to fight." He was prophetically accurate in his Commander's Assessment in that he recognized the U.S. forces were equipped with more advanced technologies available to provide increased fighting capabilities. Boomer passed on the following list of what he considered the most advanced command, control, communications and computer (C4) systems of air, ground and naval assets that helped make a difference:

- U.S./Coalition forces' complete control of Iraqi airspace
- Unmanned aerial vehicles (UAVs) and satellite imagery
- Global Positioning System (GPS) use to track "blue forces"
- Precision targeting capabilities of air and naval gunfire weapons
- M1A2 Main Battle Tanks that could outgun all Soviet armor
- Night gunsights for weapons gave the 24/7 advantage to the MNF forces.

When this list is carefully studied, it reveals that most of the systems and new warfighting capabilities were brought into the Marine Corps inventory during General Al Gray's long journey as a warrior of Marines. Beyond just equipping the force, Gray demanded higher levels of professional military education, beginning with new field- and weapon-oriented schools for sergeants and corporals, and other courses for more senior enlisted leaders. He increased combined arms exercises to exploit these new capabilities. Equally significant was his spirited demand that maneuver warfare and special operations capable (SOC) trained personnel become a mark of every MAGTF.

During the hectic days in preparing for deployment to the Middle East, Gray was the one who recognized the Army's newest M1A2 tank would play an important role in the coming armor battles. At that time, the Marine Corps was still equipped with the older M60A3 Main Battle Tank. No service or budgetary barriers held Gray back in getting the Army's consent for an emergency issue of M1A2 tanks for a limited number of Marine tank crews. Additionally, to ensure the crews were properly trained to operate the M1A2, he took immediate action to send crews to the U.S. Army's tank and gunnery schools at Fort Campbell. As the history of the Iraqi War confirmed, these preparatory actions later culminated in the MEF's Marine tankers dominating the Soviet-made armor-infested battlefields.

Years earlier, in the mid-1970s, when then-Major General Gray served as Director of the Marine Corps Combat Development Center, he became directly interested and active in literally every developmental program. This resulted in introducing Marines to unmanned aerial vehicles (UAVs) such as the Pioneer and smaller troop-launched aerial surveillance systems that flew directly over the heads of maneuvering infantry battalions. When few thought it was important to explore the use of improved night-vision systems, he had several tested and brought the best into the Corps inventory. He sought the latest and technically-advanced night-vision capabilities for infantry and reconnaissance Marines.

Other systems on the Kuwaiti battlefields proved valuable to the warfighters. The acquisition and use of Light Armored Vehicles (LAVs) gave ground units, for the first time, a highly mobile fighting capability. It had been the missing vehicle preventing the Marine Corps from conducting maneuver warfare operations.

One of Gray's most enduring transitional ideas was his constant demand for units to conduct wargaming with digital visual displays. These wargaming technologies were later linked to position location systems including the Global Positioning System (GPS). Although this initiative was rudimentary in the 1980s, by the 1990s it had become a standard technique in exercising command and control, and the effective real-time monitoring of maneuver forces. During the Iraqi War, GPS devices were to prove invaluable for units to ensure they had accurate position locations in an otherwise harsh, nondescript desert environment and the GPS devices were credited with significantly reducing the number of "friendly fire" incidents.

Gray's transformational initiatives also included numerous innovative measures to expand the traditional focus on amphibious operations from just the traditional ship-to-shore maneuvers. He became noted for his visionary statement that, "Marines must expand their thinking and planning, and look beyond the beaches to seizing inland objectives 50, 100, or 300 miles inland." It was too radical an idea for many senior leaders to fully accept. He saw that, in a rapidly changing world, emerging threats from terrorists operating in the urban terrain could easily extend beyond the littorals. Gray advocated that his Marines be prepared to respond to growing crises beyond any region's shoreline and that they must expect to move inland to operate effectively in the world's growing littorals. Many around him silently believed such a situation would never occur. It was just a matter of "Gray once again raising the bar," and he "demanded too much from his commanders and their Marines." Interestingly, it would be nearly two decades later when a Marine Air-Ground Task Force (MAGTF) Marine Expeditionary Unit (Special Operations Capable) MEU (SOC) was ordered to execute a "ship-to-objective" maneuver from the sea to a distant objective more than 400 miles away in a besieged Afghanistan site.

In every crisis, be it a small contingency of Marine expeditionary forces into such places as Liberia or Somali, or going to war in the Middle East to recapture Kuwait from the Iraqi Army, leadership comes into play. A unit commander's leadership during a turbulent period ultimately makes a difference in the outcome of a crisis.

As Commandant, Gray devoted his energies and intellect to the increased levels of operational training for his Marine units. Gray was clearly responsible for the increase in mechanized, combined arms live fire exercises, combat-leadership courses for junior enlisted Marines, and procurement of the latest advanced technological fighting tools. However, he then properly stepped aside and let his Marines go to war and fight under the operational control of General Norman Schwarzkopf, then Commander, Multinational Forces.

Gray cleverly chose the best and brightest Generals and senior officers, who had to step forward, fight, and win the desert war. And they did. The MEF's Generals—from the air wing, ground units, and logistics support commands—were all veterans of the Vietnam War. They had fought side-by-side as Captains and Majors, served with one another during the peacetime years, attended the same senior professional military schools, and often socialized with family members. They were professionals first and friends second. They were eager and exhibited strong confidence that they could meet the challenges and become winners in a coming battle.

Several common characteristics and the core values of being a U.S. Marine bring forth exceptional professional skills inherent to leading by example, and personal integrities clearly stand out. It was these common bonds that molded them into an unbeatable air, ground and logistics team.

From Lieutenant General Walt Boomer to Major Generals Rich Hearney, Bill Keys, Mike Myatt, Harry Jenkins, and Jeremiah Pearson III, to Brigadier Generals Tom Draude, Chuck Krulak, and Jim Brabham, and officers on the Joint Staff, Butch Neal and Jack Sheehan—all were totally committed and ready.

It was an unbeatable team. And it was these Generals and many of the Colonels who commanded the regimental task forces who would become the senior leaders of the Marine Corps over the next two decades. The point is that good, timely leadership always makes the difference in any crisis. Each of these individuals led skillfully and contributed to the successes of DESERT SHIELD/DESERT STORM. They would become the Corps' "new breed" of leaders, and in so doing, would reaffirm the examples of high standards that had been ingrained in them by their predecessors who fought the battles of Iwo Jima, Okinawa, and Hue City.

As the many I Marine Expeditionary Force (MEF) units began their long trip back to the States, General Gray, the 29th Commandant of the U.S. Marine Corps, was preparing to close out his 40-plus years as a Marine officer. His journey as a warrior had come a long way from his enlistment in a small town in New Jersey. In a few weeks, he would step aside as the Marine Corps' newly designated 30th Commandant assumed his duties. Freshly promoted to four stars, General Carl Mundy, a Southern gentleman and much-admired officer, would stand side-by-side with General Gray at the Marine Barracks at 8th and I Streets, Washington, DC on June 30, 1991, to receive the official Marine Corps colors that would symbolically signal the official change of command. As history will affirm, General Mundy was the right person to assume command to steer the Marine Corps into the 21st century. General Alfred Mason Gray's service as a Marine warrior was over. Well done, sir. *Semper Fi.*

EPILOGUE

More than two decades have passed since General Alfred M. Gray completed his tenure as the 29th Commandant of the U.S. Marine Corps. Subsequently, eight superb officers have served as Commandant:

30th Commandant, General Carl E. Mundy	Jul 1, 1991-Jun 30, 1995
31st Commandant, General Charles C. Krulak	Jul 1, 1995-Jun 30, 1999
32nd Commandant, General James L. Jones*	Jul 1, 1999-Jan 13, 2003
33rd Commandant, General Michael W. Hagee	Jan 13, 2003-Nov 13, 2006
34th Commandant, General James T. Conway	Nov 13, 2006-Oct 22, 2010
35th Commandant, General James F. Amos**	Oct 22, 2010-Oct 17, 2014
36th Commandant, General Joseph F. Dunford***	Oct 17, 2014-Sep 24, 2015
37th Commandant, General Robert B. Neller	Sep 24, 2015-to date
* General Jones served earlier as General Gray's military secretary.	
** General Amos had the distinction of being the first naval aviator to serve as Commandant.	
*** General Dunford's short tenure as Commandant was due to his selection and elevation as the 19th Chairman of the Joint Chiefs of Staff.	

Each of these exceptional Marine officers has demonstrated a different style of leadership and been faced with his own unique operational and political environment during his tenure as Commandant. But each at some time during his tenure sought out Gray for private, personal discussions. Gray never made a point of these special audiences, seemingly quite satisfied in the role of "silent coach," but it remains clear that no other former Commandant has enjoyed this same access or apparent respect. In 2011, Major General Buster Howes, Order of the British Empire, Commandant of the Royal Marines, lectured at the Royal United Services Institute in London. Part of his speech contained comments about an article General Alfred M. Gray wrote in 1989:

> We are a maritime nation; we rely upon the seas for commerce, to support our friends and allies, for on-scene response to

crisis where we have no access rights or permissive facilities, and for representing our national interests around the world.

The point is, the forces of choice to handle future crisis will likely continue to be aircraft carriers and amphibious forces with embarked Marines. One might also speculate, as we enter an era characterized by increasing terrorist activity, violence in drug exportation and the use of coercive tactics such as hostage taking, that amphibious forces with their evolving special capabilities will increasingly emerge as the more logical force of choice.

There is no indication whatsoever that the zeal of xenophobic radicals, messianic clerics, nihilistic students and other insurgents bent on reversing the trend of emerging, albeit weak, impoverished, democratic governments will decrease. These men of the streets and villages are better dealt with by riflemen than by supersonic aircraft and they will be dealt with in areas where we will not likely have and will not want to establish bases ashore.

Gray did indeed have a vision; it was to prepare the Marine Corps' operating forces against the emerging terrorist threats of the 21st century. Gray's long access to the nation's most sensitive intelligence provided a unique awareness of the increasing activities of terrorists operating around the globe. He noted and studied the origin of many incidents. Most terrorist attacks were originating in the festering marketplaces and in the dusty bazaars of Arab countries. Most were not affiliated with other groups, but the potential for terrorists networking was threatening. He assessed that terrorism fueled with religious fervor would be an emerging and iconic threat to the United States and other nations.

The Marine Corps has moved on in many ways since Gray's retirement. But the impact of his ideas and programs remains vibrant. One of his greatest and most lasting contributions was his initiatives to improve the professional education programs for all Marines. Not only is the library in Quantico named the Alfred M. Gray Marine Corps Research Center in his honor, but all Marines continue to be enriched by the various activities of the Marine Corps University that Gray initiated as Commandant. In addition, Gray has fundamentally changed the lives of countless deserving young men and women through his support of agencies that provide them educational assistance.

One example is The Marine Corps Scholarship Foundation, which has been recognized as a national model with its management and exceptional low overhead costs while providing focused educational grants, especially to dependents of Marines. In addition, Gray has continued to take a keen personal interest in our returning wounded Marines, continuing a tradition that I witnessed firsthand when the wounded and dead from the Beirut bombing were returning from overseas. Again, as the first combat casualties from the Iraq and Afghanistan Wars began to arrive at Bethesda and other U.S. Navy hospitals around the country, he was there to meet and comfort them and their families.

History will someday show that General Alfred M. Gray was the right man for the right time, as the Marine Corps transitioned into the 21st century. After his retirement from the Marine Corps, the intensity of his activities has not diminished. In many ways, the pace has actually increased. He became an early sponsor in the Wounded Warrior Project and continues to be the Chairman of the Injured Marine Semper Fi Fund, which provides timely assistance to servicemen and servicewomen and their families. He remains a steady visitor to the hospitals and bases where many recovering warriors are convalescing. He has continued his special interest in education and serves as a Director of the Marine Corps-Law Enforcement Foundation, which provides scholarships and other help to families who have lost their loved ones in the line of duty. Gray is also Chancellor of the Marine Military Academy, Chairman of the Marine Youth Fitness Foundation and sits on a number of University Boards.

But that's another General Al Gray story. ...

General Alfred M. Gray, Jr.

General Carl E. Mundy

General Charles C. Krulak

General James L. Jones

General Michael W. Hagee

General James T. Conway

General James F. Amos

General Joseph F. Dunford

General Robert B. Neller

29th through 37th Commandants of the U.S. Marine Corps (Source: Wikipedia).

APPENDIX A

Reduction in Seapower Memorandum (November 15, 1989)

From General Gray, Commandant of the Marine Corps
To Acting Secretary of the Navy Henry L. Garrett III
Dated November 15, 1989

Six pages

DEPARTMENT OF THE NAVY
HEADQUARTERS UNITED STATES MARINE CORPS
WASHINGTON, D.C. 20380-0001

IN REPLY REFER TO

3000
P
15 NOV 1989

MEMORANDUM FOR THE SECRETARY OF THE NAVY

Subj: REDUCTIONS IN SEAPOWER

As we go through the difficult process of identifying naval
force reductions dictated by possible sequestration and a declining
budget, I believe it essential that we recognize internally, and
emphasize in the various external fora addressing the subject, that
we are not dealing simply with business decisions. Rather, we are
potentially reducing dramatically the seapower of the United States.
Unquestionably, in an affordability crisis, it stands to reason that
our national defense capabilities must bear some of the brunt of a
smaller budget. However, it stands equally to reason that the
reductions we make need not necessarily be equitable across the
spectrum of current defense capabilities. Naval forces should not
bear proportional reductions with land and air forces for the simple
reason that the defense needs of our nation have, are, and always
will be more dependent on those capabilities provided by naval
forces than on those for which land and air forces were established,
and by which non-naval forces are constrained.

In the dramatic, rapidly changing events which seem to point
toward a world order in which the threat of major war between the
super-powers is becoming increasingly unlikely, there remain
constants: foremost among these are the oceans of the world. The
United States is a maritime nation. It has always, and always will
rely upon the seas for commerce with its trading partners, for
support of its friends and allies far from our own shores, for on-
scene response to crises where we have no access rights or
permissive facilities, and for simply representing our national
interests around the world. Our overseas basing structure is
declining and promises to do so at an accelerated rate in the
current fiscal and political environment. In 1947, we had 450 bases
overseas. Today we have 120 - and the majority of those are located
in and around Europe. In response to crises during the past decade,
we have experienced refusals of refueling, over-flight, or advanced
staging rights by nations who are our friends. In the future, there
is no question in my mind but that we will experience rejection
again. During the same period, and continuing at even an
increasing rate in the future, the emergence of independent, self-
willed nations around the globe has reduced our ability to act
quickly and decisively in regional conflicts. In earlier times, we
simply landed the Marines and worried about regional consequences -
if any - later. Today, our diplomatic interests are well served by
an ability to unilaterally position a force, and then rheostatically
control its employment to suit the scenario. For anything but major
operations, logistic support can also come from the sea, without
dependence on vulnerable facilities ashore. Land-based forces do
not provide this capability; only forces operating from sea-bases

Subj: REDUCTIONS IN SEAPOWER

offer the NCA such flexibility. Today, if we reacted to a crisis
in Panama or Honduras, we would likely respond with airborne forces.
In a decade, we would be required to seize an airfield in Panama,
and perhaps in Honduras as well. If forces were to remain there,
bases would have to be established and defended, and logistics
support developed. In smaller scale crises and contingency
operations of the future, this rheostatic, sea-based capability will
be even more important than it is today.

The foregoing, together with numerous other possible
illustrations, point to the fact that the nation will continue to
require credible seapower in the future just as it has in the past.
With regard to the elements of that seapower, I have a second
concern - which relates to the way we in the DoN assess and pass
relative value judgements on the various capabilities that provide
us effective seapower. As we deal with the hard choices of which
capabilities to pare down, it is imperative that we recognize just
why we have naval forces. To be sure, the technological
superiority and force-in-being represented by our strategic
submarines and ASW forces have been and are major factors in
constraining Soviet expansionism and bringing about the current
reshaping of the world order. We must maintain those critical
capabilities. At the same time, it is instructive to look back over
time and recognize that our continuous forward presence of balanced
fleet capabilities in both oceans has been likewise constraining.
Moreover, those capabilities have been used in a far wider spectrum
of crises and conflict than in stand-off deterrence vis-a-vis the
Soviets. In the past 44 years, naval forces - ships, aircraft,
Sailors and Marines - have responded to significant crises response
on 187 occasions. In three of those crises, we have used the Navy
to sink other navies, and in only one incident - the Persian Gulf
battle in April 1988 - did we sink a vessel larger than a patrol
boat. In that same time-frame, we responded to continental crises
with amphibious forces 100 times, and we used carriers 125 times.
The point is, as history clearly shows us, that unless crises
diminish significantly in the future, the forces of choice to handle
them will likely continue to be aircraft carriers and amphibious
forces with embarked Marines. One might also speculate, as we enter
an era characterized by increasing terrorist activities, violence in
drug exportation, and use of coercive tactics such as hostage
taking, that amphibious forces, with their evolved special
operations capabilties, will emerge increasingly as the more logical
force of choice. There is no indication whatsoever that the zeal of
xenophobic radicals, messianic clerics, nihilistic students and
other insurgents bent on reversing the trend of emerging, albeit
weak or impoverished, democratic governments will decrease. These
men of the streets and villages are better dealt with by riflemen
than by supersonic aircraft - and they must be dealt with in areas
where we will not likely have and will not want to establish, bases
ashore.

2

Subj: REDUCTIONS IN SEAPOWER

An additional philosophical point flowing from the foregoing
lies in broadly-held misperceptions of amphibious operations in
general. To the layman, an amphibious operation and an amphibious
assault are synonymous. The practitioner, however, understands that
the assault is but one type of amphibious operation. The layman
conjures up a view of the close range, human wave assaults against
Pacific islands or Normandy in World War II. Lost in perception is
the recognition that the reason we conducted such operations was
the state of technology at the time. We may need to do an
amphibious assault again in the future, as it represents the most
credible means in the U.S. arsenal for forcible projection of our
forces into a hostile area. In the event we conduct such
operations in the future, modern technology has afforded the means
to avoid the mass assaults of the past; but that is not my thesis
here. Rather, my point flows from the foregoing paragraphs which
point up the fact that consistent with the definition of the term
amphibious, such operations represent, simply, operations of a wide
variety from strategically and tactically mobile sea-bases. Just as
an aircraft carrier is a sea-based airfield, so are amphibious ships
the helicopter operating and maintenance bases, the logistics bases
and the troop assembly areas and attack positions from which we
launch operations. The popular misperception that amphibious ships
are simply troop ships by another name reflects ignorance of their
actual capabilities and utility.

The foregoing brings me to my major areas of concern with the
ongoing proposed budgetary reductions. The transfer from active
status of 15 amphibious ships in the next 2-3 years represents a
reduction of almost 25% of those ships available to support
deployment of sea-based forces. This comes at a time, when we are,
if anything, expanding the use of such ships for versatile
employment consistent with the emerging demands of low intensity
conflict. For example, there have been amphibious ships standing by
for detached duty for drug operations and LSTs are frequently
deployed for other special operations. Two amphibious ships were
used for an extended deployment in the Alaska oil spill cleanup.
Additional amphibious ships were used in the Persian Gulf for
support operations over the extended period of operation EARNEST
WILL. One ship is currently on extended deployment around the
littoral of the increasingly critical region of South America in
Exercise UNITAS, and a second ship has just returned from the
equally important, nation-building West-Africa Training Cruise. All
of these deployments represent ships and crews now constrained by
optempo/perstempo considerations. These smaller-crewed, more
economical-to-operate vessels provide great flexibility and obviate
the necessity for employment in such operations of larger, more
expensive-to-operate ships. Adding the fact that four other
amphibious platforms are detached as numbered fleet flagships, and
that an average of nine are in overhaul or maintenance at any given
point brings into focus the fact that one-third of the entire
amphibious force is "off the line" a majority of the time. To

3

Subj: REDUCTIONS IN SEAPOWER

budgetarily reduce another 25% leaves us with a critically
diminished capability to support naval presence and crisis response
missions. It would also exacerbate our woeful shortfall in
strategic mobility assets.

In determining our need for amphibious ships, we have, over
time, fallen prey to our own device of quantifying the amphibious
force in terms of gross lift characterizations. The "MEF plus MEB
Assault Echelon" lift requirement agreed to by the Navy and Marine
Corps, and prescribed in Defense Guidance, has served the useful
purpose of providing an affordability baseline for SCN plans. Our
ongoing budget review considerations address amphibious lift in
terms of fingerprint percentages categorized into troop, vehicle,
cargo, and deck-spots required for the MEF plus MEB. However, the
fact is that on a day-to-day basis, we do not operate amphibious
groups of MEF or MEB size. We maintain forward deployed MEUs, we
train MEUs or reduced scope MEBs and MEFs, and we operate ships out
of the amphibious envelope as described above. In other words, we
don't lift percentages of a force of any particular size on a day-
to-day basis; we operate numbers of ships to provide needed
capabilities in a variety of seapower requirements. To reinforce
this point, I'm advised that the nearly-completed Amphibious
Requirements Study directed by you concludes that the numbers of
amphibious ships required is not a function of wartime lift
requirements, but rather, flows from the demands of peace-to-war
operations. Thus, the reductions proposed in amphibious lift would
not only result in significant degradation of our already deficient
vehicle lift, but it would reduce dramatically - by 25% - the number
of platforms able to conduct peacetime operations. Also, in the
class of ships selected - the LST - it would eliminate our ability
to discharge equipment directly onto the beach, a significant
capability in under-developed regions. It would eliminate our
ability to conduct highspeed, underway launches of assault
amphibian vehicles. This, in turn, would consume critical space in
types of ships needed for LCACs or other landing craft. In sum, we
would be drawing down one of the most flexible, most economical,
and least manpower intensive ships in the amphibious force. The
bottom line is: the proposed retirements represent not simply a
reduction in a measurable percentage of wartime lift; they represent
a quantum degradation in our ability to conduct day-to-day fleet
operations.

A related area of concern lies in the deactivation of two
Battleship Battle Groups. Recommissioning of the battleships not
only provided the Navy with the versatile platforms represented in a
spectrum of surface fire support capabilities for a variety of
missions, but more specifically, it filled a long recognized void in
the fire support requirements for landing and supporting Marines in
any amphibious assault role. There simply is no other single
platform that can provide the devastating fire support required to
enable the projection of a landing force ashore during the very

4

413

Subj: REDUCTIONS IN SEAPOWER

vulnerable phase when the Marines are without shore-based
artillery. For over a decade, the naval services wrestled with the
problem of how to achieve adequate surface fire support to fill this
operational void. The four battleships answered the requirement in
spades. Additionally, a Battleship Battle Group can be substituted
in many instances for a CVGB, providing flexibility in force
employment and allowing fleet and theater commanders to properly
prioritize forces and efficiently meet operational requirements.
Decommissioning of two is, once again, a drastic reduction in the
nation's seapower, and should be weighed heavily, I believe, against
potential draw downs of less useful systems and capabilities -
either from within the Navy, or external to the Department.

Together, amphibious forces and Battleship Battle Groups serve
to define force presence, and underscore naval forces' unique
ability to serve as the sharp edge of diplomacy. Our status as a
global power is visibly demonstrated in port visits by amphibious
task forces and Battleship Battle Groups, and our ability to respond
in a measured manner to international provocations finds credibility
in their physical, observable presence. Gunboat diplomacy has had
its detractors, but having the ability to conduct it has proven on
occasion to be invaluable. We should reflect on the damage that
would occur from an inability to respond to hostile acts, or
threats, to U.S. personnel abroad.

My third area of concern - and not necessarily in that priority
- is the significant proposed reduction in Marine Corps manpower.
Once again, I appreciate that budgetary reductions must be
accomplished, but the potential short-term reduction of 17,000
Marines poses a crippling impact on our ability to sustain and
operate Marine forces around the world. Unlike land-based forces in
CONUS or forward-based garrisons, awaiting commitment to
hostilities, Marine forces are mobile naval operating forces. As an
example, consistent with operations in the U.S. Atlantic Fleet, in
the past three months, forces from the II Marine Expeditionary Force
have operated from the Persian Gulf, to NATO's northern flank, in
the Great Lakes, in Panama and the Caribbean, around the littoral of
South America, and up and down the West Coast of Africa. During the
same time-frame, in the Pacific, the forces of III MEF have operated
with the Pacific Fleet from the Aleutians to Korea, in Japan, the
Philippines, and Thailand. To sustain that forward deployed
expeditionary force in the Western Pacific, we draw units based in
Hawaii and California. This enables us to maintain unit
cohesiveness and personnel stability as well as to meet perstempo
requirements. Thus, while it appears budgetarily simple to "reduce
a brigade", our ability to sustain III MEF well forward would be
severely impacted by such precipitous action.

At the expense of appearing to resist any reductions at a time
when cuts in our national defense structure are clearly mandated, I
reiterate my belief that we must articulate the need to effect

5

APPENDIX A

Subj: REDUCTIONS IN SEAPOWER

significant draw-downs from forces of lesser utility than the
majority of those currently in active service in the DoN. In blunt
terms, we are continuing to build costly strategic capabilities
which will continue to contribute to nuclear deterrence, but we are
doing so at the cost of dramatic reductions in the forces we rely
upon to do the fundamental business of day-to-day peacekeeping
around the world. It is time for our decision makers to understand
that reductions of one-third share of budget decrements across-the-
board may appear managerially logical, but operationally serve to
emasculate vital crisis response capabilities. Contrary to the
events and mood driving the current reordering of the world, the
dramatic reductions being envisioned for our naval forces in
general, and our Marine Corps in particular, are likely to be the
very catalysts that provoke an increase in world disorder.

Finally, it is abundantly clear that the ability of adversarial
states and groups to openly flourish and aggressively sponsor
activities which threaten us across the spectrum of conflict has not
diminished, nor can we afford to speculate that it will. If we
agree that our peacetime presence has contributed to whatever
stability has existed in the world to date, then it follows that our
absence will increase instability and encourage a power vacuum that
could increase our vulnerability.

Very Respectfully,

A. M. GRAY

6

APPENDIX B
Personal Military Awards and Foreign Decorations General Alfred M. Gray, USMC

Defense Distinguished Service Medal with One Oak Leaf Cluster
Navy Distinguished Service Medal with Two Gold Stars
Army Distinguished Service Medal
Air Force Distinguished Service Medal
Coast Guard Distinguished Service Medal
Silver Star Medal
Bronze Star Medal with Combat "V" and Three Stars
Purple Heart Medal with Two Stars
Legion of Merit with Combat "V" and One Star
Meritorious Service Medal
Joint Service Commendation Medal with Two Bronze Oak Leaf Clusters
Navy Commendation Medal
RVN Cross of Gallantry w/1 Star and Palm

Unit Awards

Presidential Unit Citation w/1 Star
Navy Unit Commendation Medal w/2 Stars
Meritorious Unit Commendation w/1 Star
National Defense Service Medal w/2 Stars
Combat Action Medal w/2 Stars
Korean Service Medal w/1 Star
Armed Forces Expeditionary Medal w/1 Star
Humanitarian Service Medal w/1 Star
United Nations Service Medal
Vietnam Service Medal
Sea Service Deployment Ribbon
RVN Cross of Gallantry Unit Citation

Foreign Awards

Order of National Security—Korea
Medal of Merit in Gold—Netherlands
Order of Naval Merit—Brazil
Meritorious Military Service Order w/Star—Columbia
Naval Infantry Medal—Argentina
Meritorious Naval Sea Order—Korea

ENDNOTES AND SOURCES

Chapter 1: The Test

4. O'Neal, Michael, Lieutenant Colonel, USMC, "What Grand Theft Armor?" *Armed Forces Journal,* August 1994, p.4.
5. Ibid.
6. Korski, Daniel, "Interagency Military Cooperation: Just the First." Special United Press International. *The Washington Times,* 2004, p. 4.
7. Marolda, Edward J. and Schneller, Robert J., Shield and Sword. "The United States Navy and The Persian War." *Naval Institute Press,* Annapolis, MD, 2001, p. 52.
8. Marr, Phebe, *The Modern History of Iraq.* Westview Press, San Francisco, CA, 1985, p. 14.
9. Ibid, p. 15.
10. Stewart, Richard A., *Sunrise at Abadan: The British and Soviet Invasion of Iraq, 1941.* Praeger, New York, NY, p. 6.

Chapter 2: The Character of the 29th Commandant

1. Gray, Alfred M., General, USMC, Interview August 1, 2008.
2. Ibid.
3. King, Neal, Sergeant Major, USMC, Interview. HQMC History and Museum Division, 1989.
4. Ibid.
5. Bertolatus, Charles, Undated interview.
6. Frank, Benis, Interview of Major General Alfred M. Gray, USMC, on May 26, 1984. HQMC History and Museum Division.
7. Simmons, Edwin, Brigadier General, USMC (Ret.), Director, HQMC History and Museum Division. Undated anthology memorandums.

Chapter 3: The Early Years of Marine Corps Service

1. Gray, Alfred M., General, USMC, Cryptologic Warrior. Compendium of intelligence experiences. *Signal Magazine USMC,* undated.
2. Ibid.
3. Frank, Benis, interview of Major General Alfred M. Gray, at HQMC History and Museum Division, 1984
4. Gray, Alfred M., Major, USMC, Bronze Star Citation, First Award, Secretary of the Navy, November 6, 1964.
5. Gray, Alfred M., Major, USMC, Silver Star Citation, First Award (South Vietnam), May 14, 1967.
6. Gray, Alfred M., Major, USMC, Bronze Star Medal, awarded by Commanding Officer, 12th Marines, 3rd Marine Division (REIN), August 25, 1967.

7. McGee, James, Colonel, USMC (Ret.), Interviews and memorandum, 1995.
8. Ibid, p. 1.
9. Ibid, p. 2.
10. Ibid, p. 3.
11. Ibid, p. 3.
12. Ibid, pp. 4-5.

Chapter 4: The Final Collapse of South Vietnam

1. McGee, James, Colonel, USMC (Ret.), Interviews and memorandum, 1995, p. 8.
2. Gray, Alfred M., General, USMC (Ret.), Memorandum, June 2011, Note #9.
3. Butler, Dwayne. *The Fall of Saigon.* Dell Publishing Company, 1986, p. 406.
4. Gray, Alfred M., General, USMC (Ret.), Memorandum, June 2011, Note #9.
5. Ibid, Note #11.
6. Ibid, Note #15.
7. Quinlan, David, Colonel, USMC, and Dunham, George R., Major, USMC, "Marines in Vietnam: The Bitter End, 1973-1975, HQMC History and Museum, p. 146.
8. Gray, Alfred M., Colonel, USMC, Bronze Star, Fourth Award (South Vietnam), 1975.

Chapter 5: The Carolina MAGTF

1. Gardner, Dwayne, Colonel, USMC, Interviews and memorandum for the record, 1995-2005.
2. Ibid.
3. Ibid.
4. Ibid.
5. *RLT-2 After Action Report: Northern Wedding-Bold Guard.* Volume III, October 1978.
6. Ibid, p. 11.
7. *Mobile Protective Weapons System (MPWS) Study and Recommendations.* Executive Summary, July 1984, p. 2.
8. Ibid.
9. *U.S. Marines at Twentynine Palms, California.* HQMC History and Museum, 1989, pp. 72-75.

Chapter 6: "Papa Bear"

1. Anthology and Annotated Bibliography. Undated USMC document.
2. Joy, James, Brigadier General, USMC (Ret.), Undated memorandum.
3. Ibid, p. 6.

4. Otte, Dr. Paul, and Gray, Alfred M., General, USMC (Ret.), *The Conflicted Leader and Vantage Leadership*. Franklin University Press, Columbus, Ohio, 2006, p. 89.
5. Keiser, Gordon, Colonel, USMC (Ret.), Memorandum and interviews, 2005-2007.
6. Joy, James, Brigadier General USMC (Ret.), Memorandum and interviews, 2004-2007.
7. Ibid, p. 5.
8. Pierce, Terry, Captain, USN, *Warfighting and Disruptive Technologies: Disguising Innovation*. Frank Case Books, New York, NY, 2004, p. 17.
9. Smith, Ray, Major General, USMC, Multiple interviews, 1986-2006.
10. Pierce. *Warfighting and Disruptive Technologies: Disguising Innovation*. p. 17.
11. Joy, Memorandum and multiple interviews.
12. Collins, Patrick, Colonel USMC, Interviews, 1992-1994.
13. Ibid.
14. Turley, Gerald, Colonel USMCR (Ret.), Obituary for Colonel Patrick Collins, USMC, July 14, 1997.

Chapter 7: The Beirut Bombing

1. Geraghty, Timothy, Colonel USMC, *Peacekeepers at War*, Dulles, VA Potomac Books Inc. Forward written by General Alfred M. Gray, pp. viii-x.
2. Department of Defense Commission on International Terrorist Act, Oct. 23, 1983.
3. Weinberger, Caspar W., *Fighting For Peace: Seven Critical Years in the Pentagon*, Warner Books, New York, NY, 1990, p. 135.
4. Ibid, p. 152.
5. 24th Marine Amphibious Unit (MAU), Command Chronology, Beirut, Lebanon. p. 15.
6. Ibid, p. 4.
7. Perry, Mark, *Four Stars*. Houghton Mifflin Co., Boston, MA, p. 312.
8. Ibid.
9. *After Action Report: Lebanon Bombing Casualty Handling Report.* HQMC, undated.
10. Frank, Benis, Interview of Major General Alfred M. Gray, May 26, 1984.
11. *Command Chronology, Second Marine Division*, October-November 1983.
12. Inspector General's Report, HQMC.
13. Frank, Interview of Major General Alfred M. Gray.
14. Joy, James, Brigadier General USMC (Ret.), interviews.
15. Frank, Interview of Major General Alfred M. Gray.

Chapter 8: Three Stars and Force Commander

1. Millet, Allan, R., *Semper Fidelis, The History of the United States Marine Corps.* Macmillan Publishing Co., New York, NY.
2. Ibid, p. 532.
3. USMC Study, *Special Operations Capabilities.* Undated, p. 2.
4. Ibid, p. 4.
5. HQMC Memorandum for the Record. June 7, 1985, p. 2.
6. Commandant of the Marine Corps letter to Commanding General, FMFLANT, June 14, 1985, p. 1.
7. Second Marine Division, *Standard Operations Procedures for Training,* M1540.2.
8. Second Marine Division Order P1540.21, p. 2.
9. Myatt, Michael, Major General, USMC (Ret.), Interviews and memorandum, December. 2005.
10. Ibid.
11. Ibid.
12. Commandant of the Marine Corps, Memorandum for the Joint Chiefs of Staff on *The Marine Corps and Special Operations (G-3)*.
13. Keiser, Gordon, Colonel, USMC (Ret.), Interviews, 2006-2007.
14. Command Chronologies, Second Marine Division, 1983 to August 1984.
15. Commandant of the Marine Corps letter to Commanding General, FMFLANT.
16. Myatt, Michael, Major General, USMC (Ret.), interviews with author Turley on a series of interviews on or about General Gray's modus operandi.
17. Ibid.

Chapter 9: U.S. National Security and a Maritime Strategy

1. *National Security Strategy of the United States: The White House.* March 1990, p. 1.
2. Friedman, Norman, *The U.S. Maritime Strategy.* Naval Institute, Annapolis, MD, 1988, pp. 3-5.
3. Lehman, John, F., *Command of The Seas.* Scribner's and Sons, New York, NY, 1988, p. 99.
4. Ibid, p. 118.
5. Ibid, p. 119.
6. Ibid, pp. 2-3.
7. Ibid, pp. 121-150.
8. Amos, Granville, Brigadier General, USMC (Ret.), interviews and memorandums.
9. Commanding Officer, 22nd MEU, *After Action Report* and follow-on interviews.
10. Doyle, J. J., Colonel, USMC (Ret.), *After Action Report: Operation Eastern Exit.* July 9, 1991, p. 1.

Chapter 10: Commandants of the Marine Corps and Their Roles

1. Wood, Anthony A., Colonel, USMC (Ret.), *Special Briefing presented to the Chief of Naval Operations Strategy Studies Group,* 2003.
2. Boot, Max, *The Savage Wars for Peace.* Perseus Book Group, New York, NY, 2002, p. 8.
3. Krulak, Victor, Lieutenant General, USMC (Ret.), *First to Fight: An Inside View of the U.S. Marine Corps* quoting General A.A. Vandegrift, USMC, before Senate Committee on Naval Affairs. *Unification of the Armed Forces.* Seventy-Ninth Congress, Second Session, May 10, 1946. Annapolis, MD: Bluejacket Books, Naval Institute Press, 1984, p. 37.
4. Ibid, p. 324.
5. Fleming, Keith Jr., *Biography of General Randolph McCall Pate, Commandant of the Marine Corps.* Edited by Allen Millett, and Jack Shulimson, Naval Institute Press, 2004, p. 353.
6. Ibid, p. 357.
7. Ibid, p. 360.
8. Ibid, p. 402.
9. Ibid, p. 407.
10. Ibid, p. 427.
11. Ibid, p. 456.
12. Ibid, p. 450.
13. Goldwater-Nichols Department of Defense Reorganization Act of 1986, Pub. L. 99–433.
14. US House of Representatives, House Armed Services Committee, *1986 Defense Reorganization Act,* Subcommittee Report, September 16, 1987.

Chapter 11: The Changing of Command

No source documents in this chapter.

Chapter 12: The First Year

1. Gray, Alfred M., General, USMC (Ret.), Interview, March 7, 2007.
2. Comfort, Clayton, Major General, USMC (Ret.), Biography. October 10, 1987, p. 2.
3. Gray. Interview.
4. Ibid.
5. Vaughn William L. Jr., Master's Thesis: *The Extraordinary Career of General A.M. Gray.* Norwich University, February 23, 2000.
6. Ibid, p. 9.
7. Krulak, Charles, General, USMC (Ret.), *Warfighting (MCDP. 1),* June 20, 1997.
8. Gray, Interview.
9. Title 10, U.S. Code; Public Law, p. 248.

10. Gray, Interview.
11. Ibid.
12. Vaughn, *The Extraordinary Career of General A.M. Gray*, p. 20.
13. Hall, D. B., Lieutenant Colonel USMC (Ret.), *A Crucial Investment: USMC Marine Combat Training*, undated.
14. Vaughn. *The Extraordinary Career of General A.M. Gray*, p. 21.
15. Ibid, p. 28.
16. Gray, Alfred M., General, USMC, Letter to Commanding General, Marine Combat Development Command (MCCDC), October 10, 1988, p. 4.
17. Ibid, p. 6
18. Chief of Staff, HQMC, Naval Message to all Marines (ALMAR) 26/87. *Memorandum: Marine Gunner Program,* October 22, 1987.
19. Marine Combat Development Command (MCCDC) Letter. October 10, 1988, p. 420.
20. HQMC Briefing to Secretary of the Navy: *V-22 Osprey.*
21. Report by Chairman, CMC Task Force on *Women in the Marine Corps.* December 3, 1987, p. 3.
22. HQMC Notice. Subject: *Legislative History of Combat Exclusion Policy.*
23. Commandant of the Marine Corps, *White Letter No. 88.* Draft, undated.
24. Commandant of the Marine Corps letter to Secretary of the Navy: *CS: 836, Report on Women in the Marine Corps.* December 4, 1987.
25. "Top Marine Balks at Equality Report. Decision on Women Draws Rebuke from the Pentagon" *Kansas City Times,* April 26, 1988.
26. Gray, Alfred M., General, USMC, Testimony to Congressional Subcommittee.
27. Webb, James, *Letter of Resignation to Secretary of Defense,* February 23, 1988.

Chapter 13: The Second and Third Critical Years

1. *Historical Summary of Selected Strategies and Initiatives by the Marine Corps' Former Commandants Information Paper* prepared for James F. Amos, Lieutenant General, USMC, 2007, p. 5.
2. *USMC: A History of Innovative Warfighting.* HQMC History and Museums Division, June 12, 1990, p. 24.
3. Commandant of the Marine Corps Naval Message: *25000Z Reorganization of the Department of Defense; Special Operations Directorate.*
4. HQMC Conference Report. General Gray Briefing to General Officers and the Force Structure Study Group. January 6, 1988.
5. *Discriminate Deterrence Study,* Department of Defense, 1988.
6. Gray, Alfred M., General, USMC, Memorandum to the Secretary of the Navy, November 15, 1988.
7. Gray, Alfred M., General, USMC, Personal letter to the Secretary of the Navy, November 15, 1988.

8. Gray, Memorandum to the Secretary of the Navy, p. 6.
9. HQMC Conference Report. Briefing to General Officers, p. 2.
10. Gray, Alfred M., General, USMC, Statement to *Projection Forces and `Regional Defense Committee*: Senate Armed Services Committee. March 10, 1989. Operational Handbook 6-1, Section III, pp. 2-6.
11. Ibid.
12. Higgins, William Richard, Colonel, USMC, Biography dated July 21, 1993.
13. *The Hostage Tragedy of Colonel William R. Higgins, U.S. Marine Corps*. HQMC Memorandum, undated.
14. "McCain Leads Fight to Retrieve Marine's Remains" *Naval Affairs,* March 1990, p. 14.
15. Plaque placed near Colonel Higgins's gravesite, Quantico National Cemetery, Quantico, VA.
16. HQMC Marine Corps Professional Reading Program; ALMAR 127/88, July 11, 1988, Paragraph 2.
17. Ibid.
18. HQMC Activation of the Marine Corps University (MCU) ALMAR 128/88, July 13, 1988.
19. Zinni, Anthony, General, USMC, Meeting and interview, July 12, 2007.
20. Rakow, William M., Colonel, USMC, Interview and memorandum, 2006.
21. Ibid, p. 2.
22. Contingency MAGTF 2-88. *Operations Plan.* April 17, 1988.
23. Brinkley, Samuel S., Lieutenant Colonel, USMC, Operations Order and interview, August 4, 2007.
24. Rakow, Memorandum.
25. Gray, Alfred M., General, USMC, Commandant's letter to the Officer Corps, May 1, 1989.
26. Freitas, Mark and Treadway, Braddock W., Master's Thesis: "*Stygian Myth: U.S. Riverine Operations Against the Guerrilla.*" Naval Postgraduate School. Monterey, CA, December 1994, p. 101.
27. Small Craft Company Activation Order. Sequence of events ceremony brochure.
28. *Marine Corps Gazette,* May 1990.
29. Klamper, Amy, "River War" *Seapower Magazine*, February 2006.

Chapter 14: The Final Year and Moving "Into Harm's Way"

1. Brandtner, Martin, Lieutenant General, USMC (Ret.), Interviews and memorandum.
2. Drew, Elizabeth, *Washington Preparing for War*: George Bush, Forty-First President, speech August 1990. Excerpt from *The Gulf War Reader*, edited by Micah L. Sifry and Christopher Cerf. Times Books, New York, NY, Random House, 1991, p. 187.

3. Boomer, Walter, E., Lieutenant General, USMC (Ret.), Series of interviews and meetings with author Gerald Turley, 2004-2009.
4. Quilter, Charles J., Colonel, USMCR, *U.S. Marines in the Persian Gulf: 1990-1991: With the First Expeditionary Force in DESERT SHIELD and DESERT STORM.* HQMC History and Museums Division. Washington, DC, 1992, p. 35.
5. Bush, George, President of the United States address from the Oval Office, White House. *In Defense of Saudi Arabia.* Excerpt from *The Gulf War Reader*, edited by Micah L. Sifry and Christopher Cerf. Times Books, New York, NY, Random House, 1991, p. 197.
6. Quilter, *U.S. Marines in the Persian Gulf: 1990-1991,* p. 3.
7. Ibid, p. 6.
8. Ibid, p. 8.
9. Ibid, p. 23.
10. Friedman, Norman, *DESERT VICTORY,* Naval Institute Press, Annapolis, MD, p. 80.
11. Brown, Ronald J., Lieutenant Colonel, USMCR, *U.S. Marines in the Persian Gulf, 1990-99: With the Marine Forces Afloat In DESERT SHIELD And DESERT STORM.* HQMC History and Museum Division, 1998, pp. 34-37.
12. Ibid, p. 113.
13. Friedman, *DESERT VICTORY.* p. 204.
14. Brown, *U.S. Marines in the Persian Gulf, 1990-99,* p. 42.
15. Ibid, pp. 43-44.
16. Ibid, p. 113.
17. Marolda, Edward J. and Robert J. Schneller Jr., *Shield and Sword: The U.S. Navy and the Persian Gulf War.* Naval Institute Press Naval Historical Center Annapolis, MD, 1998, p. 250.
18. Ibid, p. 378.
19. Cureton, Charles H., Lieutenant Colonel, USMCR, *The U.S. Marines in the Persian Gulf, 1990-91; With the First Marine Division in DESERT SHIELD and DESERT* STORM. HQMC History and Museum Division. Washington, DC, 1993, p. 19.
20. Draude, Thomas, Interviews, 2006-2009.
21. Dunnigan, James, and Austin, Bay, *From Shield to Storm: High-Tech Weapons, Military Strategy, & Coalition Warfare in the Persian Gulf.* William Marrow and Company, Inc. New York, NY, 1991, p. 243.
22. Brown, *U.S. Marines in the Persian Gulf, 1990-99,* p. 113.
23. Friedman, *DESERT VICTORY,* p. 204.
24. Amos, Granville, Brigadier General, USMC (Ret.), Interviews, 2005-2009.
25. Sachtleben. Glen, Lieutenant Colonel, USMCR, "Operation Sharp Edge: The Corps' (SOC) Program in Action" *Marine Corps Gazette,* 1991, pp. 77-86.
26. Ibid.

27. Scales, Robert, Brigadier General, US Army, *Certain Victory: The US Army in the Gulf War.* US Army Desert Storm Study Project. Washington, DC, 1993, p. 109.
28. Bradley, William, and Richard Mullen, "Operation Eastern Edge. Marine Corps Stallions to the Rescue*" Marine Corps Gazette*, Quantico, VA, November 1991, pp. 56-57.
29. Ibid, pp. 81-86.
30. Quilter, *U.S. Marines in the Persian Gulf: 1990-1991,* p. 21.
31. Ibid, pp. 54-57.
32. Ibid.
33. Lake, Richard, Brigadier General, USMC (Ret.), Letter of July 6, 2009 and personal papers and memorandums on intelligence-related matters, DESERT STORM, and interviews, 2008.
34. Ibid.

Chapter 15: DESERT STORM: "The 100-Hour War"

1. Scales, Robert, Brigadier General, US Army, *Certain Victory: The US Army in the Gulf War.* US Army Desert Storm Study Project. Washington, DC, 1993, p. 199..
2. Lake, Richard, Brigadier General, USMC (Ret.), Interview and personal documents, July 9, 2009.
3. Chenoweth, Avery, Colonel, USMCR, with Brooks Nihart, Colonel, USMC (Ret.). *Semper Fi: The Definitive Illustrated History of the U.S. Marine Corps.* Sterling Publishing Co., New York, NY, 2005, p. 405.
4. Cureton, Charles H., Lieutenant Colonel, USMCR, *U.S. Marines in the Persian Gulf, 1990-1991, With the First Marine Division in DESERT SHIELD and DESERT STORM,* HQMC History and Museum Branch.
5. Mroczkowski, Dennis P., Lieutenant Colonel, USMCR, *U.S. Marines in the Persian Gulf, 1990-1991, with the Second Marine Division in DESERT SHIELD and DESERT STORM.* HQMC History and Museum Branch, 1993, p. 39.
6. Schwarzkopf, Norman H., General, US Army, News Briefing. February 27, 1990.
7. Quilter, Charles, J., Colonel, USMCR, *U.S. Marines in the Persian Gulf, 1990-1991: With the I Marine Expeditionary Force in DESERT SHIELD and DESERT STORM,* HQMC History and Museums Division, 1993, p. 111.

GLOSSARY OF ACRONYMS
AND ABBREVIATIONS

AAAV	Advanced Amphibious Assault Vehicle
AAF	Air Alert Force
AAV or AMTRAC	Amphibious Assault Vehicle
ACE	Aviation Combat Element
ACMC	Assistant Commandant of the Marine Corps
AOR	Area of Responsibility
ARG	Amphibious Ready Group
ARVN	Army of the Republic of Vietnam
ATF	Amphibious Task Force
BLT	Battalion Landing Team
BSG	Brigade Support Group
BSSG	Brigade Service Support Group
BWT	Basic Warrior Training
C2	Command and Control
C3	Command, Control and Communications
C3I	Command, Control, Communications and Intelligence
C4I	Command, Control, Communications, Computers and Intelligence
CAO	Combined Arms Operations
CAX	Combined Arms Exercise
CENTCOM	Central Command
CINCEUR	Commander-in-Chief, Europe
CINCLANT	Commander-in-Chief, Atlantic
CJCS	Chairman, Joint Chiefs of Staff
CMC	Commandant of the Marine Corps
CNA	Center of Naval Analysis
CNO	Chief of Naval Operations

CO	Commanding Officer
COC	Combat Operations Center
COMEX	Communications Exercise
COMMAR-FORCENT	Commander, Marine Forces Central Command
COMUS-NAVCENT	Commander, U.S. Naval Forces Central Command
CPX	Command Post Exercise
DACOWITS	Defense Advisory Committee on Women in the Military Services
DAO	Defense Attaché Office
DI	Drill Instructor
DMZ	Demilitarized Zone
DoD	Department of Defense
FBI	Federal Bureau of Investigation
FMF	Fleet Marine Force
FMFLANT	Fleet Marine Force Atlantic
FMFM	Fleet Marine Force Manual
FMFPAC	Fleet Marine Forces Pacific
FROST	Fast Response on Short Transmission
FSSG	Force Service Support Group
G-3 Alpha	Brigade's Assistant Operations Officer
GCE	Ground Combat Element
GOSP	Global Oil Separation Plant
GPS	Global Positioning System
HF	High Frequency
HMM	Heavy Helicopter Squadron
HMMWV or Humvee	High Mobility Multipurpose Wheeled Vehicle
HQMC	Headquarters, U.S. Marine Corps
IG	Inspector General
IRR	Individual Ready Reserve

JCS	Joint Chiefs of Staff
JSOC	Joint Special Operations Command
JTFME	Joint Task Force Middle East
KIA	Killed in Action
LAV	Light Armored Vehicle
LAW	Light Anti-Armor Weapon
LCAC	Landing Craft Air Cushion
LFTC	Landing Force Training Command
L-Hour	Landing Hour
LIC	Low-Intensity Conflict
LOGEX	Logistic Exercise
LSD	Amphibious Dock Landing Ship
LSU	Logistics Support Unit
LVT	Landing Vehicle Tracked
MAB	Marine Amphibious Brigade
MAF	Marine Amphibious Force
MAG	Marine Aircraft Group
MAGTF	Marine Air-Ground Task Force
MAPEX	Map Exercise
MARCENT	Marine Corps Forces Central Command
MARG	Mediterranean Amphibious Ready Group
MARSOC	Marine Corps Forces Special Operations Command
MAU	Marine Amphibious Unit
MAW	Marine Aircraft Wing
MCAGTC	Marine Corps Air-Ground Combined Arms Training Center
MCCDC	Marine Corps Combat Development Command
MCCP	Marine Corps Campaign Plan
MCDC	Marine Corps Development Center
MCDEC	Marine Corps Development and Education Command
MCI	Marine Corps Institute

MCRC	Marine Corps Research Center
MCU	Marine Corps University
MEB	Marine Expeditionary Brigade
MEF	Marine Expeditionary Force
MEU (SOC)	Marine Expeditionary Unit (Special Operations Capable)
MFA	Marine Corps Forces Africa
MFA	Marine Forces Afloat
MNF	Multinational Force
MOS	Military Occupational Specialty
MOUT	Military Operations in Urban Terrain
MPS	Maritime Prepositioning Shipping
MPWS	Mobile Protective Weapons System
MSB	Marine Security Battalion
MSC	Military Sealift Command
NATO	North Atlantic Treaty Organization
NCA	National Command Authority
NCO	Noncommissioned Officer
NEO	Noncombatant Evacuation Operation
NSA	National Security Agency
NSG	Naval Security Group
NVA	North Vietnamese Army
PHIBRON	Amphibious Squadron
PLO	Palestine Liberation Organization
PME	Professional Military Education
POW	Prisoner of War
PP&O	Plans, Programs and Operations
RD&A	Research Development and Acquisitions
RLT	Regimental Landing Team
ROC	Required Operational Capability
RPV	Remotely Piloted Vehicle

RRP	Rapid Response Planning
SES	Senior Exectutive Service
SIGINT	Sensitive Intelligence
SO	Special Operations
SOC	Special Operations Capable
SOCOM	Special Operation Command
SOF	Special Operations Force
SOTG	Special Operations Training Group
SRI	Surveillance, Reconnaissance, and Intelligence
STX	Situation Training Exercise
SWAT	Special Weapons and Tactics
TACTEST	Tactical Test
TAOR	Tactical Area of Responsibility
TBS	The Basic School
TECG	Tactical Exercise Control Group
TEEP	Training Exercise and Employment Plan
TOW	Tube-launched, Optically Tracked, Wire-Guided
TRAP	Tactical Recovery of Aircraft and Personnel
TWSEAS	Tactical Warfare Simulations Evaluation Analysis System
UAV	Unmanned Aerial Vehicle
UN	United Nations
USSR	Union of Soviet Socialist Republics
VHF	Very High Frequency
VNMC	South Vietnamese Marine Corps
WIA	Wounded in Action
WMD	Weapons of Mass Destruction

INDEX

Italicized entries refer to publications and ship names.

investigation of Saigon evacuation
operation, 74
Iran, 21, 127, 137, 175, 199, 248, 309,
311, 315, 322-325, 357
IRAQI FREEDOM, 127
Iraqi invasion/military forces, viii, 4,
31, 33, 53, 62, 65, 163, 188, 312,
335
Iraqi threat to I MEF, 347, 379
Israel, 17, 108, 138, 139, 156, 221, 309,
314, 316, 373

J

Japan, 31, 32, 33, 43, 64, 211, 226, 256,
278, 279, 338, 348, 349, 397
Jaskilka, Samuel, 52
Jazirat Qurah Island, 358
Jenkins, Harry W Jr., 10, 119, 196, 346,
353, 354, 367, 394, 403
Johnston, Robert B., 357
Joint Chiefs of Staff (JCS), 7, 76, 77,
336, 431
joint exercise, 233
joint operations, 70, 83, 159, 167, 223
Joint Special Operations Command
(JSOC), 159, 163, 172, 431
Jones, James L., 253, 274, 277, 279, 405,
408
Joy, Jim, xiii, 119, 120, 122, 123, 130,
148, 420, 421
Judge, Darwin, 76, 77
JUST CAUSE II OPERATION, 193,
362
JUST CAUSE OPERATION, 193

K

Keane (Major), 72, 76
Kelley, Paul X., 5, 47, 150, 158, 160,
168, 172, 198, 221, 222, 225-227,
229, 237, 242, 243, 252, 256
as Commandant, 5, 47, 150, 158, 160,
168, 172, 198, 221, 222, 225-227,
229, 237, 242, 243, 252, 256
at Beirut memorial services, 149, 150

maritime prepositioning shipping
(MPS), 170, 171, 222, 308,
343-345, 349, 361, 398, 432
special operation capabilities, 158,
177
Kennedy, John F., 39, 41, 45, 46, 48, 77,
214
Keys, William M., 347, 377, 385, 403
Commanding General 2nd Marine
Division, 347, 377, 385, 403
minefield breaching concept, 377
Vietnam, 347, 377, 385, 403
kidnapping incidents, 315
King, Martin Luther, 45, 48, 54
King, Neal, 419
Koh Tang Island, 79
Korean War, 30, 144, 208, 210, 221, 297
Krulak, Charles C., 115, 132, 225, 258,
371, 388, 403, 405, 423
Krulak, Victor, 214, 237, 423
Kuwait, viii, 2-4, 19, 21, 22, 40, 116,
130, 191, 192, 322, 334, 335, 338-
340, 344, 346, 348, 352, 356-361,
365, 371-374, 380, 385, 388, 389,
391-396, 398, 399, 402
International Airport, 391, 393, 395
invasion of Kuwait by Iraq/war to
liberate, 335, 339
Kuwait City, 3, 116, 282, 359, 372,
374, 380, 388, 389, 393, 394

L

Labutti, Frank, 119
Laidig, Scott, 52
Lake, Richard, 427
Landing Craft Air Cushion (LCAC), 5,
223, 298, 332, 431
landing forces, 82, 112, 116, 208,
350, 356. See also amphibious
landings/warfare
Landing Force Training Command, 82,
431
LaPlante (Rear Admiral), 351

Secretary of State, 196, 367
Secretary of the Navy, 165, 179, 183,
    188, 189, 219, 222, 229, 230, 242,
    247, 257, 285, 286, 288, 289, 291,
    293, 294, 295, 300, 302, 306, 309,
    312, 409, 419, 424, 425
security guard duty, 72, 197, 294, 364,
    365, 368
sensor technology, 49
sexual harassment, 287, 290, 293
Shaltila refugee camp, 138
SHARP EDGE OPERATION, 194, 195,
    362-365
Sheehan, John J. (Jack), 56, 63, 403
Shepherd, Lemuel C., 211
Shepherd Task Force, 387
Sheridan, Michael, 97
Shetland Islands, 93-95, 104
ship-to-shore movements, 87, 94, 97,
    104, 125, 210, 297, 402
Shoup, David, 205, 212, 213
SIGINT (sensitive intelligence)
    material, 43, 46, 433
Silver Star Medal, 50, 132, 219, 226,
    347, 417, 419
Simmons, Edwin, 40, 119, 219, 237, 419
Skelton, Ike, 272
Slade, George, 72, 75
Smith, Keith A., 255, 311
Smith, Ray, 63, 129, 377, 421
Snepp, Frank, 74
softball game, 321
SOLID SHIELD exercise, 180, 233, 339,
    358
Somalia, 192, 195, 196, 366-370
Southeast Asia, 11, 41, 49, 82
South Korea. See Korean War
South Vietnam. See Vietnam
Southwest Asia, 336, 352, 399
Soviet Union, 12, 32, 45, 182, 187, 189,
    238, 239, 279. See also Cold War
special operations capable (SOC), 61,
    101, 108, 135, 150, 158, 164, 171,
    172, 177, 178, 192, 195, 322, 323,
    327, 364, 365, 400, 402, 426, 432,
    433

special operations forces (SOFs), 158,
    223, 332, 433
SRI (surveillance, reconnaissance, and
    intelligence) activities, 331, 433
SS Mayaguez, 78, 79
Stanley, Clifford, 275, 352, 356
stealth technology, 185
Steele (Admiral), 73
Steele, Marty, 355, 356, 376
Stiner, Carl, 141
Stokes, Tom, 119
Strategic Reserve forces, 14, 239
strategic thinking, 265
succession, 227, 310
Sullivan, Gordon R., 251
Summers, David W., 9, 277, 279
surveillance, 42, 49, 52, 107, 117, 143,
    184, 187, 331, 342, 401. See
    also SRI (surveillance, reconnais-
    sance, intelligence) activities
Sutton, Russell H., 352
Syracuse Study, 133, 134
Syria, 137, 138, 139, 141

T

tactical exercise control group (TECG),
    172, 350, 433
tactical exercises, 127, 172, 350
Tactical Recovery of Aircraft and
    Personnel (TRAP), 135, 172,
    174, 433
Tactical Warfare Simulations Evaluation
    Analysis System (TWSEAS),
    127, 128, 433
Taft, William, 162
tank battalion, 5, 6, 13, 388
Tan Son Nhut Air Base, 69, 70, 73, 76
targeting systems, 184
task force teams, 260
Taylor, Charles, 193, 362
TBS (The Basic School). See Basic
    School, The
teaching, 123, 153, 160, 174, 270. See
    also education

Tennous (Lebanese general), 141
terrorism and terrorists, 22, 106, 108,
        126, 133, 135, 138, 139, 141, 143,
        144, 149, 150, 157, 158, 171, 175,
        182, 198, 268, 293, 299, 301, 302,
        305, 314-316, 327, 330-333, 406
Tet Offensive, 215, 228
thermosights, 341, 354
Third World, 33, 238, 257, 301, 304,
        305, 329, 330. See also developing
        nations
Tiger Brigade, 387
TIGER OPERATION, 353, 357
"Top of the Roof Gang", 42
trade protection, 129
training programs, ix, 13, 16, 53, 120,
        132, 135, 260, 274, 332. See
        also education
Travis Trophy Award, 231
Troy, Task Force, 359
Truman, Harry S., 32, 33, 209, 210
Turkey, 21, 58, 84, 105, 125, 156, 168
Turley, Bunny, iii, 109, 110, 225, 243,
        278, 316
Turley, Gerald H., iii, 22, 81, 83, 220,
        243, 277, 278, 314, 421, 422, 426
Twentynine Palms, Marine Corps
        Ground Combat Center, 8, 15,
        63, 109-113, 115, 129, 164, 218,
        247, 339, 344, 349, 350, 420
Twomey, David, 119, 120

U

U-2 spy plane downing, 45
Umm Al Monida, 358
unconventional actions/warfare,
        126, 158, 182, 198, 305. See
        also terrorism and terrorists
UNITAS XXV OPERATION, 166
United States and the World in the 1985
        Era (University of Syracuse),
        133
unmanned aerial vehicles (UAVs), 331,
        342, 400, 401, 433
urban environments, 46, 134, 156, 164,
        174, 175, 402

US Air Force, 3, 6, 32, 66, 67, 69, 70, 72,
        74, 79, 109, 117, 118, 166, 169,
        184, 189, 201, 203, 209, 271, 272,
        288, 303, 316, 343, 353, 356, 417
USCENTCOM (US Central
        Command), 202, 345, 351-353,
        357, 372, 429
U.S. Navy, Central Command
        (COMUSNAVCENT), 351, 352,
        354, 430
USS Blue Ridge, 67, 69, 73, 75, 76, 351,
        352, 356
USS Dubuque, 67
USS Edgar F. Luckenbach, 26
USS Guam, 196, 198, 368, 370
USS Hancock, 67, 79
USS Holt, 80
USS Independence, 192, 343, 360
USS McCormick, 325
USS Merrill, 325
USS Midway, 67, 76
USS Missouri, 3, 384
USS Mobile, 79
USS Mount Whitney, 83, 85, 93, 94, 96,
        233
USS Princeton, 357
USS Saipan, 2, 195, 364
USS Salem, 226
USS Samuel B. Roberts, 323, 324
USS Tarawa, 298
USS Trenton, 196, 198, 325, 368, 370
USS Tripoli, 357
USS Whidbey Island, 219
USS Wilson, 80
USS Wisconsin, 3, 384

V

V-22 (tiltrotor) Osprey helicopter, 5,
        223, 285, 286, 298, 308, 331, 424
Vandegrift, A. A., 209, 210, 211, 423
Van Riper, Paul, 115, 244, 275
Vaughn, William, 268, 423, 424
Vessey, John, 233
VHF radio, 85, 87, 433

www.ingramcontent.com/pod-product-compliance
Lightning Source LLC
Chambersburg PA
CBHW062355090426
42740CB00010B/1284